4 **Of the titles that are serialized in SHONEN JUMP Magazine, have you purchased the Graphic Novels?**

- ☐ Yes
- ☐ No

If **YES**, which ones have you purchased? (check all that apply)

- ☐ Dragon Ball Z
- ☐ Hikaru no Go
- ☐ Naruto
- ☐ One Piece
- ☐ Shaman King
- ☐ Yu-Gi-Oh!
- ☐ YuYu Hakusho

If **YES**, what were your reasons for purchasing? (please pick up to 3)

- ☐ A favorite title
- ☐ A favorite creator/artist
- ☐ I want to read it in one go
- ☐ I want to read it over and over again
- ☐ There are extras that aren't in the magazine
- ☐ The quality of printing is better than the magazine
- ☐ Recommendation
- ☐ Special offer
- ☐ Other

If **NO**, why did/would you not purchase it?

- ☐ I'm happy just reading it in the magazine
- ☐ It's not worth buying the graphic novel
- ☐ All the manga pages are in black and white unlike the magazine
- ☐ There are other graphic novels that I prefer
- ☐ There are too many to collect for each title
- ☐ It's too small
- ☐ Other ____________________

5 **Of the titles NOT serialized in the Magazine, which ones have you purchased?** **(check all that apply)**

- ☐ Beet the Vandel Buster
- ☐ Bleach
- ☐ Dragon Ball
- ☐ Dr. Slump
- ☐ Eyeshield 21
- ☐ Hunter x Hunter
- ☐ I"s
- ☐ Knights of the Zodiac
- ☐ Legendz
- ☐ The Prince of Tennis
- ☐ Rurouni Kenshin
- ☐ Whistle!
- ☐ Yu-Gi-Oh!: Duelist
- ☐ None
- ☐ Other ____________________

If you did purchase any of the above, what were your reasons for purchase?

- ☐ A favorite title
- ☐ A favorite creator/artist
- ☐ Read a preview in SHONEN JUMP Magazine and wanted to read the rest of the story
- ☐ Recommendation
- ☐ Other

Will you purchase subsequent volumes?

- ☐ Yes
- ☐ No

6 **What race/ethnicity do you consider yourself?** **(please check one)**

- ☐ Asian/Pacific Islander
- ☐ Black/African American
- ☐ Hispanic/Latino
- ☐ Native American/Alaskan Native
- ☐ White/Caucasian
- ☐ Other

THANK YOU! Please send the completed form to:

VIZ Survey
42 Catharine St.
Poughkeepsie, NY 12601

All information provided will be used for internal purposes only. We promise not to sell or otherwise divulge your information.

SHONEN JUMP
THE WORLD'S MOST POPULAR MANGA

COMPLETE OUR SURVEY AND LET US KNOW WHAT YOU THINK!

☐ Please do NOT send me information about VIZ and SHONEN JUMP products, news and events, special offers, or other information.

☐ Please do NOT send me information from VIZ's trusted business partners.

Name: _____

Address: _____

City: _____ **State:** _____ **Zip:** _____

E-mail: _____

☐ Male ☐ Female **Date of Birth** (mm/dd/yyyy): ___ / ___ / ___ (Under 13? Parental consent required)

❶ Do you purchase SHONEN JUMP Magazine?

☐ Yes   ☐ No (if no, skip the next two questions)

If **YES**, do you subscribe?
☐ Yes   ☐ No

If **NO**, how often do you purchase SHONEN JUMP Magazine?
☐ 1-3 issues a year
☐ 4-6 issues a year
☐ more than 7 issues a year

❷ Which SHONEN JUMP Graphic Novel did you purchase? (please check one)

☐ Beet the Vandel Buster   ☐ Bleach   ☐ Dragon Ball
☐ Dragon Ball Z   ☐ Dr. Slump   ☐ Eyeshield 21
☐ Hikaru no Go   ☐ Hunter x Hunter   ☐ I"s
☐ Knights of the Zodiac   ☐ Legendz   ☐ Naruto
☐ One Piece   ☐ Rurouni Kenshin   ☐ Shaman King
☐ The Prince of Tennis   ☐ Ultimate Muscle   ☐ Whistle!
☐ Yu-Gi-Oh!   ☐ Yu-Gi-Oh!: Duelist   ☐ YuYu Hakusho
☐ Other _____

Will you purchase subsequent volumes?
☐ Yes   ☐ No

❸ How did you learn about this title? (check all that apply)

☐ Favorite title   ☐ Advertisement   ☐ Article
☐ Gift   ☐ Read excerpt in SHONEN JUMP Magazine
☐ Recommendation   ☐ Special offer   ☐ Through TV animation
☐ Website   ☐ Other _____

Check us out
on the web!

www.shonenjump.com

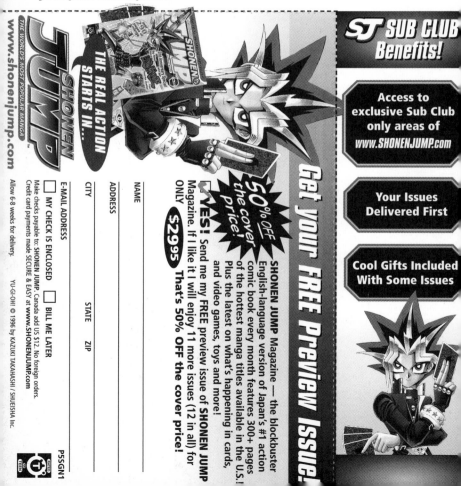

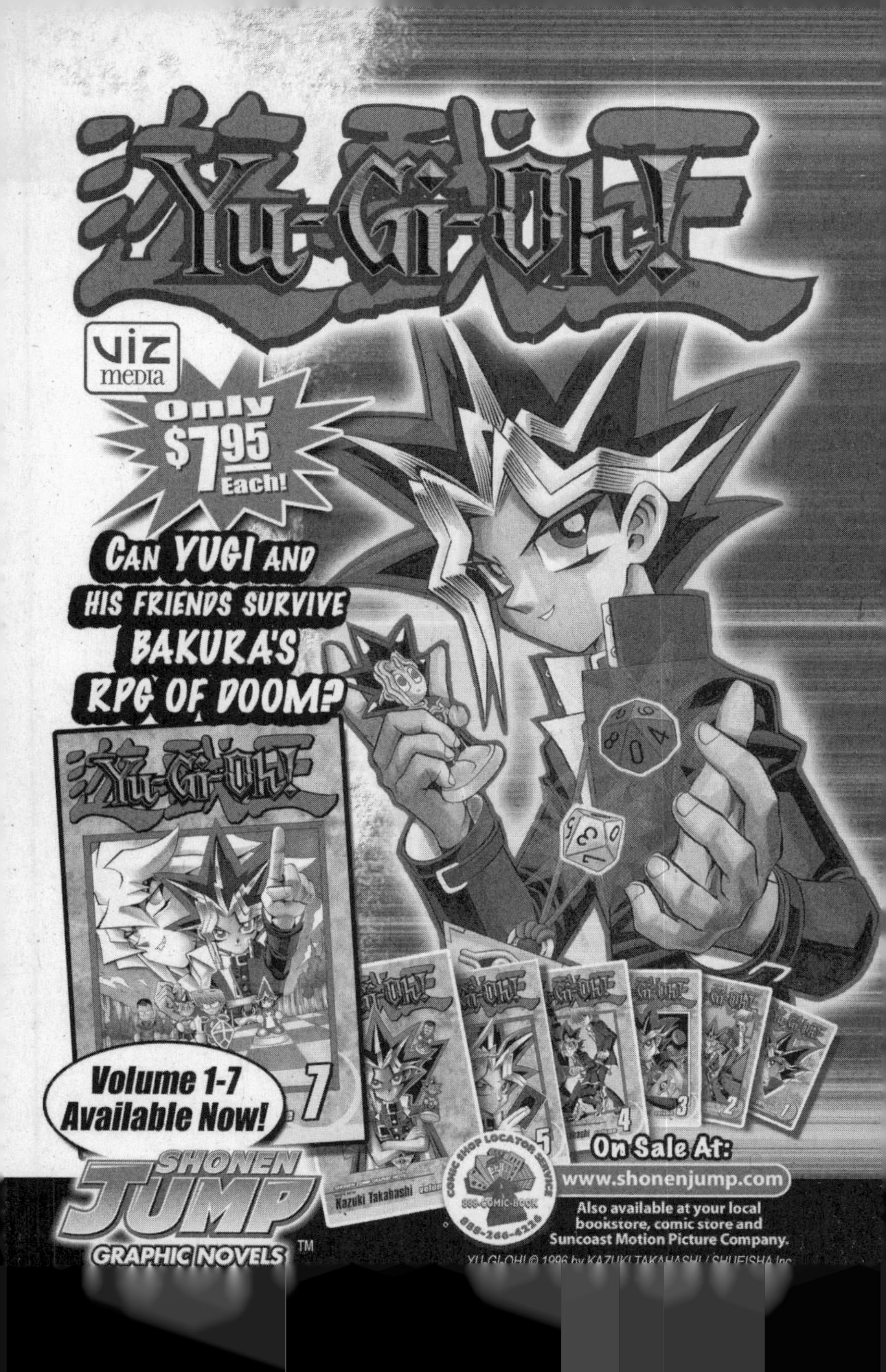

Yu-Gi-Oh!™
viz media
Only $7.95 Each!
Can Yugi and his friends survive Bakura's RPG of doom?
Yu-Gi-Oh!
7
Volume 1-7
Available Now!
5
4
3
2
1
Kazuki Takahashi
Shonen Jump Graphic Novels™
Comic Shop Locator Service
888-COMIC-BOOK
888-266-4226
On Sale At:
www.shonenjump.com
Also available at your local bookstore, comic store and Suncoast Motion Picture Company.
YU-GI-OH! © 1996 by KAZUKI TAKAHASHI / SHUEISHA Inc.

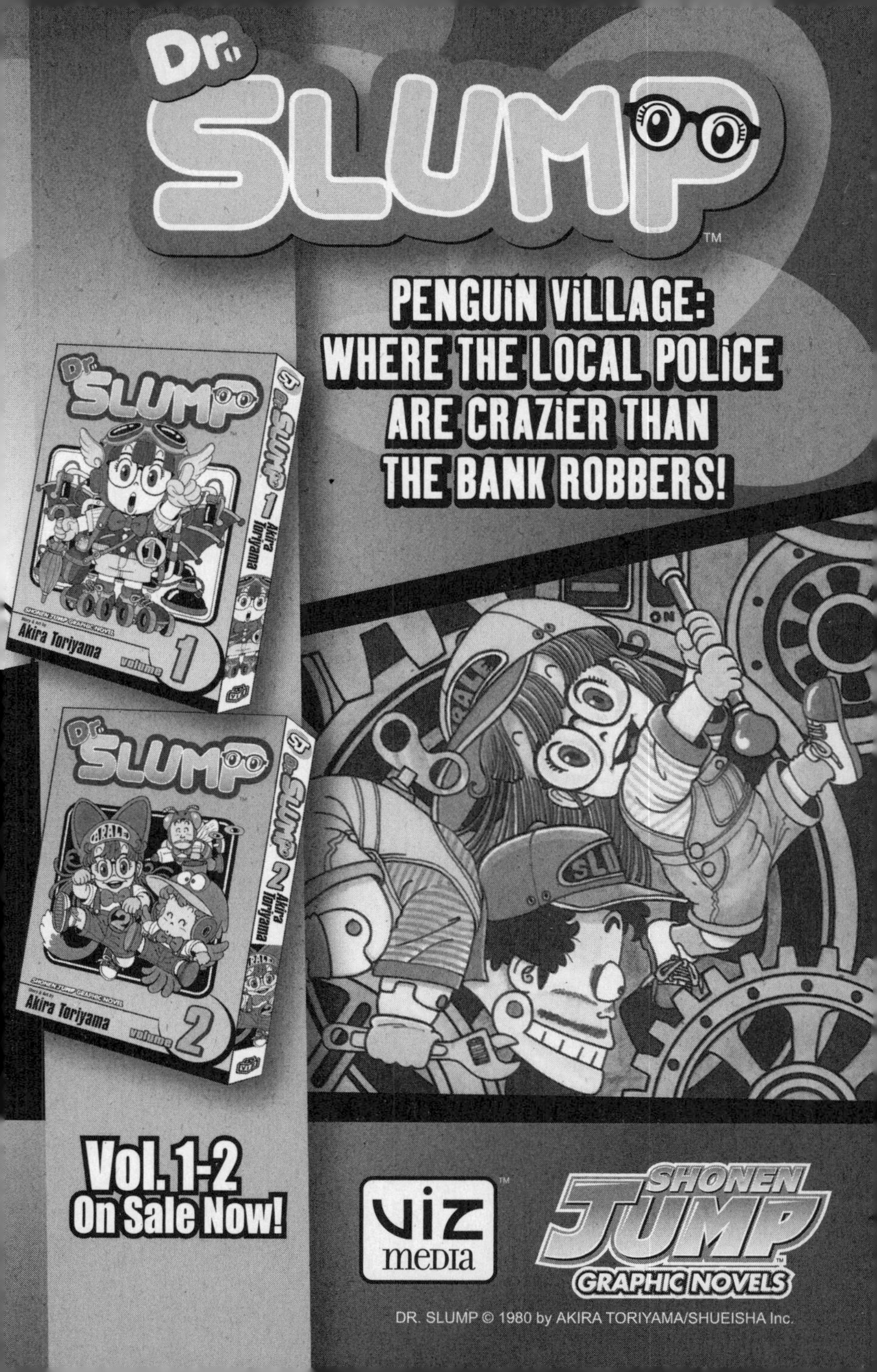
Dr. SLUMP™
PENGUIN VILLAGE: WHERE THE LOCAL POLICE ARE CRAZIER THAN THE BANK ROBBERS!
Dr. SLUMP
Akira Toriyama
volume 1
Dr. SLUMP
Akira Toriyama
volume 2
Vol. 1-2
On Sale Now!
viz media
SHONEN JUMP GRAPHIC NOVELS
DR. SLUMP © 1980 by AKIRA TORIYAMA/SHUEISHA Inc.

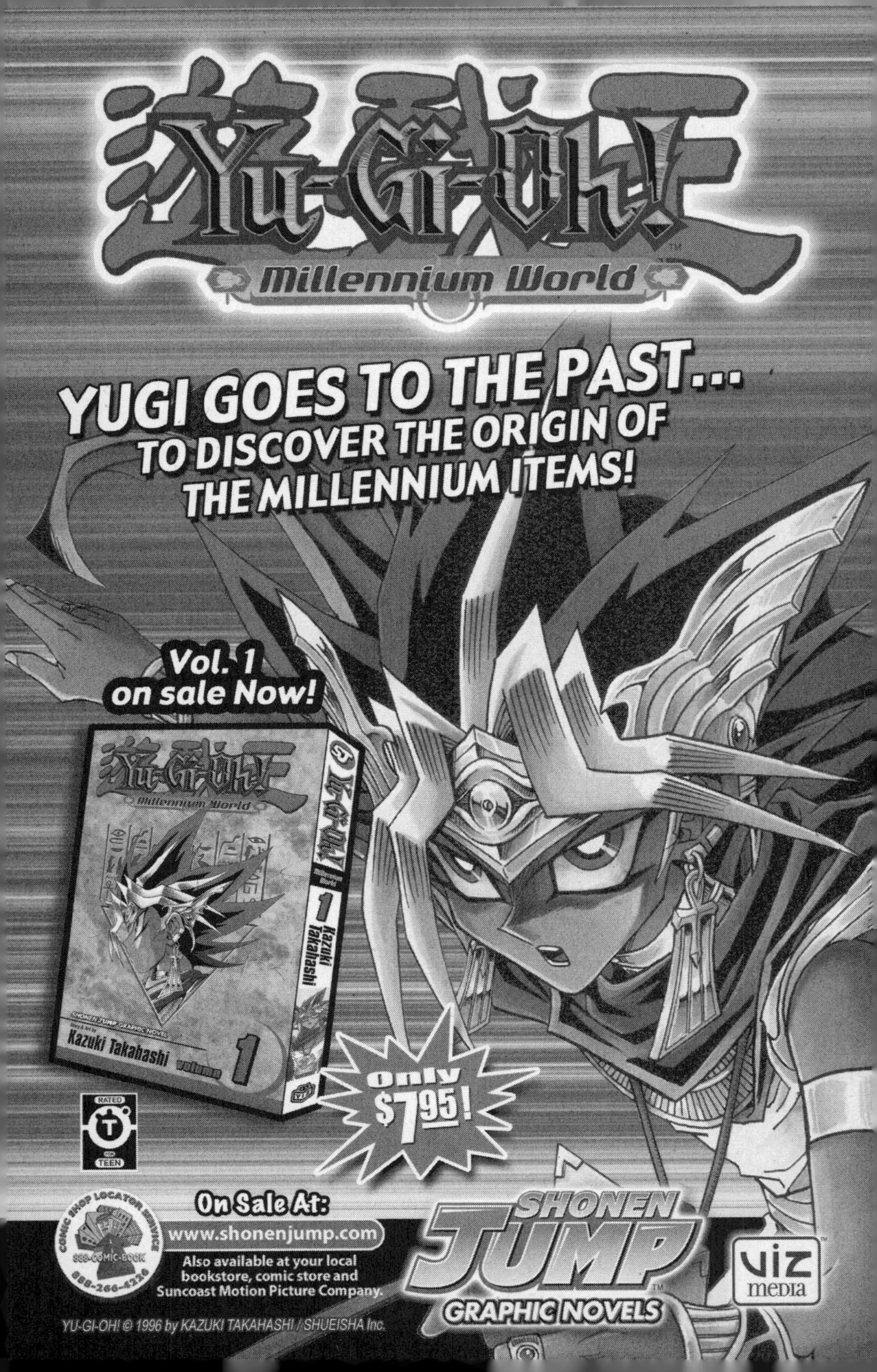

SHONEN JUMP GRAPHIC NOVEL

Vol. 7

HEAVY METAL RAIDERS
STORY AND ART BY
KAZUKI TAKAHASHI

《MAIN CAST》

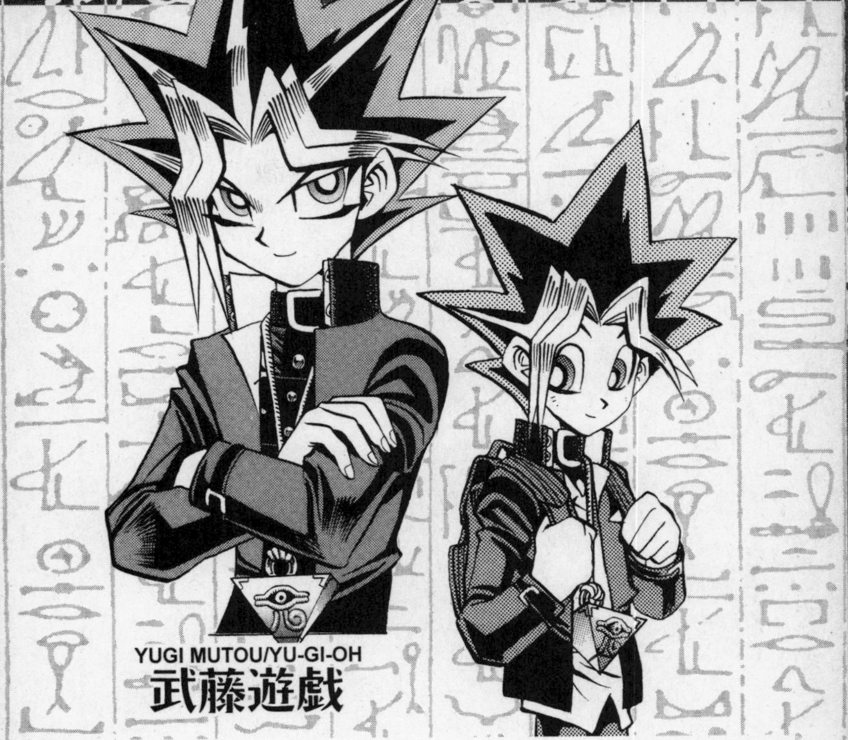
YUGI MUTOU/YU-GI-OH
武藤遊戯

Using the power of his Millennium Eye, Pegasus stole the soul of Yugi's grandpa, and forced Yugi to enter a "Duel Monsters" tournament on his private island, Duelist Kingdom. Yugi's archrival, Kaiba, also entered the tournament to protect his company from a takeover by Pegasus...and to rescue his little brother Mokuba. In a shocking upset, Kaiba beat Yugi for the first time ever, and advanced to fight Pegasus, only to be utterly defeated. Now, four duelists remain for the final rounds of the tournament…and the first match is Yugi vs. Mai…

MAXIMILLION J. PEGASUS
ペガサス・J・クロフォード

SETO KAIBA
海馬瀬人

SUGOROKU MUTOU
武藤双六

HIROTO HONDA
本田ヒロト

ANZU MAZAKI
真崎杏子

KATSUYA JONOUCHI
城之内克也

RYO BAKURA
獏良 了

MAI KUJAKU
孔雀 舞

THE STORY SO FAR...

When 10th grader Yugi solved the Millennium Puzzle, he became
Yu-Gi-Oh, the King of Games, a dark avenger who challenged
evildoers to "Shadow Games" of life and death. Using his gaming
skills, he faced deadly adversaries like Seto Kaiba, obsessive
gamer and teenage corporate president, and Ryo Bakura, whose
friendly personality turned evil when he was possessed by the
spirit of the Millennium Ring. But Yugi's toughest opponent was
Maximillion Pegasus, bearer of the Millennium Eye and super-rich
creator of "Duel Monsters," the world's most popular collectible
card game.

Yu-Gi-Oh! Duelist

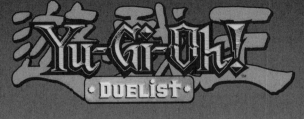

Vol. 7

CONTENTS

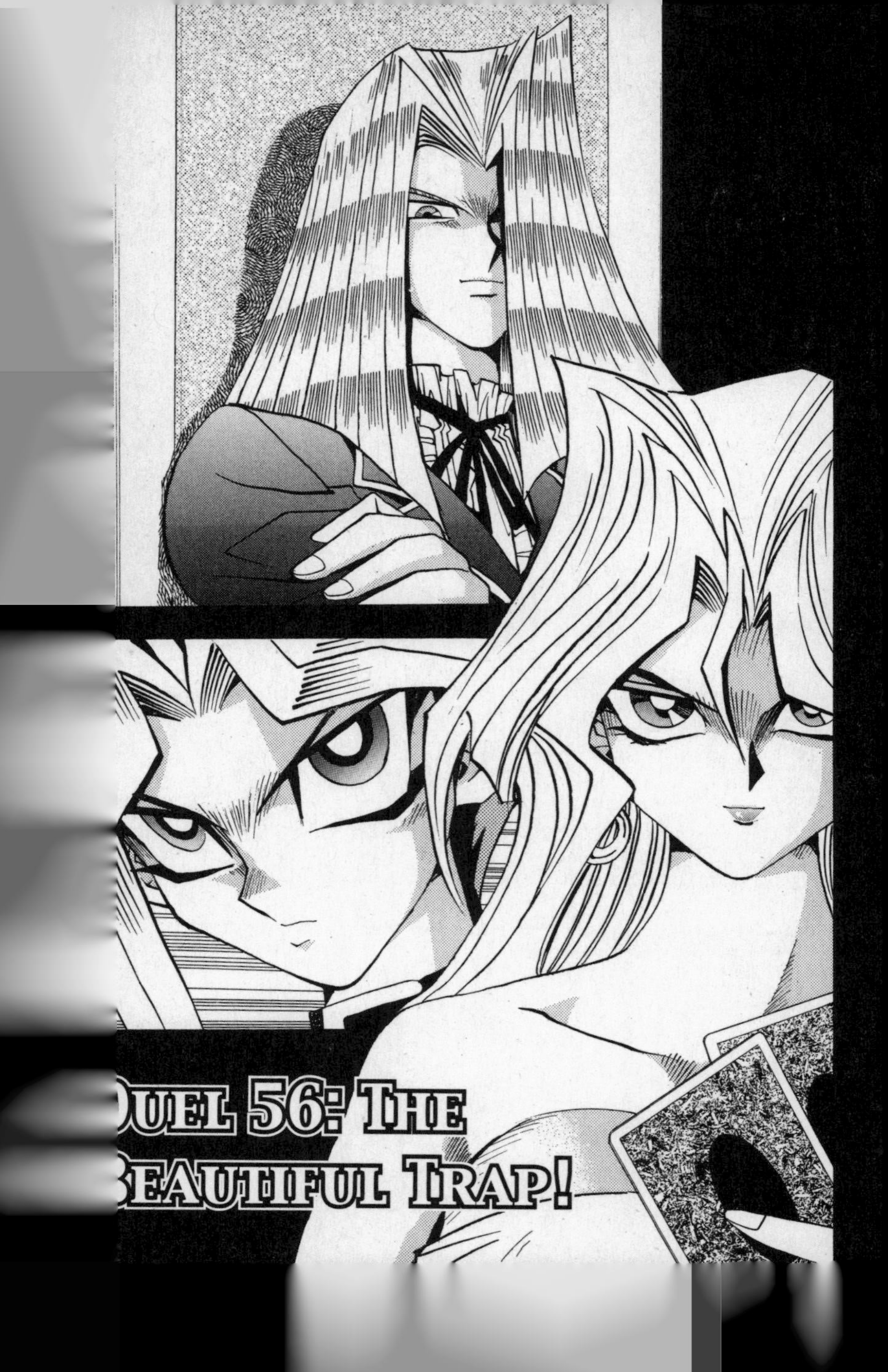
Duel 56: The
Beautiful Trap!

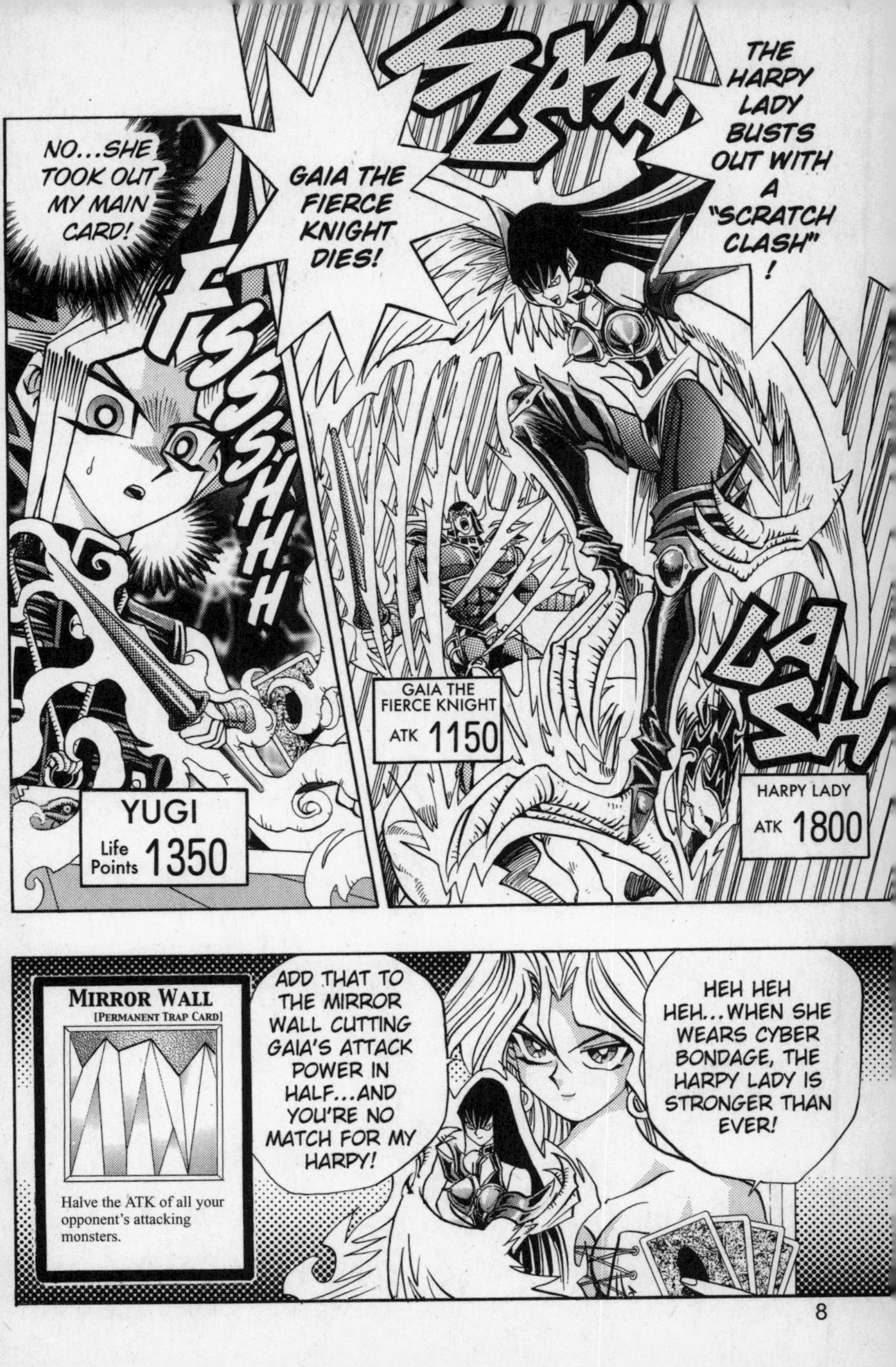
SLASH
THE HARPY LADY BUSTS OUT WITH A "SCRATCH CLASH"!
GAIA THE FIERCE KNIGHT DIES!
GAIA THE FIERCE KNIGHT ATK 1150
HARPY LADY ATK 1800
NO...SHE TOOK OUT MY MAIN CARD!
FSSSSHHHH
YUGI Life Points 1350
HEH HEH HEH...WHEN SHE WEARS CYBER BONDAGE, THE HARPY LADY IS STRONGER THAN EVER!
ADD THAT TO THE MIRROR WALL CUTTING GAIA'S ATTACK POWER IN HALF...AND YOU'RE NO MATCH FOR MY HARPY!
MIRROR WALL
[PERMANENT TRAP CARD]
Halve the ATK of all your opponent's attacking monsters.

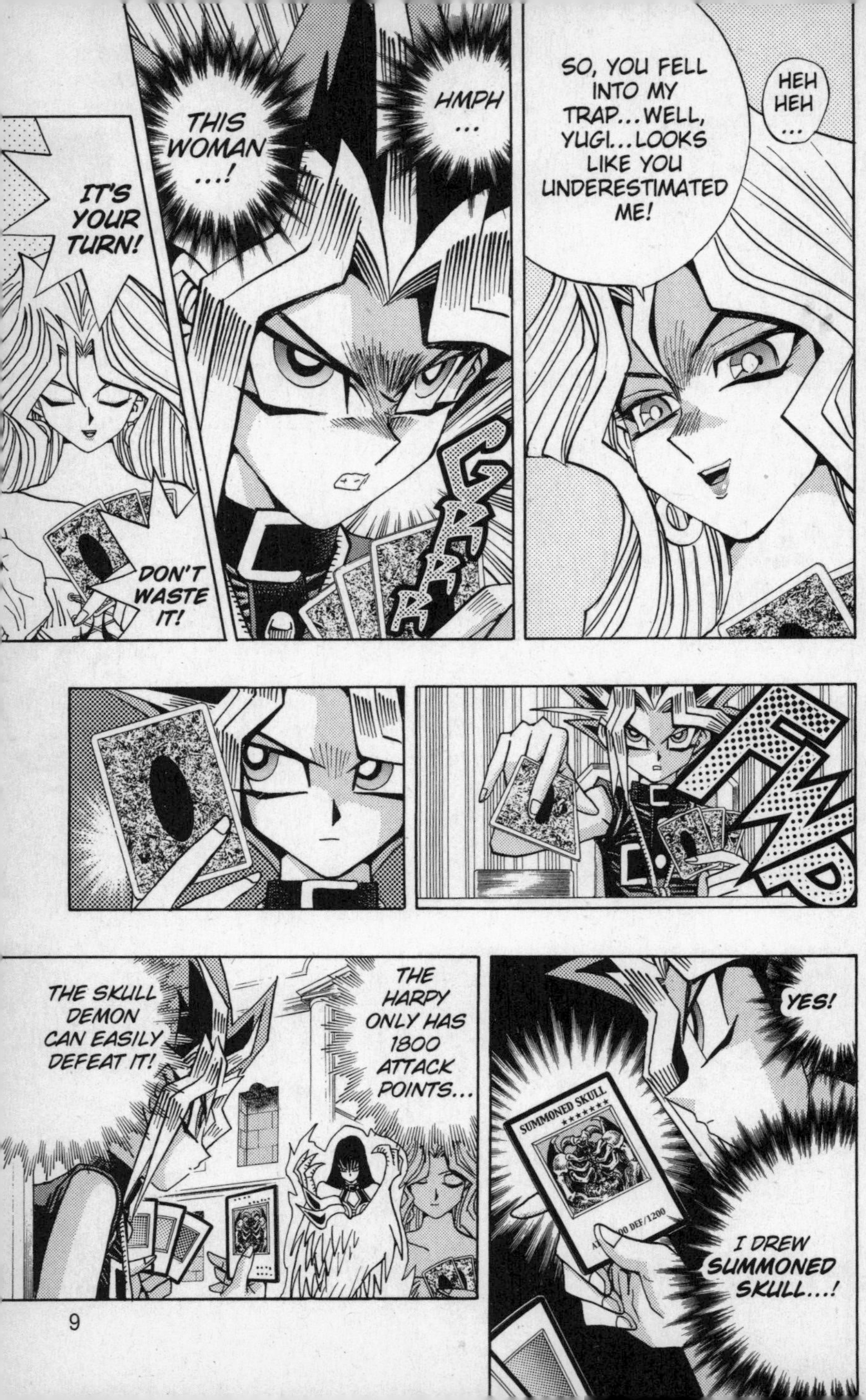
HEH HEH ...
SO, YOU FELL INTO MY TRAP...WELL, YUGI...LOOKS LIKE YOU UNDERESTIMATED ME!
HMPH ...
THIS WOMAN ...!
IT'S YOUR TURN!
DON'T WASTE IT!
YES!
SUMMONED SKULL
I DREW SUMMONED SKULL...!
THE HARPY ONLY HAS 1800 ATTACK POINTS...
THE SKULL DEMON CAN EASILY DEFEAT IT!

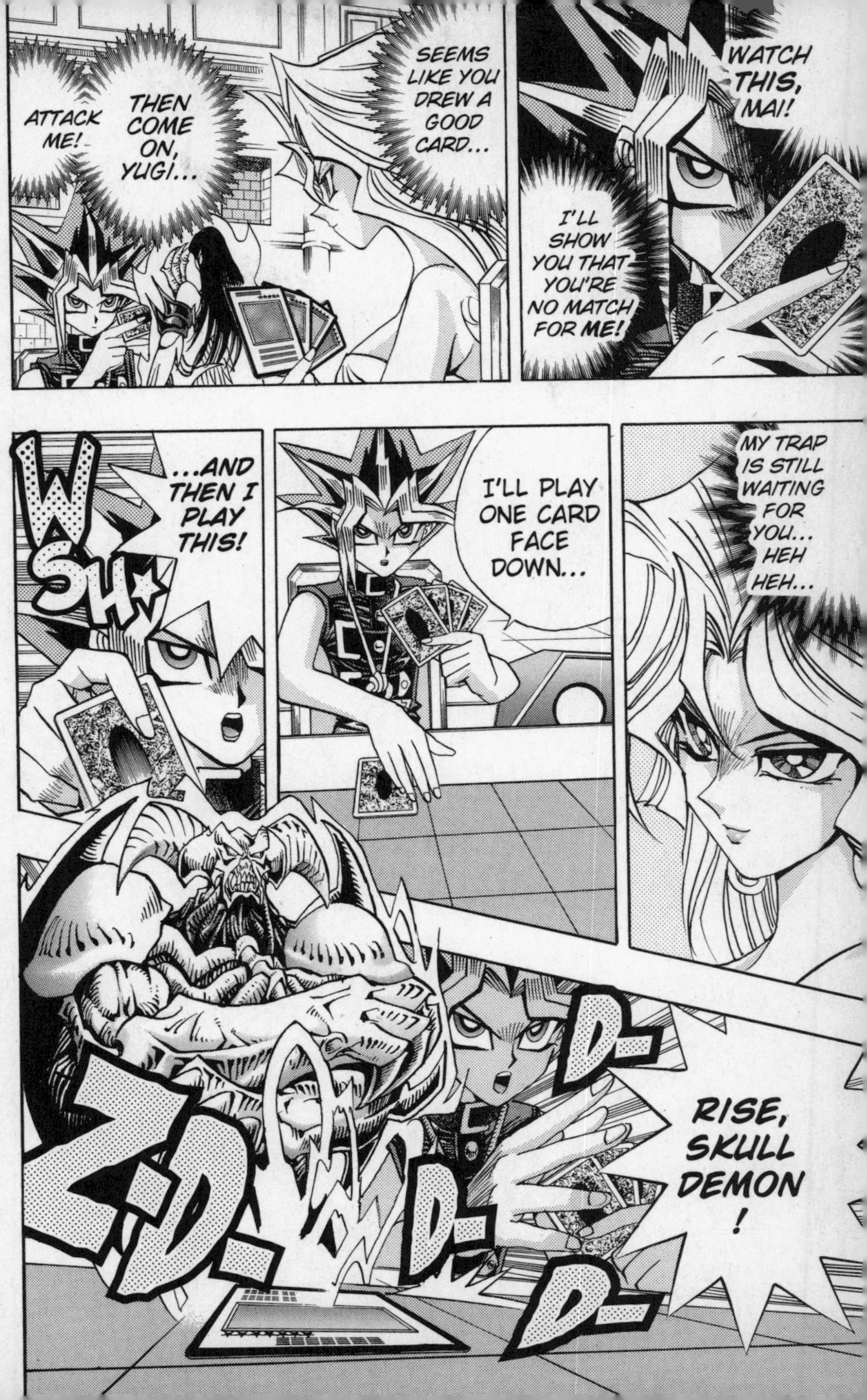
WATCH THIS, MAI!
I'LL SHOW YOU THAT YOU'RE NO MATCH FOR ME!
SEEMS LIKE YOU DREW A GOOD CARD...
THEN COME ON, YUGI...
ATTACK ME!
MY TRAP IS STILL WAITING FOR YOU... HEH HEH...
I'LL PLAY ONE CARD FACE DOWN...
...AND THEN I PLAY THIS!
WSH
RISE, SKULL DEMON!
D-
D-
D-
Z-D-

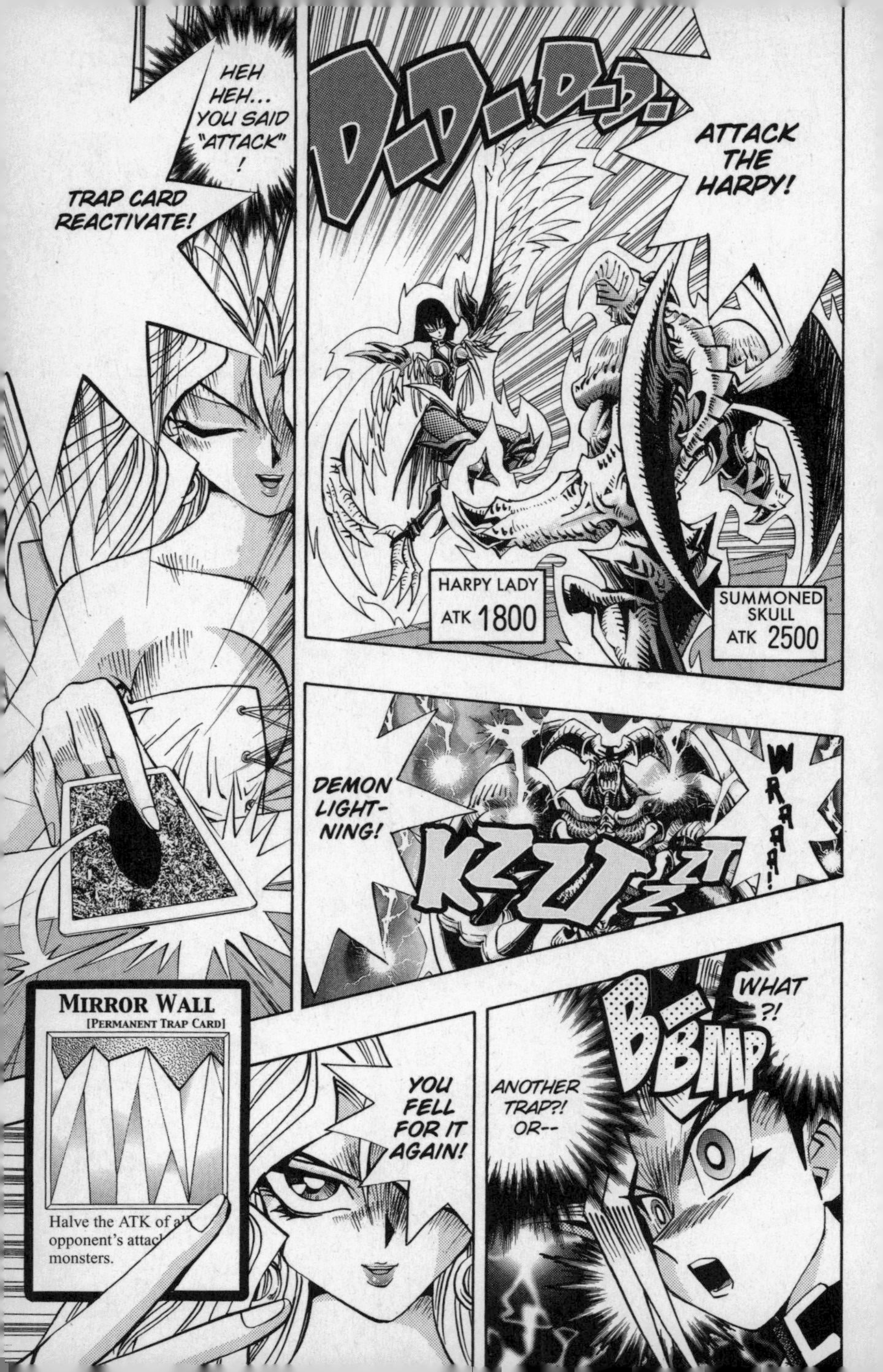

ATTACK THE HARPY!
D..D..D..D..
HARPY LADY ATK 1800
SUMMONED SKULL ATK 2500
DEMON LIGHTNING!
WRAAA!
KZZTZZT
HEH HEH... YOU SAID "ATTACK"!
TRAP CARD REACTIVATE!
MIRROR WALL
[PERMANENT TRAP CARD]
Halve the ATK of all opponent's attacking monsters.
WHAT?!
B-BMP
ANOTHER TRAP?! OR--
YOU FELL FOR IT AGAIN!

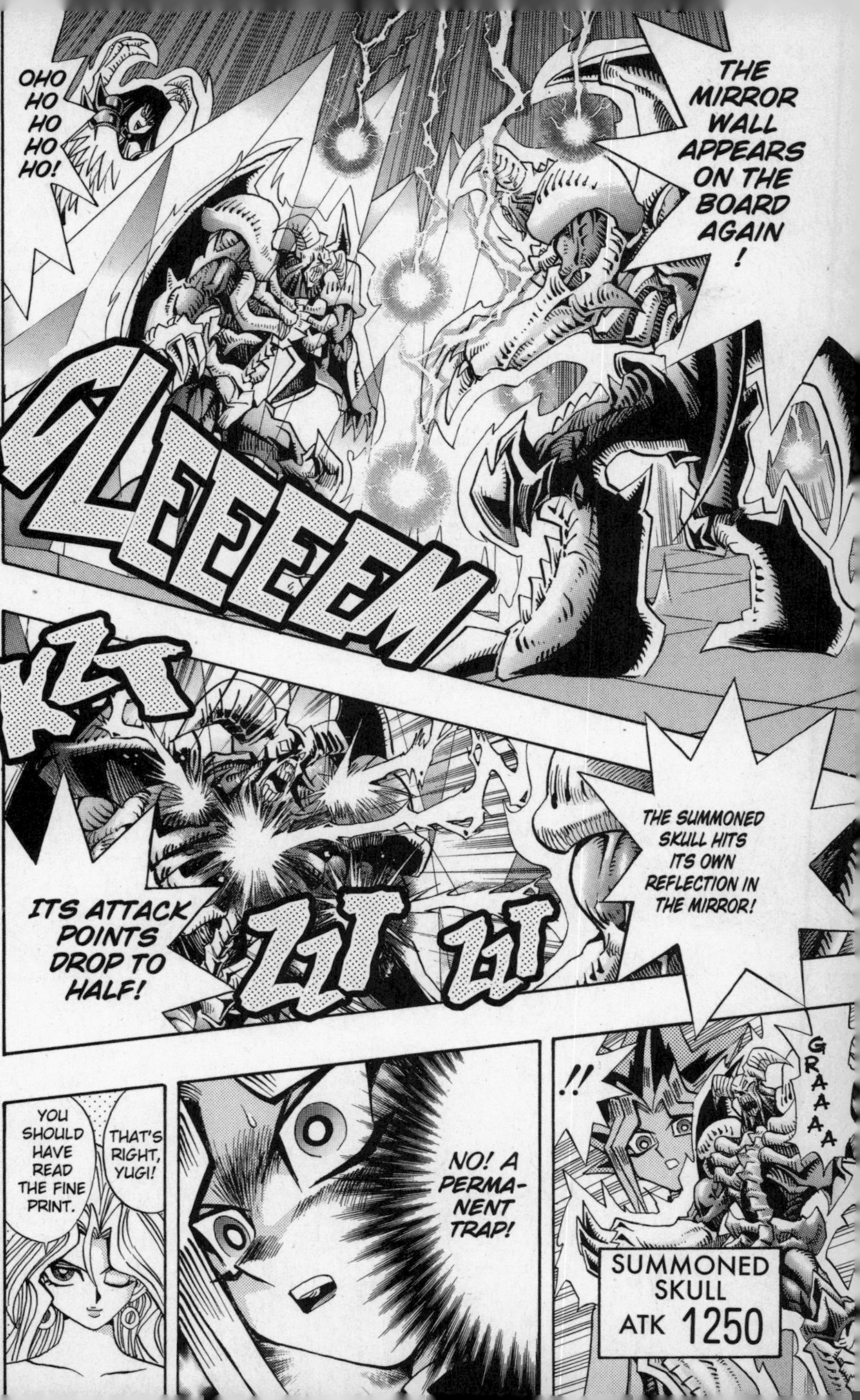
THE MIRROR WALL APPEARS ON THE BOARD AGAIN!
OHO HO HO HO HO!
THE SUMMONED SKULL HITS ITS OWN REFLECTION IN THE MIRROR!
ITS ATTACK POINTS DROP TO HALF!
!!
GRAAAA
SUMMONED SKULL
ATK 1250
NO! A PERMA-NENT TRAP!
THAT'S RIGHT, YUGI!
YOU SHOULD HAVE READ THE FINE PRINT.

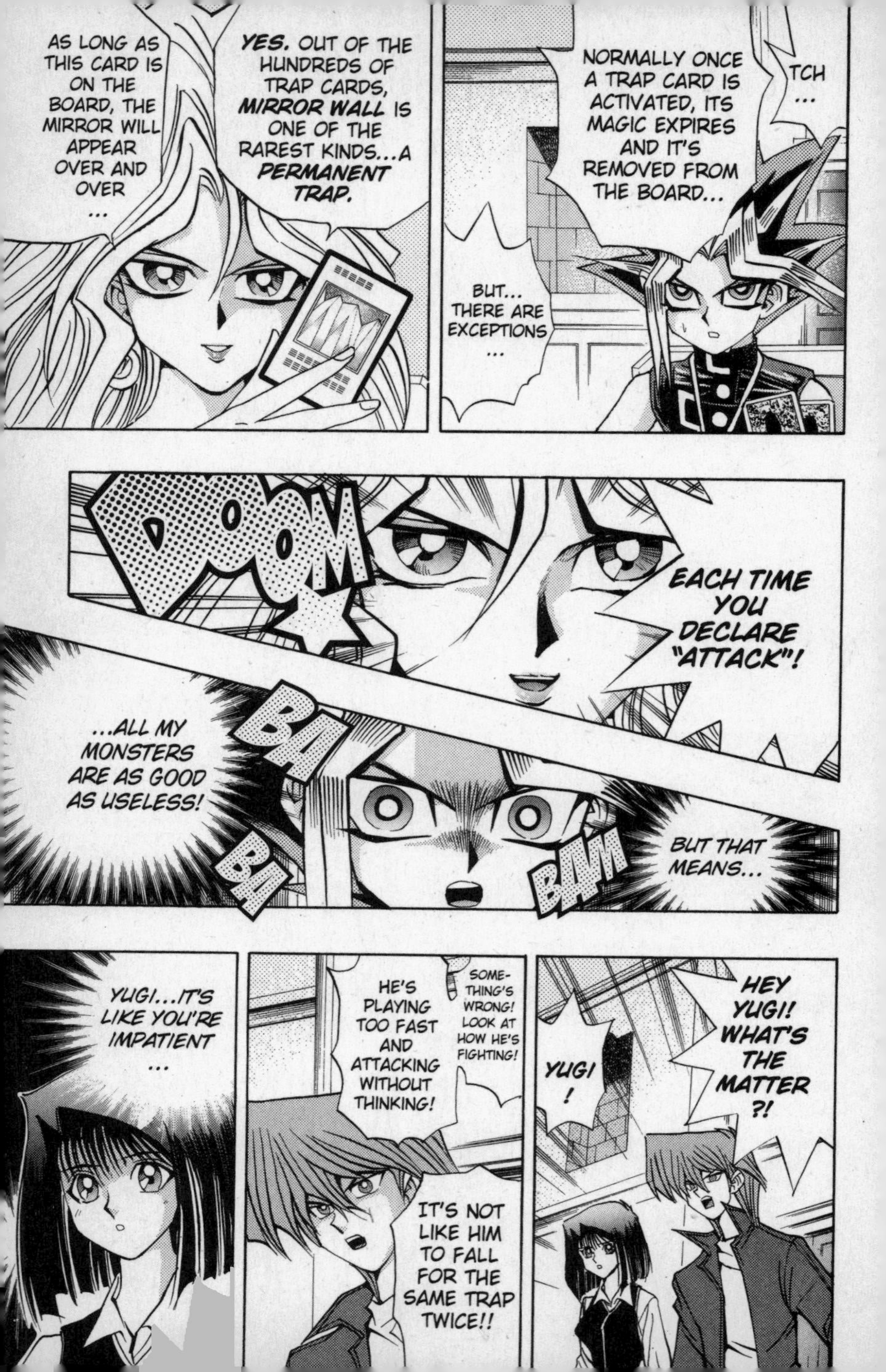
TCH ...
NORMALLY ONCE A TRAP CARD IS ACTIVATED, ITS MAGIC EXPIRES AND IT'S REMOVED FROM THE BOARD...
BUT... THERE ARE EXCEPTIONS ...
YES. OUT OF THE HUNDREDS OF TRAP CARDS, MIRROR WALL IS ONE OF THE RAREST KINDS...A PERMANENT TRAP.
AS LONG AS THIS CARD IS ON THE BOARD, THE MIRROR WILL APPEAR OVER AND OVER ...
DOOM
EACH TIME YOU DECLARE "ATTACK"!
BA
BA
BAM
BUT THAT MEANS...
...ALL MY MONSTERS ARE AS GOOD AS USELESS!
HEY YUGI! WHAT'S THE MATTER ?!
YUGI !
SOME-THING'S WRONG! LOOK AT HOW HE'S FIGHTING!
HE'S PLAYING TOO FAST AND ATTACKING WITHOUT THINKING!
IT'S NOT LIKE HIM TO FALL FOR THE SAME TRAP TWICE!!
YUGI...IT'S LIKE YOU'RE IMPATIENT ...

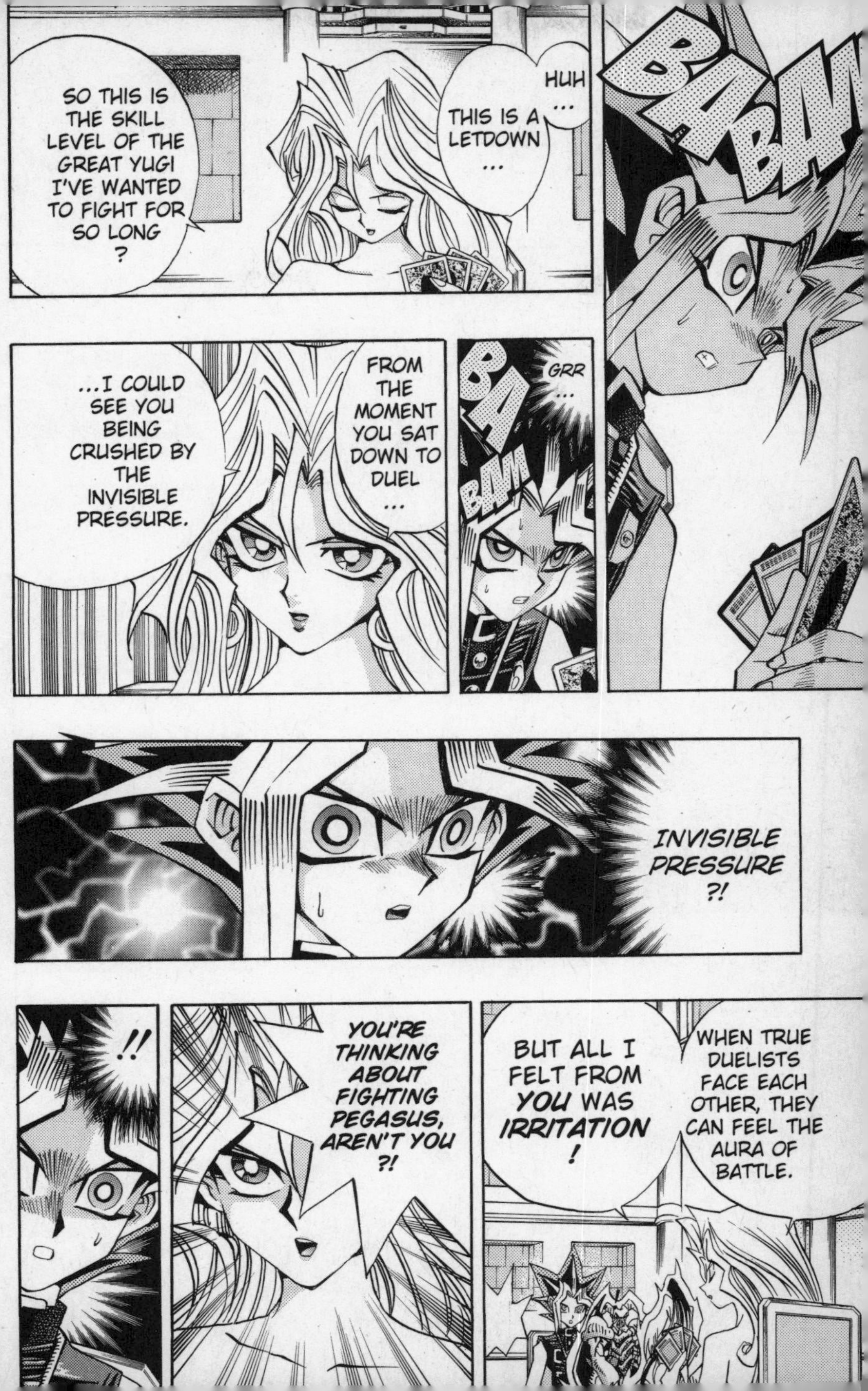
BABA
HUH ...
THIS IS A LETDOWN ...
SO THIS IS THE SKILL LEVEL OF THE GREAT YUGI I'VE WANTED TO FIGHT FOR SO LONG ?
GRR ...
BA BAM
FROM THE MOMENT YOU SAT DOWN TO DUEL ...
...I COULD SEE YOU BEING CRUSHED BY THE INVISIBLE PRESSURE.
INVISIBLE PRESSURE ?!
WHEN TRUE DUELISTS FACE EACH OTHER, THEY CAN FEEL THE AURA OF BATTLE.
BUT ALL I FELT FROM YOU WAS IRRITATION !
YOU'RE THINKING ABOUT FIGHTING PEGASUS, AREN'T YOU ?!
!!

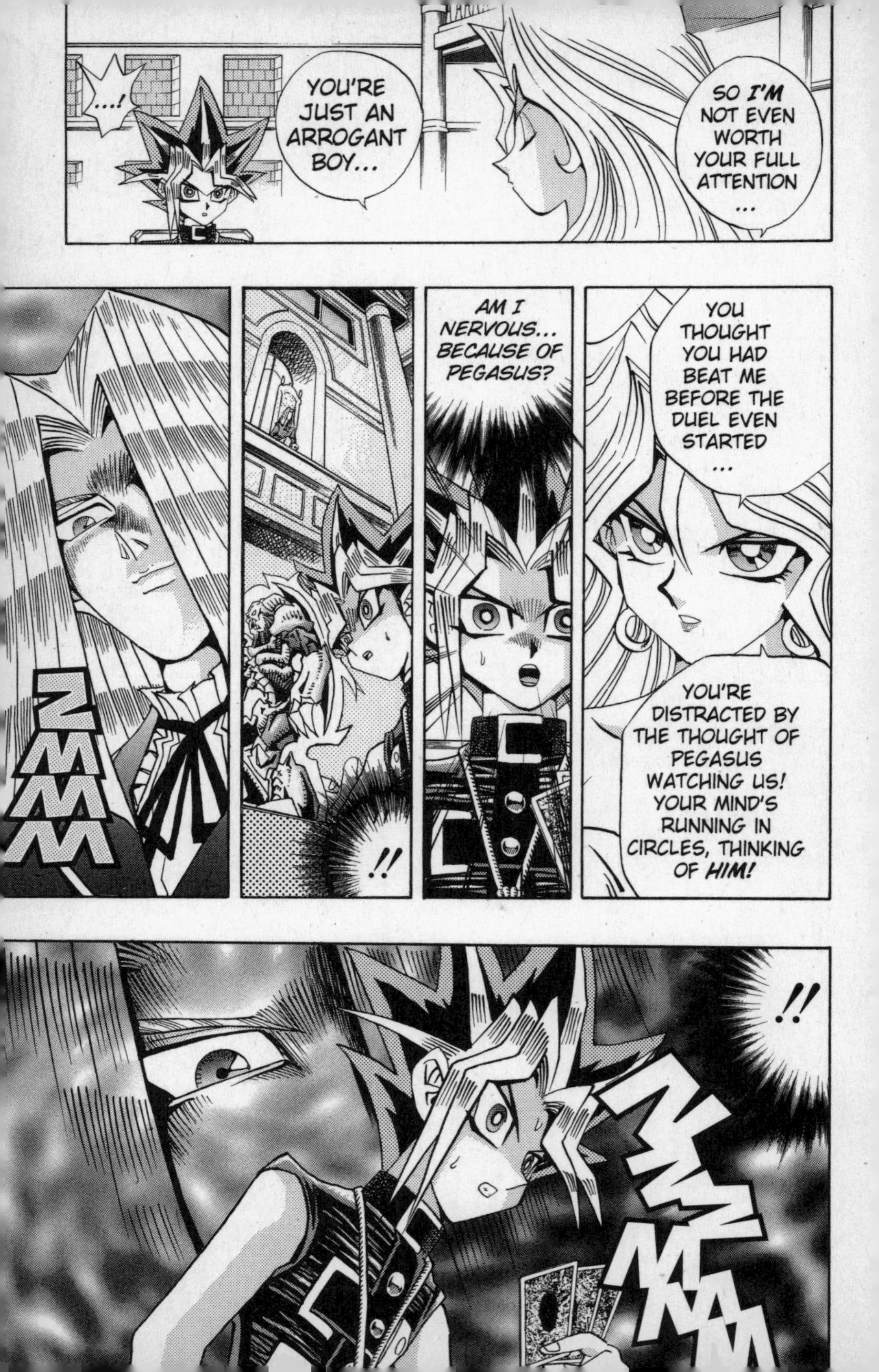
SO *I'M* NOT EVEN WORTH YOUR FULL ATTENTION ...
YOU'RE JUST AN ARROGANT BOY...
...!
YOU THOUGHT YOU HAD BEAT ME BEFORE THE DUEL EVEN STARTED ...
YOU'RE DISTRACTED BY THE THOUGHT OF PEGASUS WATCHING US! YOUR MIND'S RUNNING IN CIRCLES, THINKING OF *HIM!*
AM I NERVOUS... BECAUSE OF PEGASUS?
!!
!!

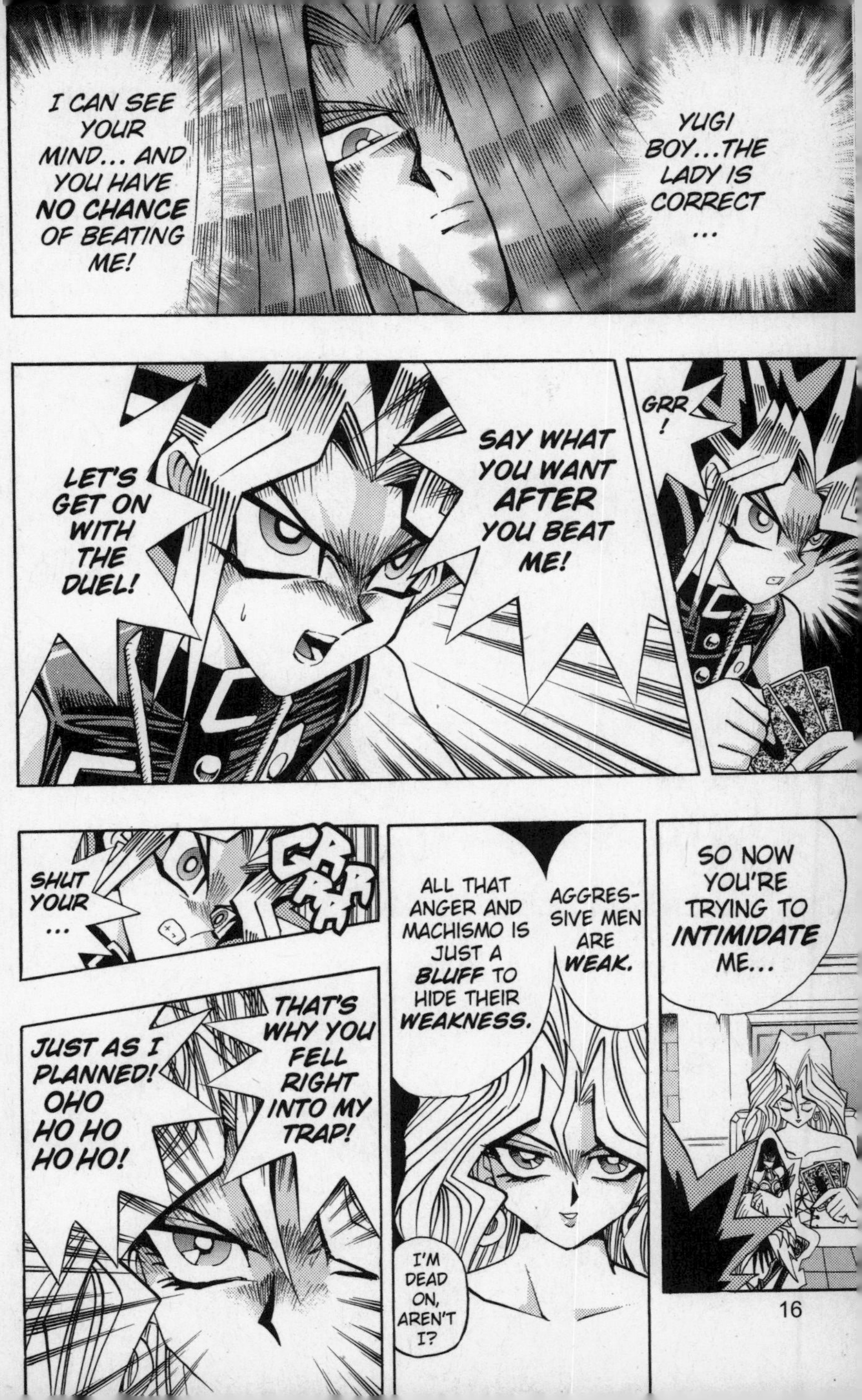
YUGI BOY...THE LADY IS CORRECT ...
I CAN SEE YOUR MIND... AND YOU HAVE NO CHANCE OF BEATING ME!
GRR!
SAY WHAT YOU WANT AFTER YOU BEAT ME!
LET'S GET ON WITH THE DUEL!
SO NOW YOU'RE TRYING TO INTIMIDATE ME...
AGGRES-SIVE MEN ARE WEAK.
ALL THAT ANGER AND MACHISMO IS JUST A BLUFF TO HIDE THEIR WEAKNESS.
I'M DEAD ON, AREN'T I?
GRRRR
SHUT YOUR ...
THAT'S WHY YOU FELL RIGHT INTO MY TRAP!
JUST AS I PLANNED! OHO HO HO HO HO!

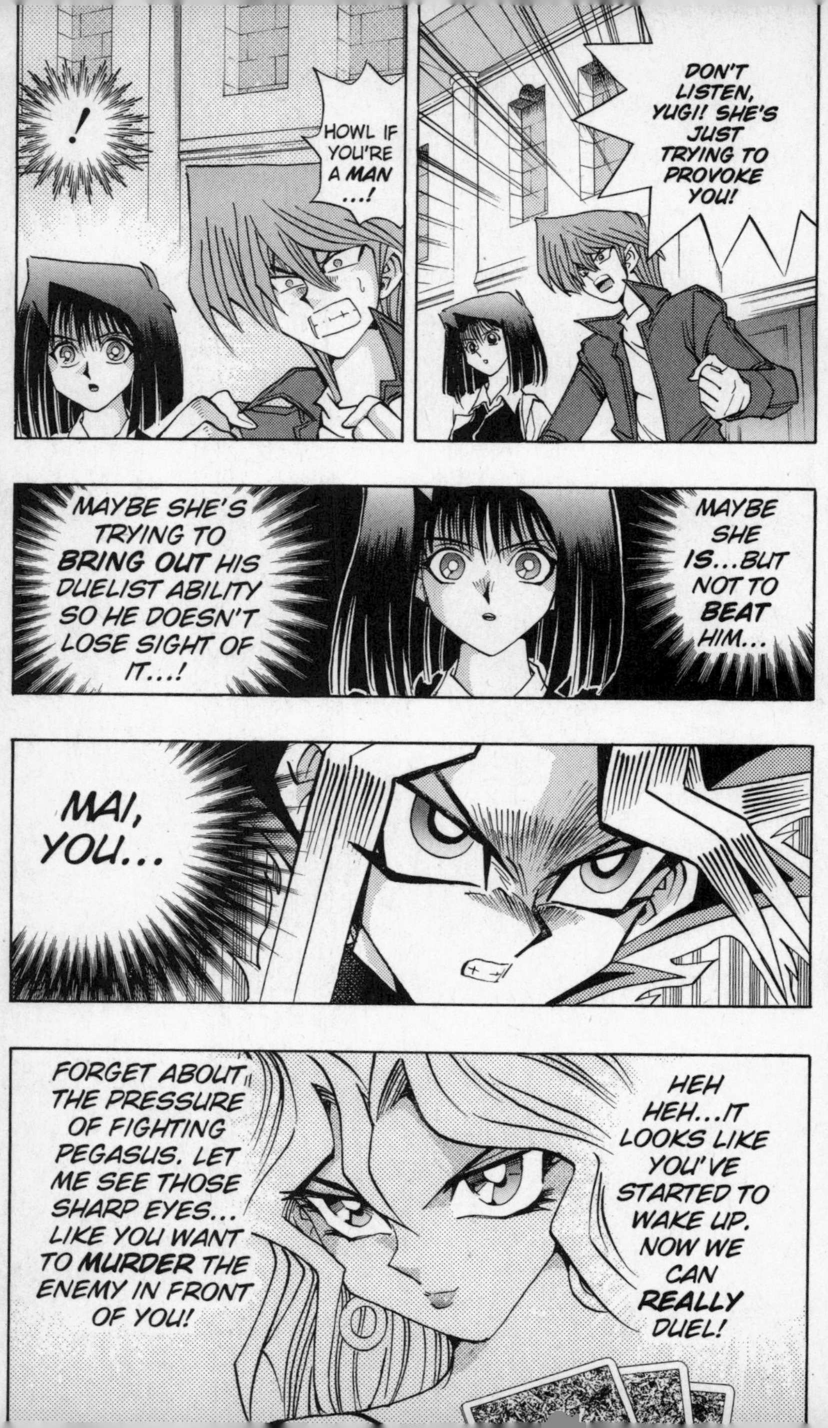
DON'T LISTEN, YUGI! SHE'S JUST TRYING TO PROVOKE YOU!
!
HOWL IF YOU'RE A MAN ...!
MAYBE SHE IS...BUT NOT TO BEAT HIM...
MAYBE SHE'S TRYING TO BRING OUT HIS DUELIST ABILITY SO HE DOESN'T LOSE SIGHT OF IT...!
MAI, YOU...
HEH HEH...IT LOOKS LIKE YOU'VE STARTED TO WAKE UP. NOW WE CAN REALLY DUEL!
FORGET ABOUT THE PRESSURE OF FIGHTING PEGASUS. LET ME SEE THOSE SHARP EYES... LIKE YOU WANT TO MURDER THE ENEMY IN FRONT OF YOU!

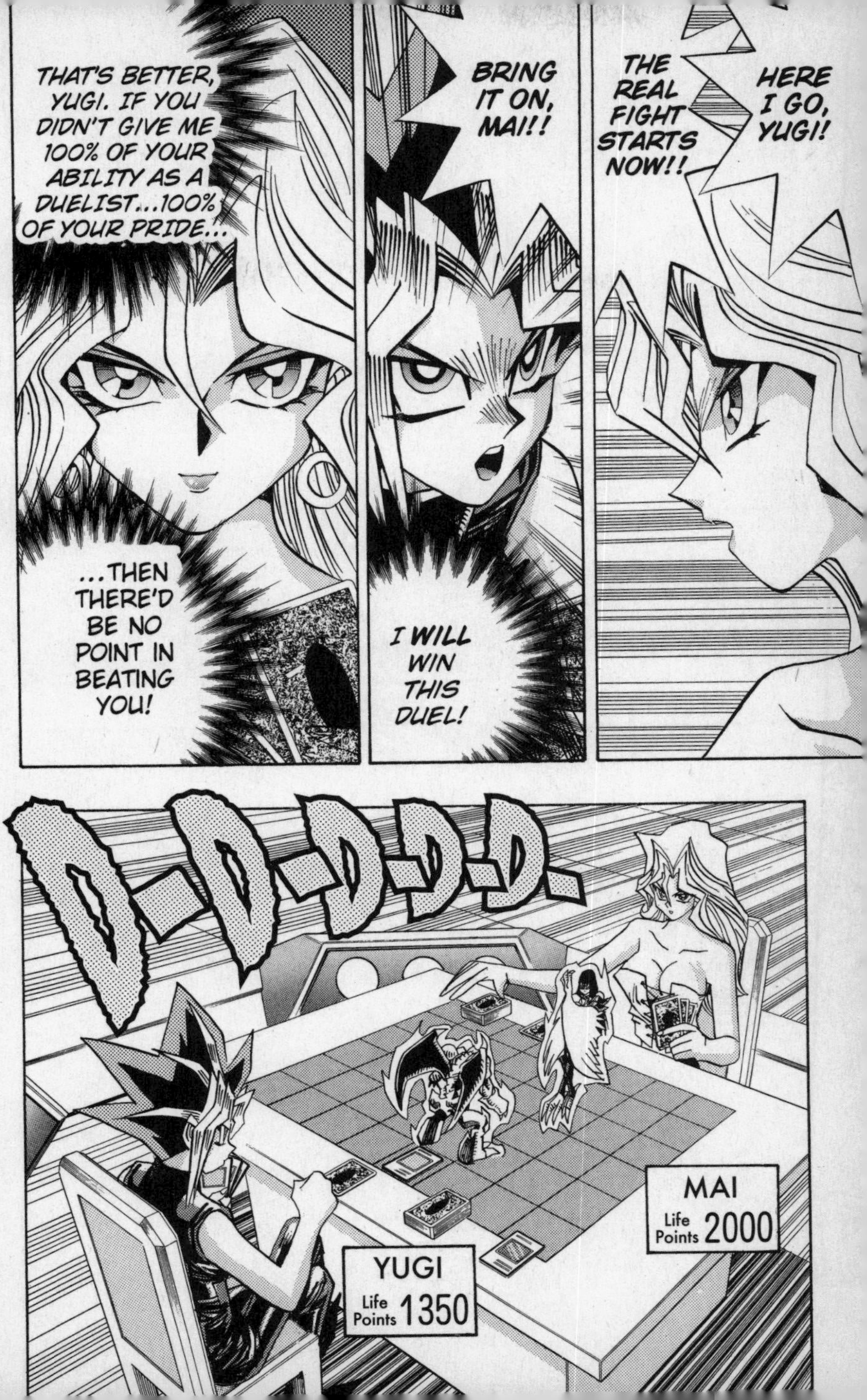
HERE I GO, YUGI!
THE REAL FIGHT STARTS NOW!!
BRING IT ON, MAI!!
I WILL WIN THIS DUEL!
THAT'S BETTER, YUGI. IF YOU DIDN'T GIVE ME 100% OF YOUR ABILITY AS A DUELIST...100% OF YOUR PRIDE...
...THEN THERE'D BE NO POINT IN BEATING YOU!
D-D-D-D-D.
MAI
Life Points 2000
YUGI
Life Points 1350

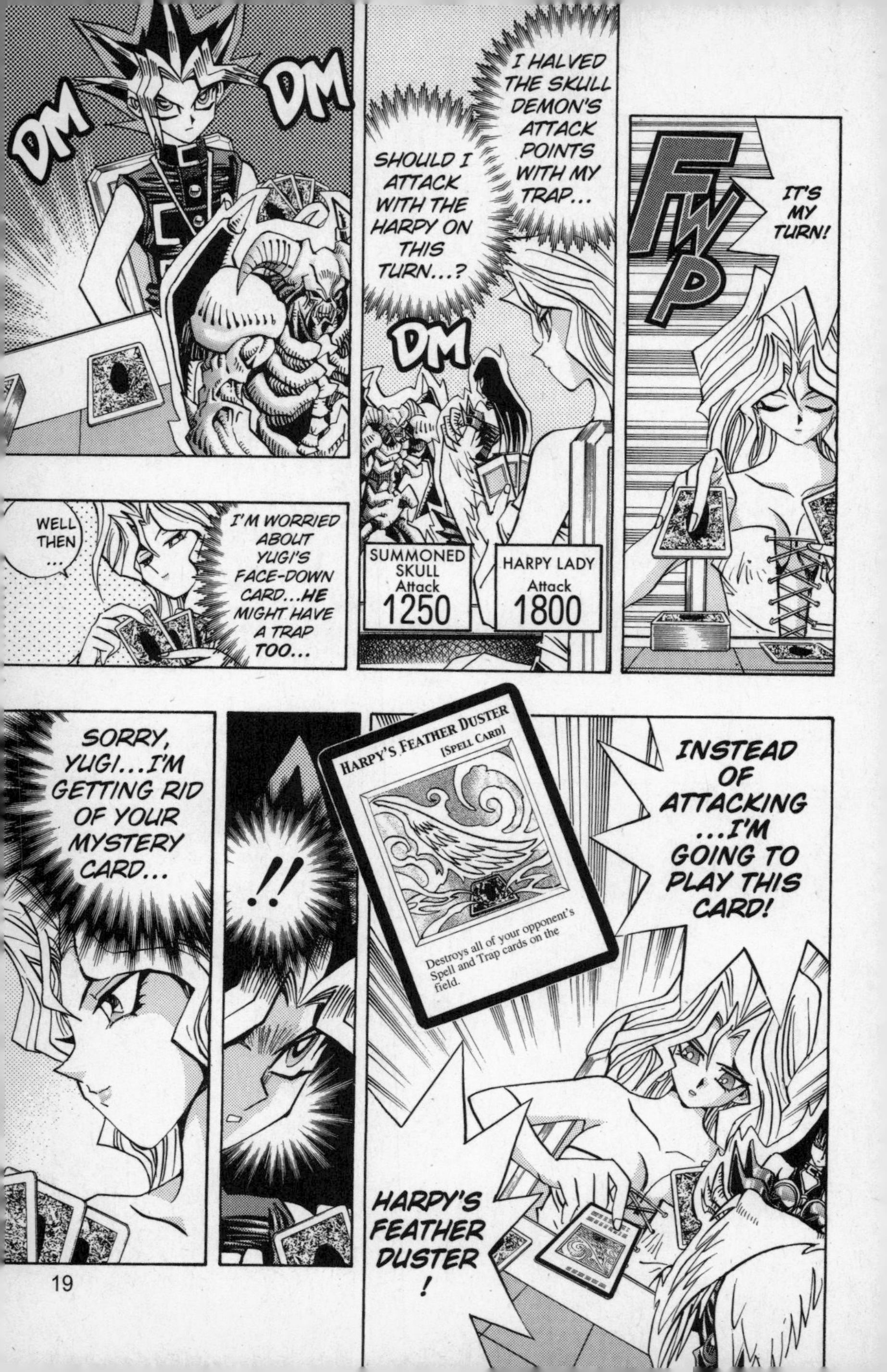
FWP
IT'S MY TURN!
I HALVED THE SKULL DEMON'S ATTACK POINTS WITH MY TRAP...
SHOULD I ATTACK WITH THE HARPY ON THIS TURN...?
DM
SUMMONED SKULL Attack 1250
HARPY LADY Attack 1800
DM
DM
I'M WORRIED ABOUT YUGI'S FACE-DOWN CARD...HE MIGHT HAVE A TRAP TOO...
WELL THEN ...
INSTEAD OF ATTACKING ...I'M GOING TO PLAY THIS CARD!
HARPY'S FEATHER DUSTER [SPELL CARD]
Destroys all of your opponent's Spell and Trap cards on the field.
HARPY'S FEATHER DUSTER!
!!
SORRY, YUGI...I'M GETTING RID OF YOUR MYSTERY CARD...

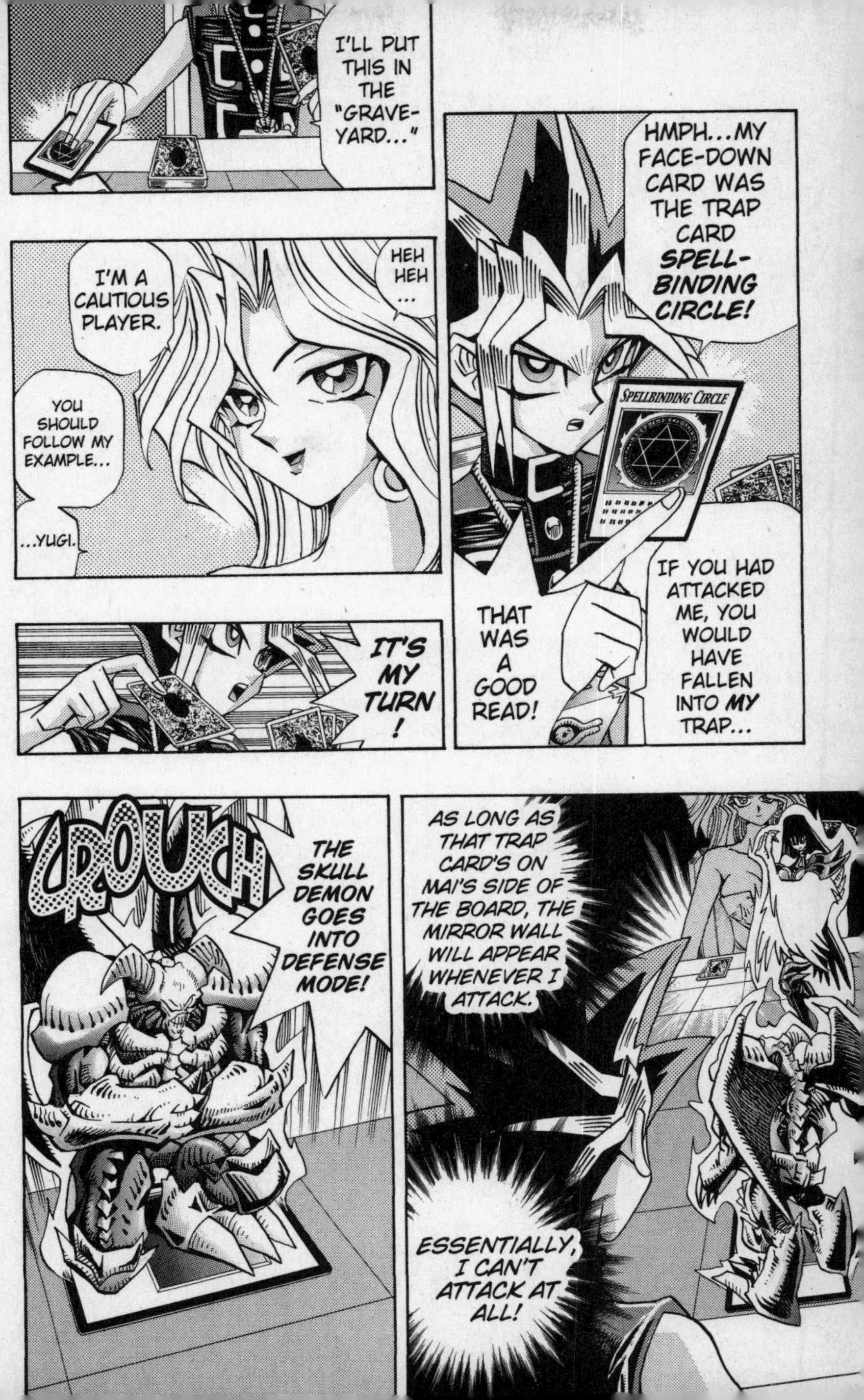
I'LL PUT THIS IN THE "GRAVEYARD..."
HMPH...MY FACE-DOWN CARD WAS THE TRAP CARD SPELL-BINDING CIRCLE!
SPELLBINDING CIRCLE
IF YOU HAD ATTACKED ME, YOU WOULD HAVE FALLEN INTO MY TRAP...
THAT WAS A GOOD READ!
HEH HEH ...
I'M A CAUTIOUS PLAYER.
YOU SHOULD FOLLOW MY EXAMPLE...
...YUGI.
IT'S MY TURN!
AS LONG AS THAT TRAP CARD'S ON MAI'S SIDE OF THE BOARD, THE MIRROR WALL WILL APPEAR WHENEVER I ATTACK.
ESSENTIALLY, I CAN'T ATTACK AT ALL!
CROUCH
THE SKULL DEMON GOES INTO DEFENSE MODE!

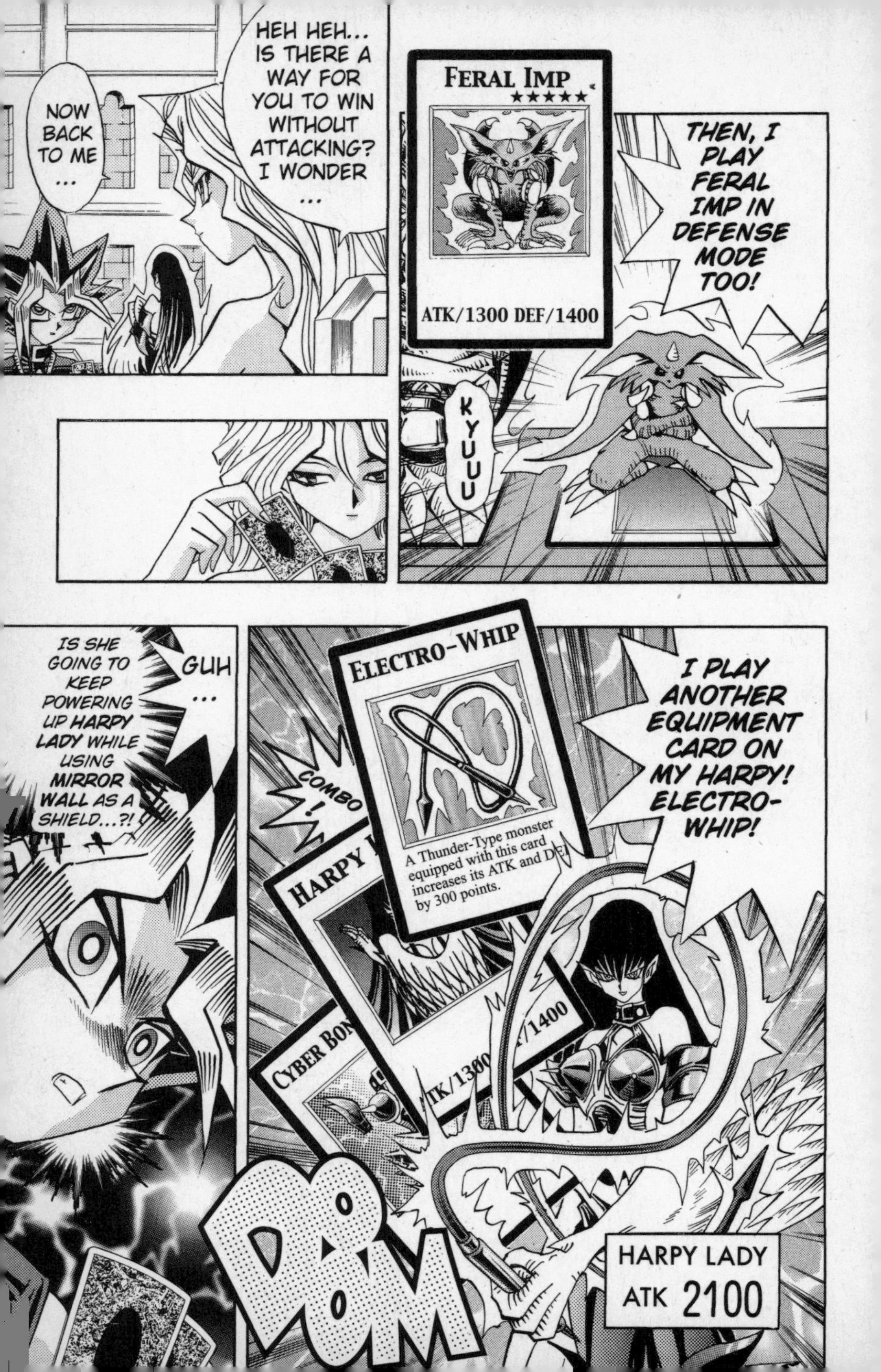

Feral Imp
ATK/1300 DEF/1400
THEN, I PLAY FERAL IMP IN DEFENSE MODE TOO!
KYUUU
HEH HEH... IS THERE A WAY FOR YOU TO WIN WITHOUT ATTACKING? I WONDER ...
NOW BACK TO ME ...
I PLAY ANOTHER EQUIPMENT CARD ON MY HARPY! ELECTRO-WHIP!
Electro-Whip
A Thunder-Type monster equipped with this card increases its ATK and DE
by 300 points.
COMBO!
HARPY
CYBER BON
/1400
TK/1300
DOOM
HARPY LADY
ATK 2100
GUH ...
IS SHE GOING TO KEEP POWERING UP HARPY LADY WHILE USING MIRROR WALL AS A SHIELD...?!

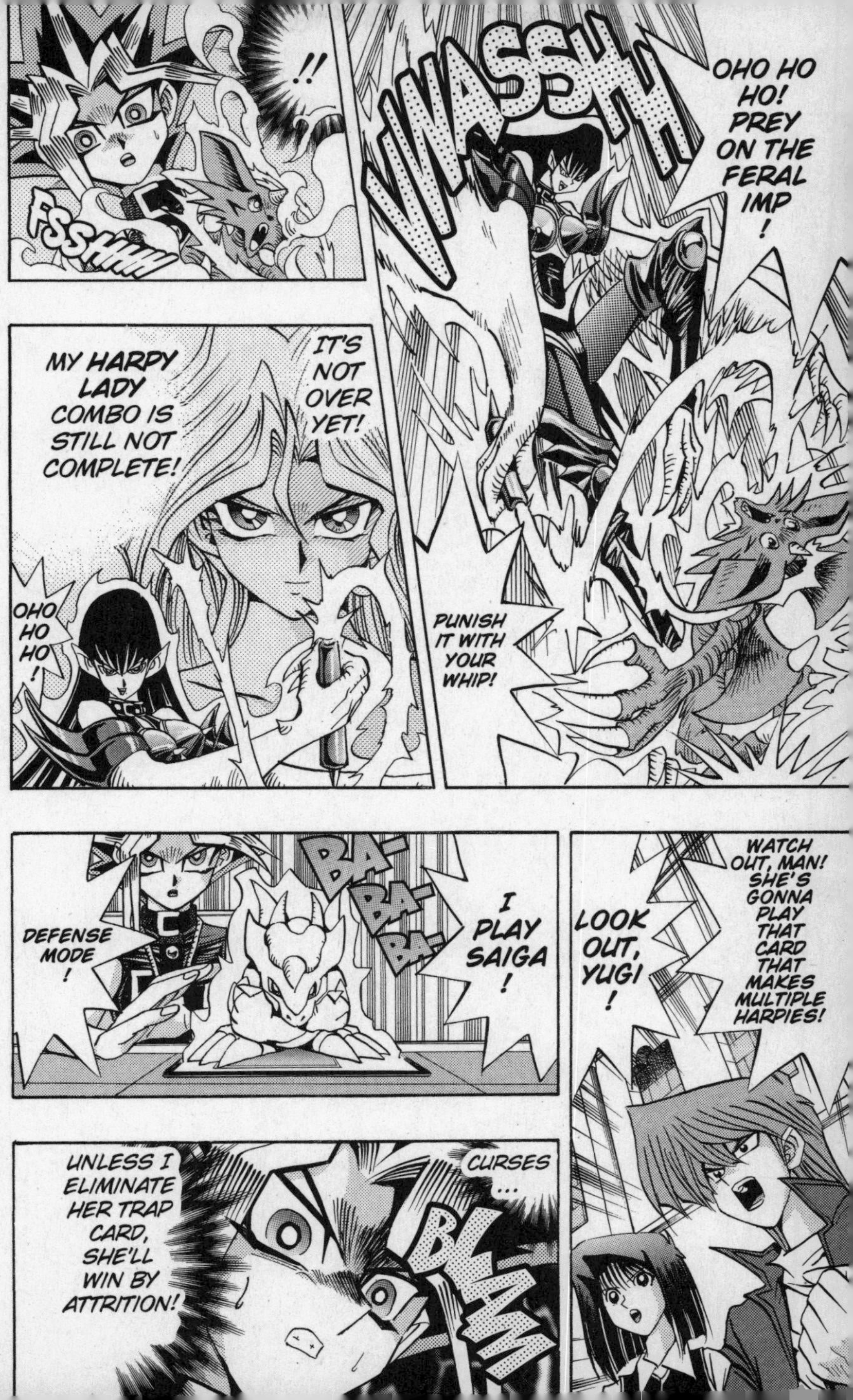
WHASSH
OHO HO HO! PREY ON THE FERAL IMP!
PUNISH IT WITH YOUR WHIP!
!!
FSSHHH
IT'S NOT OVER YET!
MY HARPY LADY COMBO IS STILL NOT COMPLETE!
OHO HO HO!
WATCH OUT, MAN! SHE'S GONNA PLAY THAT CARD THAT MAKES MULTIPLE HARPIES!
LOOK OUT, YUGI!
BA-BA-BA-
I PLAY SAIGA!
DEFENSE MODE!
CURSES...
BLAM
UNLESS I ELIMINATE HER TRAP CARD, SHE'LL WIN BY ATTRITION!

READ THIS WAY

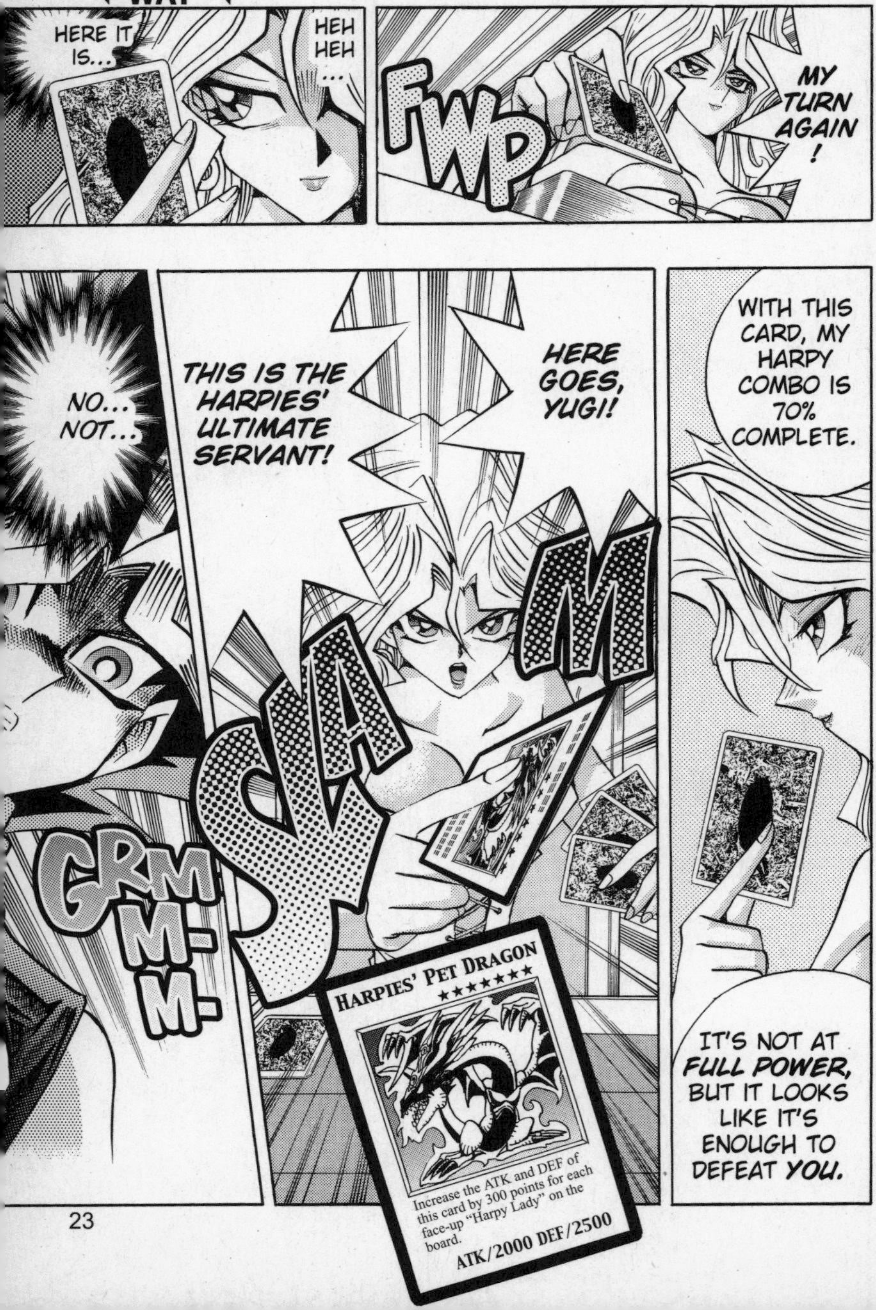
FWP
MY TURN AGAIN!
HEH HEH...
HERE IT IS...
WITH THIS CARD, MY HARPY COMBO IS 70% COMPLETE.
IT'S NOT AT FULL POWER, BUT IT LOOKS LIKE IT'S ENOUGH TO DEFEAT YOU.
HERE GOES, YUGI!
THIS IS THE HARPIES' ULTIMATE SERVANT!
SLAM
HARPIES' PET DRAGON
★★★★★★★
Increase the ATK and DEF of this card by 300 points for each face-up "Harpy Lady" on the board.
ATK/2000 DEF/2500
NO... NOT...
GRMM-M-

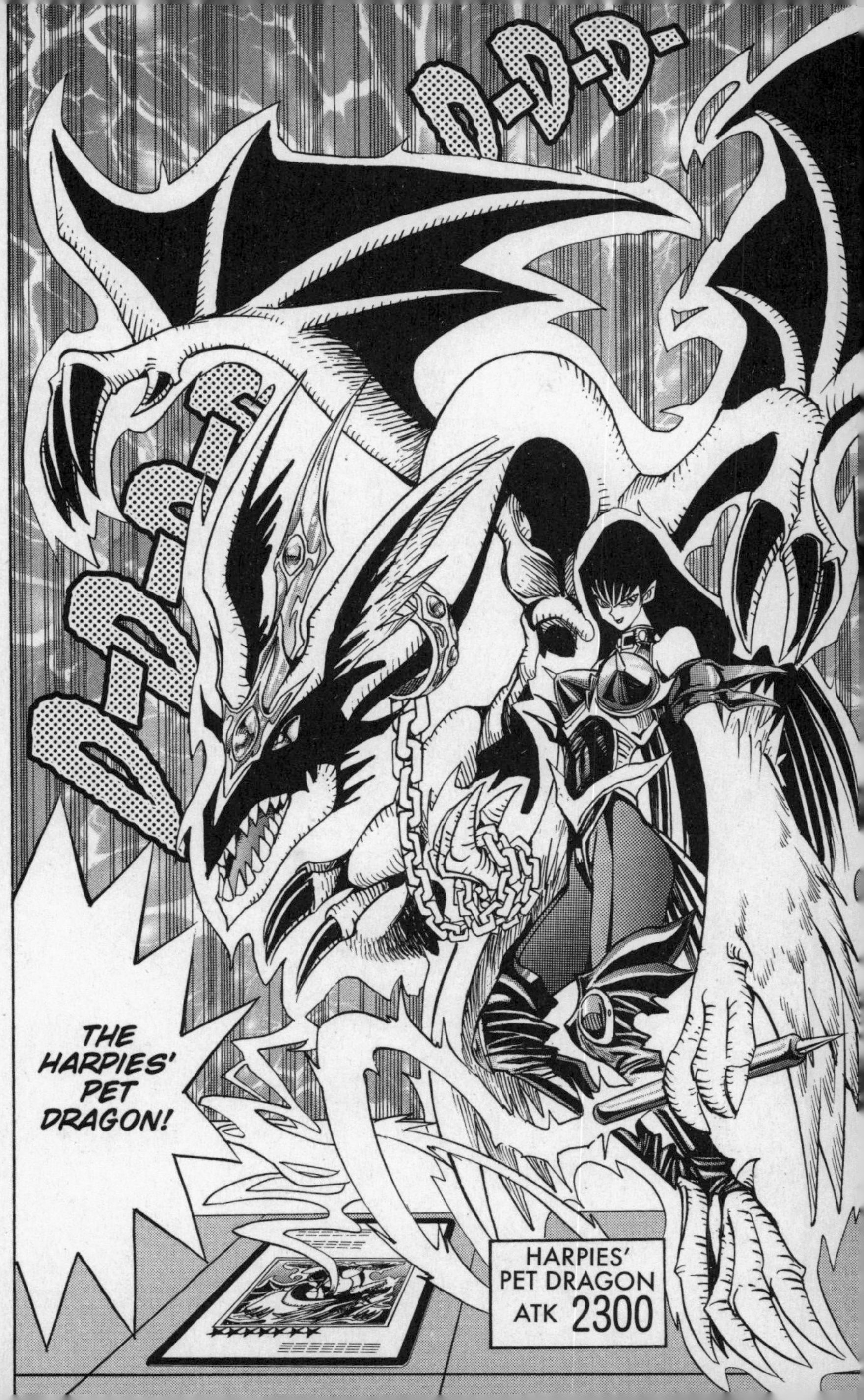
D-D-D-
D-D-D-
THE HARPIES' PET DRAGON!
HARPIES' PET DRAGON ATK 2300

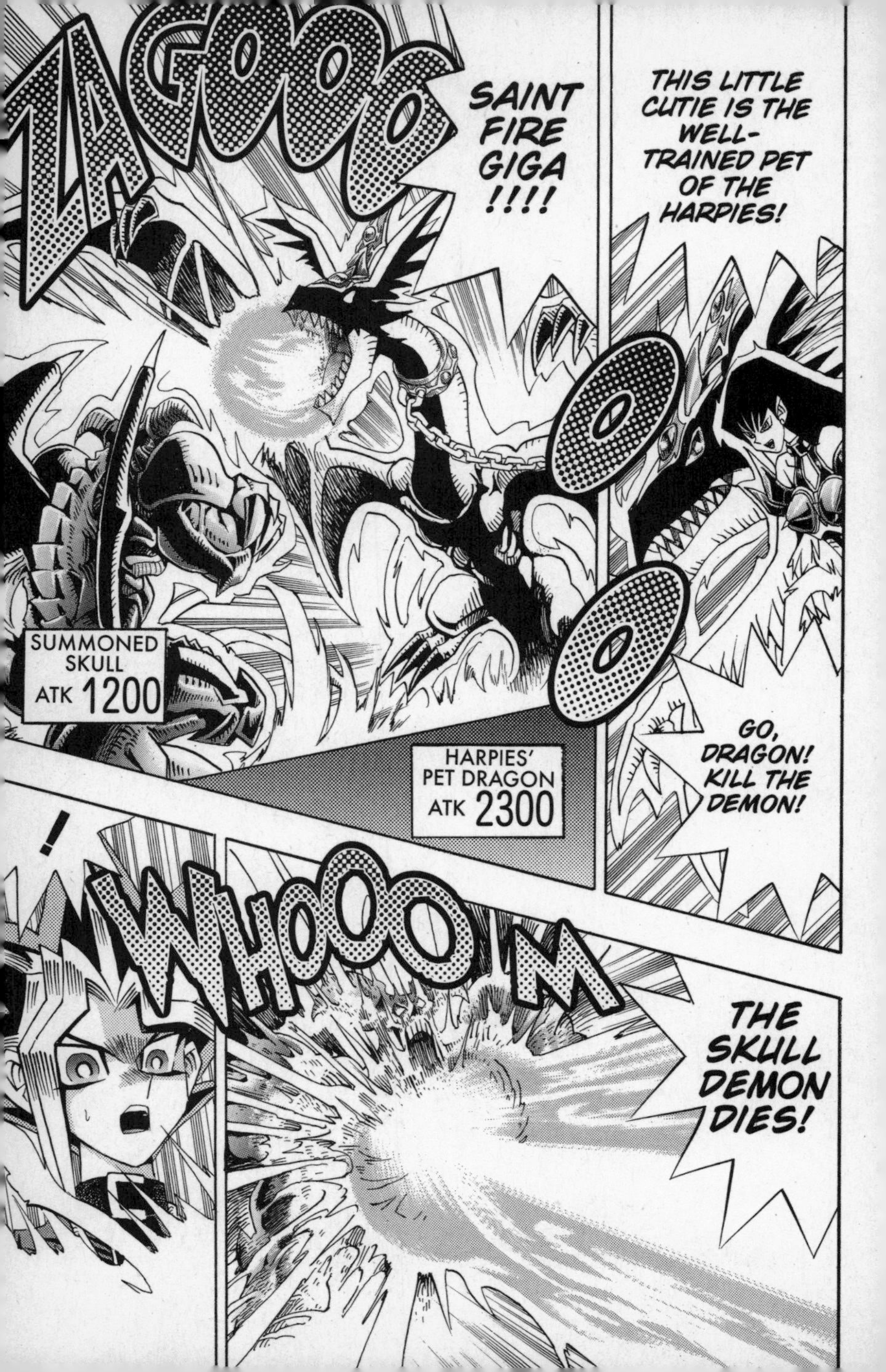
THIS LITTLE CUTIE IS THE WELL-TRAINED PET OF THE HARPIES!
GO, DRAGON! KILL THE DEMON!
ZAGOOO
SAINT FIRE GIGA!!!!
SUMMONED SKULL ATK 1200
HARPIES' PET DRAGON ATK 2300
WHOOOM
THE SKULL DEMON DIES!
!

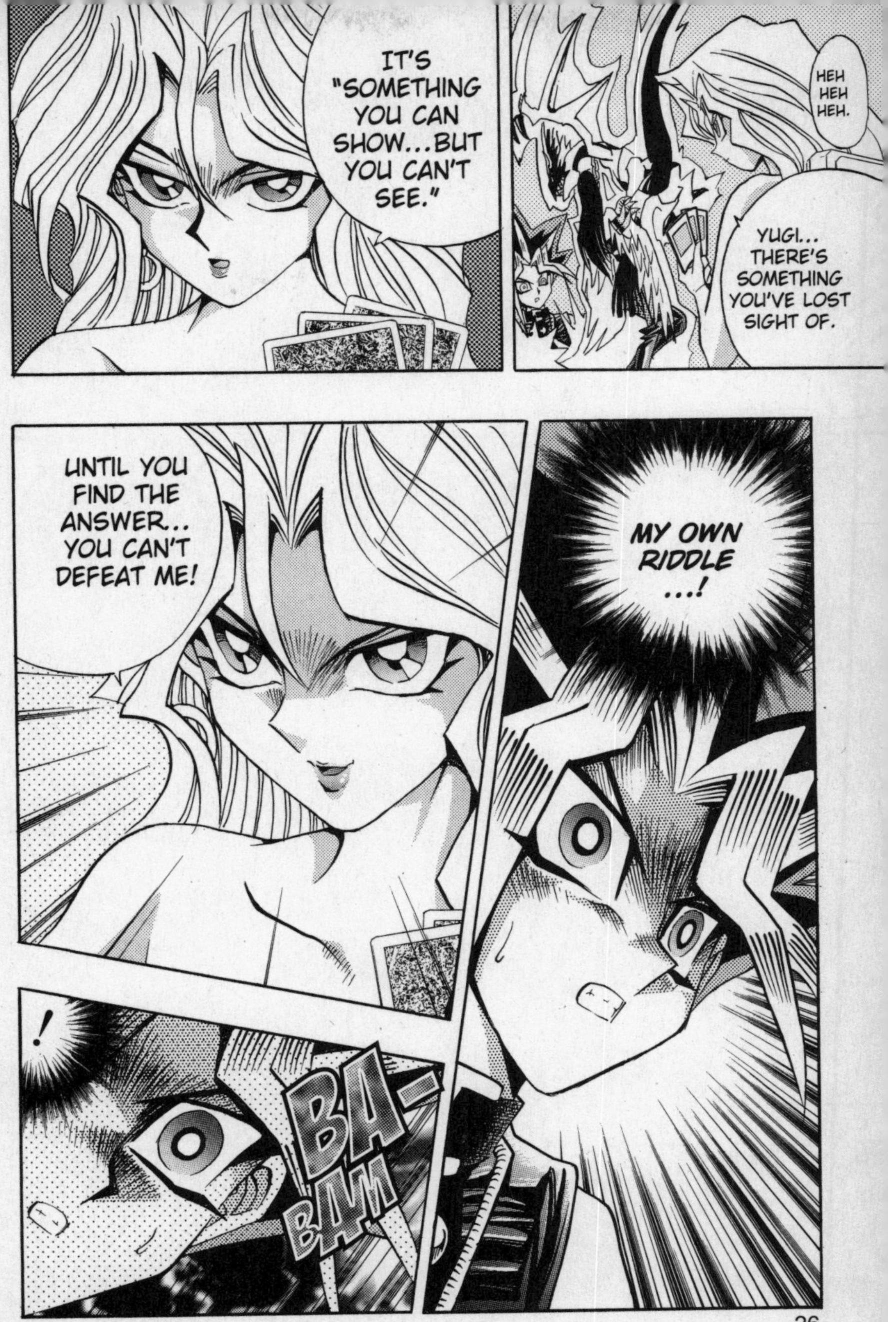
HEH HEH HEH.
YUGI... THERE'S SOMETHING YOU'VE LOST SIGHT OF.
IT'S "SOMETHING YOU CAN SHOW...BUT YOU CAN'T SEE."
MY OWN RIDDLE ...!
UNTIL YOU FIND THE ANSWER... YOU CAN'T DEFEAT ME!
!
BA-BAM

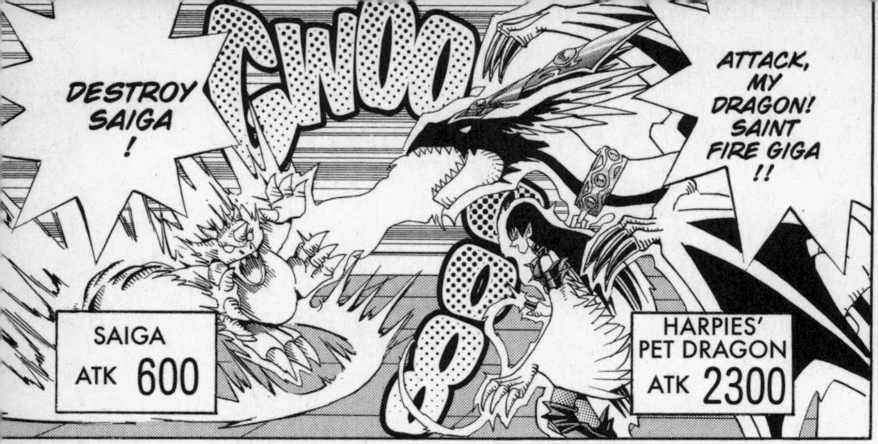
ATTACK, MY DRAGON! SAINT FIRE GIGA !!
DESTROY SAIGA !
HARPIES' PET DRAGON ATK 2300
SAIGA ATK 600

Duel 57: Find Yourself!

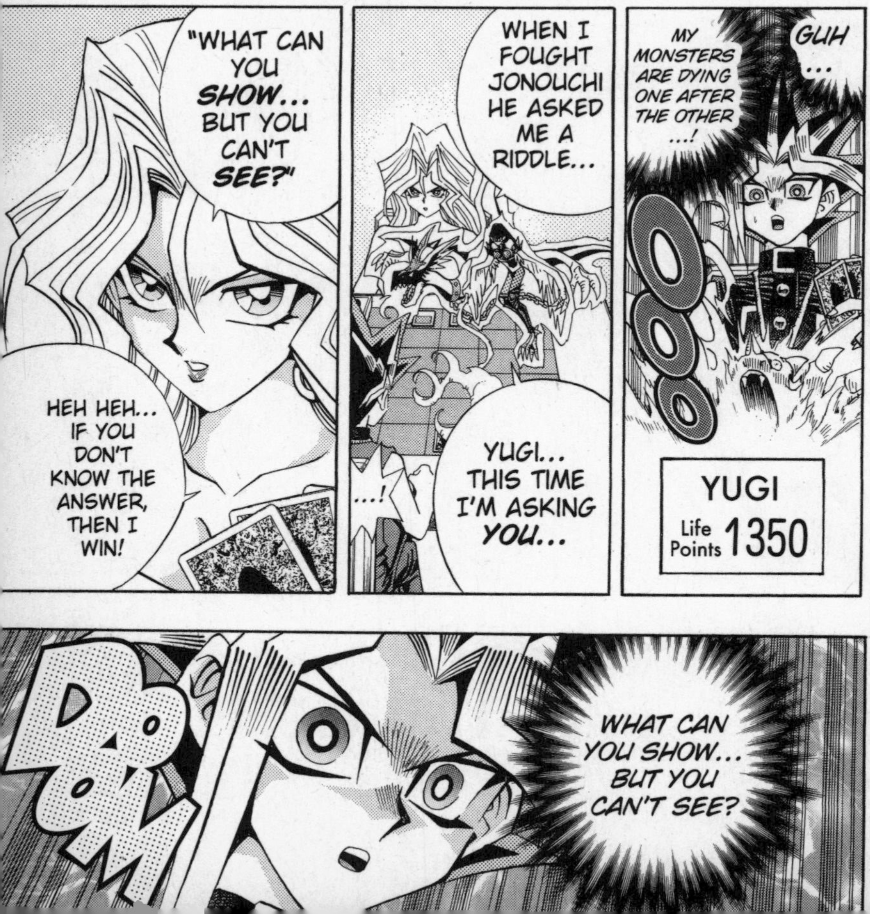
GUH ...
MY MONSTERS ARE DYING ONE AFTER THE OTHER ...!
YUGI Life Points 1350
WHEN I FOUGHT JONOUCHI HE ASKED ME A RIDDLE...
YUGI... THIS TIME I'M ASKING YOU...
...!
"WHAT CAN YOU SHOW... BUT YOU CAN'T SEE?"
HEH HEH... IF YOU DON'T KNOW THE ANSWER, THEN I WIN!
WHAT CAN YOU SHOW... BUT YOU CAN'T SEE?

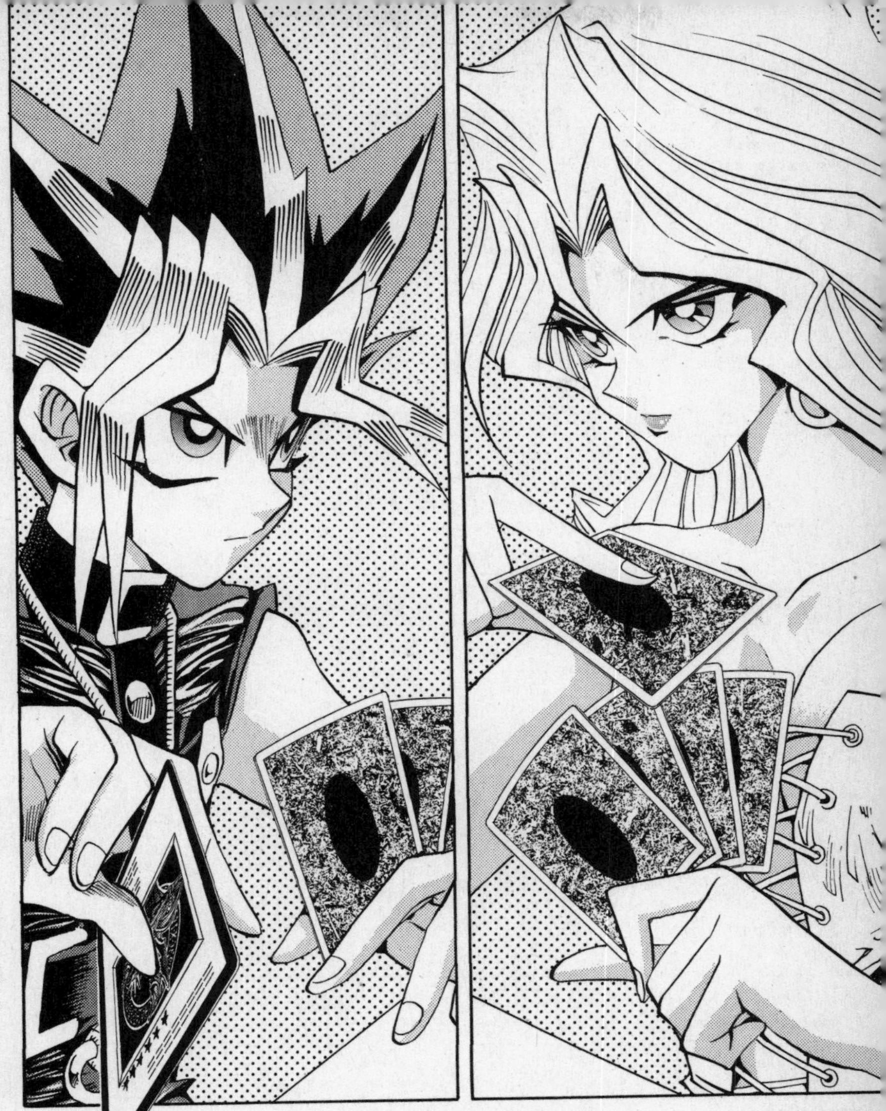

DUEL 57: FIND YOURSELF!

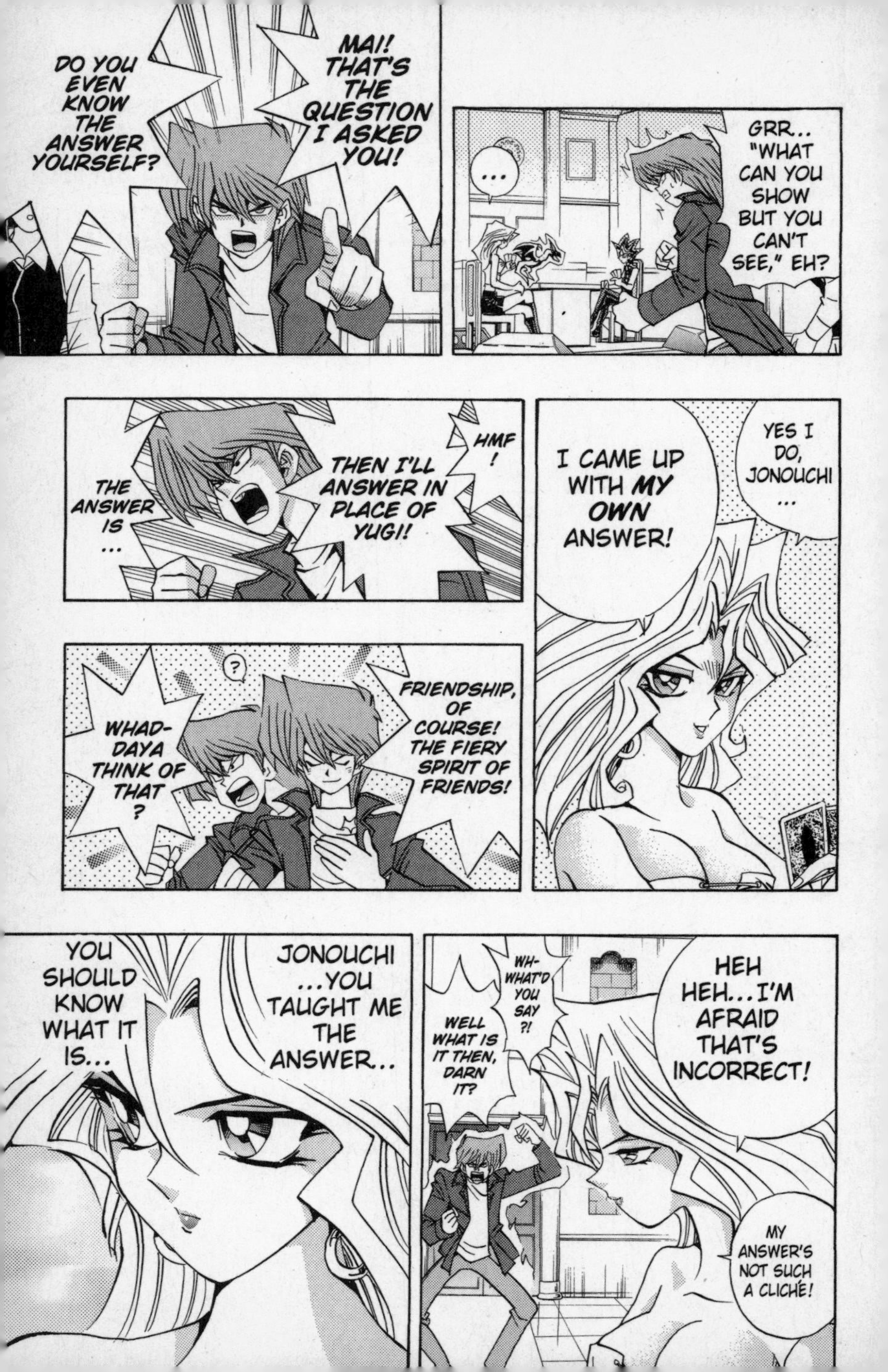
GRR... "WHAT CAN YOU SHOW BUT YOU CAN'T SEE," EH?
...
MAI! THAT'S THE QUESTION I ASKED YOU!
DO YOU EVEN KNOW THE ANSWER YOURSELF?
YES I DO, JONOUCHI...
I CAME UP WITH MY OWN ANSWER!
HMF!
THEN I'LL ANSWER IN PLACE OF YUGI!
THE ANSWER IS...
FRIENDSHIP, OF COURSE! THE FIERY SPIRIT OF FRIENDS!
?
WHAD-DAYA THINK OF THAT?
HEH HEH...I'M AFRAID THAT'S INCORRECT!
WH-WHAT'D YOU SAY?!
WELL WHAT IS IT THEN, DARN IT?
MY ANSWER'S NOT SUCH A CLICHÉ!
JONOUCHI ...YOU TAUGHT ME THE ANSWER...
YOU SHOULD KNOW WHAT IT IS...

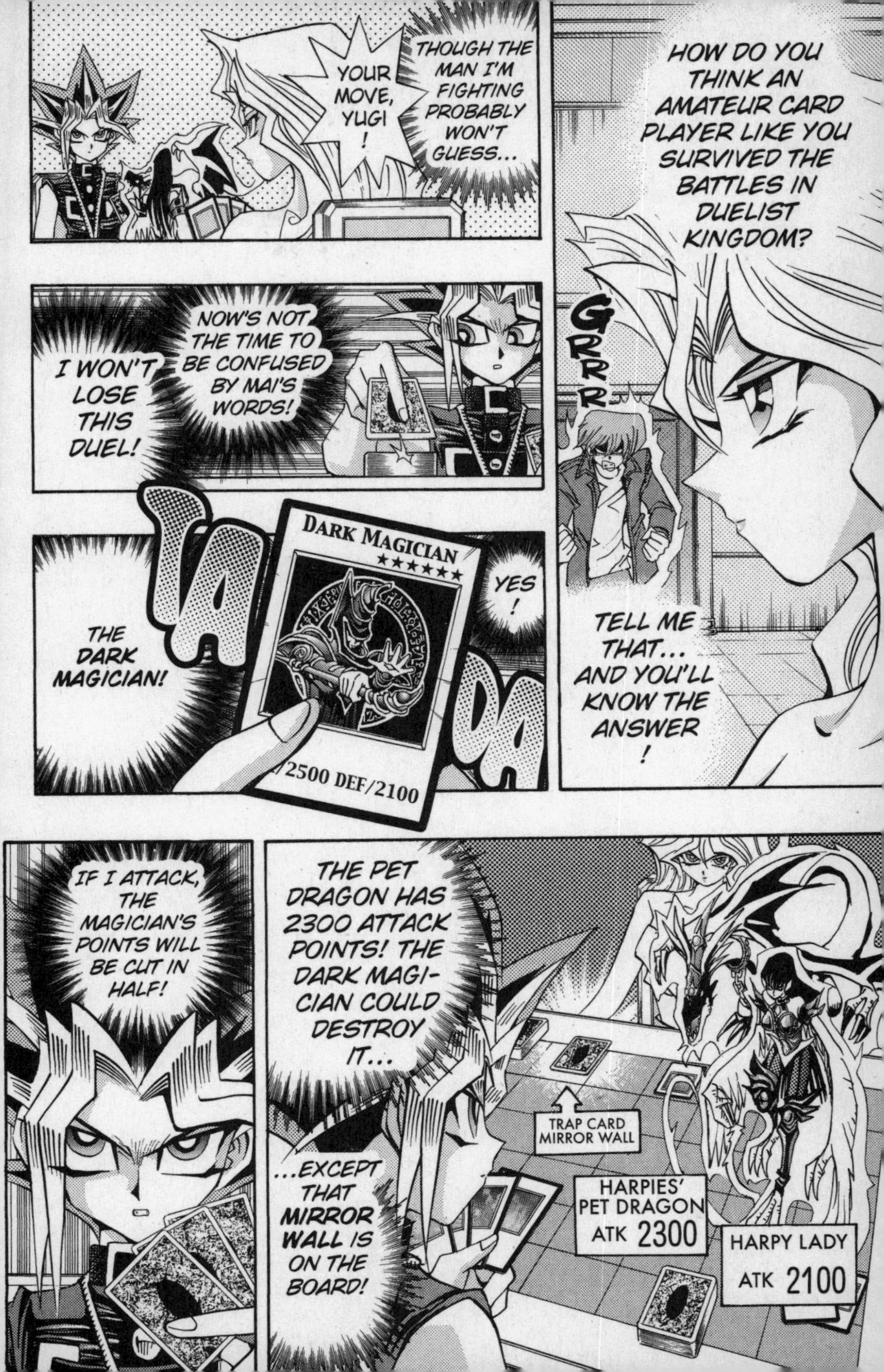
HOW DO YOU THINK AN AMATEUR CARD PLAYER LIKE YOU SURVIVED THE BATTLES IN DUELIST KINGDOM?
GRRR
TELL ME THAT... AND YOU'LL KNOW THE ANSWER!
THOUGH THE MAN I'M FIGHTING PROBABLY WON'T GUESS...
YOUR MOVE, YUGI!
NOW'S NOT THE TIME TO BE CONFUSED BY MAI'S WORDS!
I WON'T LOSE THIS DUEL!
YES!
DARK MAGICIAN
/2500 DEF/2100
THE DARK MAGICIAN!
THE PET DRAGON HAS 2300 ATTACK POINTS! THE DARK MAGICIAN COULD DESTROY IT...
TRAP CARD MIRROR WALL
HARPIES' PET DRAGON ATK 2300
HARPY LADY ATK 2100
...EXCEPT THAT MIRROR WALL IS ON THE BOARD!
IF I ATTACK, THE MAGICIAN'S POINTS WILL BE CUT IN HALF!

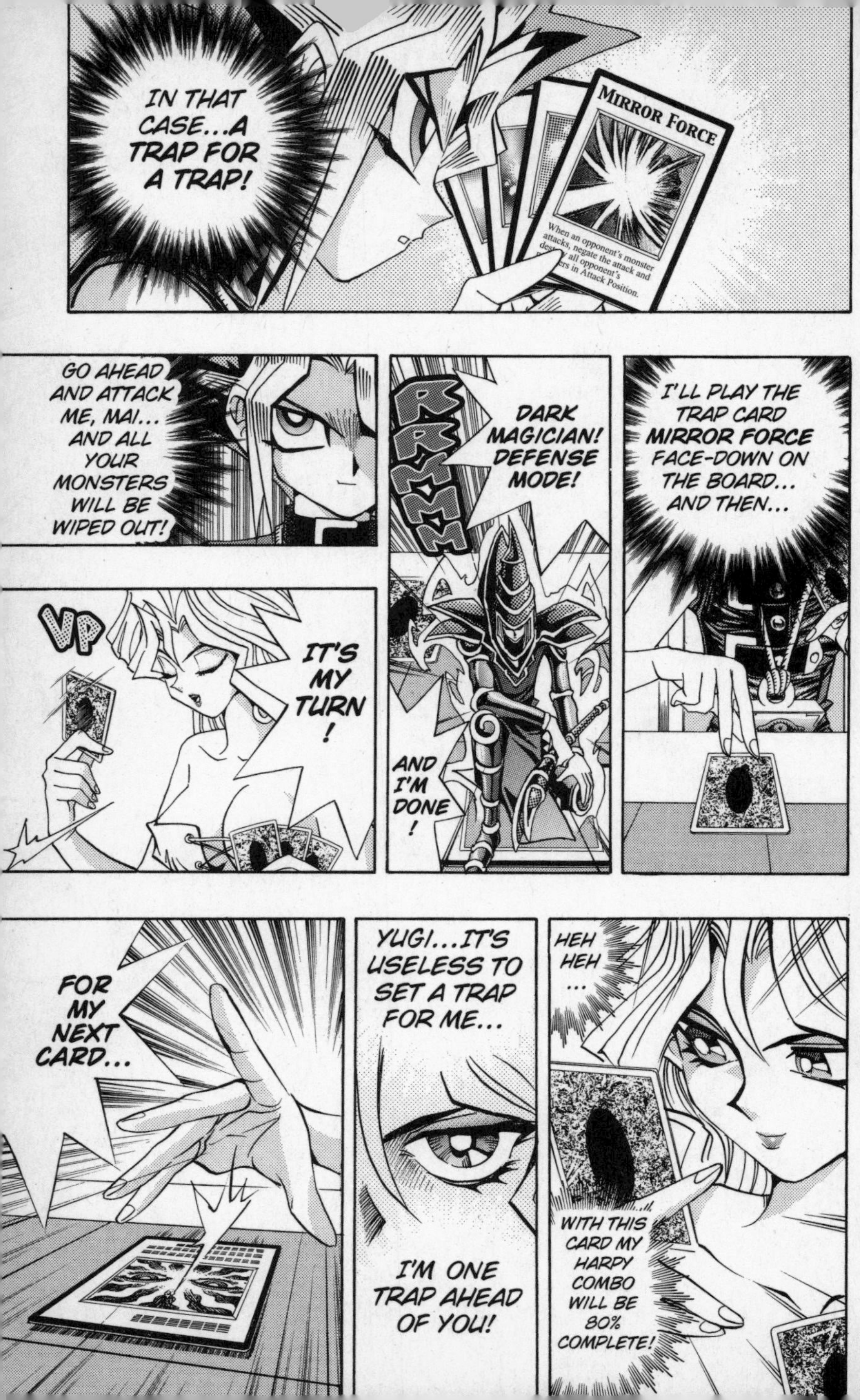
IN THAT CASE...A TRAP FOR A TRAP!
MIRROR FORCE
When an opponent's monster attacks, negate the attack and
I'LL PLAY THE TRAP CARD MIRROR FORCE FACE-DOWN ON THE BOARD... AND THEN...
RRMMM
DARK MAGICIAN! DEFENSE MODE!
AND I'M DONE!
GO AHEAD AND ATTACK ME, MAI... AND ALL YOUR MONSTERS WILL BE WIPED OUT!
VP
IT'S MY TURN!
HEH HEH ...
WITH THIS CARD MY HARPY COMBO WILL BE 80% COMPLETE!
YUGI...IT'S USELESS TO SET A TRAP FOR ME...
I'M ONE TRAP AHEAD OF YOU!
FOR MY NEXT CARD...

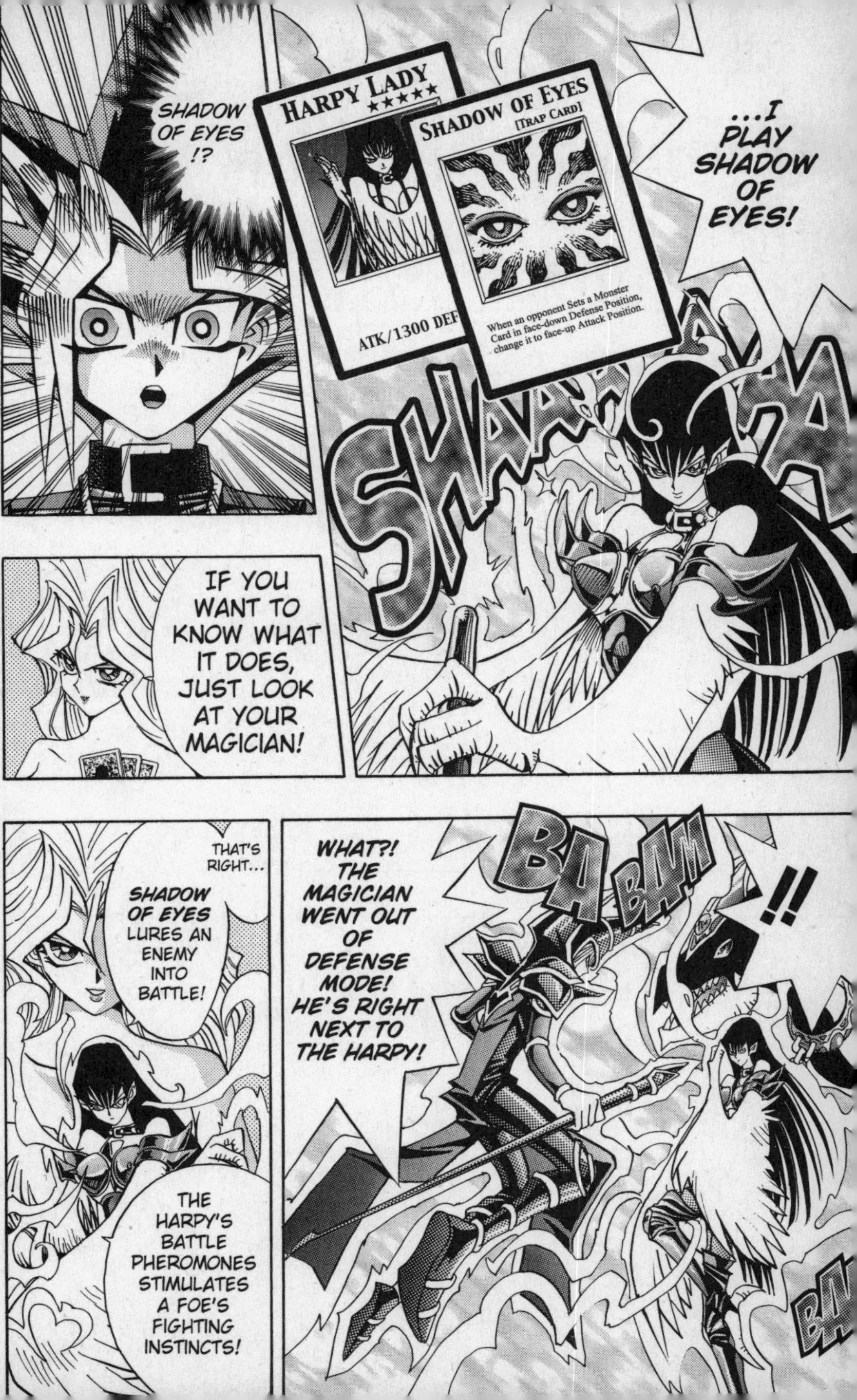

...I PLAY SHADOW OF EYES!
HARPY LADY ★★★★★
ATK/1300 DEF
SHADOW OF EYES
[TRAP CARD]
When an opponent Sets a Monster Card in face-down Defense Position, change it to face-up Attack Position.
SHAAAA
SHADOW OF EYES !?
IF YOU WANT TO KNOW WHAT IT DOES, JUST LOOK AT YOUR MAGICIAN!
BA BAM
!!
WHAT?! THE MAGICIAN WENT OUT OF DEFENSE MODE! HE'S RIGHT NEXT TO THE HARPY!
THAT'S RIGHT...
SHADOW OF EYES LURES AN ENEMY INTO BATTLE!
THE HARPY'S BATTLE PHEROMONES STIMULATES A FOE'S FIGHTING INSTINCTS!

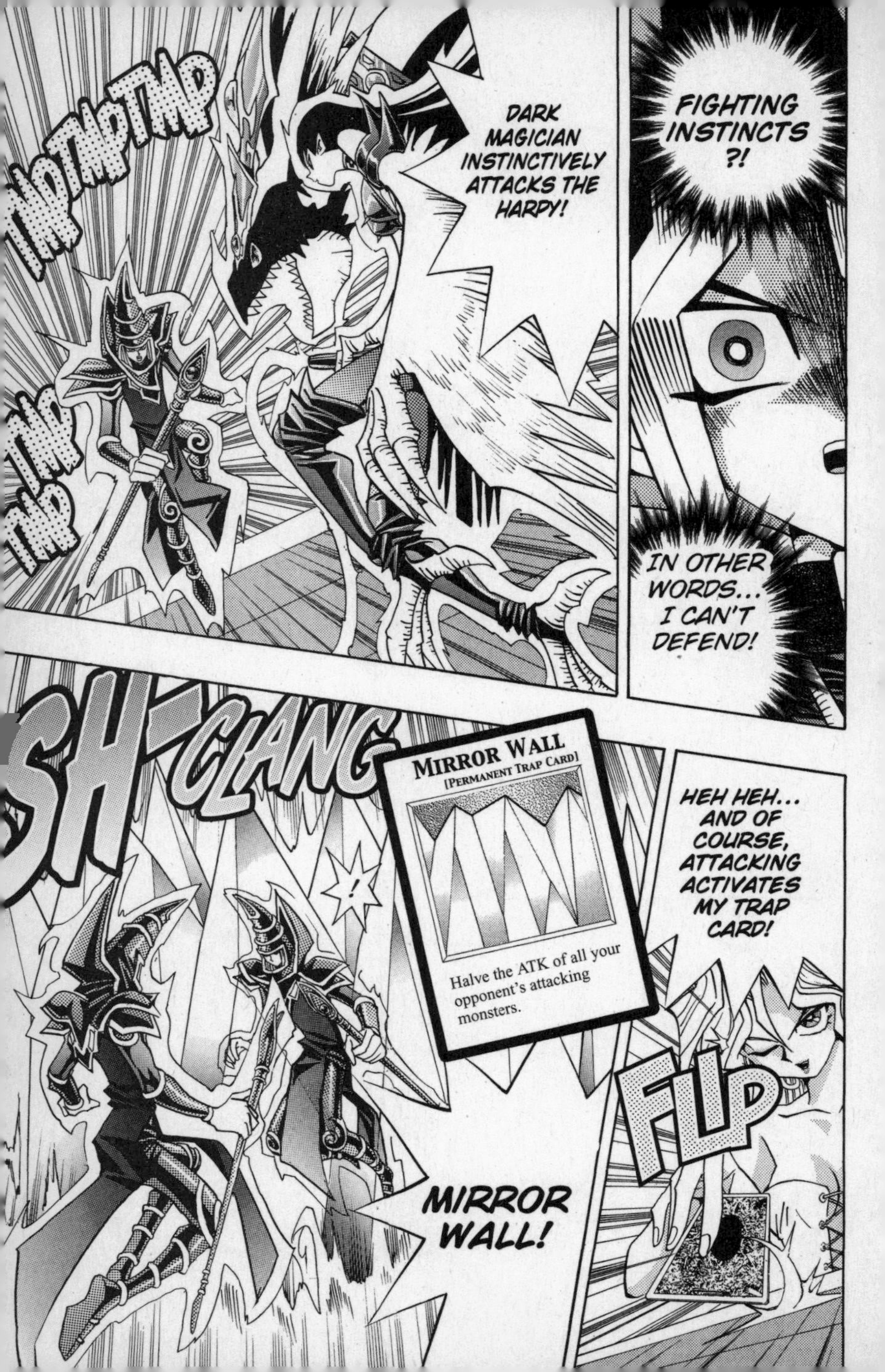
FIGHTING INSTINCTS ?!
IN OTHER WORDS... I CAN'T DEFEND!
DARK MAGICIAN INSTINCTIVELY ATTACKS THE HARPY!
TMPTMPTMP
TMP TMP
HEH HEH... AND OF COURSE, ATTACKING ACTIVATES MY TRAP CARD!
FLIP
SH-CLANG
MIRROR WALL
[PERMANENT TRAP CARD]
Halve the ATK of all your opponent's attacking monsters.
!
MIRROR WALL!

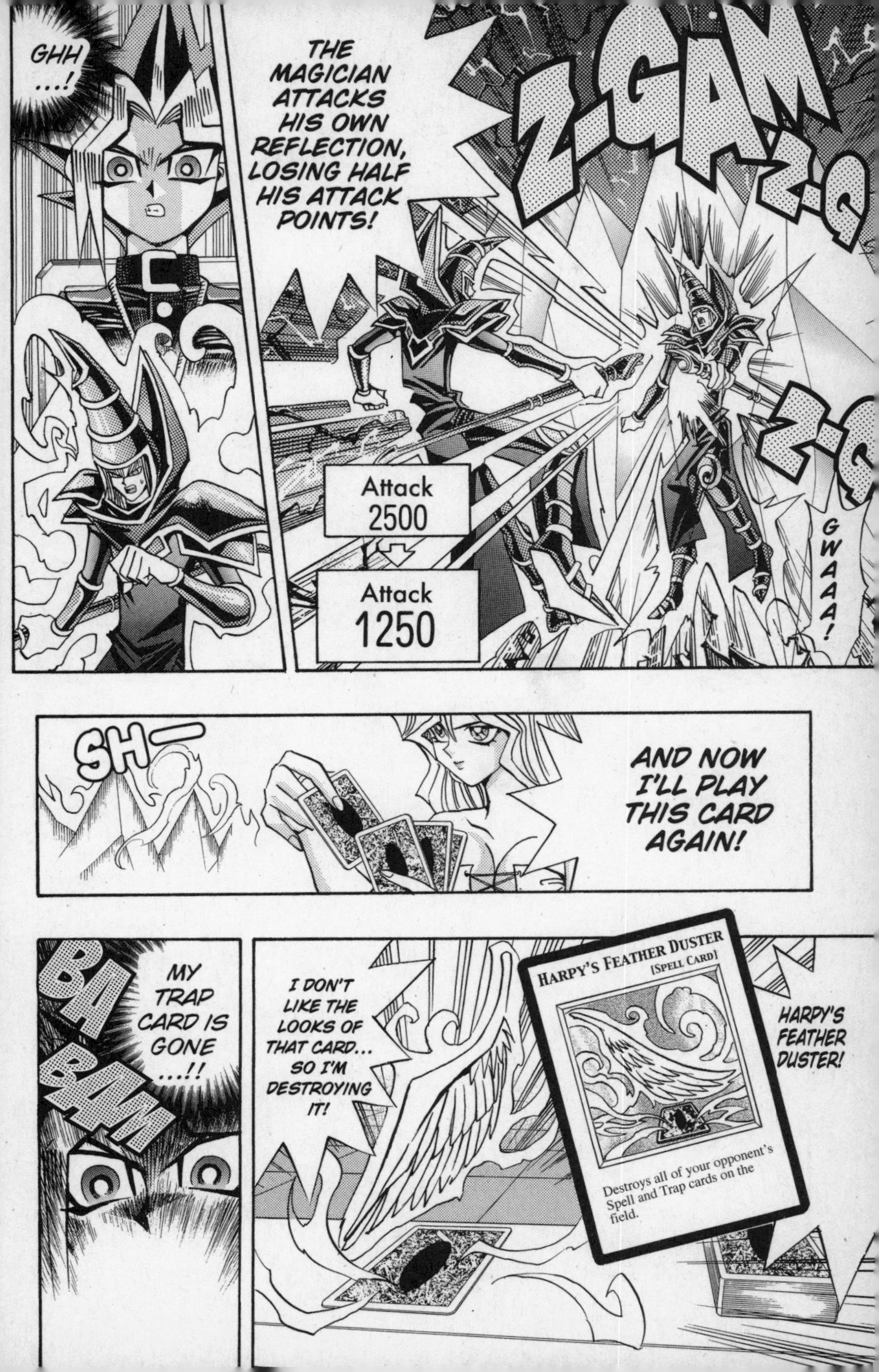
Z-GAM
Z-G
Z-G
THE MAGICIAN ATTACKS HIS OWN REFLECTION, LOSING HALF HIS ATTACK POINTS!
GWAAAA!
Attack 2500
Attack 1250
GHH ...!
AND NOW I'LL PLAY THIS CARD AGAIN!
SH—
HARPY'S FEATHER DUSTER!
HARPY'S FEATHER DUSTER
[SPELL CARD]
Destroys all of your opponent's Spell and Trap cards on the field.
I DON'T LIKE THE LOOKS OF THAT CARD... SO I'M DESTROYING IT!
MY TRAP CARD IS GONE ...!!
BA BAM

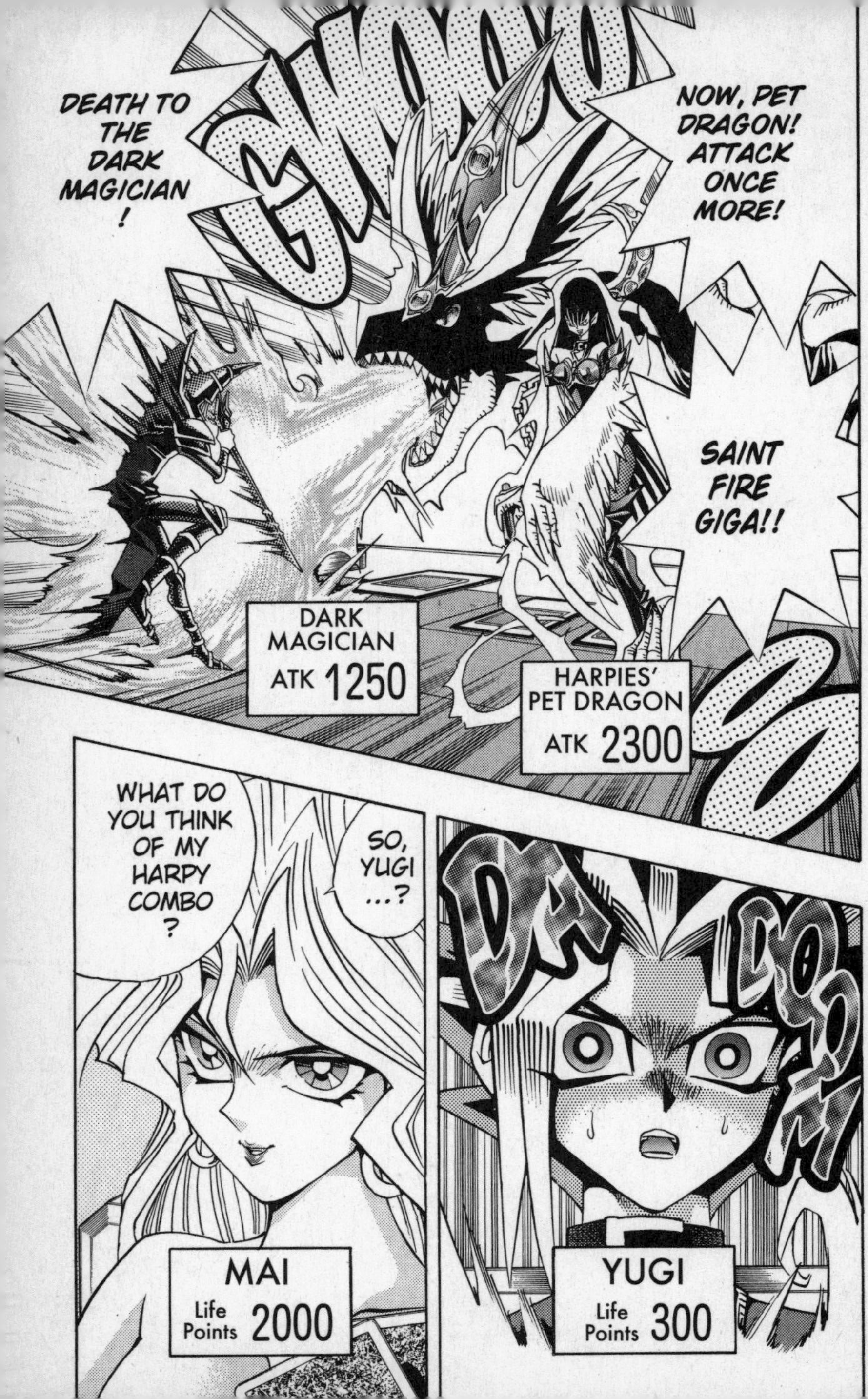
NOW, PET DRAGON! ATTACK ONCE MORE!
SAINT FIRE GIGA!!
DEATH TO THE DARK MAGICIAN!
HARPIES' PET DRAGON ATK 2300
DARK MAGICIAN ATK 1250
DA DOOM
YUGI Life Points 300
SO, YUGI...?
WHAT DO YOU THINK OF MY HARPY COMBO?
MAI Life Points 2000

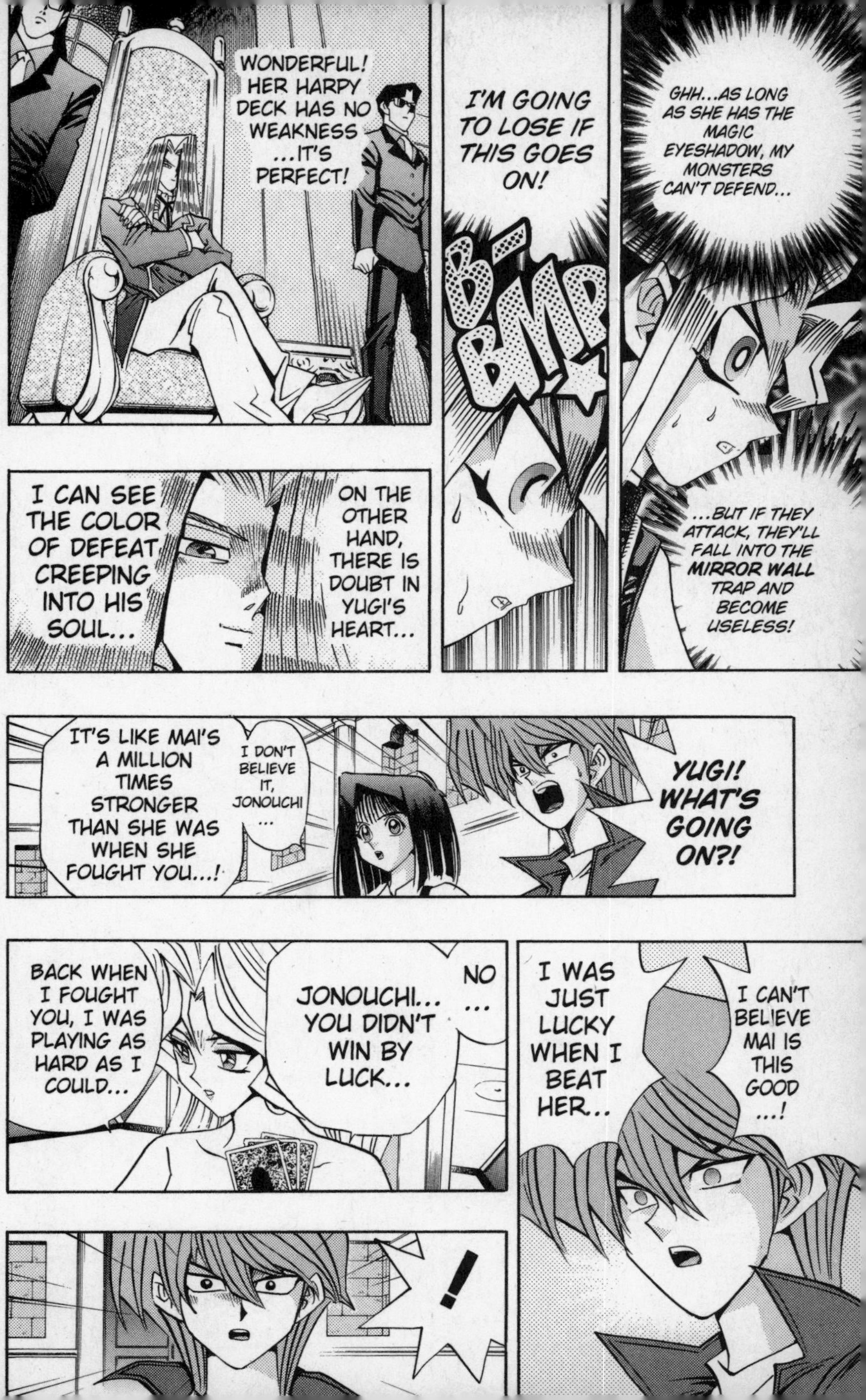
GHH...AS LONG AS SHE HAS THE MAGIC EYESHADOW, MY MONSTERS CAN'T DEFEND...
...BUT IF THEY ATTACK, THEY'LL FALL INTO THE MIRROR WALL TRAP AND BECOME USELESS!
I'M GOING TO LOSE IF THIS GOES ON!
B-BMP
WONDERFUL! HER HARPY DECK HAS NO WEAKNESS ...IT'S PERFECT!
ON THE OTHER HAND, THERE IS DOUBT IN YUGI'S HEART...
I CAN SEE THE COLOR OF DEFEAT CREEPING INTO HIS SOUL...
YUGI! WHAT'S GOING ON?!
I DON'T BELIEVE IT, JONOUCHI ...
IT'S LIKE MAI'S A MILLION TIMES STRONGER THAN SHE WAS WHEN SHE FOUGHT YOU...!
I CAN'T BELIEVE MAI IS THIS GOOD ...!
I WAS JUST LUCKY WHEN I BEAT HER...
NO ...
JONOUCHI... YOU DIDN'T WIN BY LUCK...
BACK WHEN I FOUGHT YOU, I WAS PLAYING AS HARD AS I COULD...
!

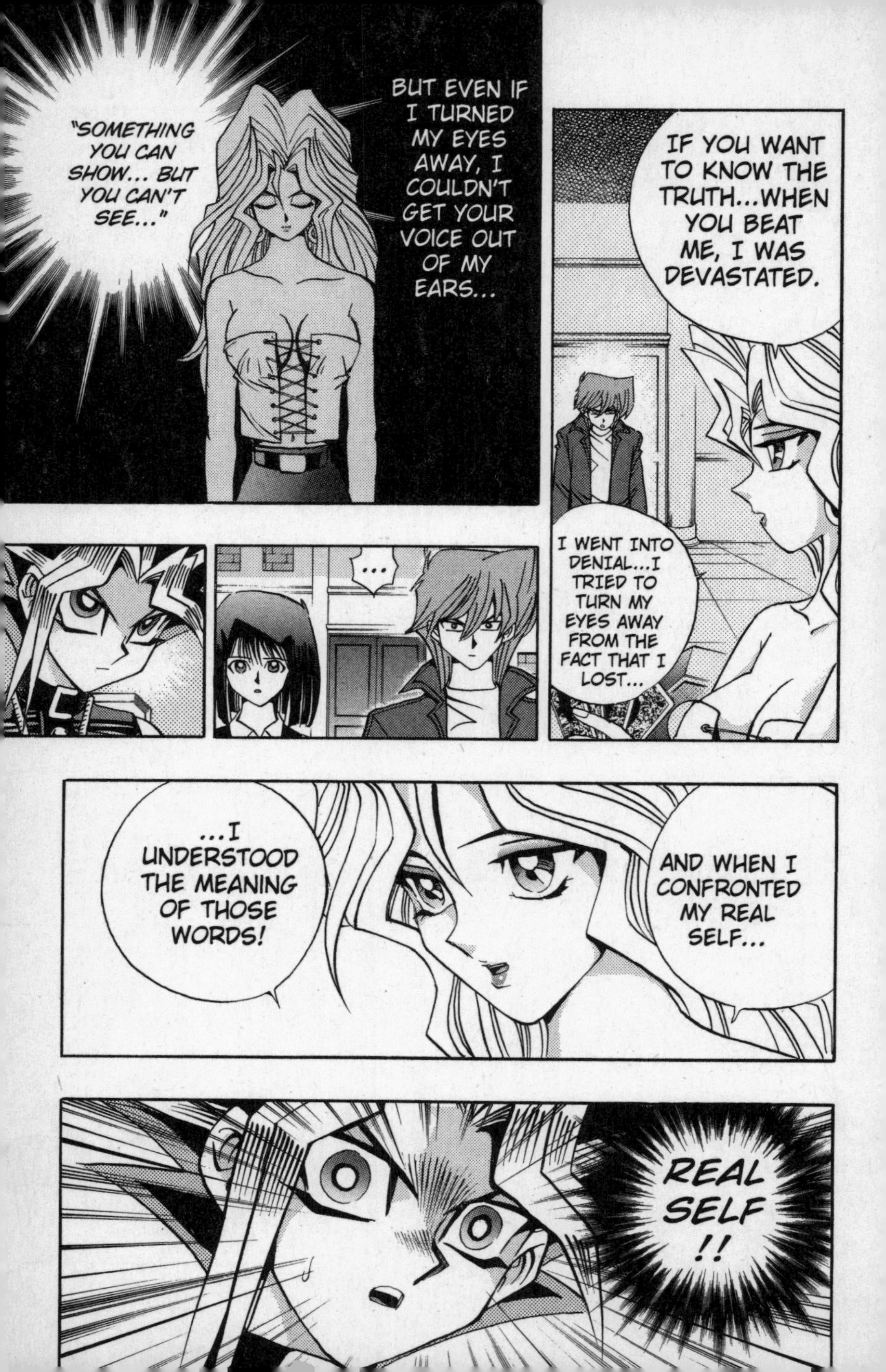
IF YOU WANT TO KNOW THE TRUTH...WHEN YOU BEAT ME, I WAS DEVASTATED.
I WENT INTO DENIAL...I TRIED TO TURN MY EYES AWAY FROM THE FACT THAT I LOST...
BUT EVEN IF I TURNED MY EYES AWAY, I COULDN'T GET YOUR VOICE OUT OF MY EARS...
"SOMETHING YOU CAN SHOW... BUT YOU CAN'T SEE..."
...
AND WHEN I CONFRONTED MY REAL SELF...
...I UNDERSTOOD THE MEANING OF THOSE WORDS!
REAL SELF!!

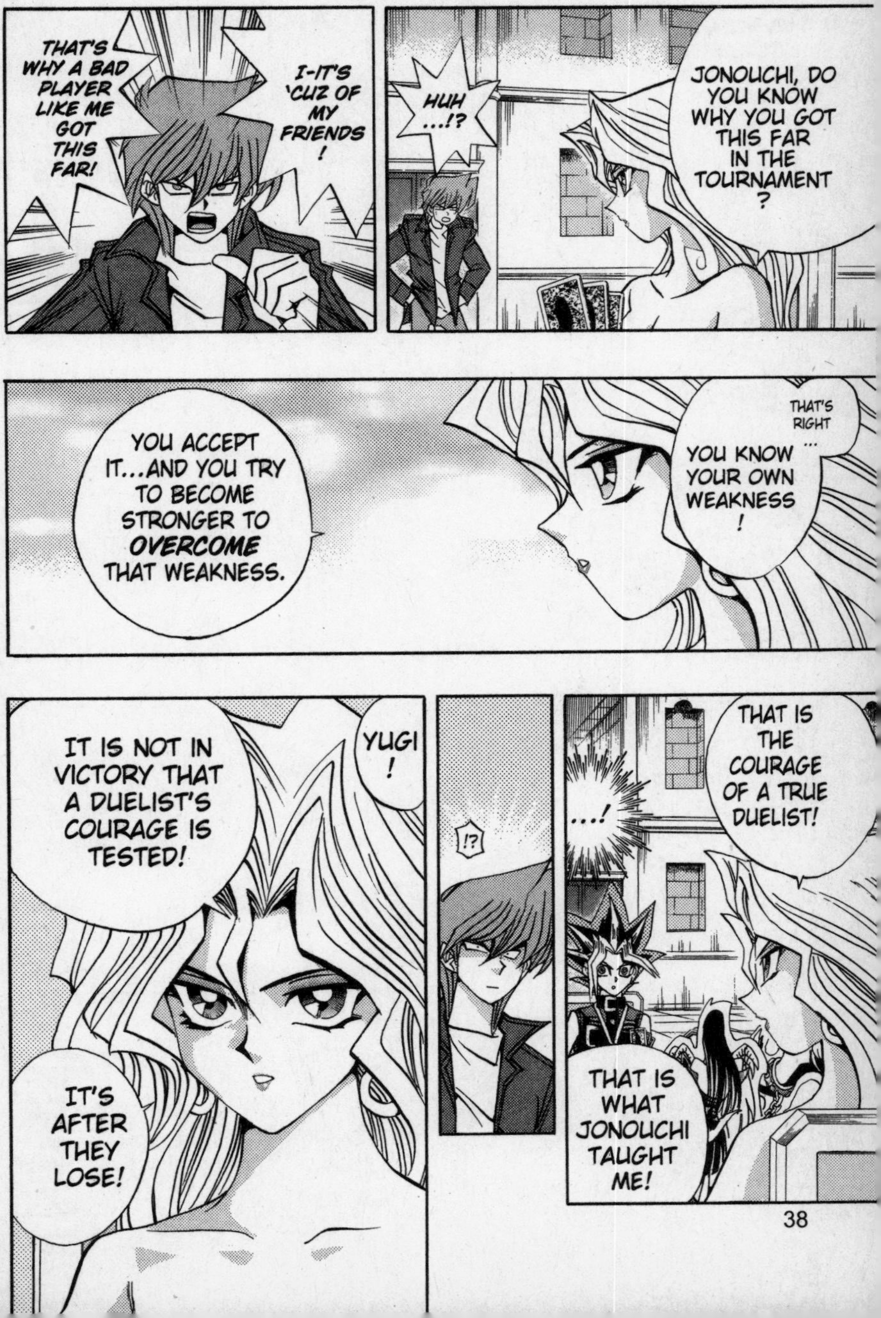
JONOUCHI, DO YOU KNOW WHY YOU GOT THIS FAR IN THE TOURNAMENT?
HUH ...!?
I-IT'S 'CUZ OF MY FRIENDS!
THAT'S WHY A BAD PLAYER LIKE ME GOT THIS FAR!
THAT'S RIGHT ...
YOU KNOW YOUR OWN WEAKNESS!
YOU ACCEPT IT...AND YOU TRY TO BECOME STRONGER TO OVERCOME THAT WEAKNESS.
THAT IS THE COURAGE OF A TRUE DUELIST!
...!
THAT IS WHAT JONOUCHI TAUGHT ME!
!?
YUGI!
IT IS NOT IN VICTORY THAT A DUELIST'S COURAGE IS TESTED!
IT'S AFTER THEY LOSE!

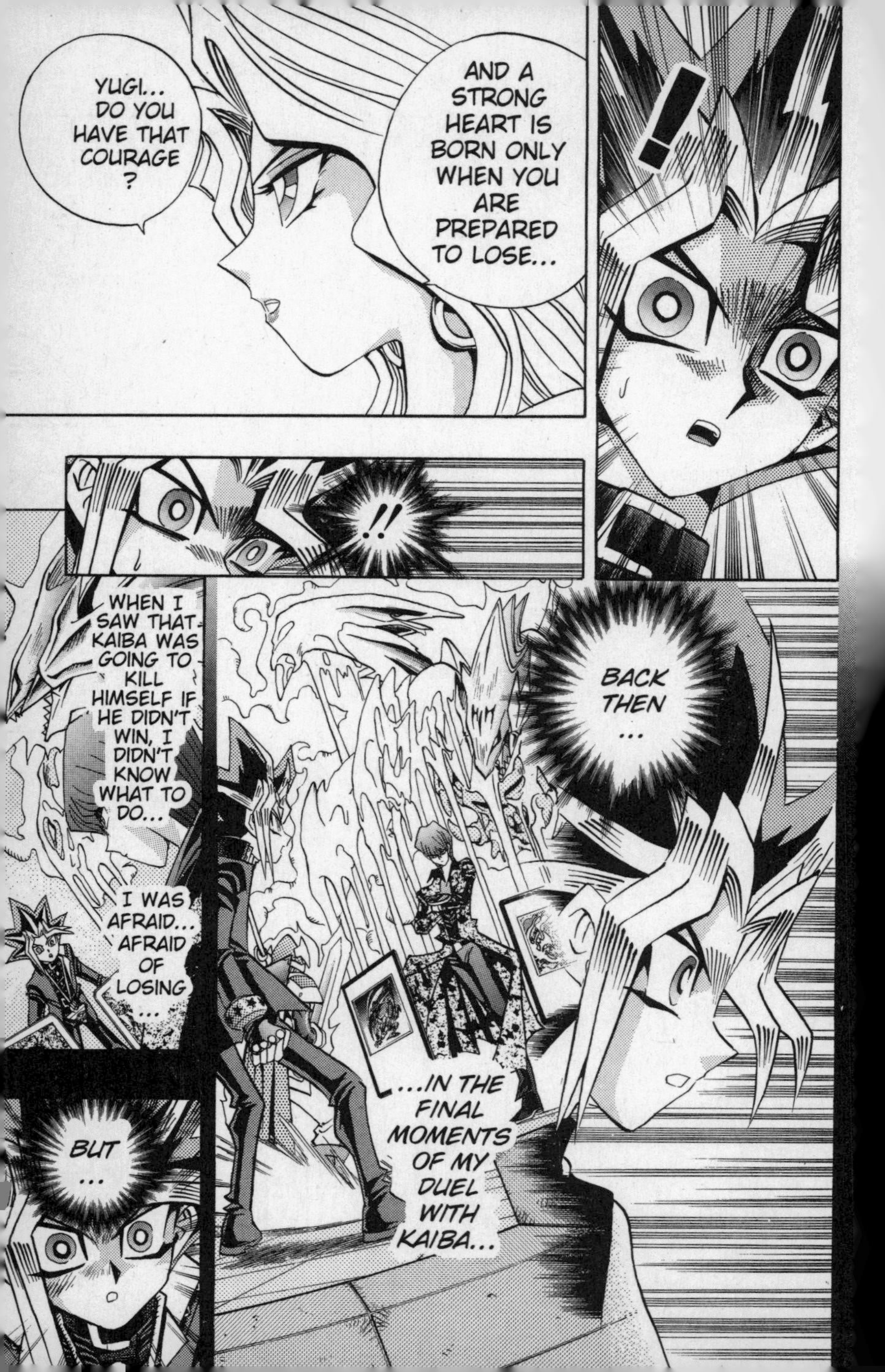
!
AND A STRONG HEART IS BORN ONLY WHEN YOU ARE PREPARED TO LOSE...
YUGI... DO YOU HAVE THAT COURAGE?
!!
BACK THEN...
...IN THE FINAL MOMENTS OF MY DUEL WITH KAIBA...
WHEN I SAW THAT KAIBA WAS GOING TO KILL HIMSELF IF HE DIDN'T WIN, I DIDN'T KNOW WHAT TO DO...
I WAS AFRAID... AFRAID OF LOSING...
BUT...

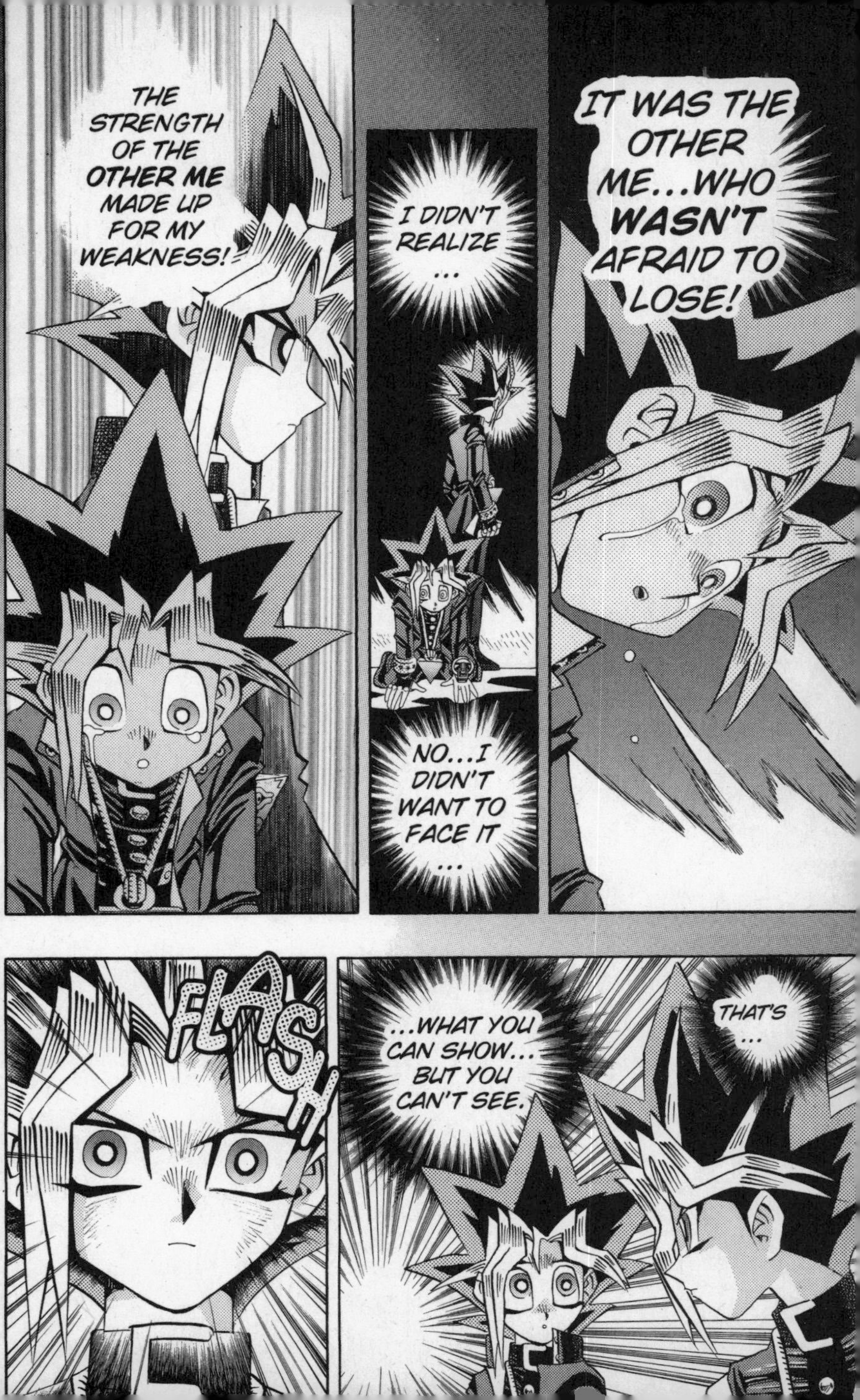
IT WAS THE OTHER ME...WHO WASN'T AFRAID TO LOSE!
I DIDN'T REALIZE ...
NO...I DIDN'T WANT TO FACE IT ...
THE STRENGTH OF THE OTHER ME MADE UP FOR MY WEAKNESS!
THAT'S ...
...WHAT YOU CAN SHOW... BUT YOU CAN'T SEE.
FLASH

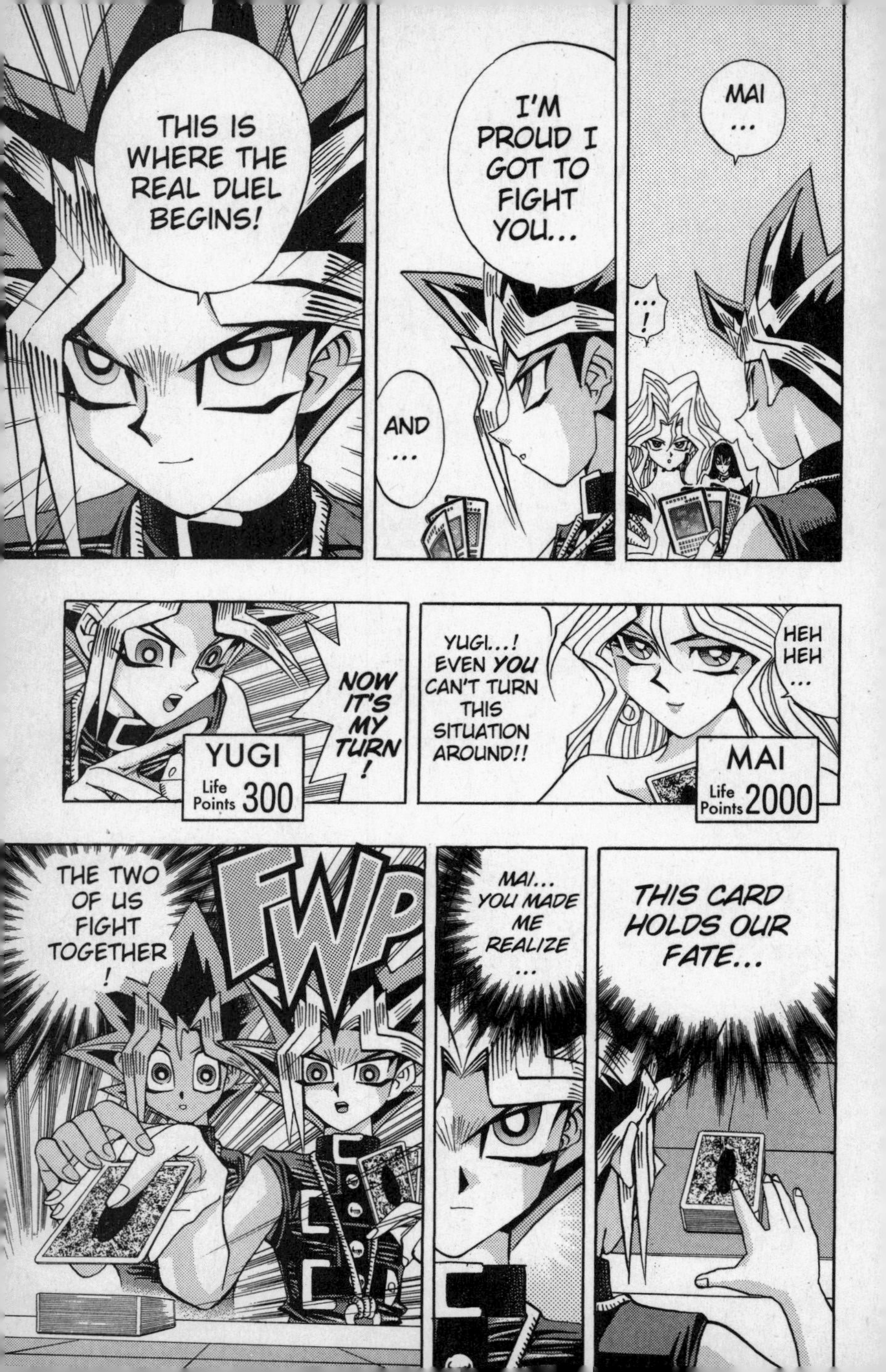
MAI ...
... !
I'M PROUD I GOT TO FIGHT YOU...
AND ...
THIS IS WHERE THE REAL DUEL BEGINS!
HEH HEH ...
YUGI...! EVEN *YOU* CAN'T TURN THIS SITUATION AROUND!!
MAI Life Points 2000
NOW IT'S MY TURN!
YUGI Life Points 300
THIS CARD HOLDS OUR FATE...
MAI... YOU MADE ME REALIZE ...
THE TWO OF US FIGHT TOGETHER!
FWP

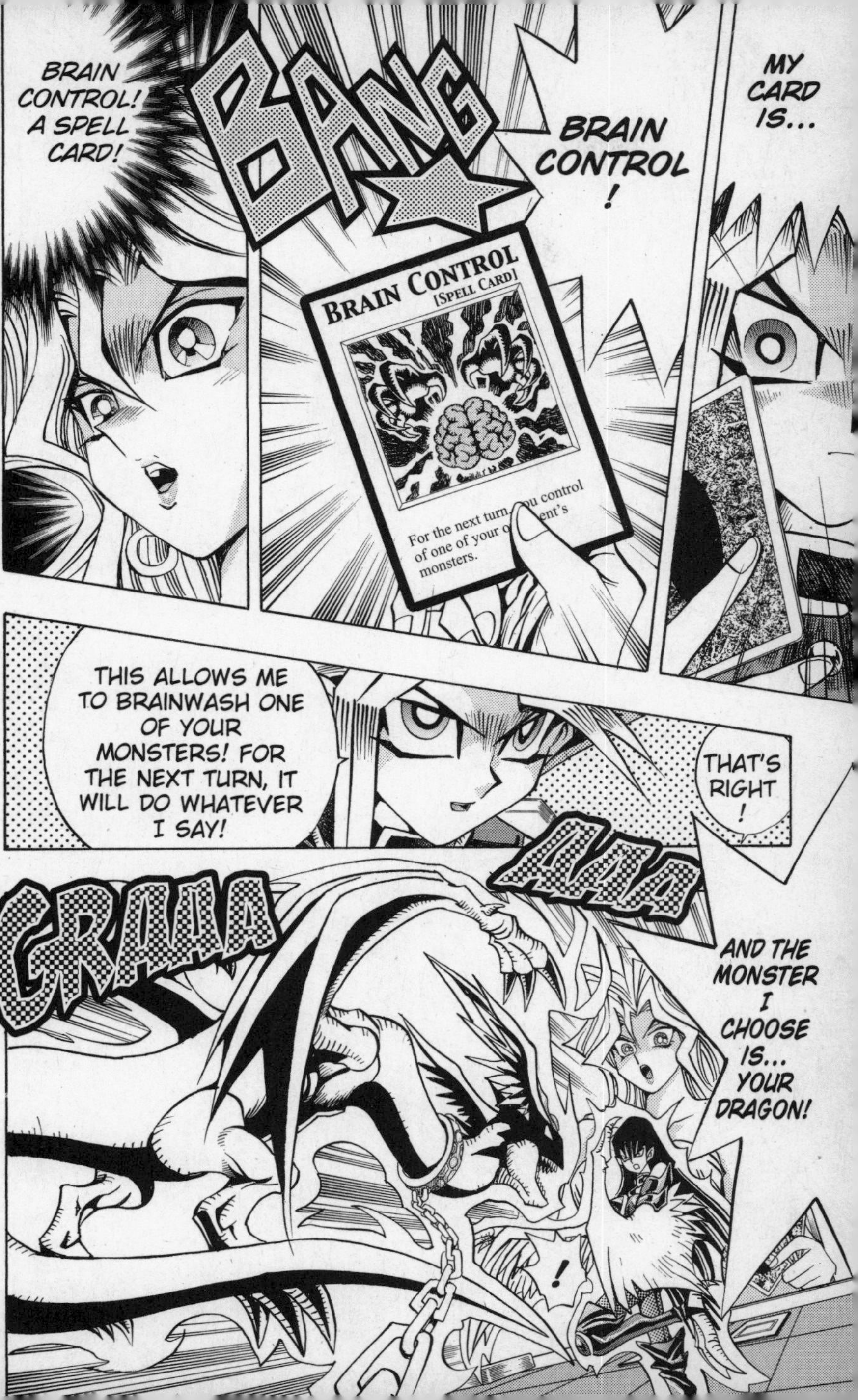
MY CARD IS...
BANG
BRAIN CONTROL!
BRAIN CONTROL
[SPELL CARD]
For the next turn, ou control
of one of your o ent's
monsters.
BRAIN CONTROL! A SPELL CARD!
THAT'S RIGHT!
THIS ALLOWS ME TO BRAINWASH ONE OF YOUR MONSTERS! FOR THE NEXT TURN, IT WILL DO WHATEVER I SAY!
AAAA
AND THE MONSTER I CHOOSE IS... YOUR DRAGON!
GRAAA
!

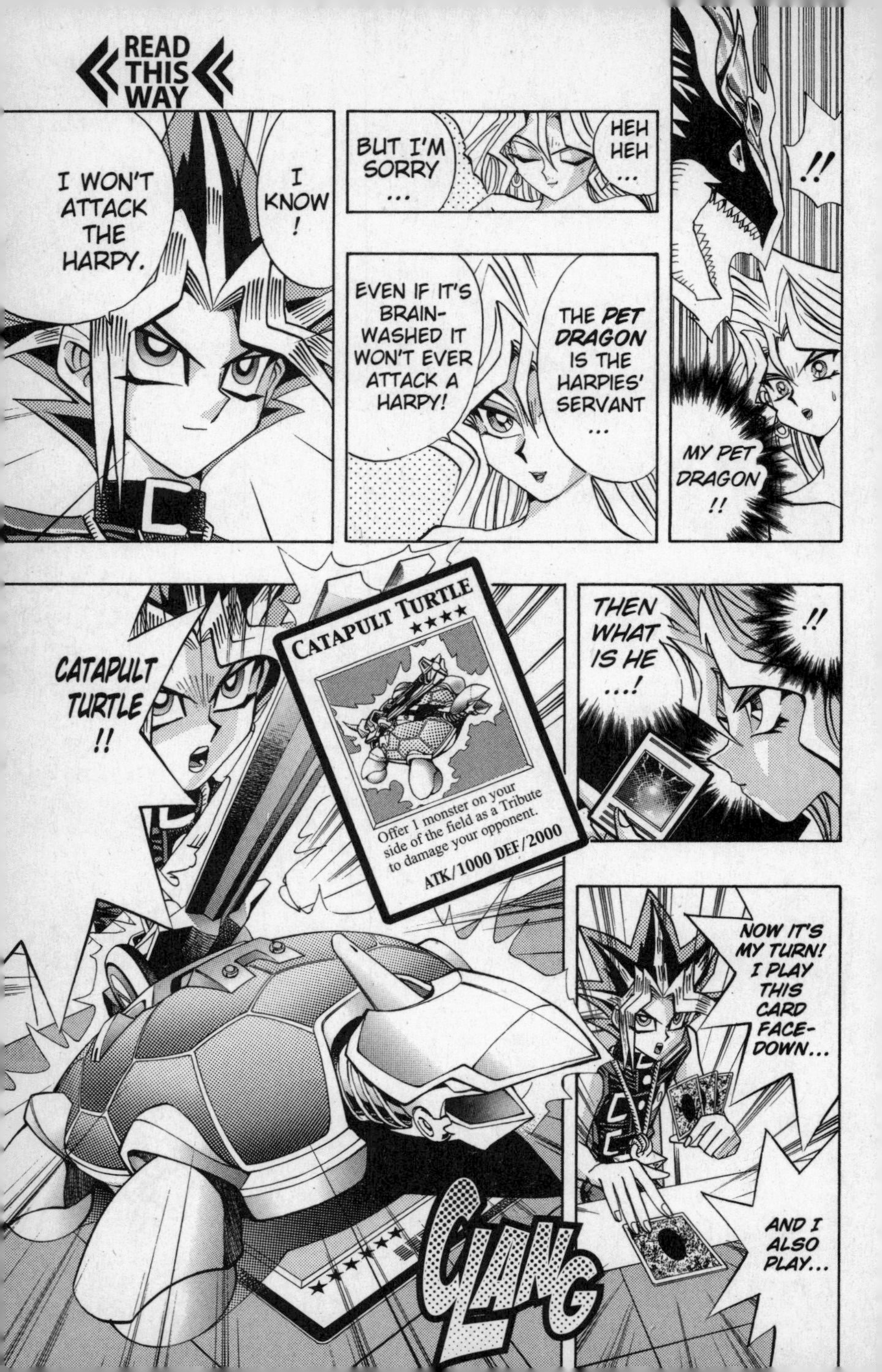
READ THIS WAY
!!
MY PET DRAGON !!
HEH HEH ...
BUT I'M SORRY ...
THE PET DRAGON IS THE HARPIES' SERVANT ...
EVEN IF IT'S BRAIN-WASHED IT WON'T EVER ATTACK A HARPY!
I KNOW !
I WON'T ATTACK THE HARPY.
!!
THEN WHAT IS HE ...!
NOW IT'S MY TURN! I PLAY THIS CARD FACE-DOWN...
AND I ALSO PLAY...
CATAPULT TURTLE ★★★★
Offer 1 monster on your side of the field as a Tribute to damage your opponent.
ATK/1000 DEF/2000
CATAPULT TURTLE !!
CLANG

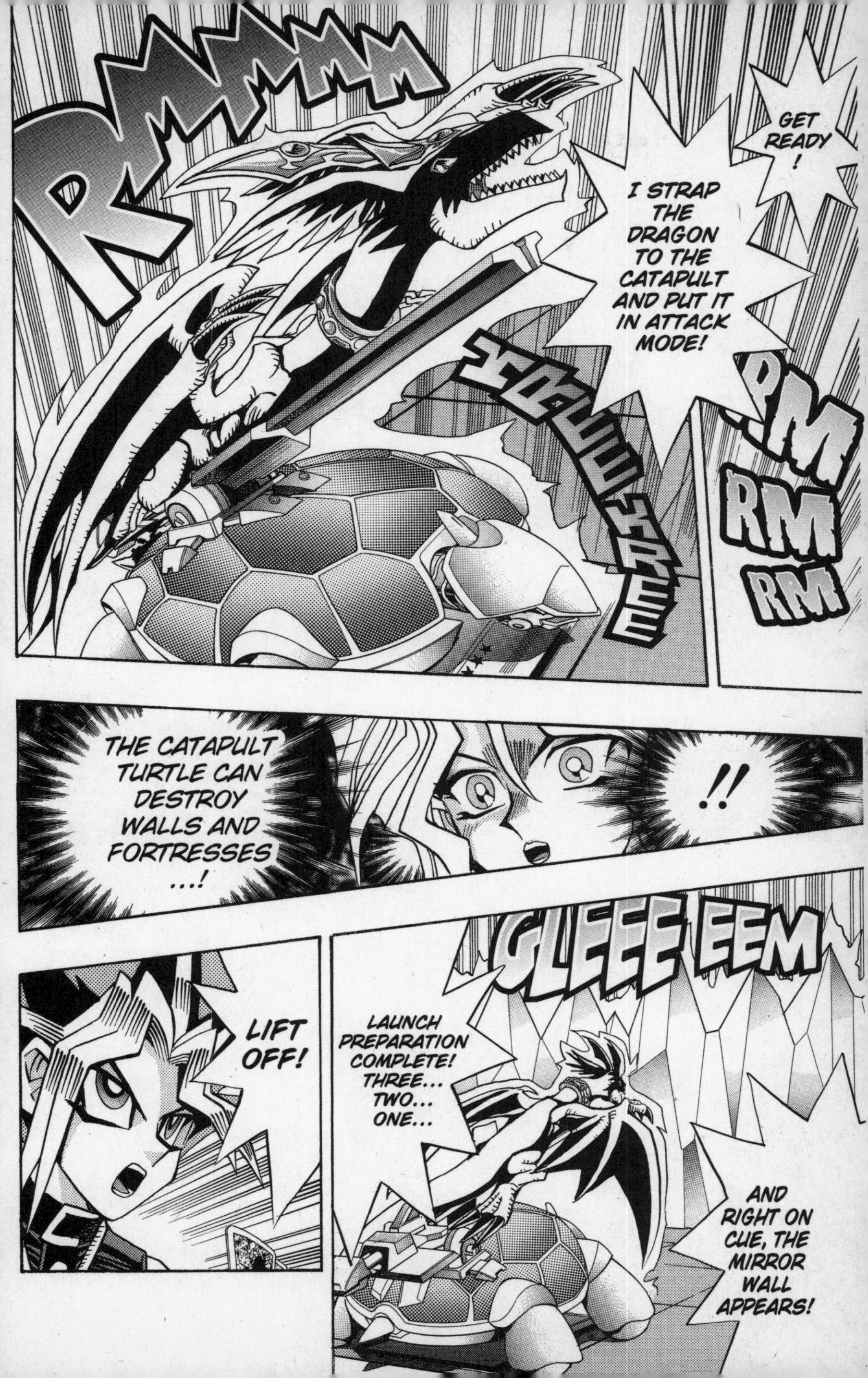
GET READY!
I STRAP THE DRAGON TO THE CATAPULT AND PUT IT IN ATTACK MODE!
RM RM RM
RAMMMM
!!
THE CATAPULT TURTLE CAN DESTROY WALLS AND FORTRESSES ...!
GLEEE EEM
LAUNCH PREPARATION COMPLETE! THREE... TWO... ONE...
AND RIGHT ON CUE, THE MIRROR WALL APPEARS!
LIFT OFF!

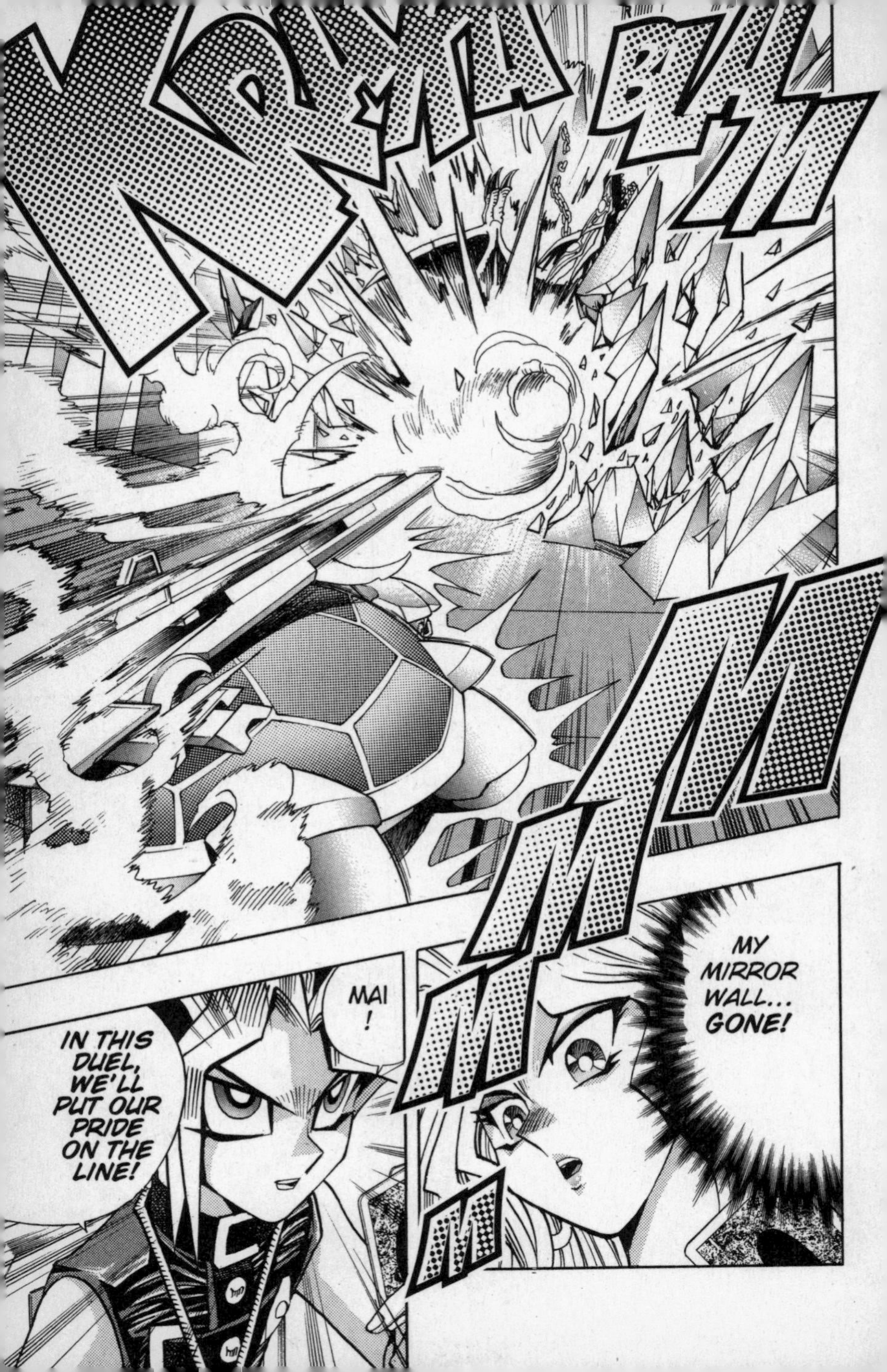
MY MIRROR WALL... GONE!
MAI!
IN THIS DUEL, WE'LL PUT OUR PRIDE ON THE LINE!

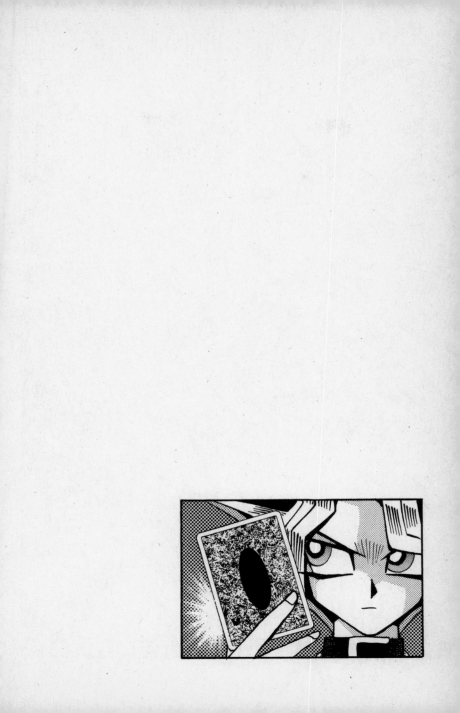

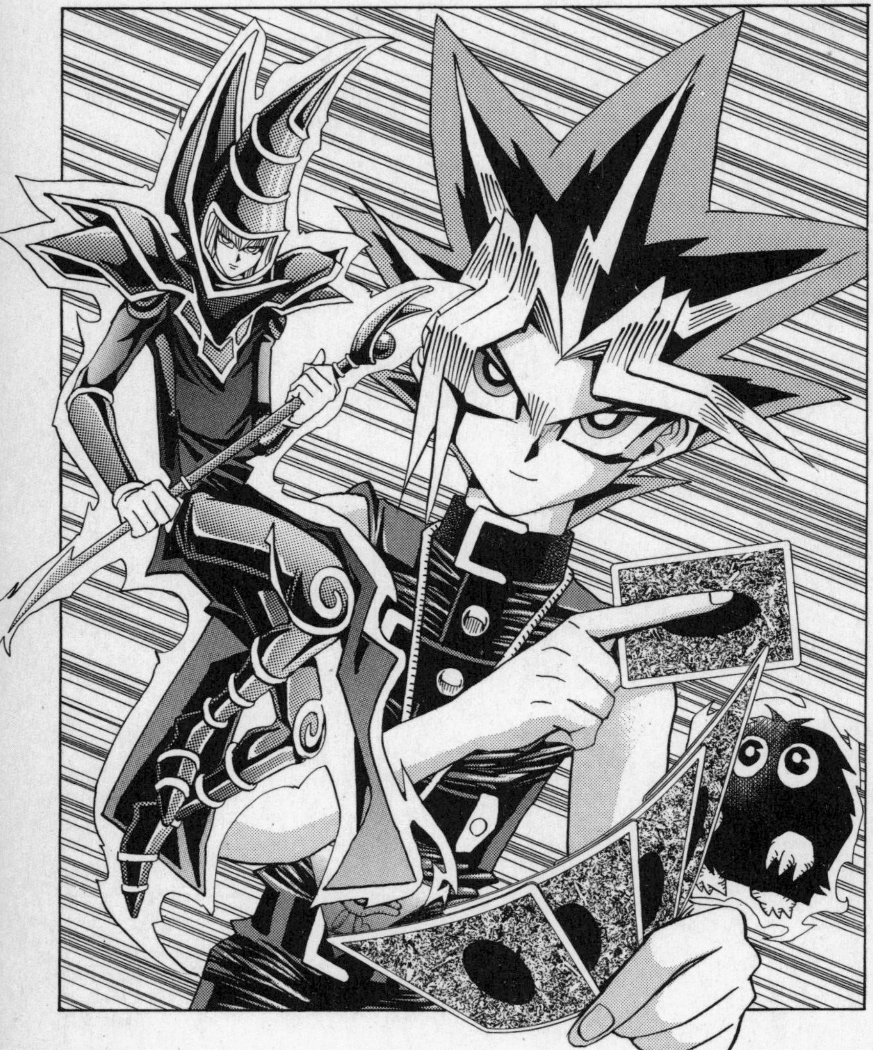

Duel 58: Running on the Edge!

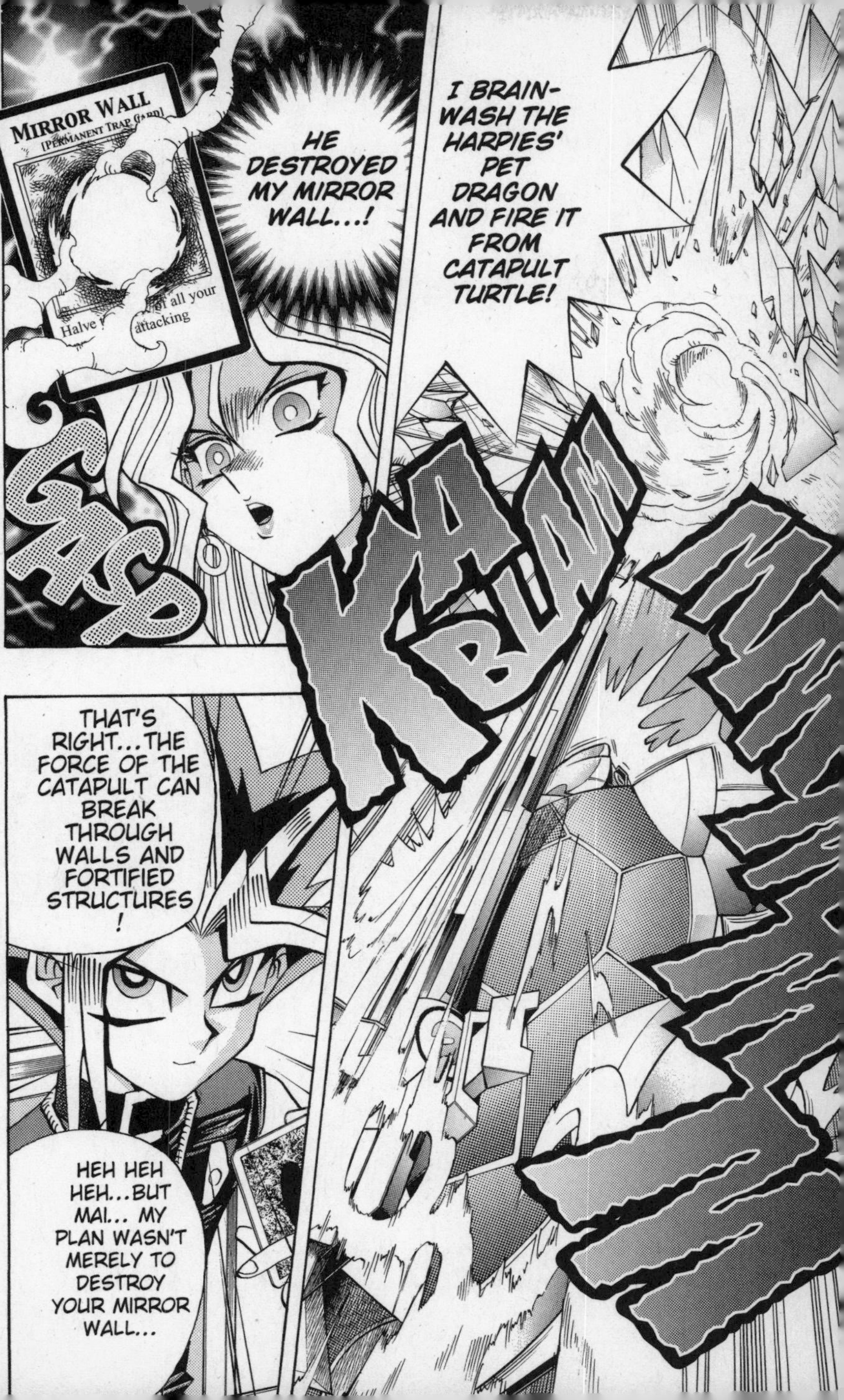
I BRAIN-WASH THE HARPIES' PET DRAGON AND FIRE IT FROM CATAPULT TURTLE!
KABOOM
MIRROR WALL
HE DESTROYED MY MIRROR WALL...!
GASP
THAT'S RIGHT...THE FORCE OF THE CATAPULT CAN BREAK THROUGH WALLS AND FORTIFIED STRUCTURES!
HEH HEH HEH...BUT MAI... MY PLAN WASN'T MERELY TO DESTROY YOUR MIRROR WALL...

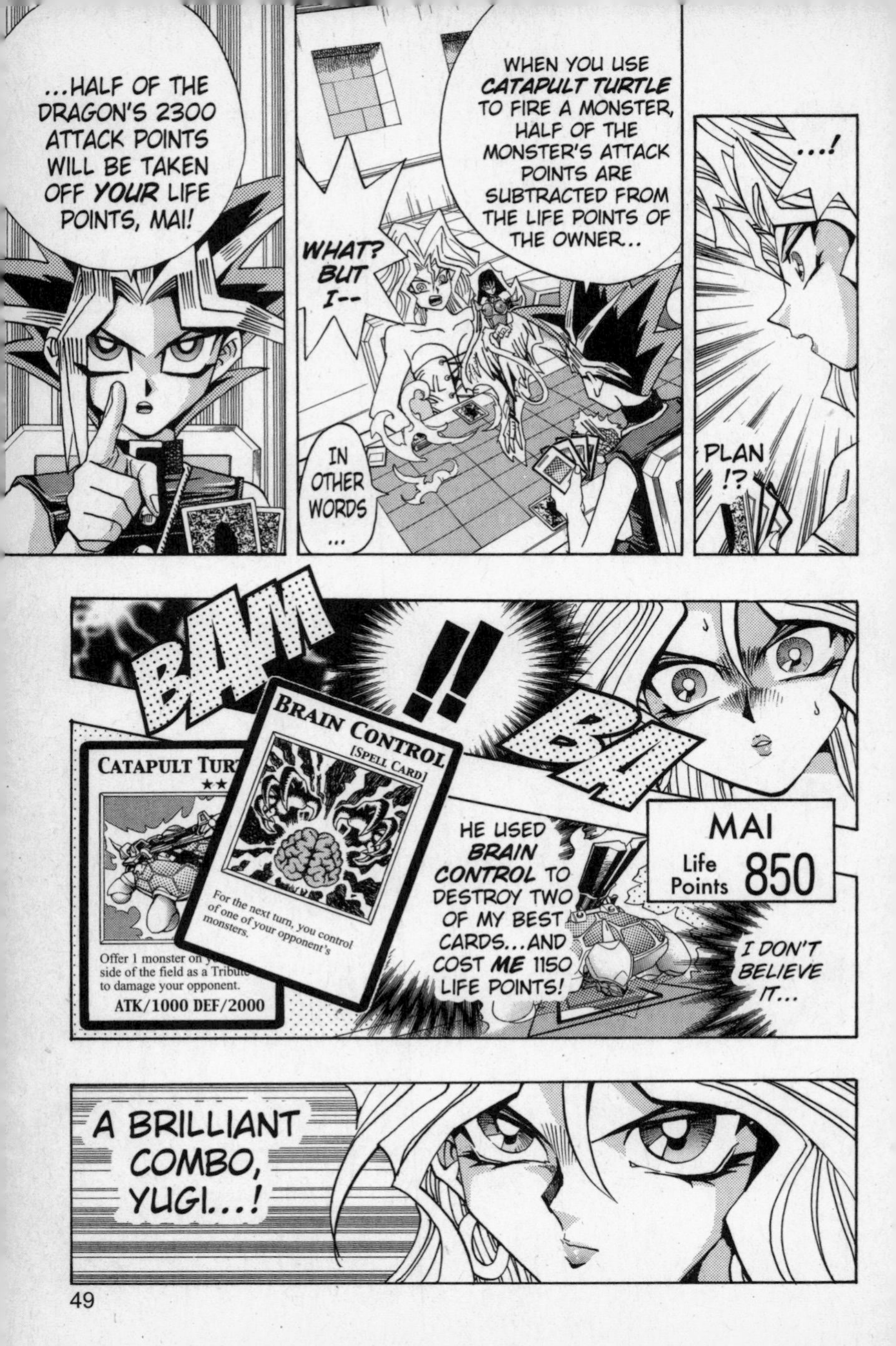
...!
PLAN !?
WHEN YOU USE CATAPULT TURTLE TO FIRE A MONSTER, HALF OF THE MONSTER'S ATTACK POINTS ARE SUBTRACTED FROM THE LIFE POINTS OF THE OWNER...
WHAT? BUT I--
IN OTHER WORDS...
...HALF OF THE DRAGON'S 2300 ATTACK POINTS WILL BE TAKEN OFF YOUR LIFE POINTS, MAI!
BAM !! BA
MAI Life Points 850
I DON'T BELIEVE IT...
HE USED BRAIN CONTROL TO DESTROY TWO OF MY BEST CARDS...AND COST ME 1150 LIFE POINTS!
BRAIN CONTROL
[SPELL CARD]
For the next turn, you control of one of your opponent's monsters.
CATAPULT TURT
Offer 1 monster on y
side of the field as a Tribute
to damage your opponent.
ATK/1000 DEF/2000
A BRILLIANT COMBO, YUGI...!

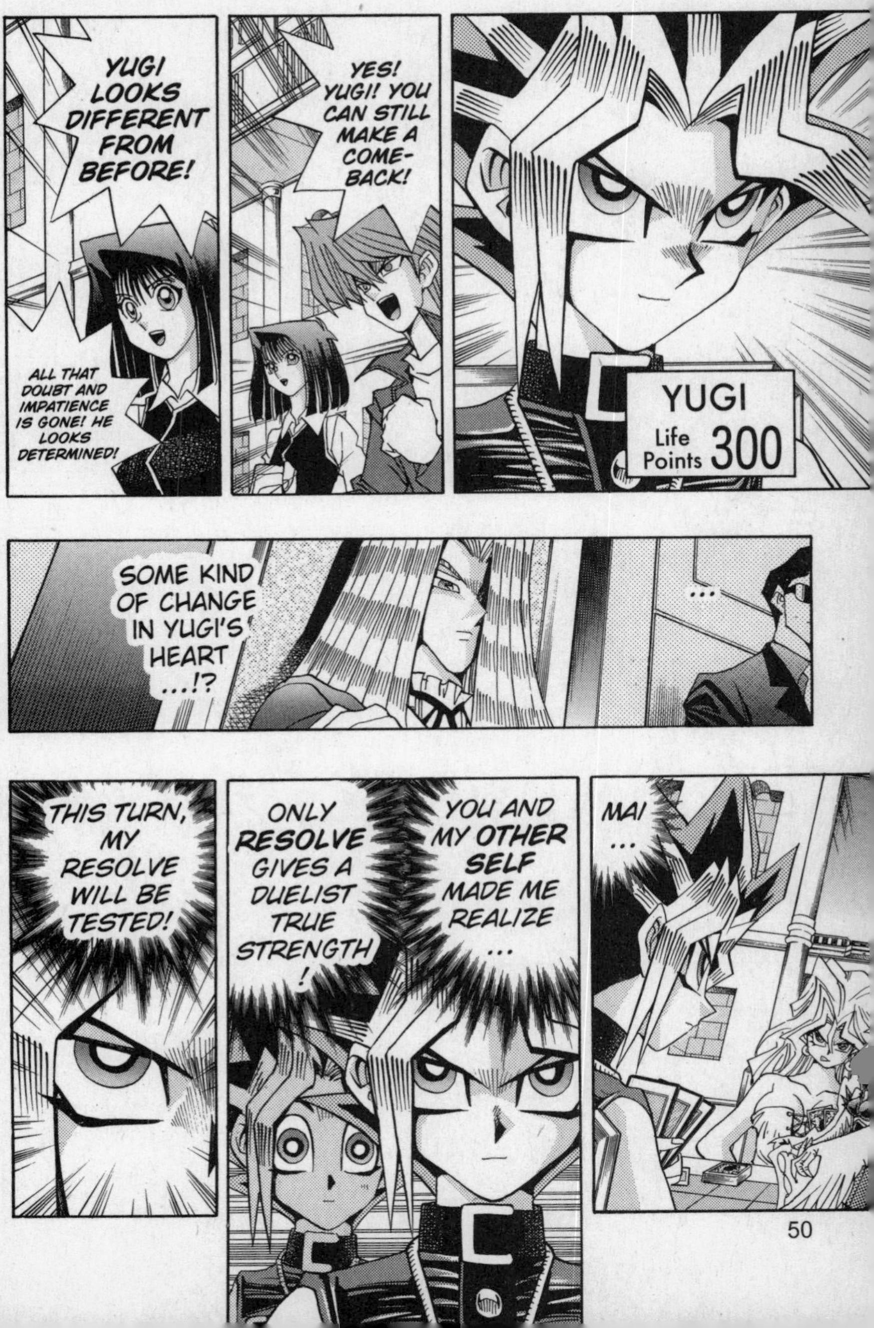
YUGI
Life Points 300
YES! YUGI! YOU CAN STILL MAKE A COME-BACK!
YUGI LOOKS DIFFERENT FROM BEFORE!
ALL THAT DOUBT AND IMPATIENCE IS GONE! HE LOOKS DETERMINED!
...
SOME KIND OF CHANGE IN YUGI'S HEART ...!?
MAI ...
YOU AND MY OTHER SELF MADE ME REALIZE ...
ONLY RESOLVE GIVES A DUELIST TRUE STRENGTH!
THIS TURN, MY RESOLVE WILL BE TESTED!

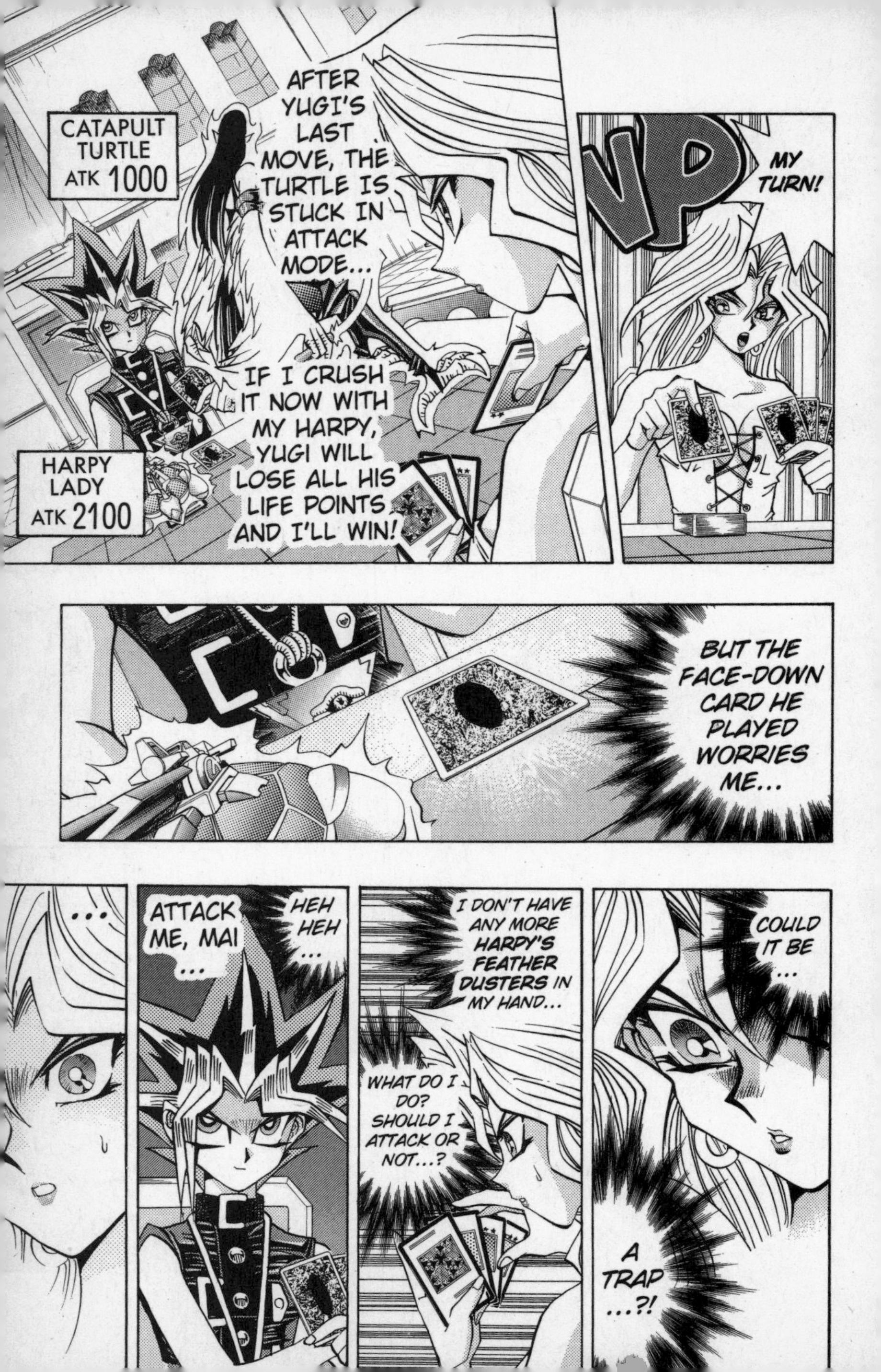
MY TURN!
AFTER YUGI'S LAST MOVE, THE TURTLE IS STUCK IN ATTACK MODE...
CATAPULT TURTLE ATK 1000
IF I CRUSH IT NOW WITH MY HARPY, YUGI WILL LOSE ALL HIS LIFE POINTS AND I'LL WIN!
HARPY LADY ATK 2100
BUT THE FACE-DOWN CARD HE PLAYED WORRIES ME...
COULD IT BE ...
A TRAP ...?!
I DON'T HAVE ANY MORE HARPY'S FEATHER DUSTERS IN MY HAND...
WHAT DO I DO? SHOULD I ATTACK OR NOT...?
HEH HEH ...
ATTACK ME, MAI ...
...

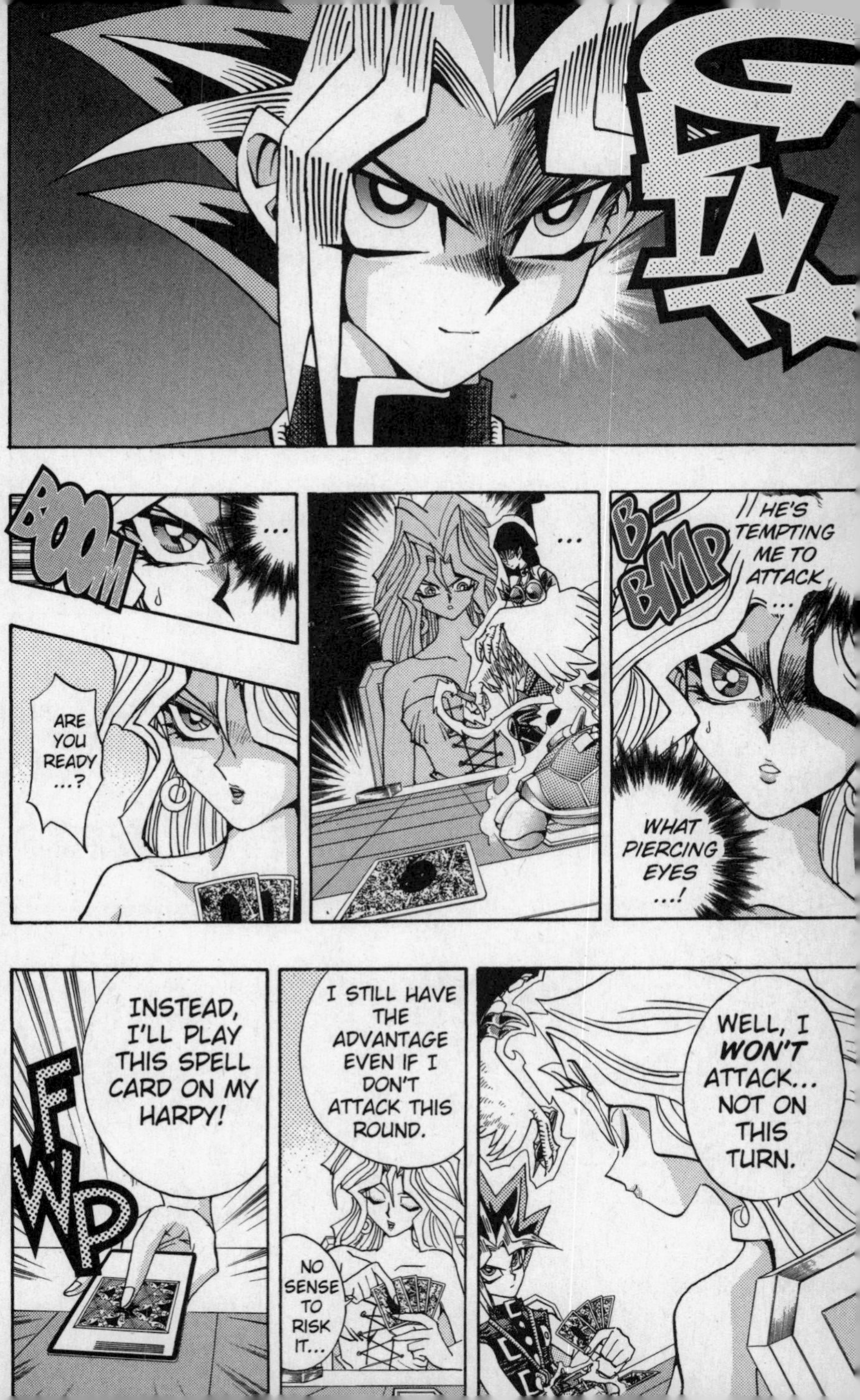
B-BMP
HE'S TEMPTING ME TO ATTACK...
WHAT PIERCING EYES...!
...
BOOM
...
ARE YOU READY...?
WELL, I *WON'T* ATTACK... NOT ON THIS TURN.
I STILL HAVE THE ADVANTAGE EVEN IF I DON'T ATTACK THIS ROUND.
NO SENSE TO RISK IT...
INSTEAD, I'LL PLAY THIS SPELL CARD ON MY HARPY!
FWP

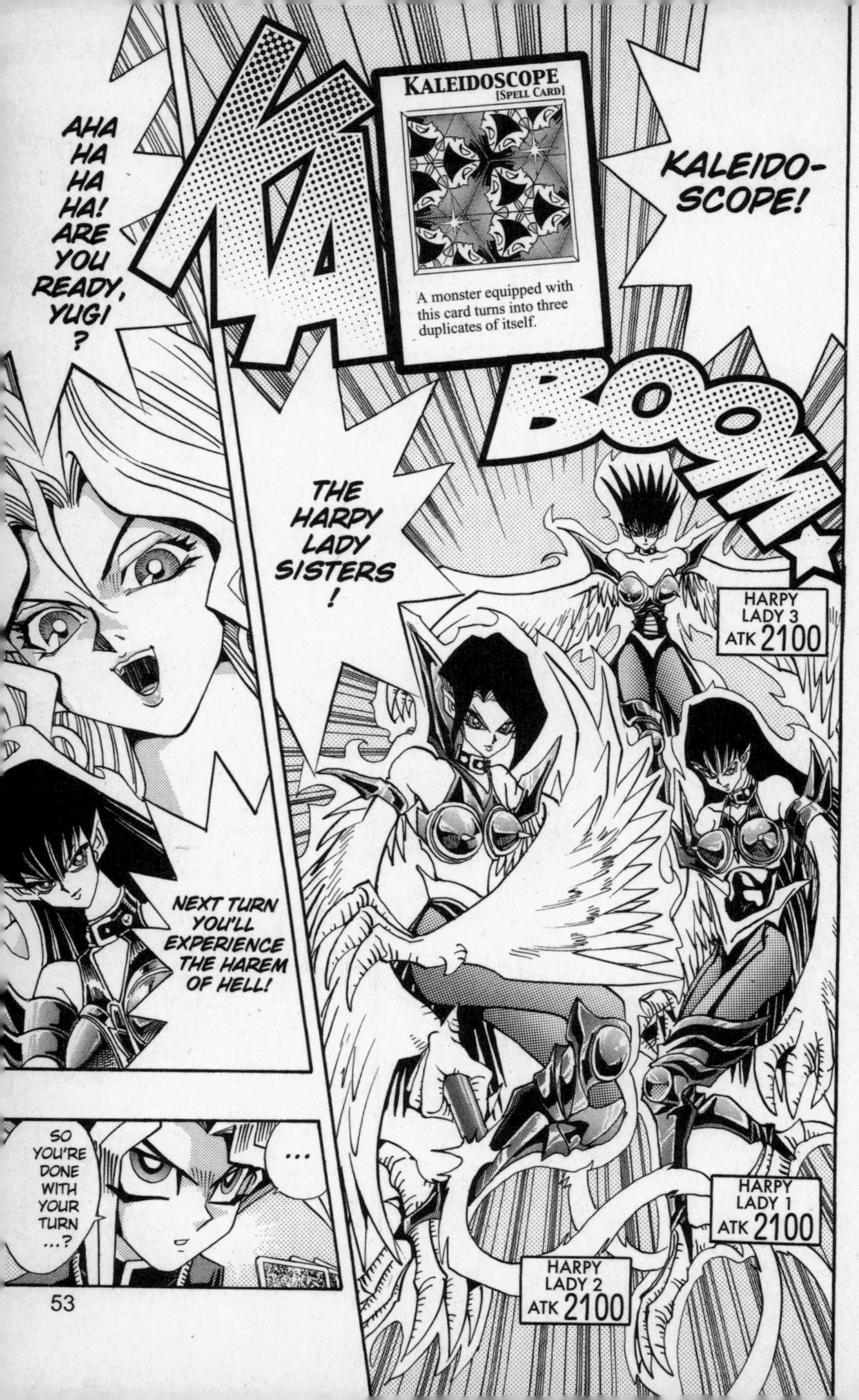

KALEIDO-SCOPE!
KALEIDOSCOPE
[SPELL CARD]
A monster equipped with this card turns into three duplicates of itself.
KA BOOM
AHA HA HA HA! ARE YOU READY, YUGI?
THE HARPY LADY SISTERS!
HARPY LADY 3 ATK 2100
HARPY LADY 1 ATK 2100
HARPY LADY 2 ATK 2100
NEXT TURN YOU'LL EXPERIENCE THE HAREM OF HELL!
...
SO YOU'RE DONE WITH YOUR TURN...?

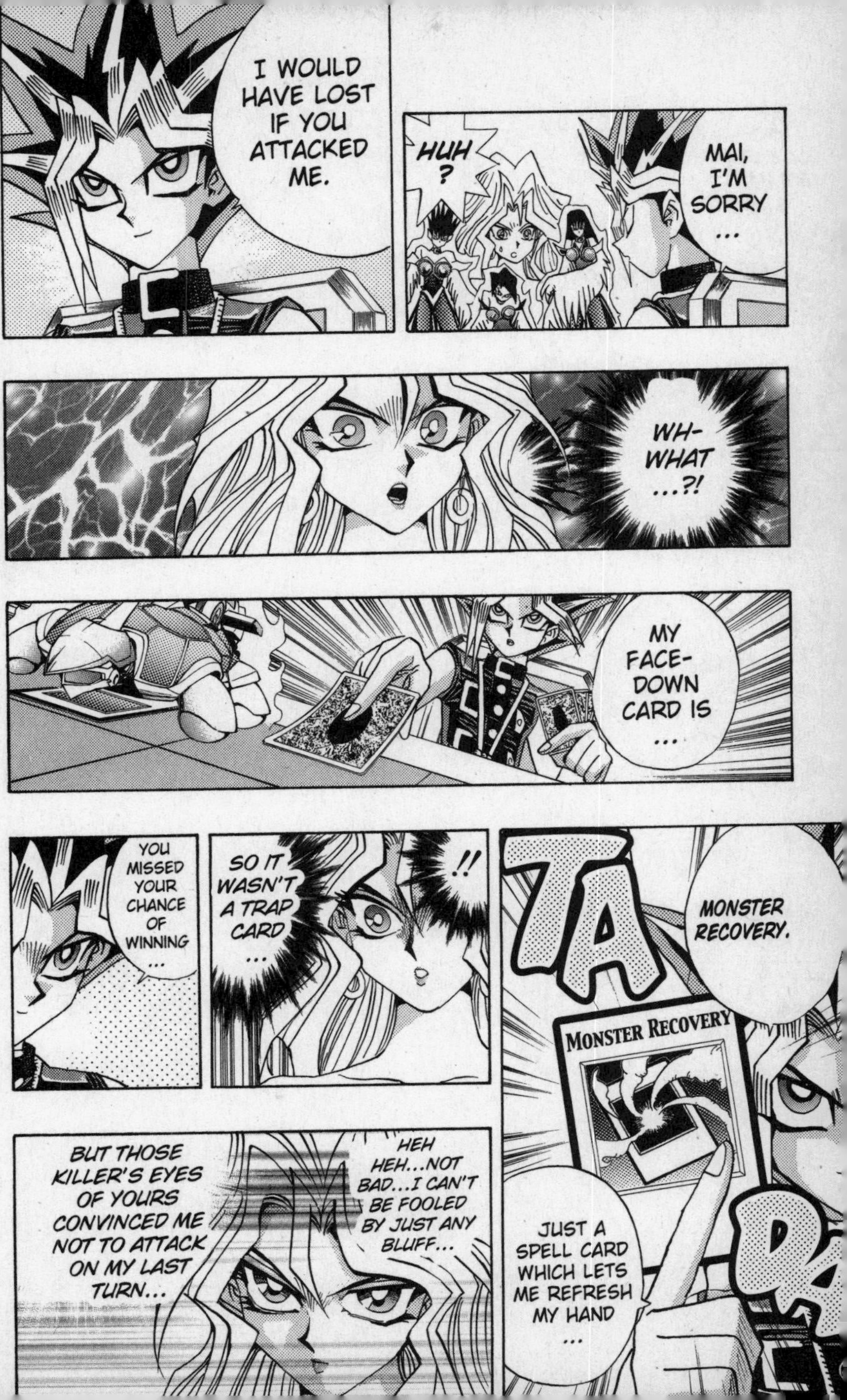
MAI, I'M SORRY ...
HUH ?
I WOULD HAVE LOST IF YOU ATTACKED ME.
WH-WHAT ...?!
MY FACE-DOWN CARD IS ...
TA
MONSTER RECOVERY.
MONSTER RECOVERY
JUST A SPELL CARD WHICH LETS ME REFRESH MY HAND ...
!!
SO IT WASN'T A TRAP CARD ...
YOU MISSED YOUR CHANCE OF WINNING ...
HEH HEH...NOT BAD...I CAN'T BE FOOLED BY JUST ANY BLUFF...
BUT THOSE KILLER'S EYES OF YOURS CONVINCED ME NOT TO ATTACK ON MY LAST TURN...

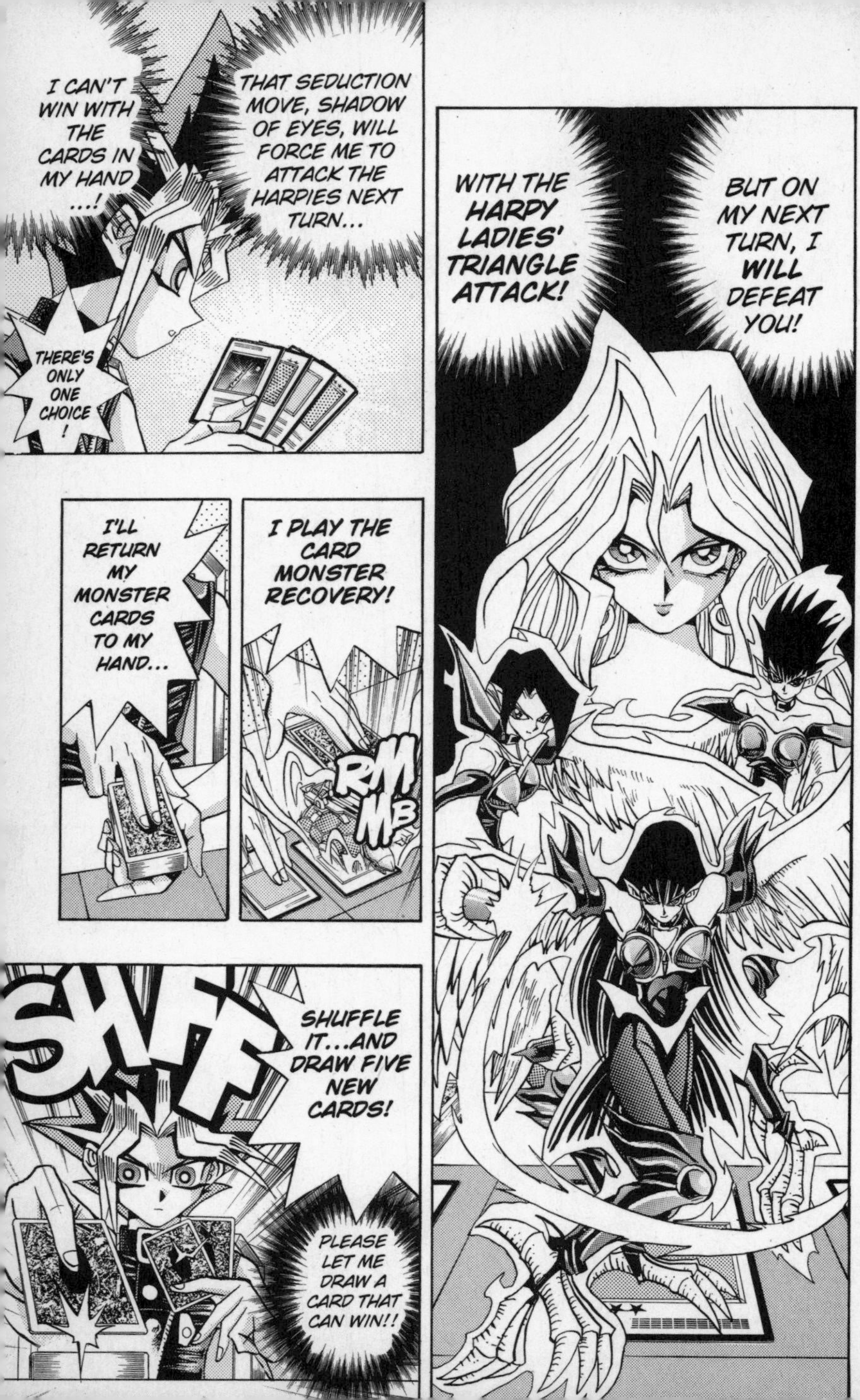
BUT ON MY NEXT TURN, I WILL DEFEAT YOU!
WITH THE HARPY LADIES' TRIANGLE ATTACK!
THAT SEDUCTION MOVE, SHADOW OF EYES, WILL FORCE ME TO ATTACK THE HARPIES NEXT TURN...
I CAN'T WIN WITH THE CARDS IN MY HAND ...!
THERE'S ONLY ONE CHOICE !
I PLAY THE CARD MONSTER RECOVERY!
RMMB
I'LL RETURN MY MONSTER CARDS TO MY HAND...
SHUFFLE IT...AND DRAW FIVE NEW CARDS!
SHF
PLEASE LET ME DRAW A CARD THAT CAN WIN!!

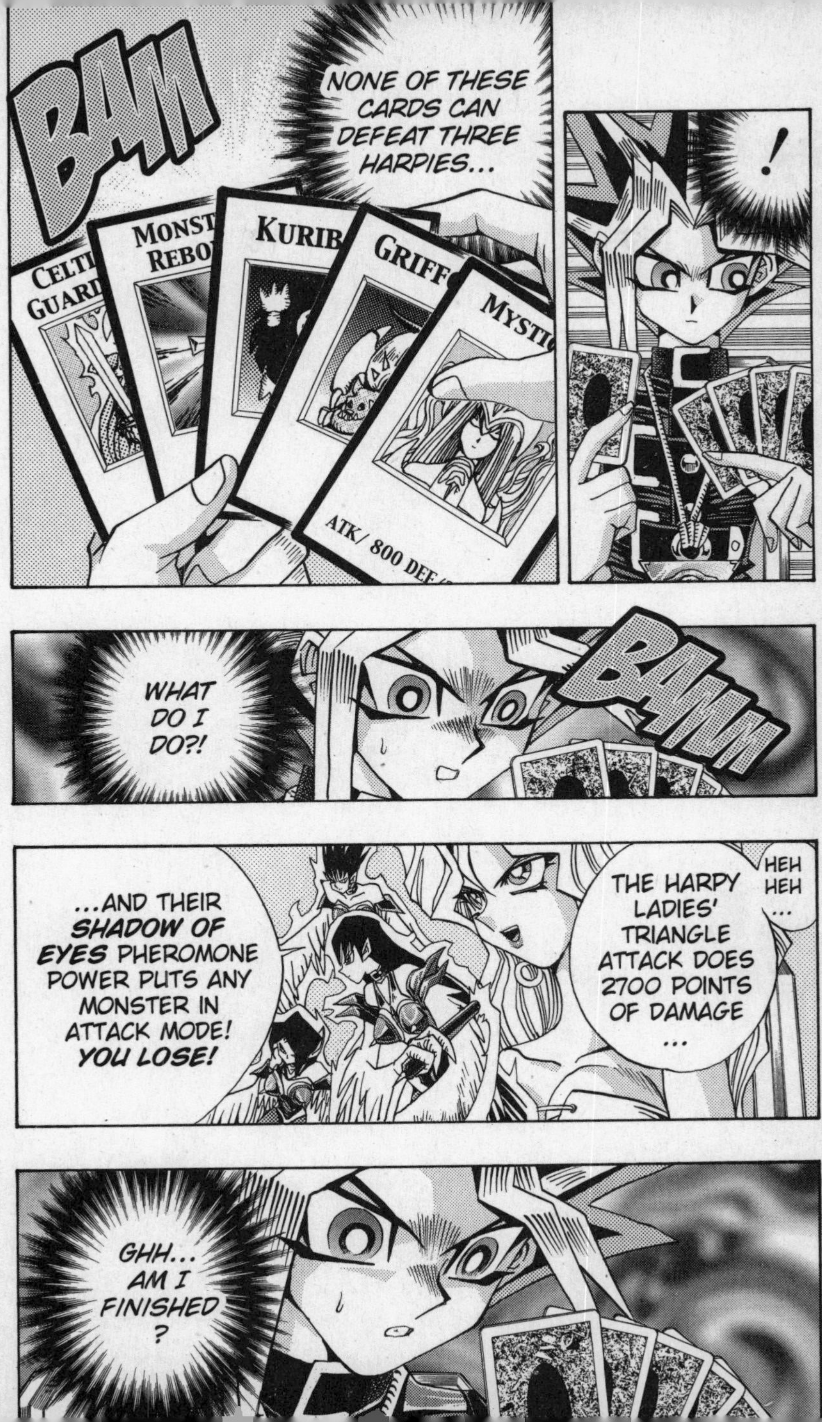
!
BAM
NONE OF THESE CARDS CAN DEFEAT THREE HARPIES...
CELTI GUARD
MONST REBO
KURIB
GRIFF
MYSTI
ATK/ 800 DEF
BAM
WHAT DO I DO?!
HEH HEH ...
THE HARPY LADIES' TRIANGLE ATTACK DOES 2700 POINTS OF DAMAGE ...
...AND THEIR SHADOW OF EYES PHEROMONE POWER PUTS ANY MONSTER IN ATTACK MODE! YOU LOSE!
GHH... AM I FINISHED ?

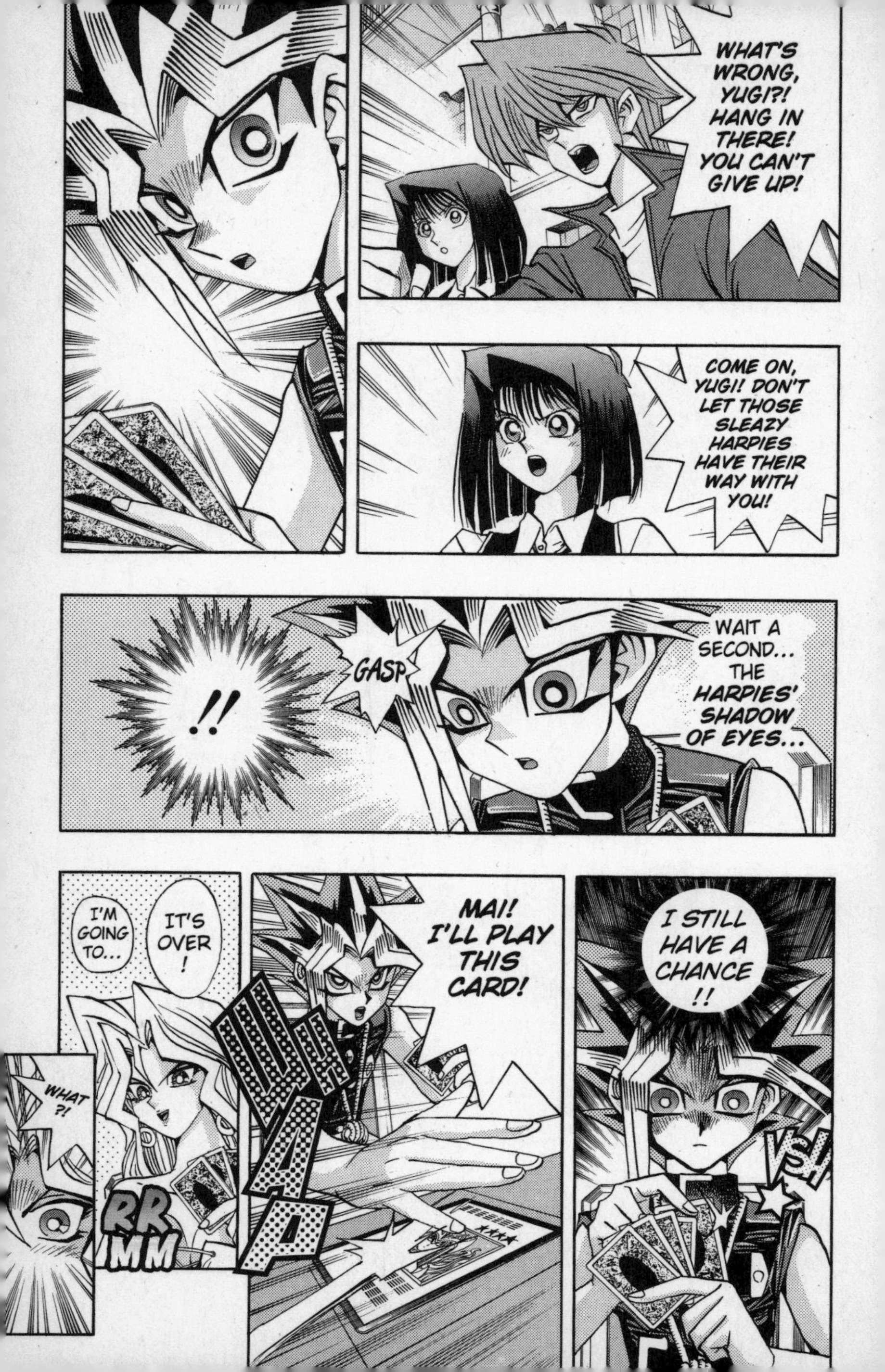
WHAT'S WRONG, YUGI?! HANG IN THERE! YOU CAN'T GIVE UP!
COME ON, YUGI! DON'T LET THOSE SLEAZY HARPIES HAVE THEIR WAY WITH YOU!
WAIT A SECOND... THE HARPIES' SHADOW OF EYES...
GASP
!!
I STILL HAVE A CHANCE!!
VSH
MAI! I'LL PLAY THIS CARD!
IT'S OVER!
I'M GOING TO...
RRMM
WHAT?!

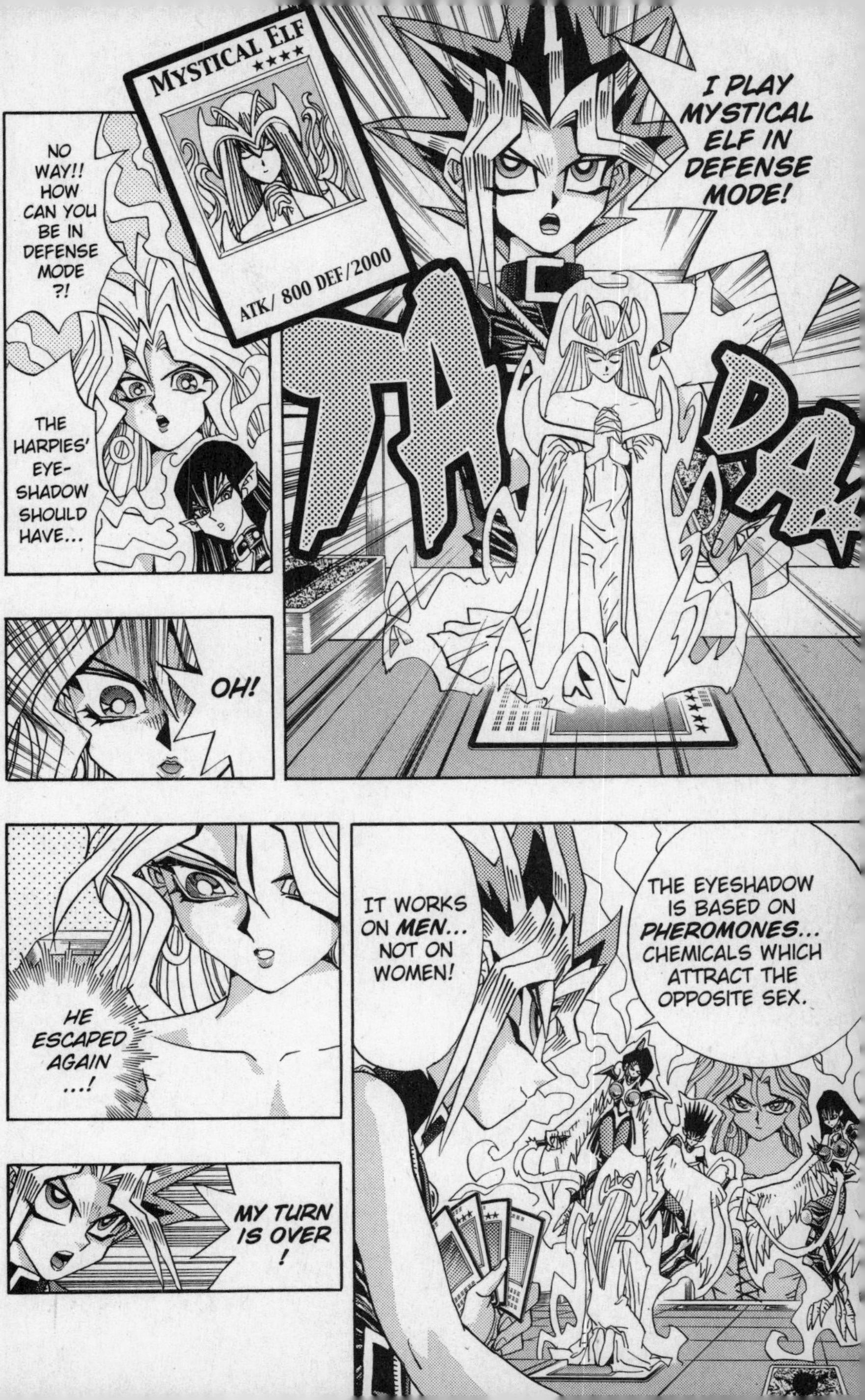
MYSTICAL ELF
★★★★
ATK/ 800 DEF/2000
I PLAY MYSTICAL ELF IN DEFENSE MODE!
TA DA
NO WAY!! HOW CAN YOU BE IN DEFENSE MODE ?!
THE HARPIES' EYE-SHADOW SHOULD HAVE...
OH!
THE EYESHADOW IS BASED ON PHEROMONES... CHEMICALS WHICH ATTRACT THE OPPOSITE SEX.
IT WORKS ON MEN... NOT ON WOMEN!
HE ESCAPED AGAIN ...!
MY TURN IS OVER !

READ THIS WAY

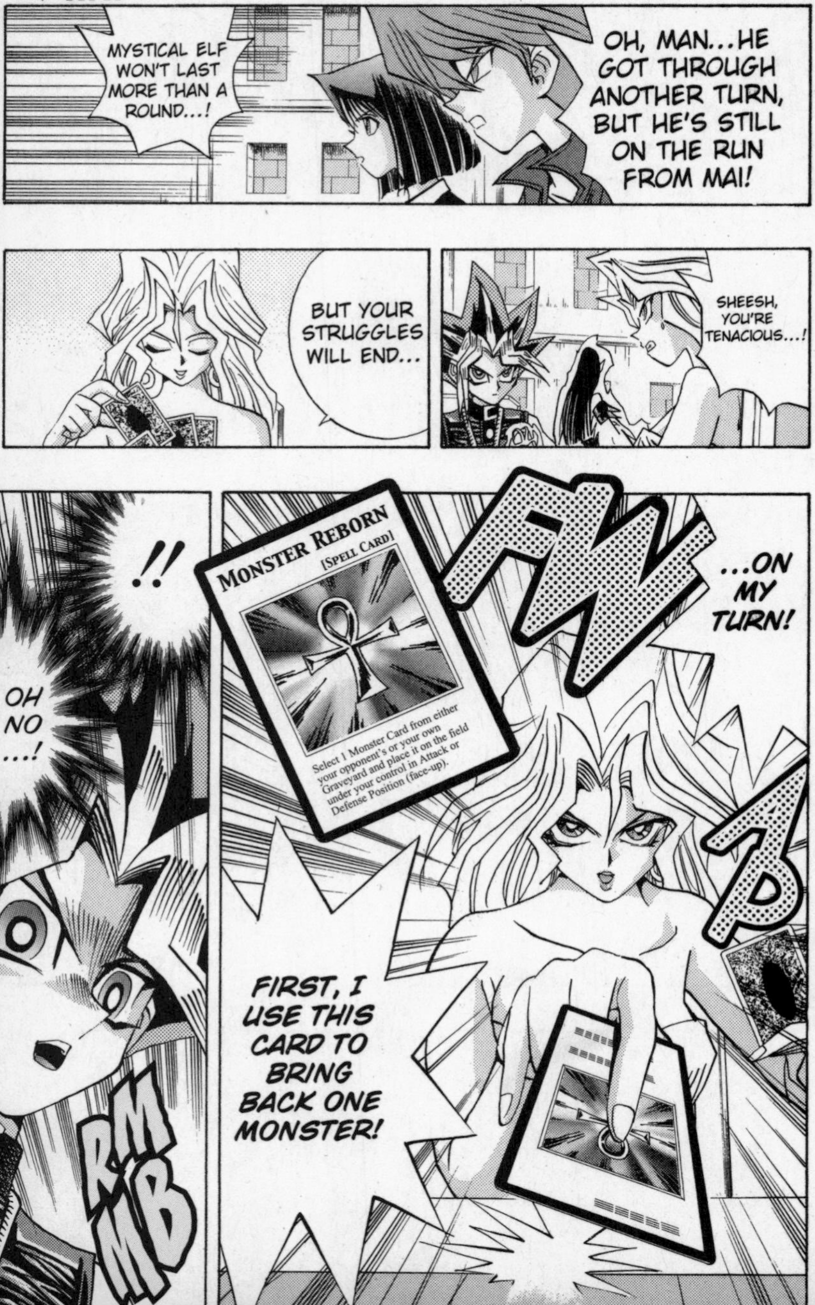
OH, MAN...HE GOT THROUGH ANOTHER TURN, BUT HE'S STILL ON THE RUN FROM MAI!
MYSTICAL ELF WON'T LAST MORE THAN A ROUND...!
SHEESH, YOU'RE TENACIOUS...!
BUT YOUR STRUGGLES WILL END...
FWAP
...ON MY TURN!
MONSTER REBORN
[SPELL CARD]
Select 1 Monster Card from either your opponent's or your own Graveyard and place it on the field under your control in Attack or Defense Position (face-up).
FIRST, I USE THIS CARD TO BRING BACK ONE MONSTER!
!!
OH NO ...!
RMMB

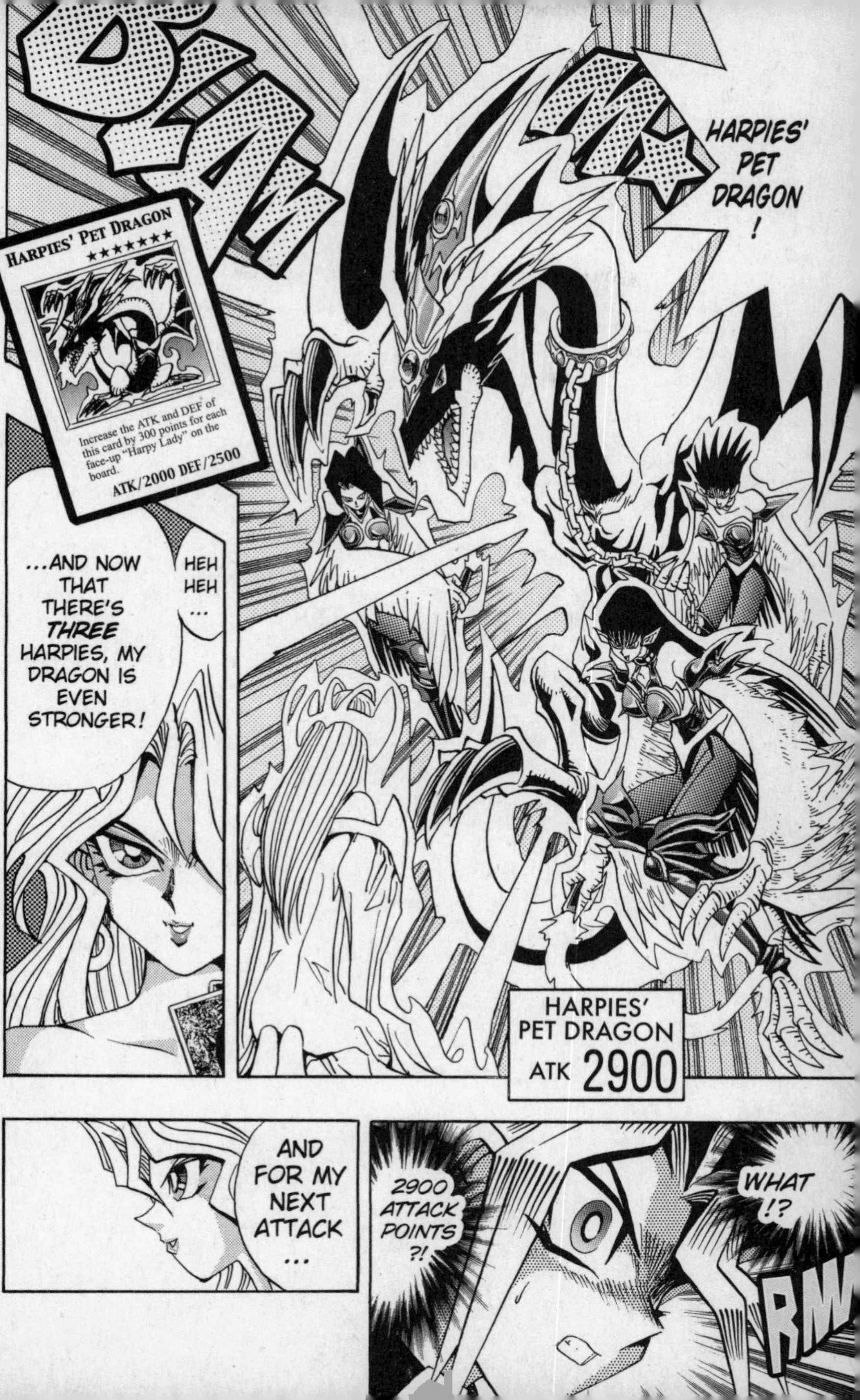
HARPIES' PET DRAGON!
HARPIES' PET DRAGON
★★★★★★★
Increase the ATK and DEF of this card by 300 points for each face-up "Harpy Lady" on the board.
ATK/2000 DEF/2500
HARPIES' PET DRAGON ATK 2900
HEH HEH ...
...AND NOW THAT THERE'S *THREE* HARPIES, MY DRAGON IS EVEN STRONGER!
WHAT !?
2900 ATTACK POINTS ?!
AND FOR MY NEXT ATTACK ...

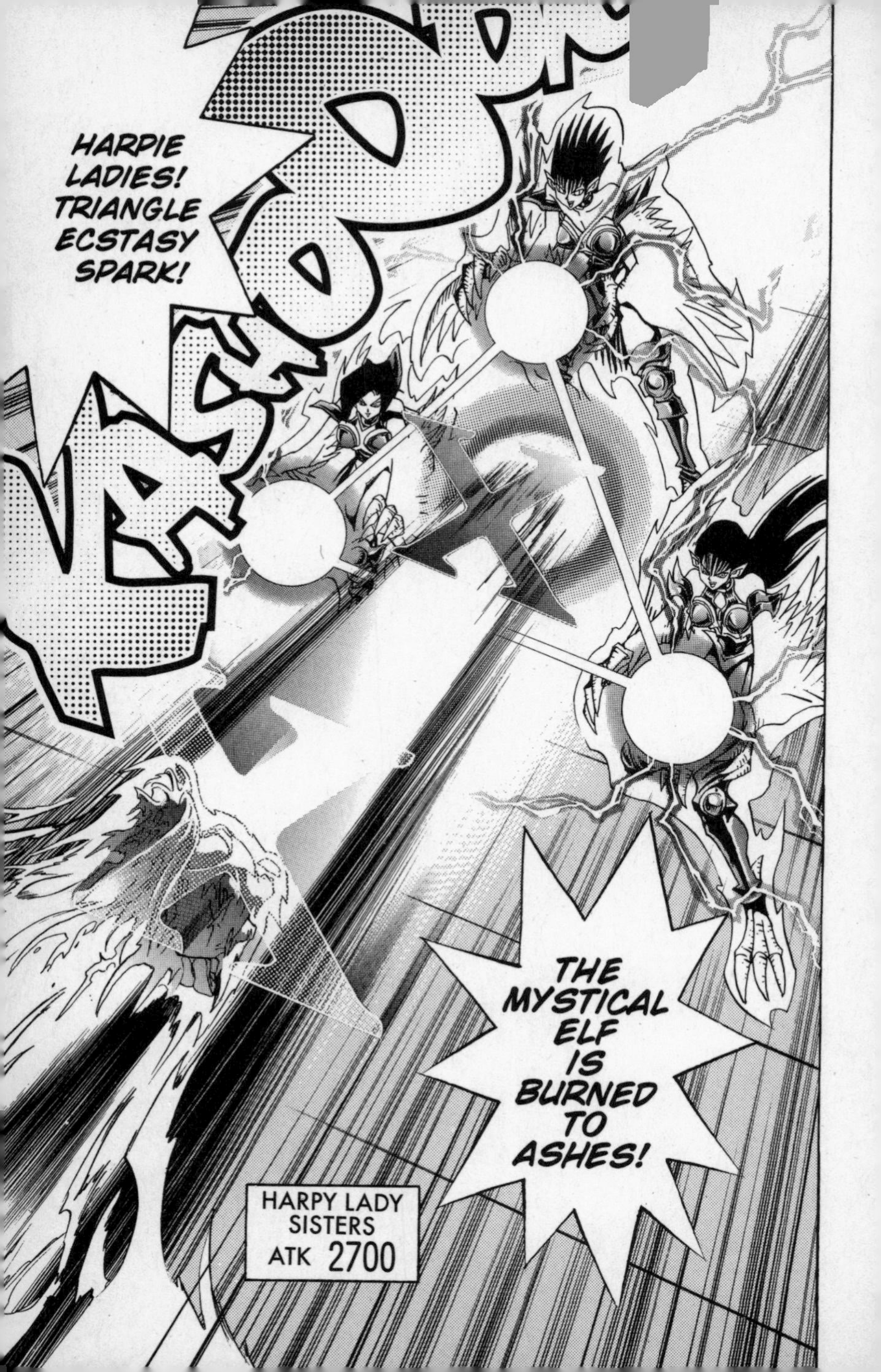
HARPIE LADIES! TRIANGLE ECSTASY SPARK!
THE MYSTICAL ELF IS BURNED TO ASHES!
HARPY LADY SISTERS ATK 2700

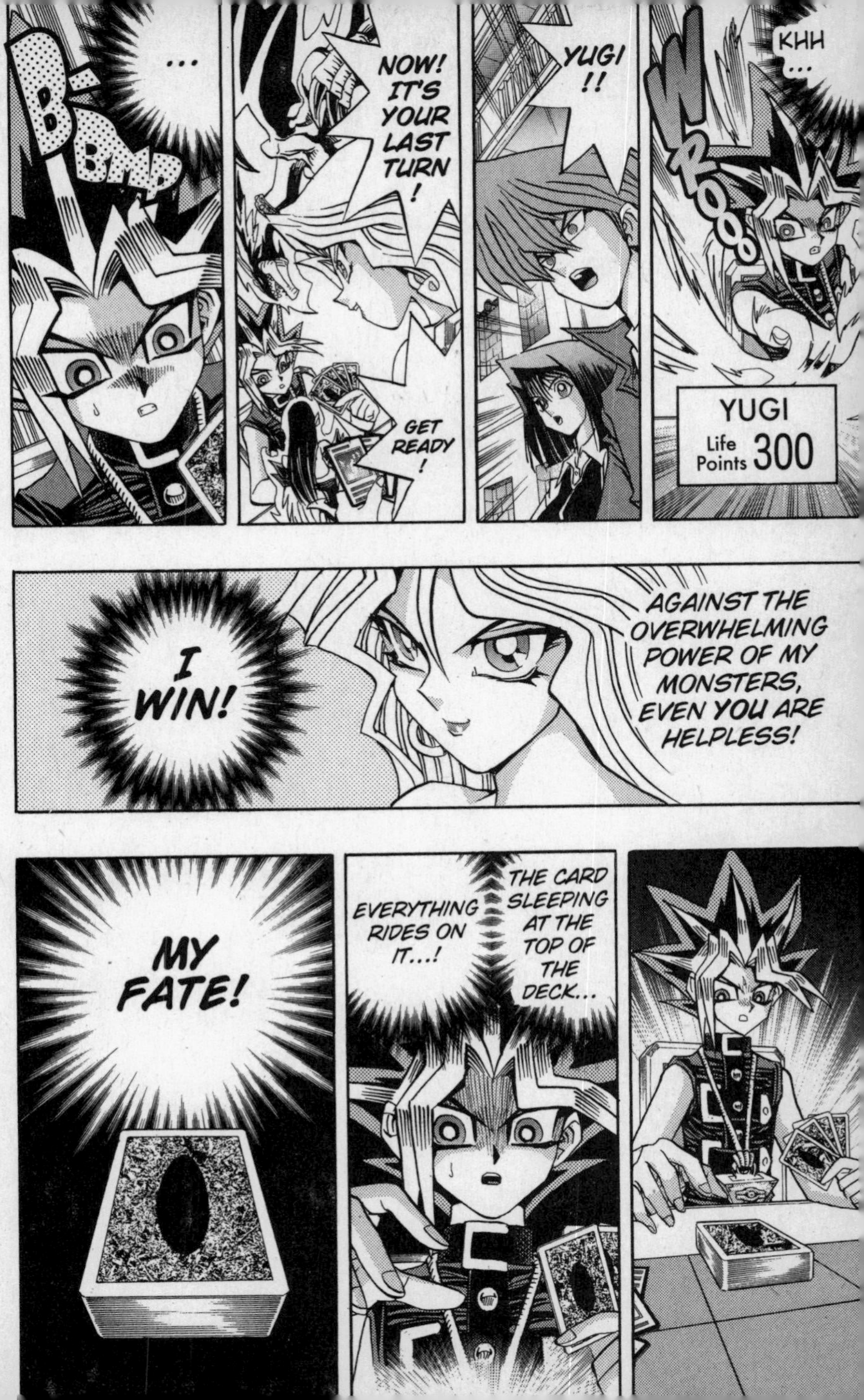
KHH ...
WROOO
YUGI
Life Points 300
YUGI !!
NOW! IT'S YOUR LAST TURN!
GET READY!
...
B-BMP
AGAINST THE OVERWHELMING POWER OF MY MONSTERS, EVEN YOU ARE HELPLESS!
I WIN!
THE CARD SLEEPING AT THE TOP OF THE DECK...
EVERYTHING RIDES ON IT...!
MY FATE!

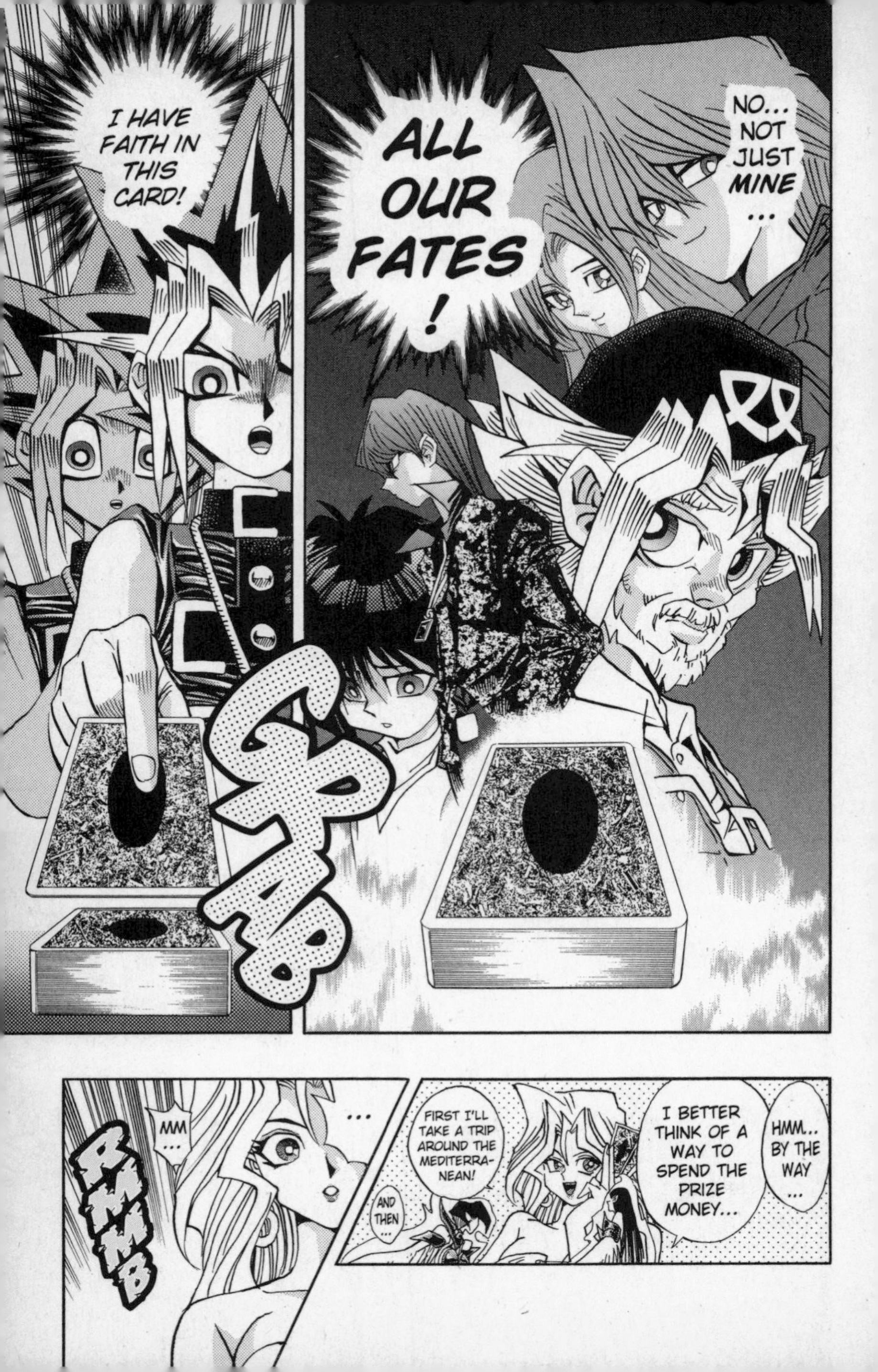
NO... NOT JUST MINE ...
ALL OUR FATES!
GRAB
I HAVE FAITH IN THIS CARD!
HMM... BY THE WAY ...
I BETTER THINK OF A WAY TO SPEND THE PRIZE MONEY...
FIRST I'LL TAKE A TRIP AROUND THE MEDITERRA-NEAN!
AND THEN ...
...
MM ...
RMMB

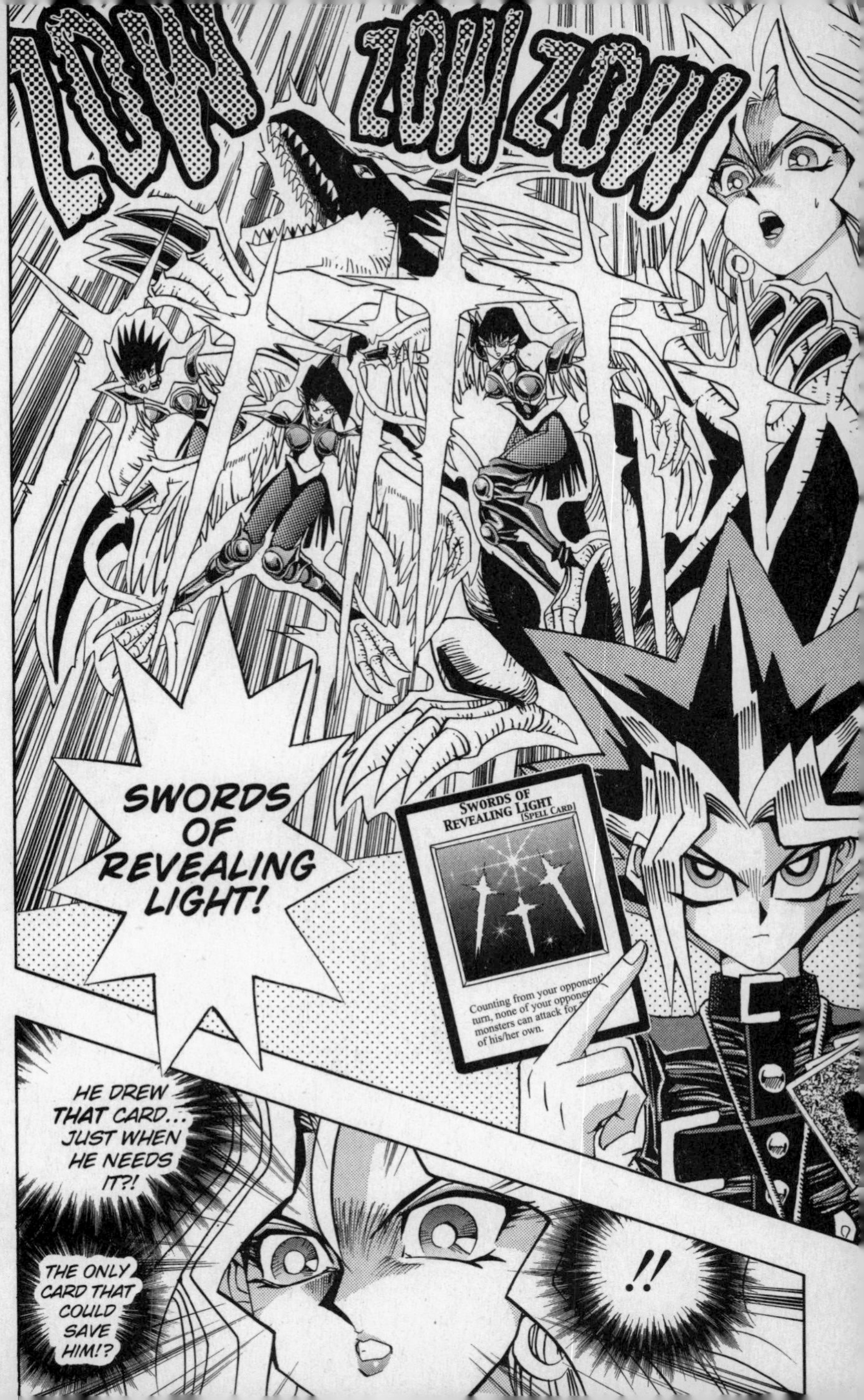
ZOW ZOW
ZOW
SWORDS OF REVEALING LIGHT!
SWORDS OF REVEALING LIGHT [SPELL CARD]
Counting from your opponent' turn, none of your opponen monsters can attack for of his/her own.
!!
HE DREW THAT CARD... JUST WHEN HE NEEDS IT?!
THE ONLY CARD THAT COULD SAVE HIM!?

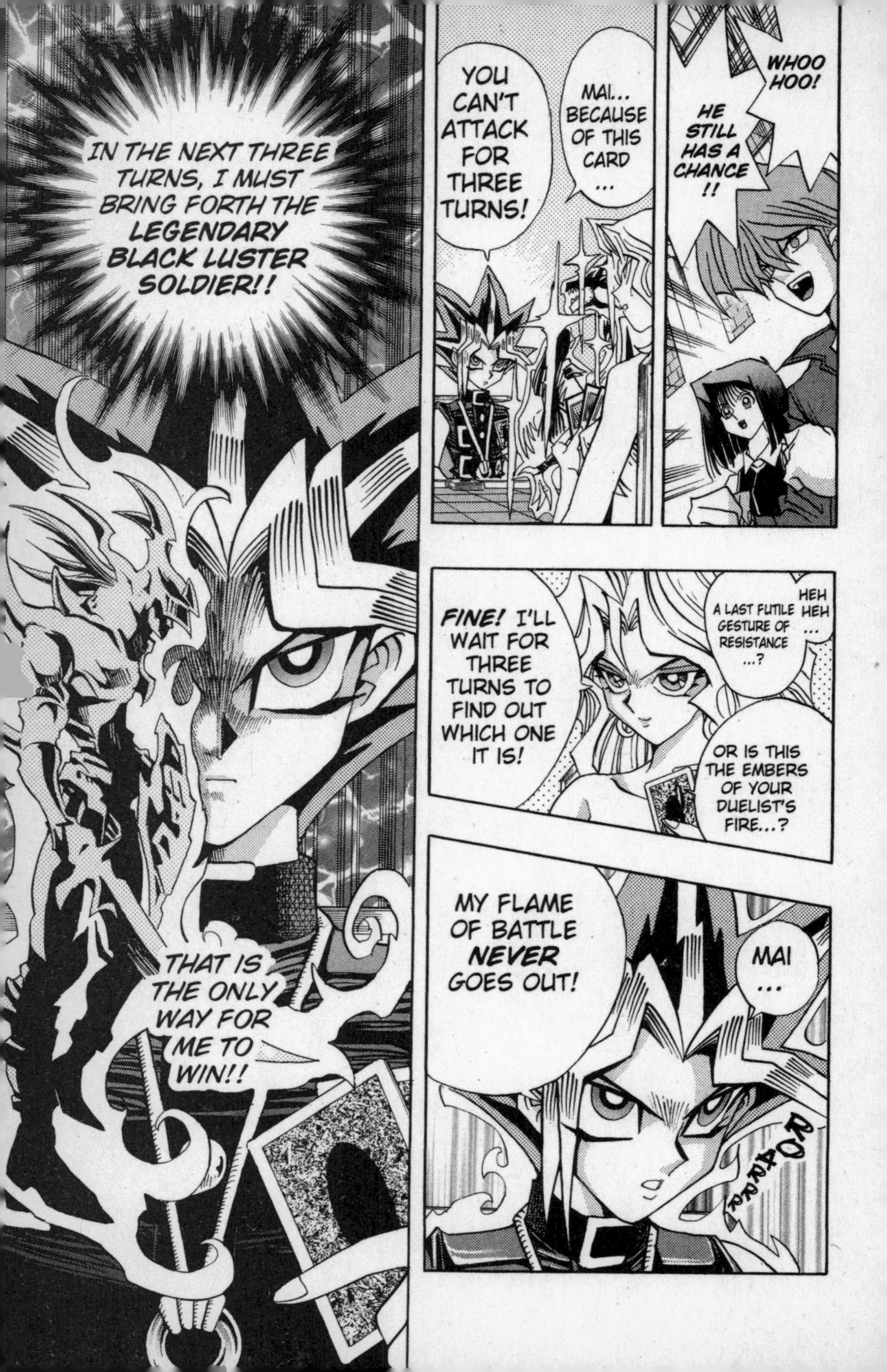

WHOO HOO!
HE STILL HAS A CHANCE!!
MAI... BECAUSE OF THIS CARD...
YOU CAN'T ATTACK FOR THREE TURNS!
HEH HEH...
A LAST FUTILE GESTURE OF RESISTANCE...?
OR IS THIS THE EMBERS OF YOUR DUELIST'S FIRE...?
FINE! I'LL WAIT FOR THREE TURNS TO FIND OUT WHICH ONE IT IS!
MAI...
MY FLAME OF BATTLE NEVER GOES OUT!
ROARRRR
IN THE NEXT THREE TURNS, I MUST BRING FORTH THE LEGENDARY BLACK LUSTER SOLDIER!!
THAT IS THE ONLY WAY FOR ME TO WIN!!

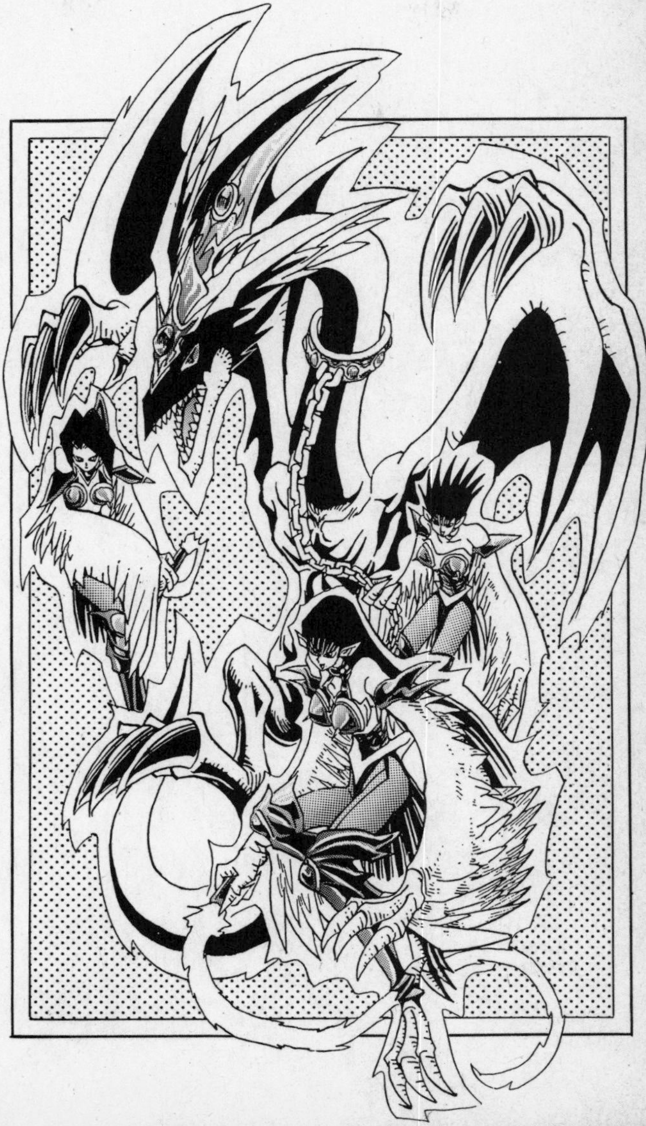

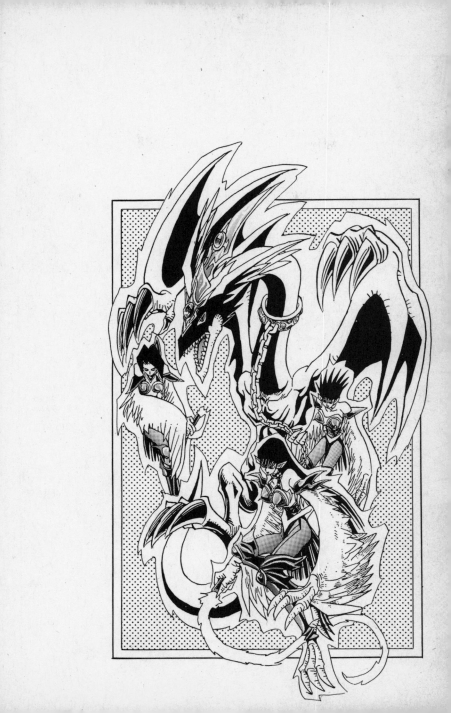

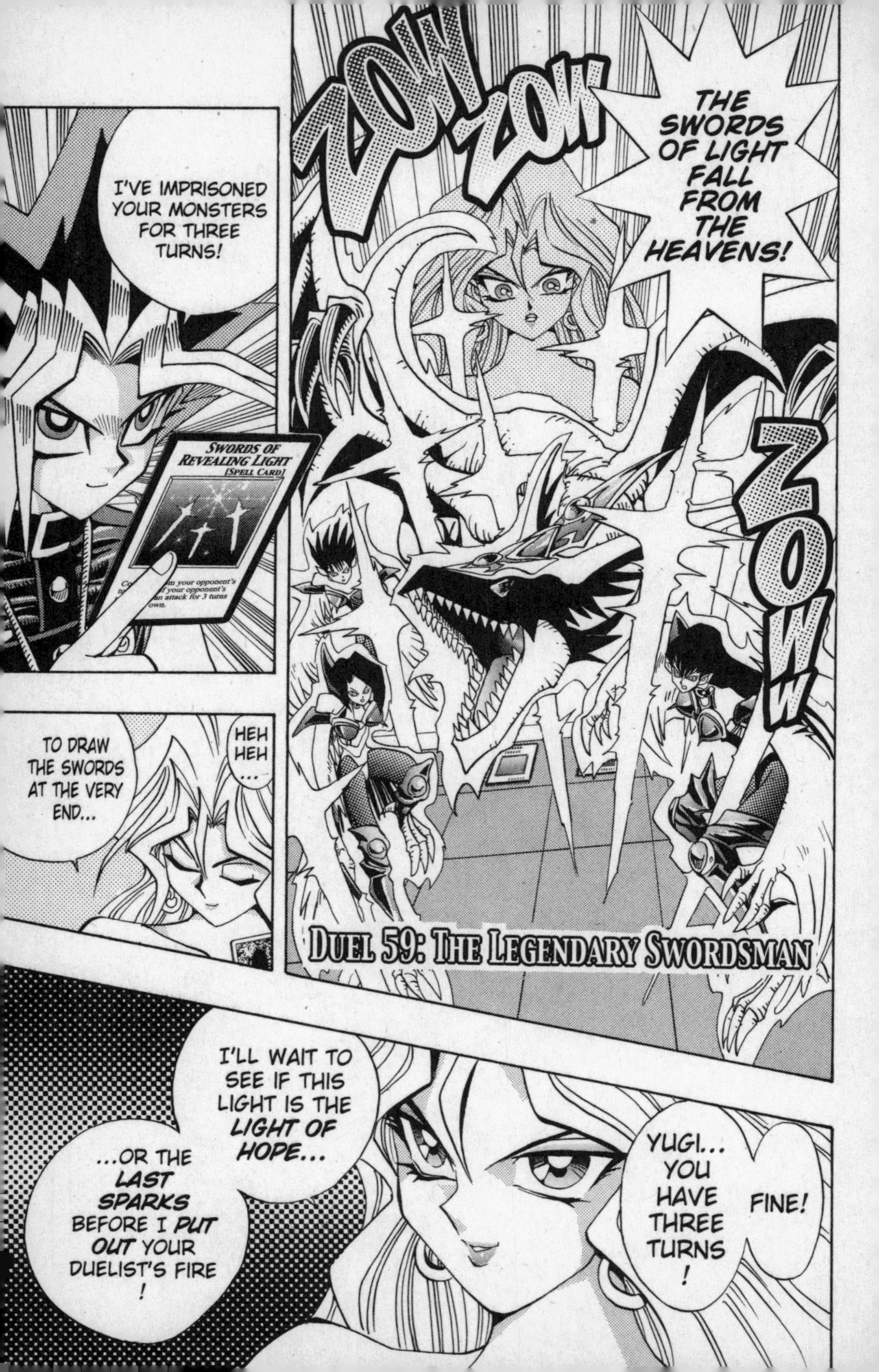
ZOW ZOW
THE SWORDS OF LIGHT FALL FROM THE HEAVENS!
ZOWW
DUEL 59: THE LEGENDARY SWORDSMAN
I'VE IMPRISONED YOUR MONSTERS FOR THREE TURNS!
SWORDS OF REVEALING LIGHT
[SPELL CARD]
HEH HEH ...
TO DRAW THE SWORDS AT THE VERY END...
FINE!
YUGI... YOU HAVE THREE TURNS!
I'LL WAIT TO SEE IF THIS LIGHT IS THE LIGHT OF HOPE...
...OR THE LAST SPARKS BEFORE I PUT OUT YOUR DUELIST'S FIRE!

Duel 59: The Legendary Swordsman

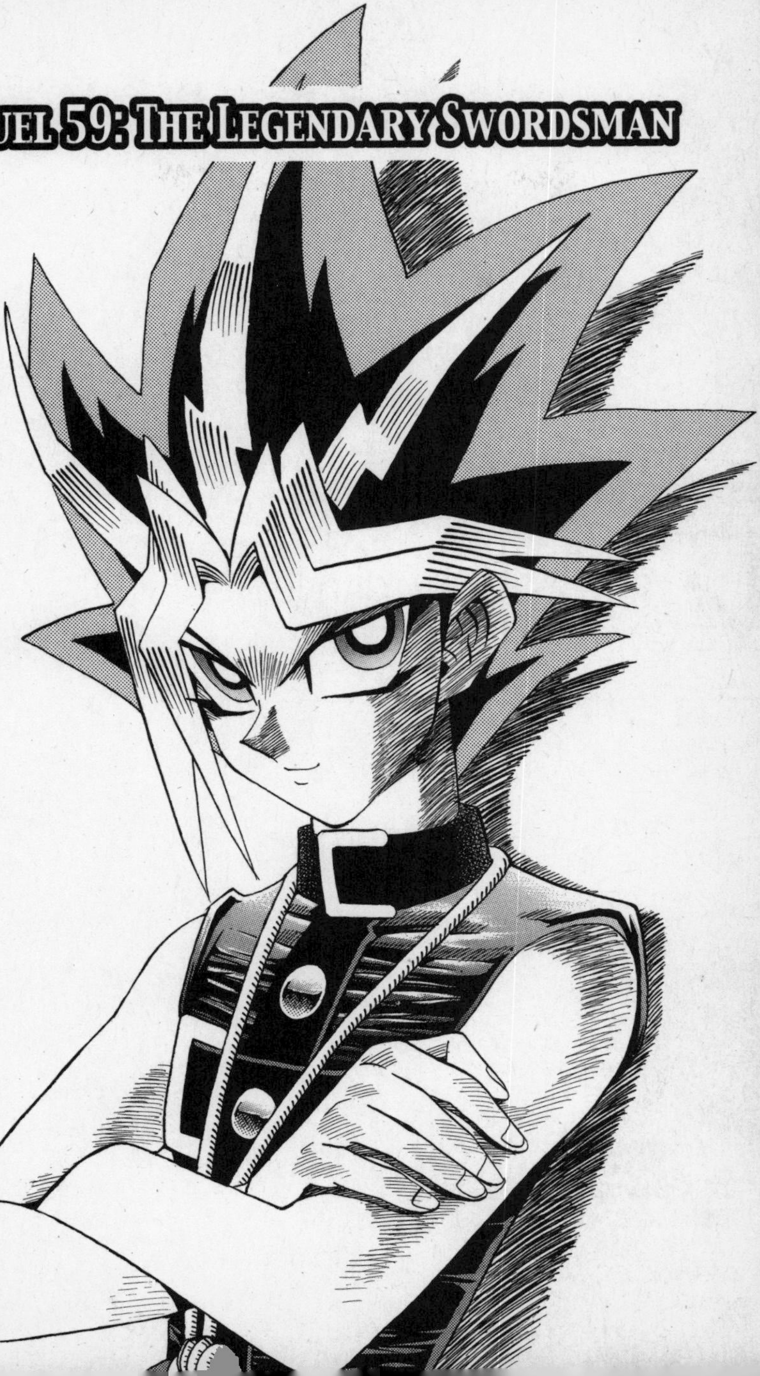

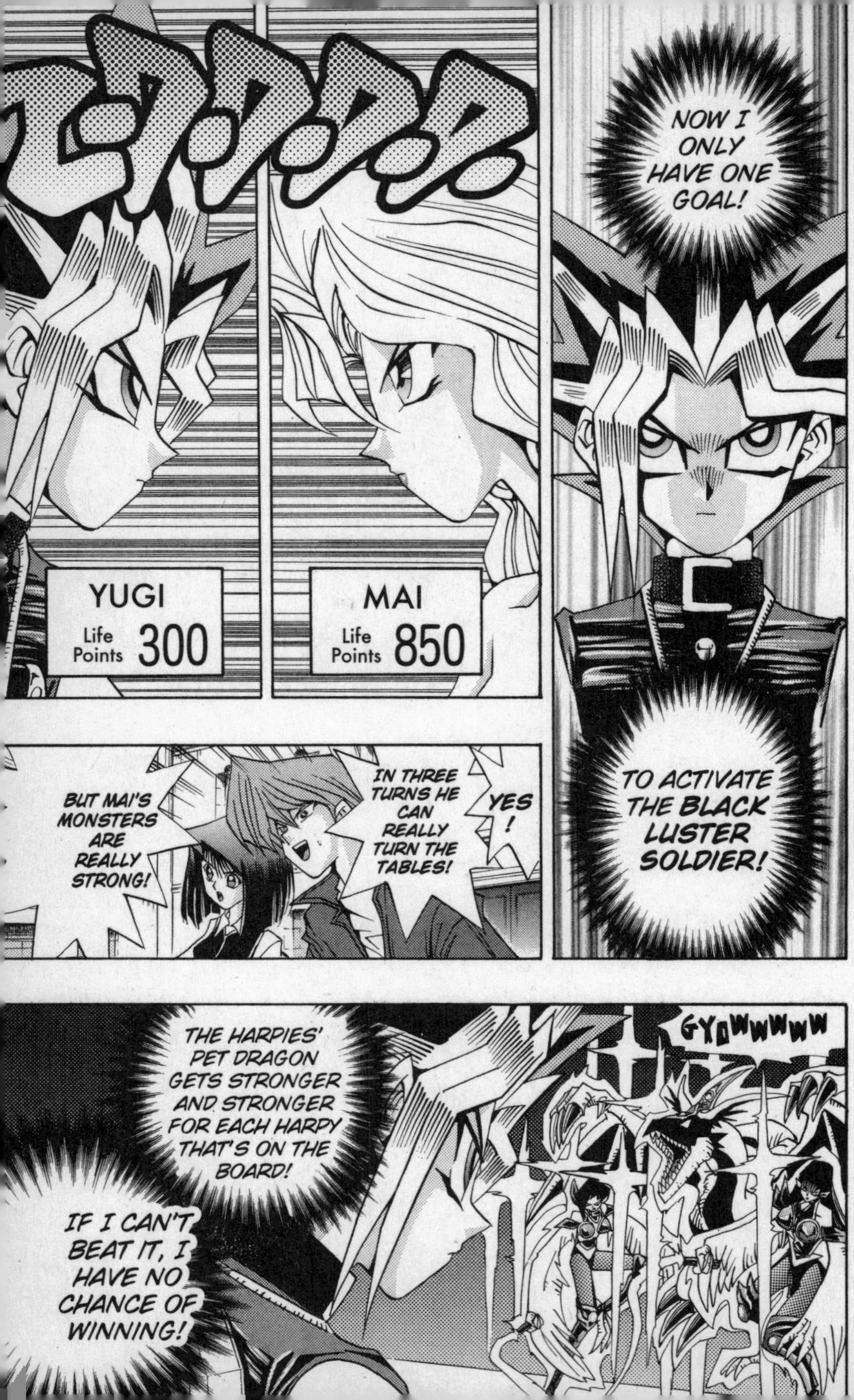
NOW I ONLY HAVE ONE GOAL!
TO ACTIVATE THE BLACK LUSTER SOLDIER!
MAI
Life Points 850
YUGI
Life Points 300
YES!
IN THREE TURNS HE CAN REALLY TURN THE TABLES!
BUT MAI'S MONSTERS ARE REALLY STRONG!
GYOWWWWW
THE HARPIES' PET DRAGON GETS STRONGER AND STRONGER FOR EACH HARPY THAT'S ON THE BOARD!
IF I CAN'T BEAT IT, I HAVE NO CHANCE OF WINNING!

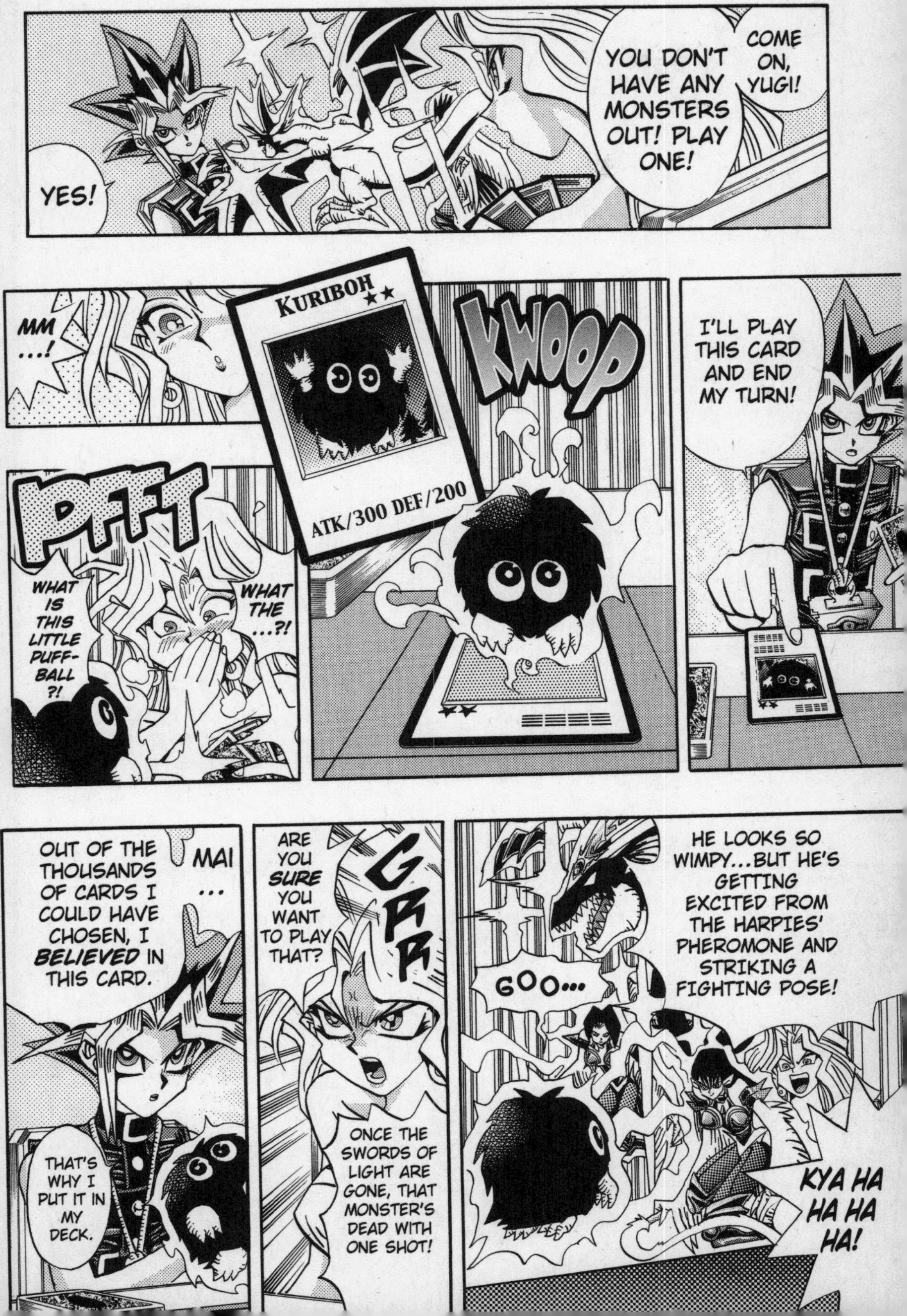
COME ON, YUGI!
YOU DON'T HAVE ANY MONSTERS OUT! PLAY ONE!
YES!
I'LL PLAY THIS CARD AND END MY TURN!
KWOOP
KURIBOH ★★
ATK/300 DEF/200
MM ...!
PFFT
WHAT THE ...?!
WHAT IS THIS LITTLE PUFF-BALL ?!
HE LOOKS SO WIMPY...BUT HE'S GETTING EXCITED FROM THE HARPIES' PHEROMONE AND STRIKING A FIGHTING POSE!
GOO...
KYA HA HA HA HA!
GRR
ARE YOU SURE YOU WANT TO PLAY THAT?
ONCE THE SWORDS OF LIGHT ARE GONE, THAT MONSTER'S DEAD WITH ONE SHOT!
MAI ...
OUT OF THE THOUSANDS OF CARDS I COULD HAVE CHOSEN, I BELIEVED IN THIS CARD.
THAT'S WHY I PUT IT IN MY DECK.

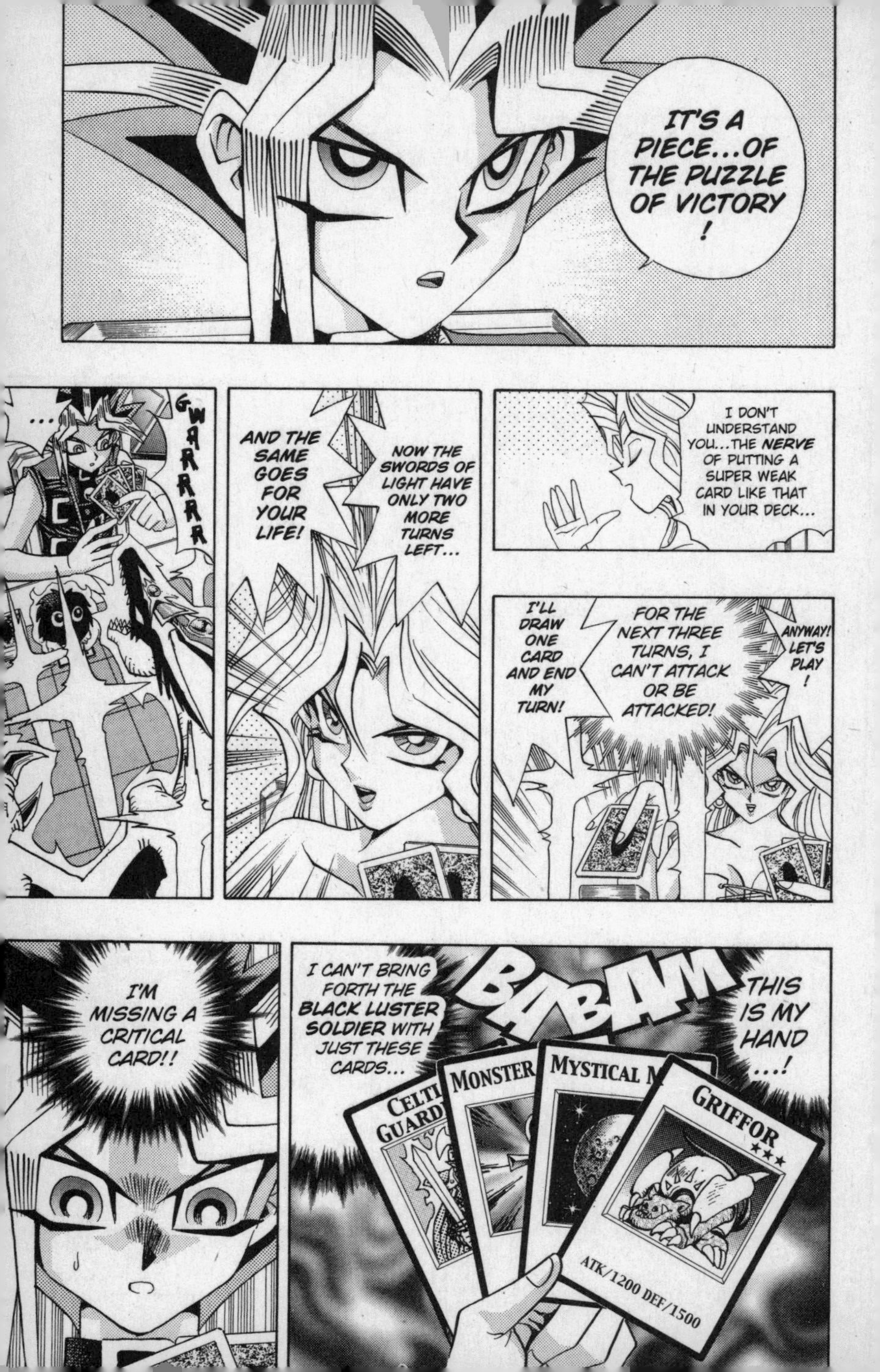
IT'S A PIECE...OF THE PUZZLE OF VICTORY !
I DON'T UNDERSTAND YOU...THE NERVE OF PUTTING A SUPER WEAK CARD LIKE THAT IN YOUR DECK...
ANYWAY! LET'S PLAY !
FOR THE NEXT THREE TURNS, I CAN'T ATTACK OR BE ATTACKED!
I'LL DRAW ONE CARD AND END MY TURN!
NOW THE SWORDS OF LIGHT HAVE ONLY TWO MORE TURNS LEFT...
AND THE SAME GOES FOR YOUR LIFE!
GWARRRRR
...
THIS IS MY HAND ...!
BABAM
I CAN'T BRING FORTH THE BLACK LUSTER SOLDIER WITH JUST THESE CARDS...
CELTI GUARD
MONSTER
MYSTICAL M
GRIFFOR
ATK/1200 DEF/1500
I'M MISSING A CRITICAL CARD!!

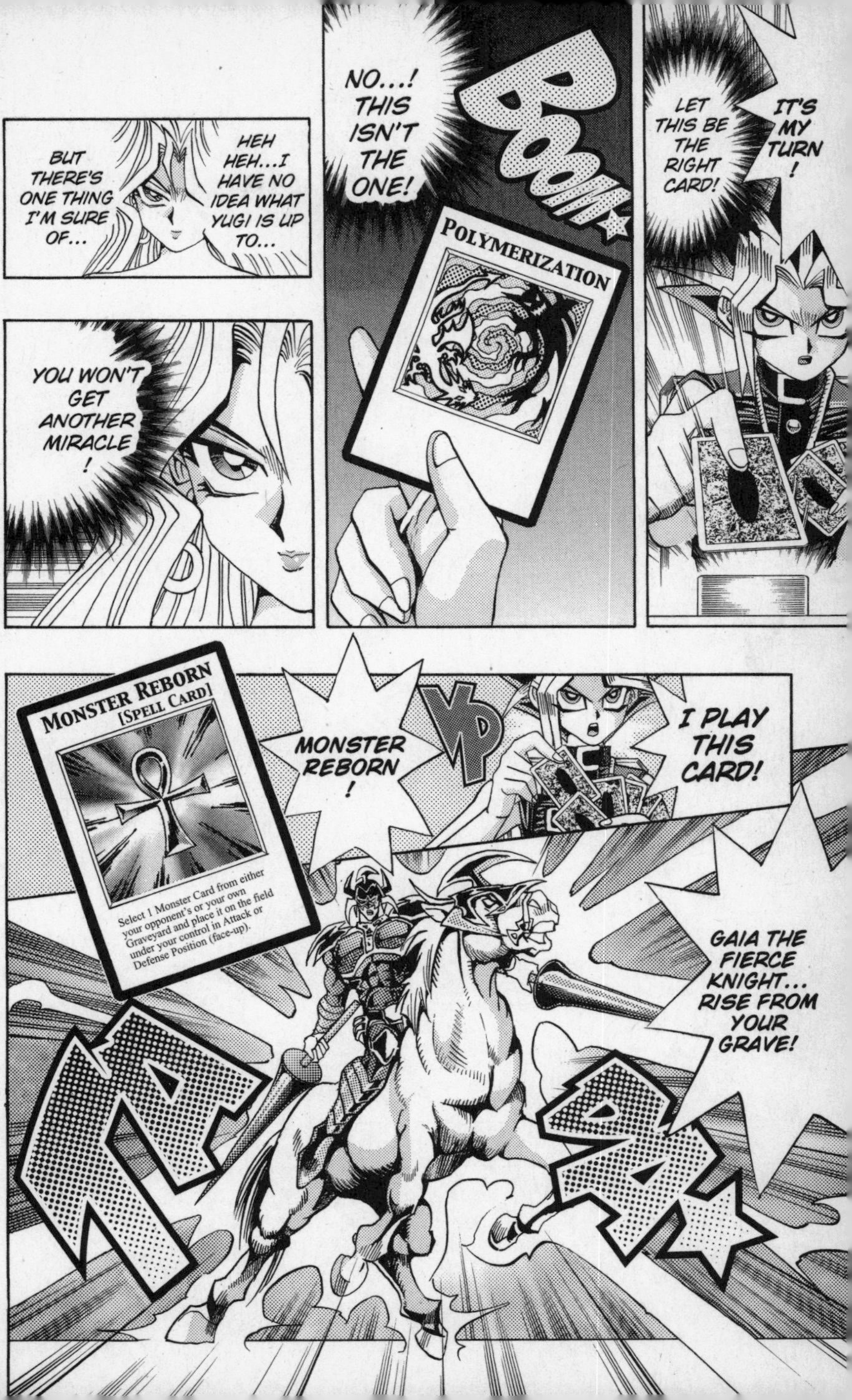
IT'S MY TURN!
LET THIS BE THE RIGHT CARD!
BOOM
NO...! THIS ISN'T THE ONE!
POLYMERIZATION
HEH HEH...I HAVE NO IDEA WHAT YUGI IS UP TO...
BUT THERE'S ONE THING I'M SURE OF...
YOU WON'T GET ANOTHER MIRACLE!
I PLAY THIS CARD!
MONSTER REBORN!
MONSTER REBORN
[SPELL CARD]
Select 1 Monster Card from either your opponent's or your own Graveyard and place it on the field under your control in Attack or Defense Position (face-up).
GAIA THE FIERCE KNIGHT... RISE FROM YOUR GRAVE!

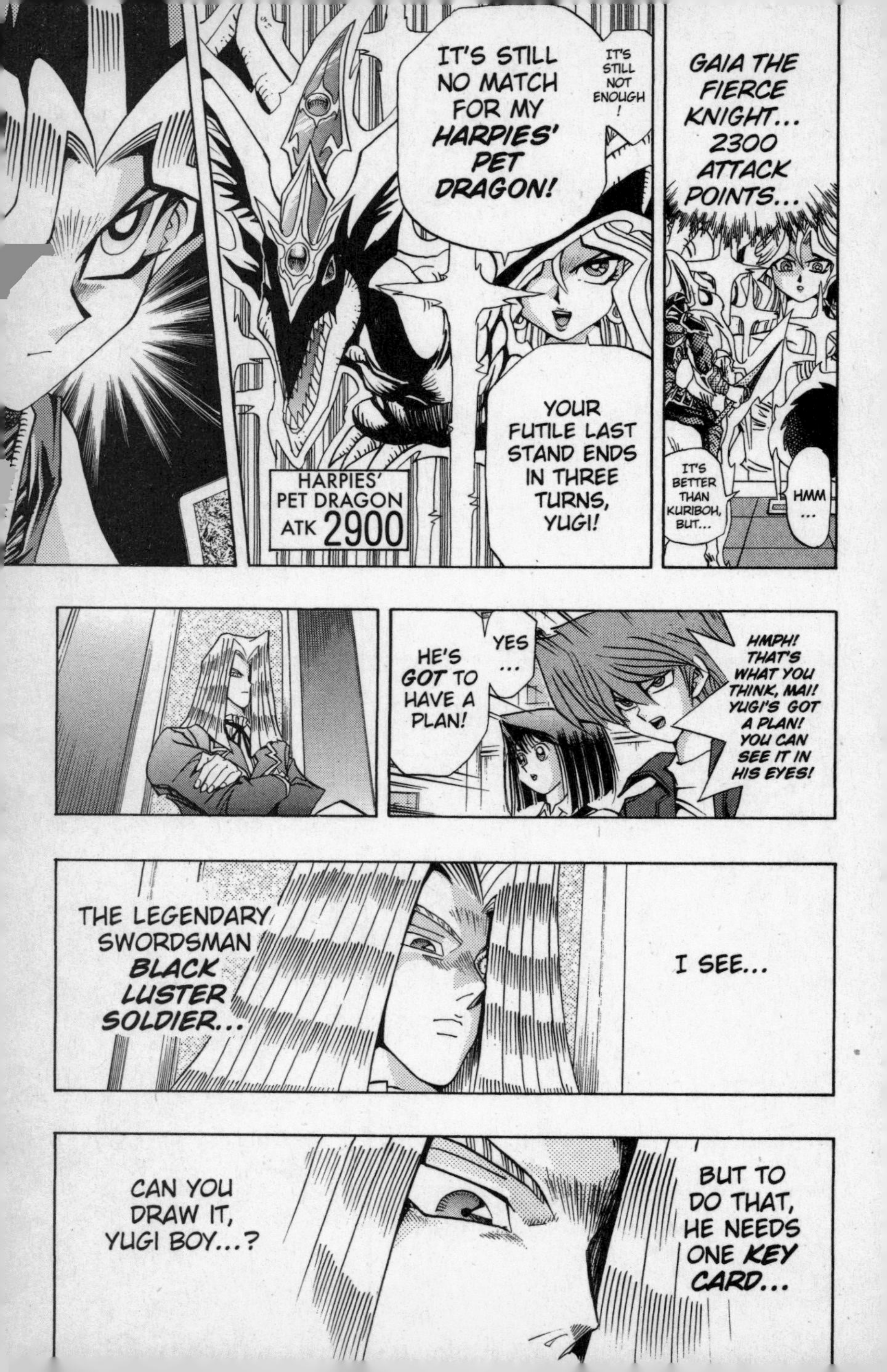
GAIA THE FIERCE KNIGHT... 2300 ATTACK POINTS...
HMM...
IT'S BETTER THAN KURIBOH, BUT...
IT'S STILL NOT ENOUGH!
IT'S STILL NO MATCH FOR MY HARPIES' PET DRAGON!
YOUR FUTILE LAST STAND ENDS IN THREE TURNS, YUGI!
HARPIES' PET DRAGON ATK 2900
HMPH! THAT'S WHAT YOU THINK, MAI! YUGI'S GOT A PLAN! YOU CAN SEE IT IN HIS EYES!
YES...
HE'S GOT TO HAVE A PLAN!
I SEE...
THE LEGENDARY SWORDSMAN BLACK LUSTER SOLDIER...
BUT TO DO THAT, HE NEEDS ONE KEY CARD...
CAN YOU DRAW IT, YUGI BOY...?

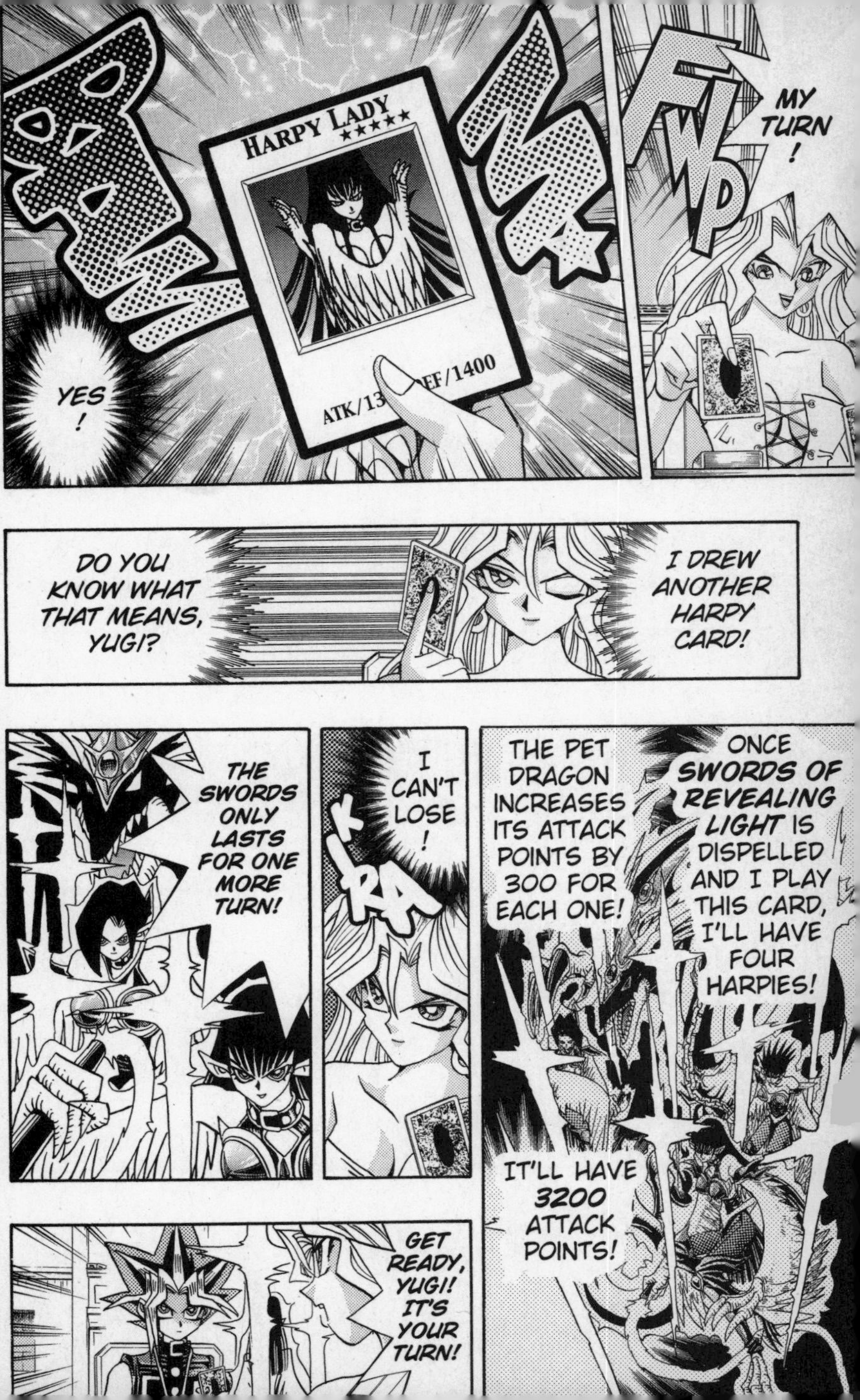
FWP
MY TURN!
HARPY LADY
YES!
I DREW ANOTHER HARPY CARD!
DO YOU KNOW WHAT THAT MEANS, YUGI?
ONCE SWORDS OF REVEALING LIGHT IS DISPELLED AND I PLAY THIS CARD, I'LL HAVE FOUR HARPIES!
THE PET DRAGON INCREASES ITS ATTACK POINTS BY 300 FOR EACH ONE!
IT'LL HAVE 3200 ATTACK POINTS!
I CAN'T LOSE!
THE SWORDS ONLY LASTS FOR ONE MORE TURN!
GET READY, YUGI! IT'S YOUR TURN!

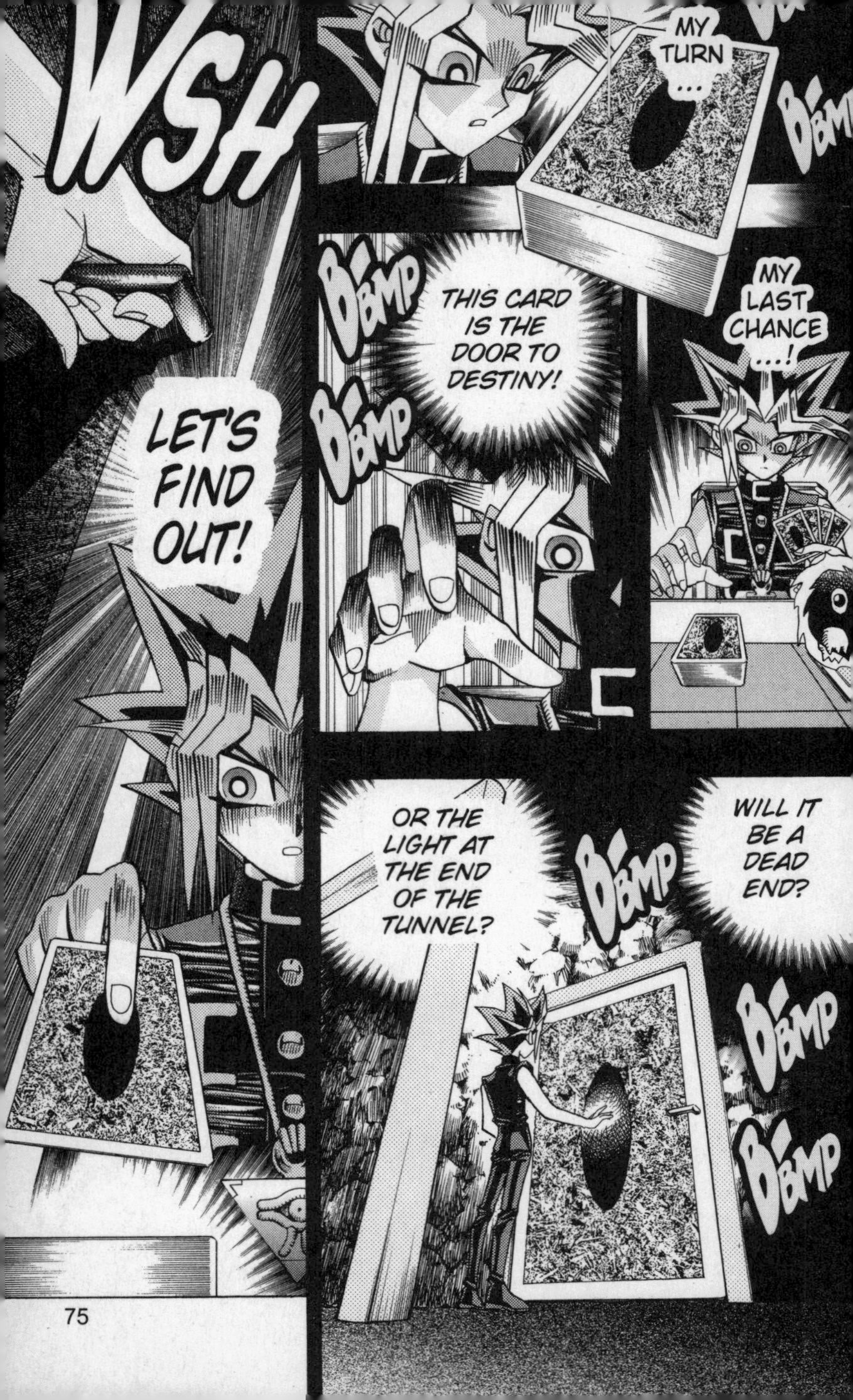
MY TURN ...
BBMP
MY LAST CHANCE ...!
BBMP
THIS CARD IS THE DOOR TO DESTINY!
BBMP
WILL IT BE A DEAD END?
BBMP
OR THE LIGHT AT THE END OF THE TUNNEL?
BBMP
BBMP
BBMP
WSH
LET'S FIND OUT!

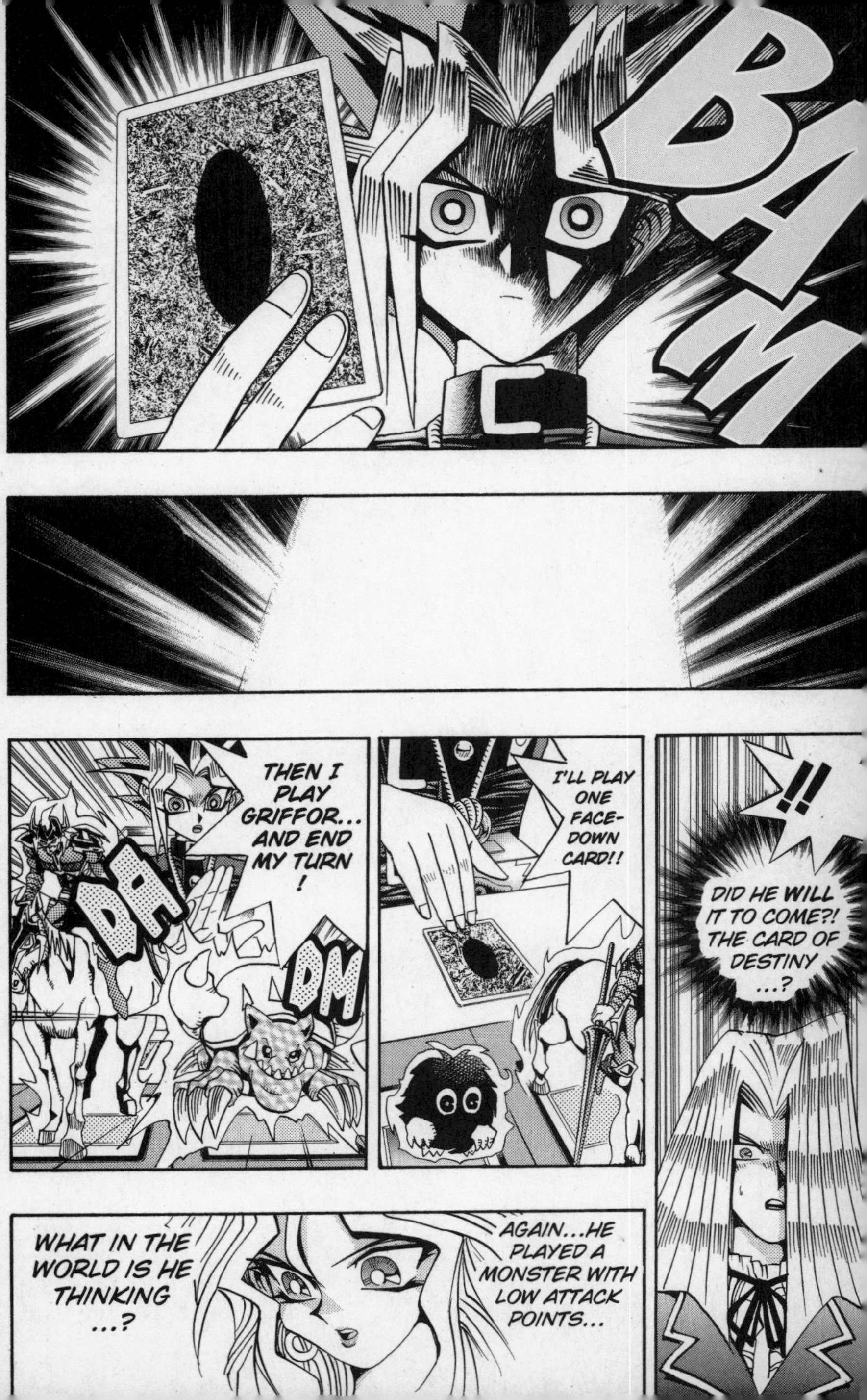
BAM
!!
DID HE WILL IT TO COME?! THE CARD OF DESTINY ...?
I'LL PLAY ONE FACE-DOWN CARD!!
THEN I PLAY GRIFFOR... AND END MY TURN!
DA
DM
AGAIN...HE PLAYED A MONSTER WITH LOW ATTACK POINTS...
WHAT IN THE WORLD IS HE THINKING ...?

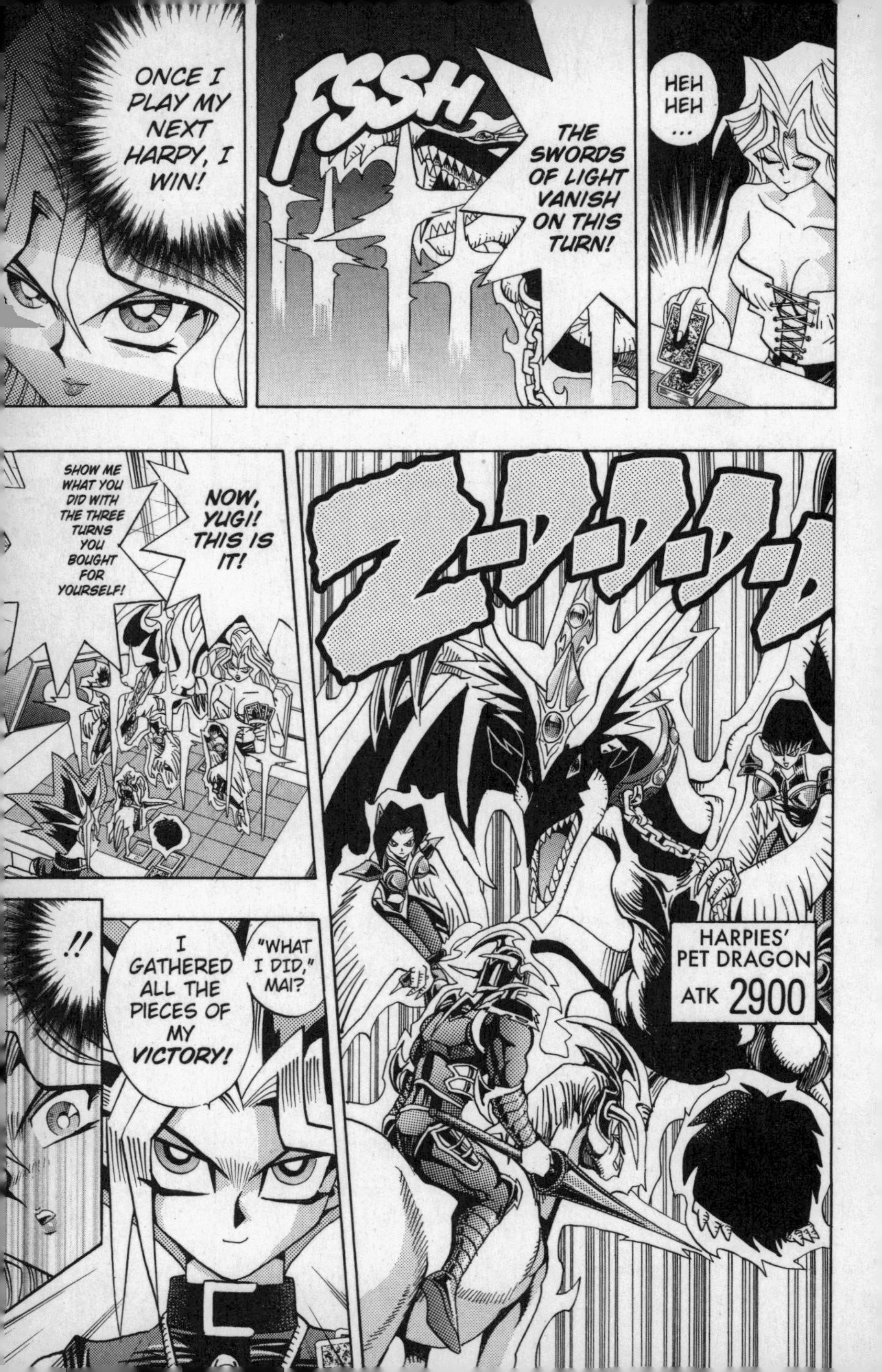
HEH HEH ...
FSSH
THE SWORDS OF LIGHT VANISH ON THIS TURN!
ONCE I PLAY MY NEXT HARPY, I WIN!
Z-D-D-D-D
HARPIES' PET DRAGON ATK 2900
NOW, YUGI! THIS IS IT!
SHOW ME WHAT YOU DID WITH THE THREE TURNS YOU BOUGHT FOR YOURSELF!
"WHAT I DID," MAI?
I GATHERED ALL THE PIECES OF MY VICTORY!
!!

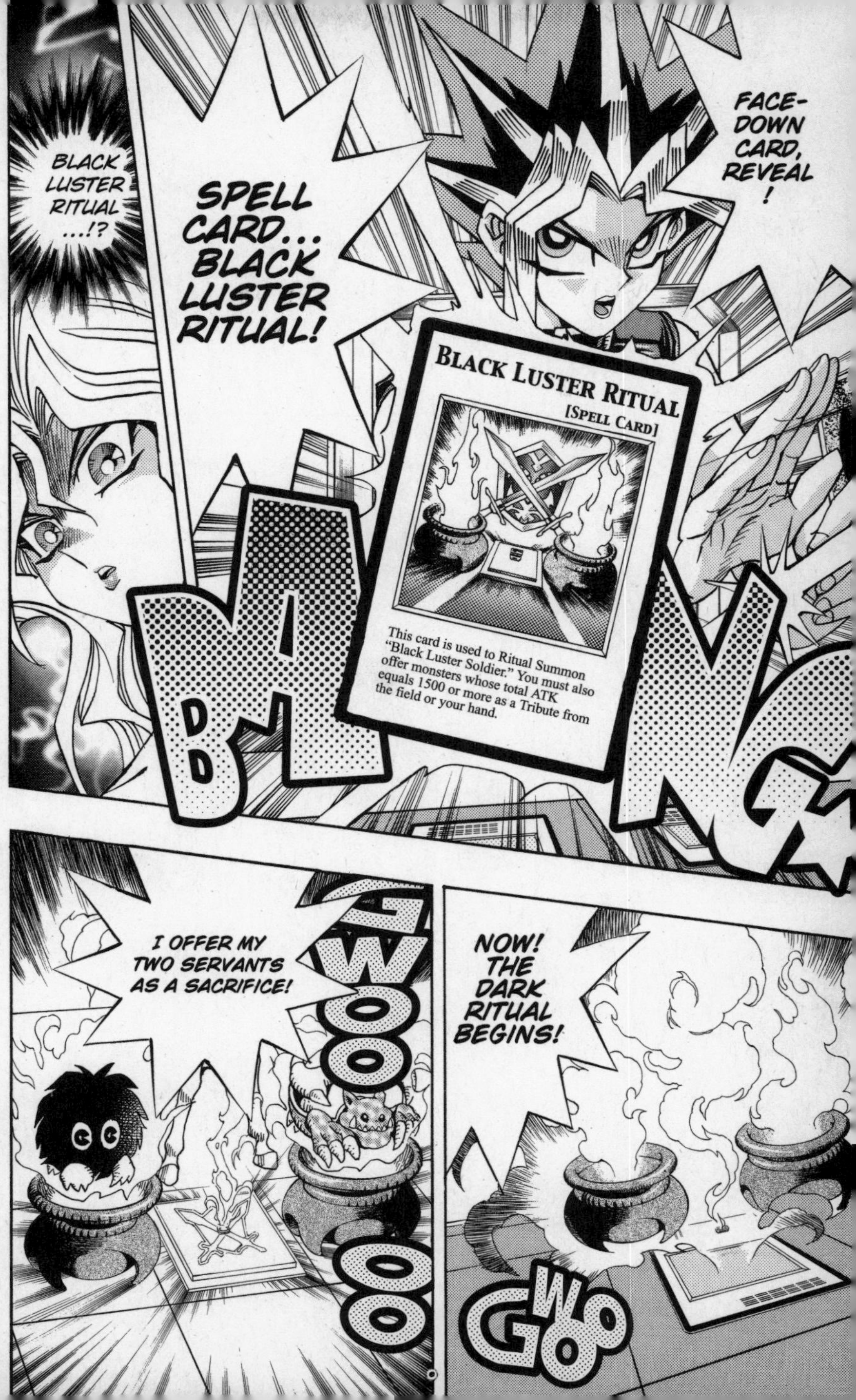
FACE-DOWN CARD, REVEAL!
SPELL CARD... BLACK LUSTER RITUAL!
BLACK LUSTER RITUAL ...!?
BLACK LUSTER RITUAL
[SPELL CARD]
This card is used to Ritual Summon "Black Luster Soldier." You must also offer monsters whose total ATK equals 1500 or more as a Tribute from the field or your hand.
NOW! THE DARK RITUAL BEGINS!
I OFFER MY TWO SERVANTS AS A SACRIFICE!

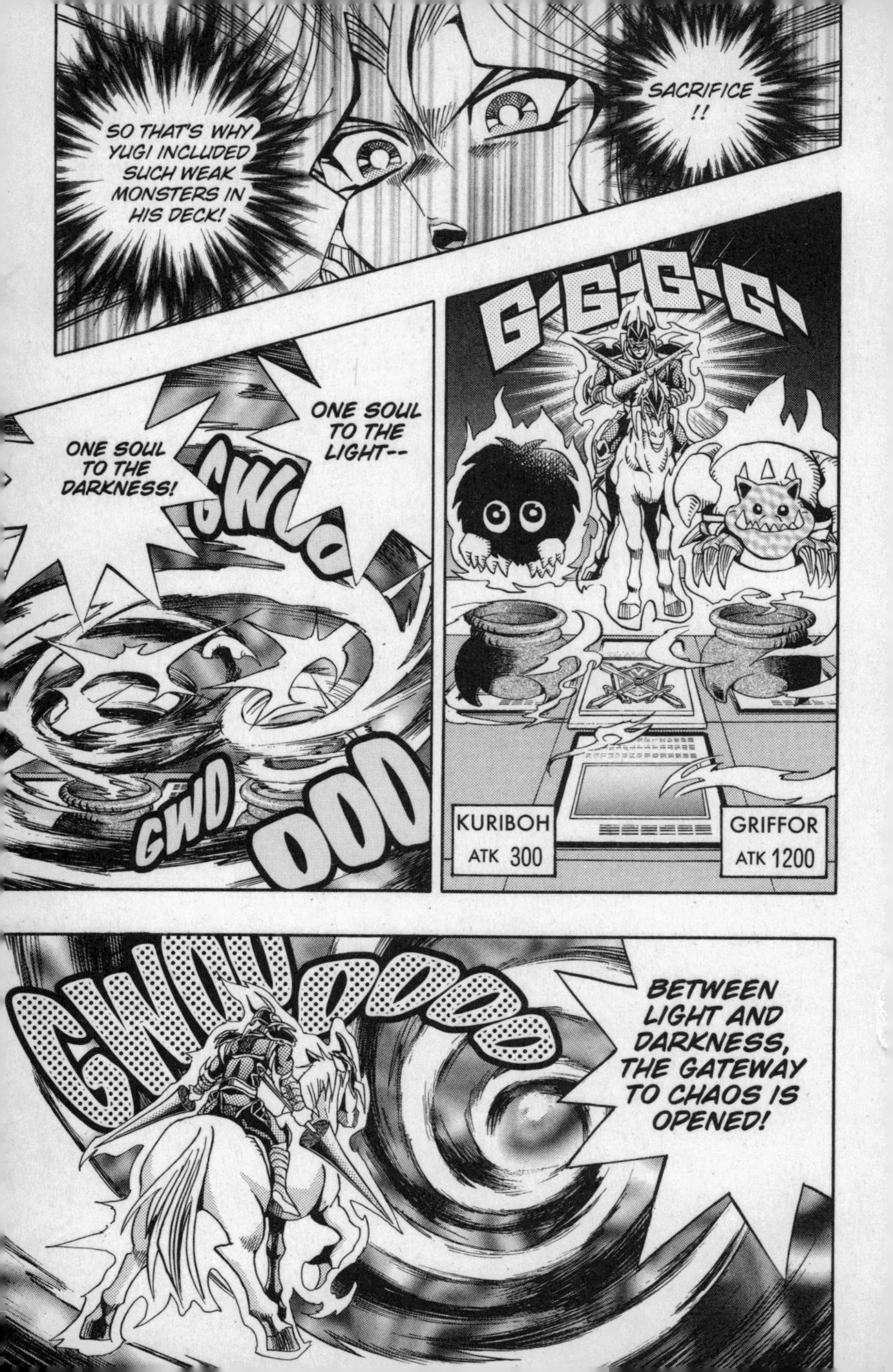
SACRIFICE !!
SO THAT'S WHY YUGI INCLUDED SUCH WEAK MONSTERS IN HIS DECK!
G-G-G-G
KURIBOH ATK 300
GRIFFOR ATK 1200
ONE SOUL TO THE LIGHT--
ONE SOUL TO THE DARKNESS!
GWO DOOO
BETWEEN LIGHT AND DARKNESS, THE GATEWAY TO CHAOS IS OPENED!

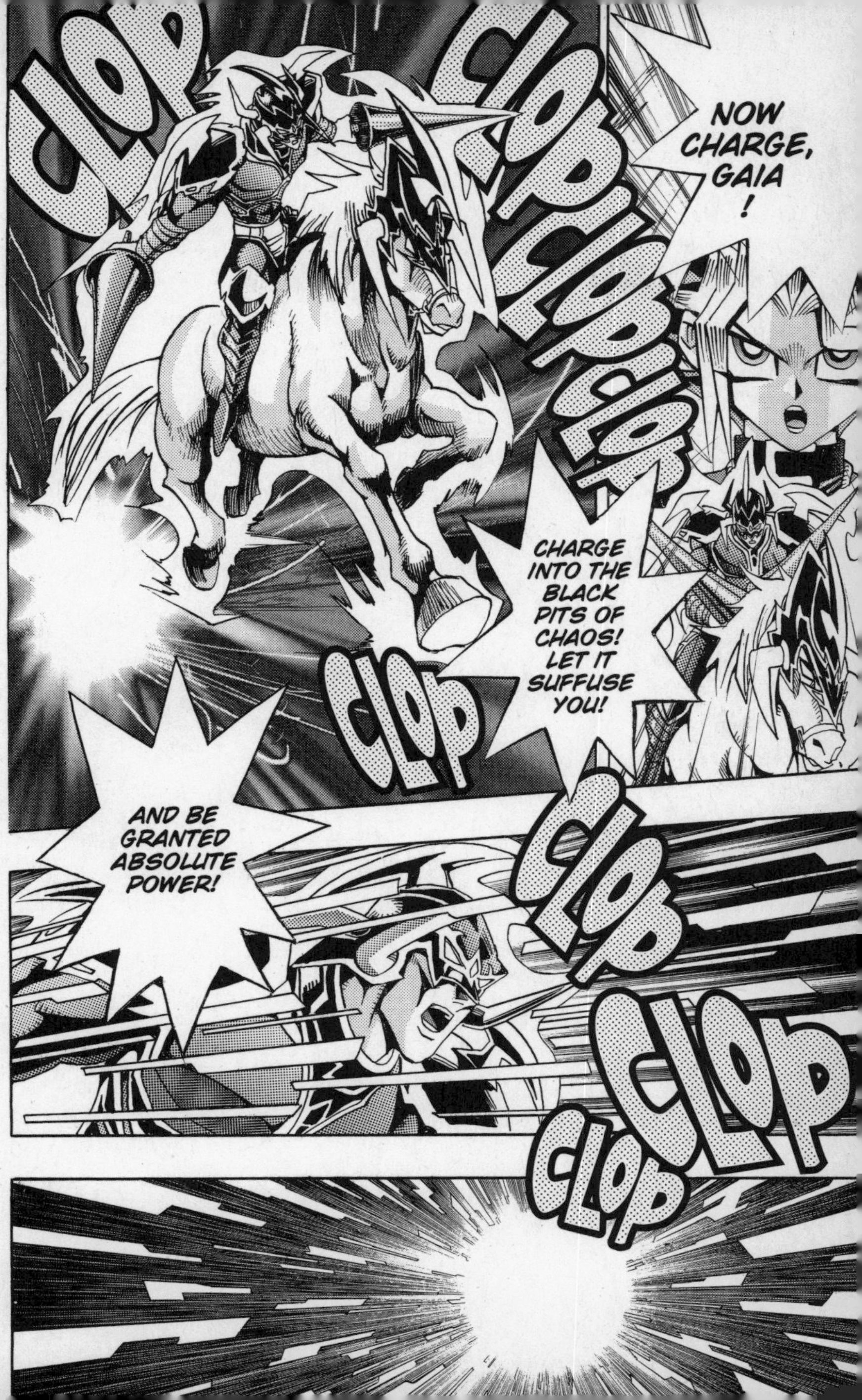
NOW CHARGE, GAIA!
CLOP CLOP CLOP CLOP
CLOP
CHARGE INTO THE BLACK PITS OF CHAOS! LET IT SUFFUSE YOU!
CLOP
AND BE GRANTED ABSOLUTE POWER!
CLOP CLOP
CLOP
CLOP CLOP

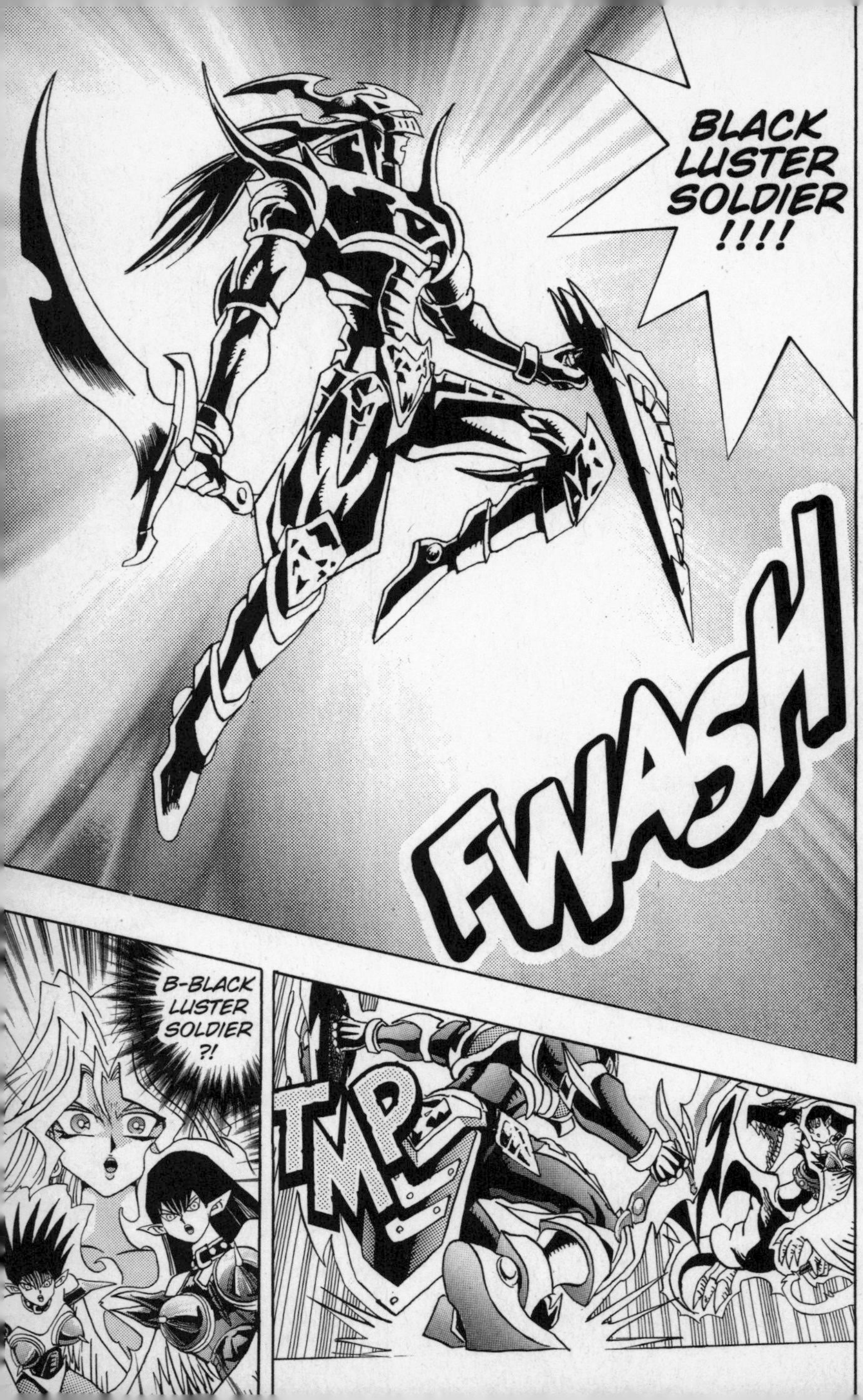
BLACK LUSTER SOLDIER !!!!
FWASH
TMP
B-BLACK LUSTER SOLDIER ?!

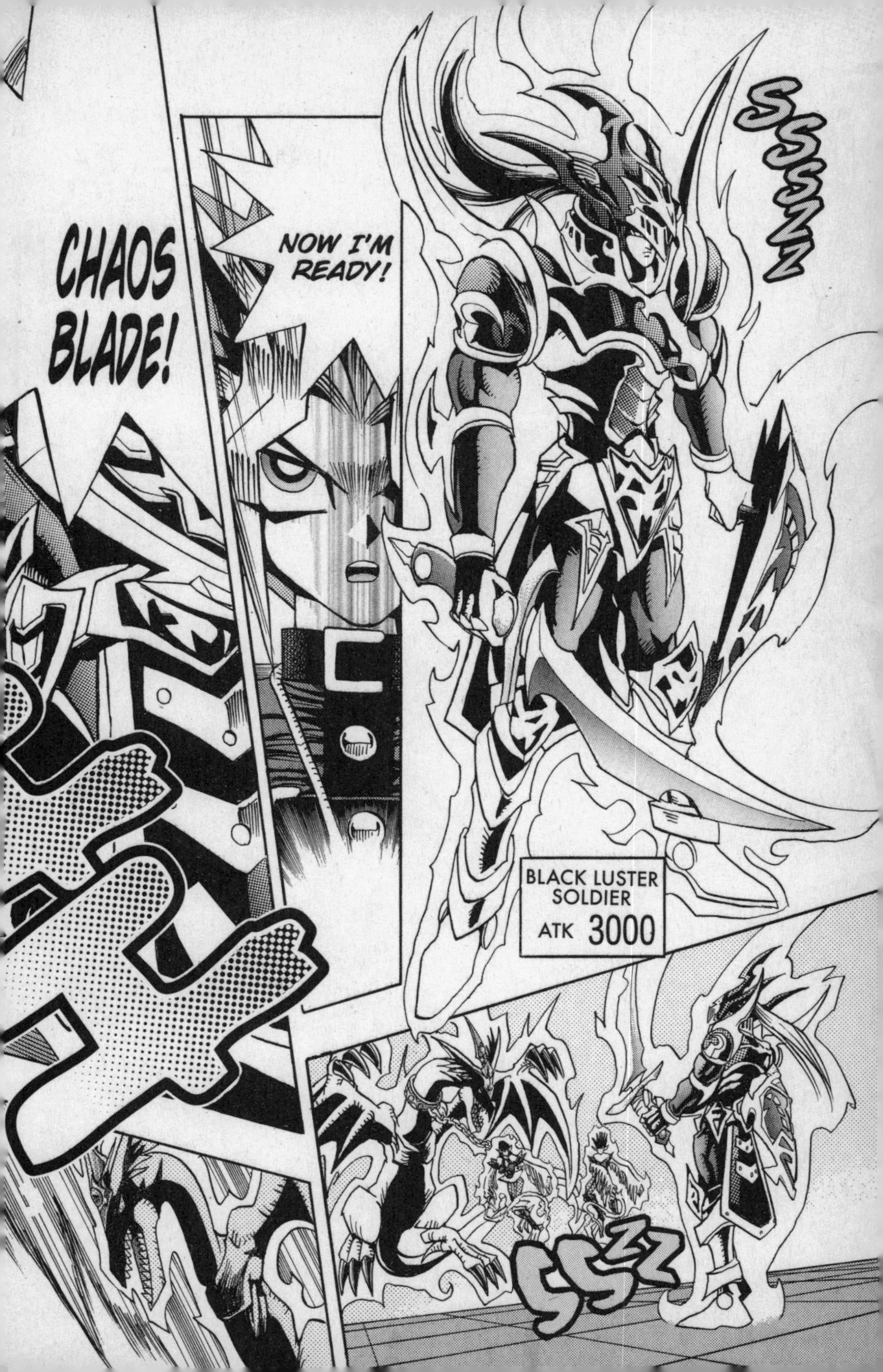
SSSWN
BLACK LUSTER SOLDIER ATK 3000
NOW I'M READY!
CHAOS BLADE!
SSZZ

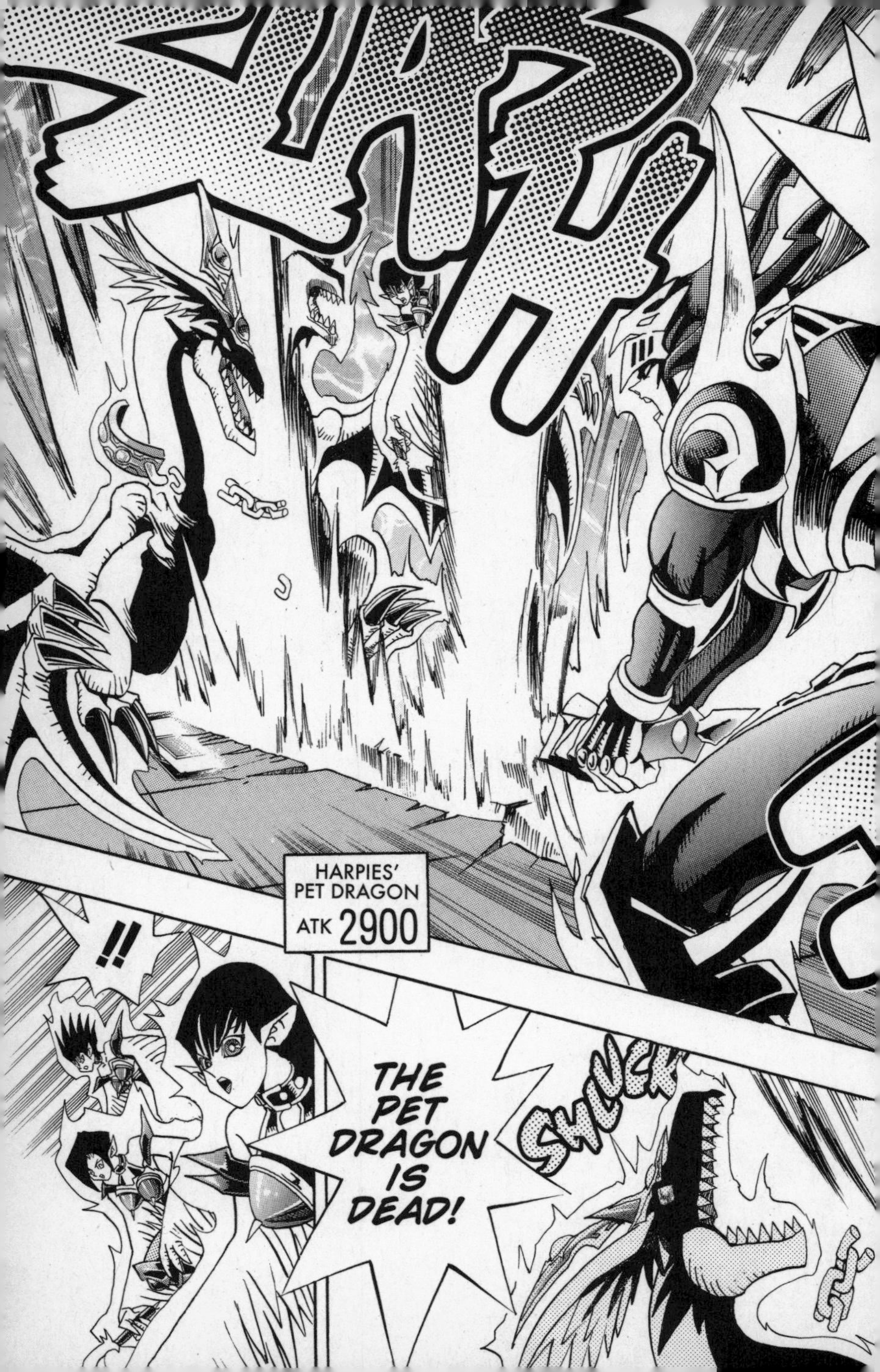
HARPIES' PET DRAGON
ATK 2900
SHUCK
!!
THE PET DRAGON IS DEAD!

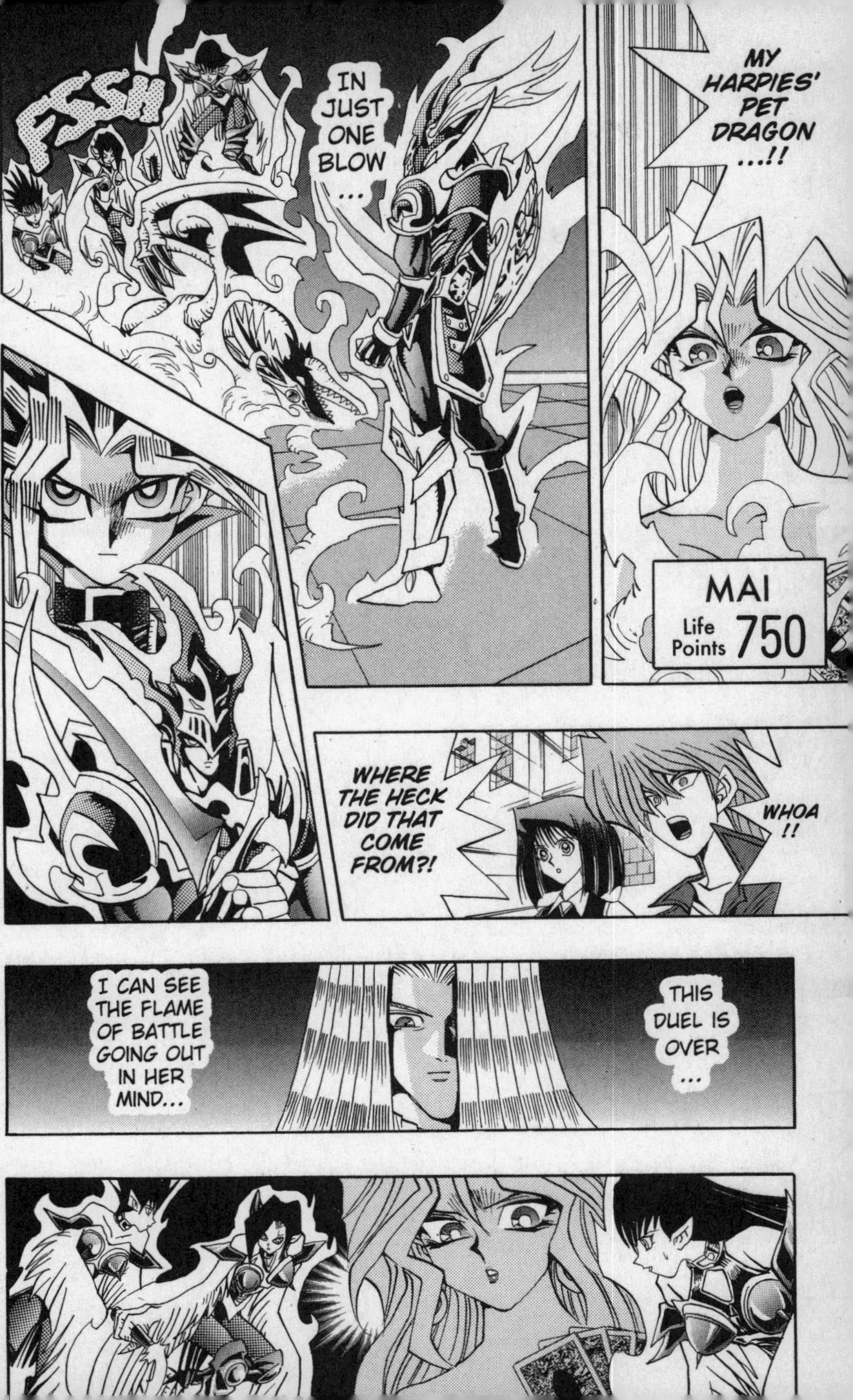

MY HARPIES' PET DRAGON ...!!
MAI
Life Points 750
IN JUST ONE BLOW ...
FSSH
WHOA !!
WHERE THE HECK DID THAT COME FROM?!
THIS DUEL IS OVER ...
I CAN SEE THE FLAME OF BATTLE GOING OUT IN HER MIND...

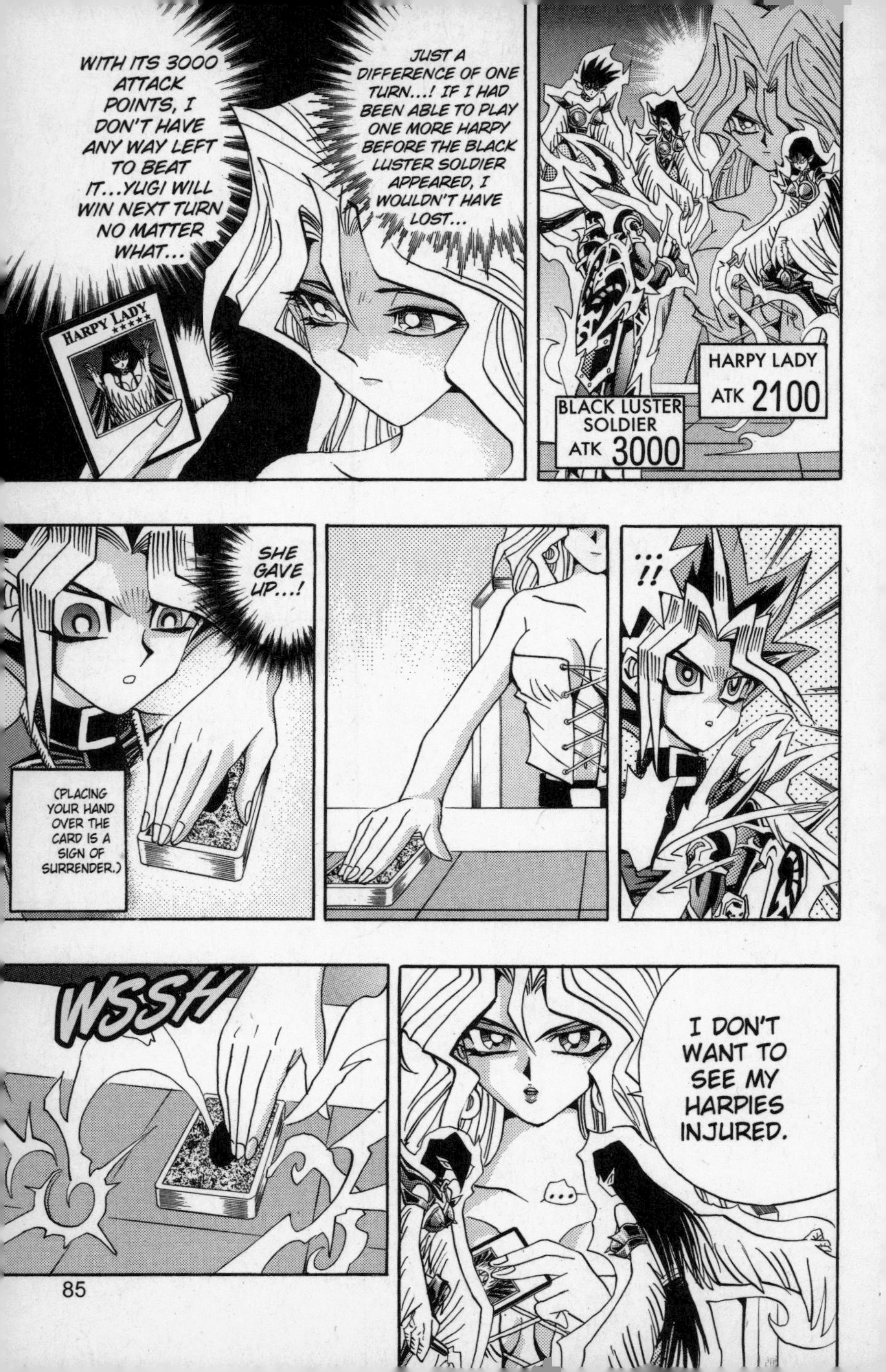
HARPY LADY
ATK 2100
BLACK LUSTER SOLDIER
ATK 3000
JUST A DIFFERENCE OF ONE TURN...! IF I HAD BEEN ABLE TO PLAY ONE MORE HARPY BEFORE THE BLACK LUSTER SOLDIER APPEARED, I WOULDN'T HAVE LOST...
WITH ITS 3000 ATTACK POINTS, I DON'T HAVE ANY WAY LEFT TO BEAT IT...YUGI WILL WIN NEXT TURN NO MATTER WHAT...
HARPY LADY
...!!
SHE GAVE UP...!
(PLACING YOUR HAND OVER THE CARD IS A SIGN OF SURRENDER.)
I DON'T WANT TO SEE MY HARPIES INJURED.
...
WSSH

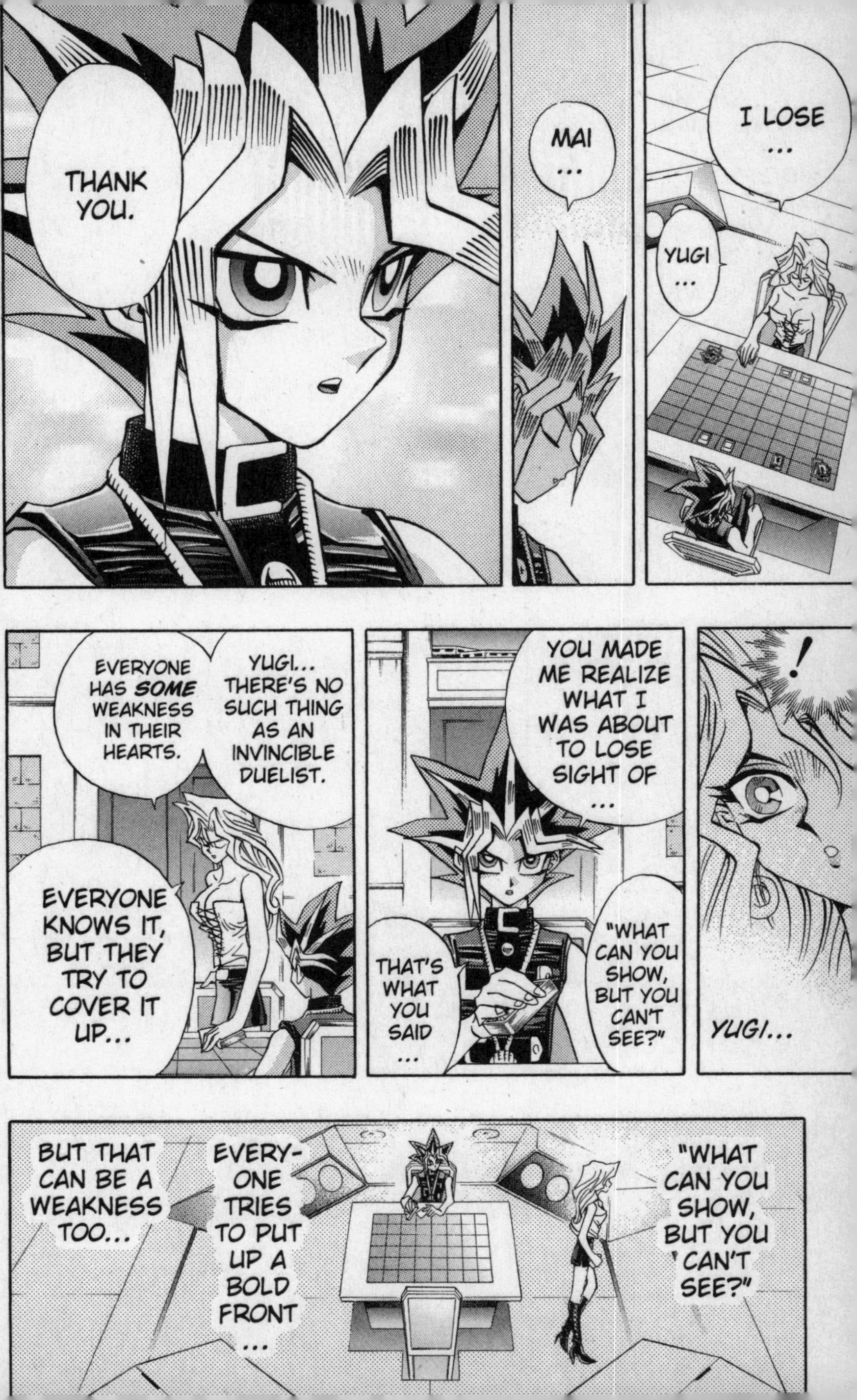
I LOSE ...
YUGI ...
MAI ...
THANK YOU.
!
YUGI...
YOU MADE ME REALIZE WHAT I WAS ABOUT TO LOSE SIGHT OF ...
"WHAT CAN YOU SHOW, BUT YOU CAN'T SEE?"
THAT'S WHAT YOU SAID ...
YUGI... THERE'S NO SUCH THING AS AN INVINCIBLE DUELIST.
EVERYONE HAS **SOME** WEAKNESS IN THEIR HEARTS.
EVERYONE KNOWS IT, BUT THEY TRY TO COVER IT UP...
"WHAT CAN YOU SHOW, BUT YOU CAN'T SEE?"
EVERY-ONE TRIES TO PUT UP A BOLD FRONT ...
BUT THAT CAN BE A WEAKNESS TOO...

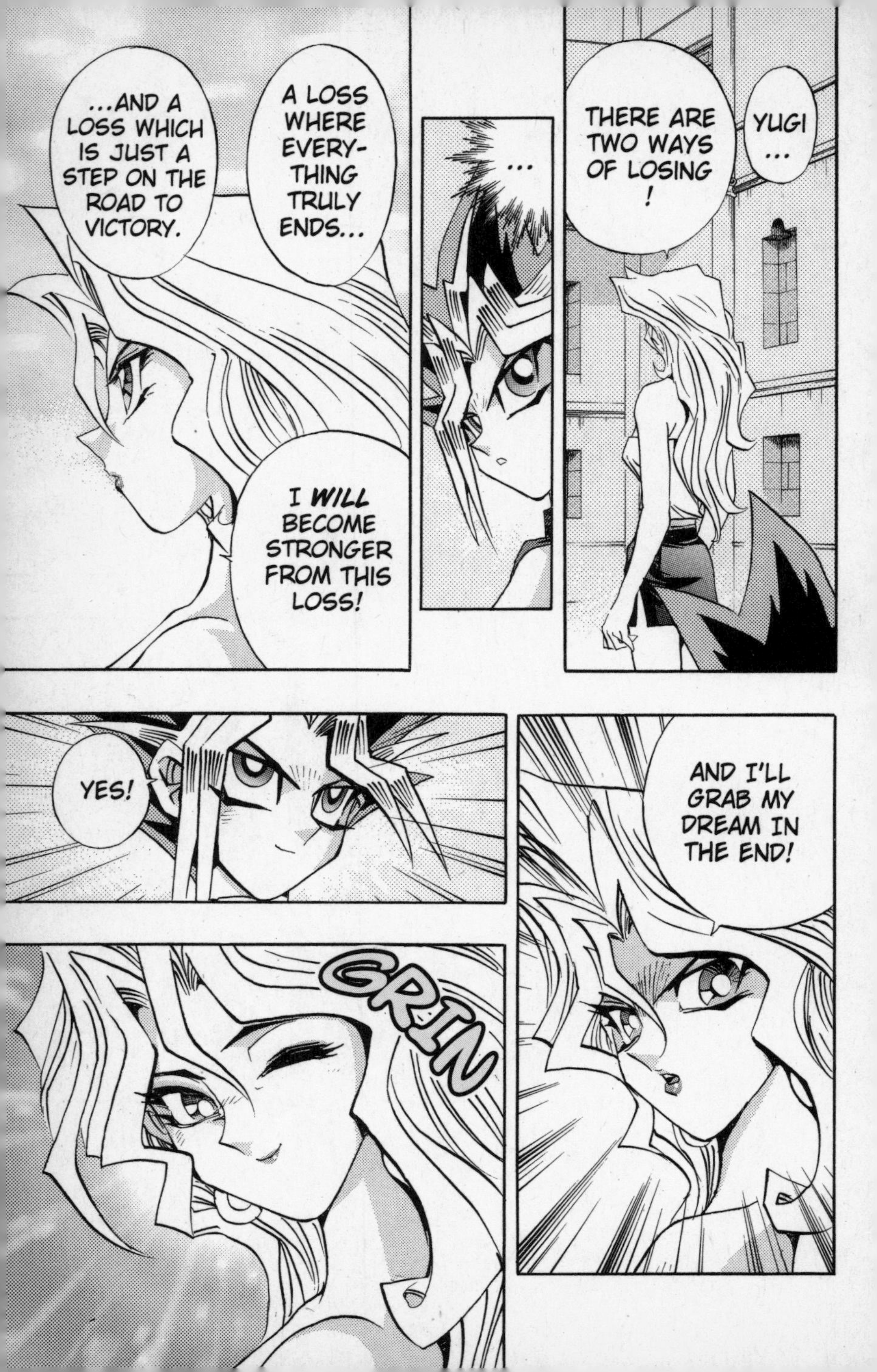
YUGI ...
THERE ARE TWO WAYS OF LOSING!
...
A LOSS WHERE EVERY-THING TRULY ENDS...
...AND A LOSS WHICH IS JUST A STEP ON THE ROAD TO VICTORY.
I *WILL* BECOME STRONGER FROM THIS LOSS!
AND I'LL GRAB MY DREAM IN THE END!
YES!
GRIN

Duel 60: Because We're Friends

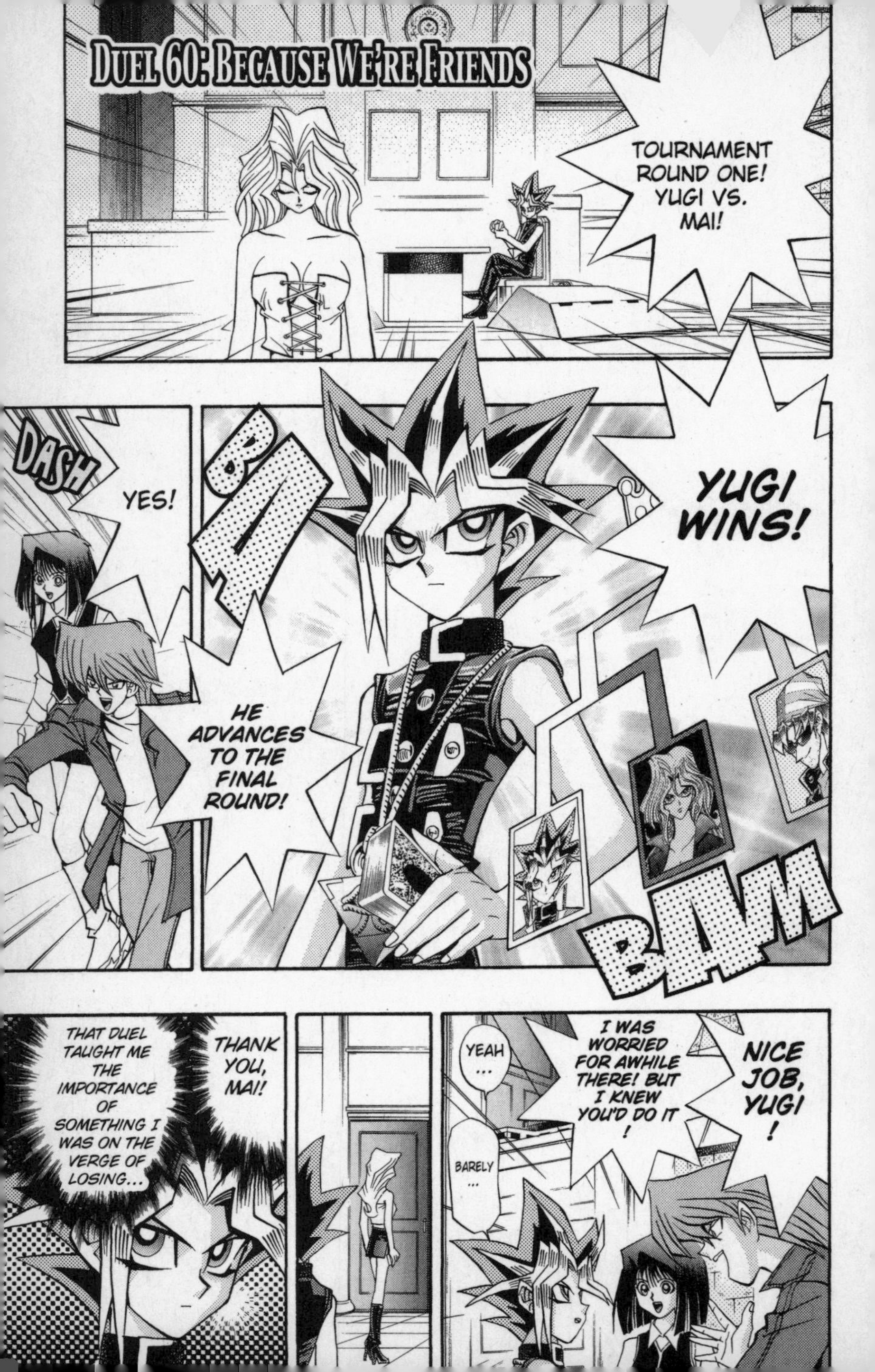
TOURNAMENT ROUND ONE! YUGI VS. MAI!
BA
YUGI WINS!
HE ADVANCES TO THE FINAL ROUND!
BAM
DASH
YES!
NICE JOB, YUGI!
I WAS WORRIED FOR AWHILE THERE! BUT I KNEW YOU'D DO IT!
YEAH...
BARELY...
THANK YOU, MAI!
THAT DUEL TAUGHT ME THE IMPORTANCE OF SOMETHING I WAS ON THE VERGE OF LOSING...

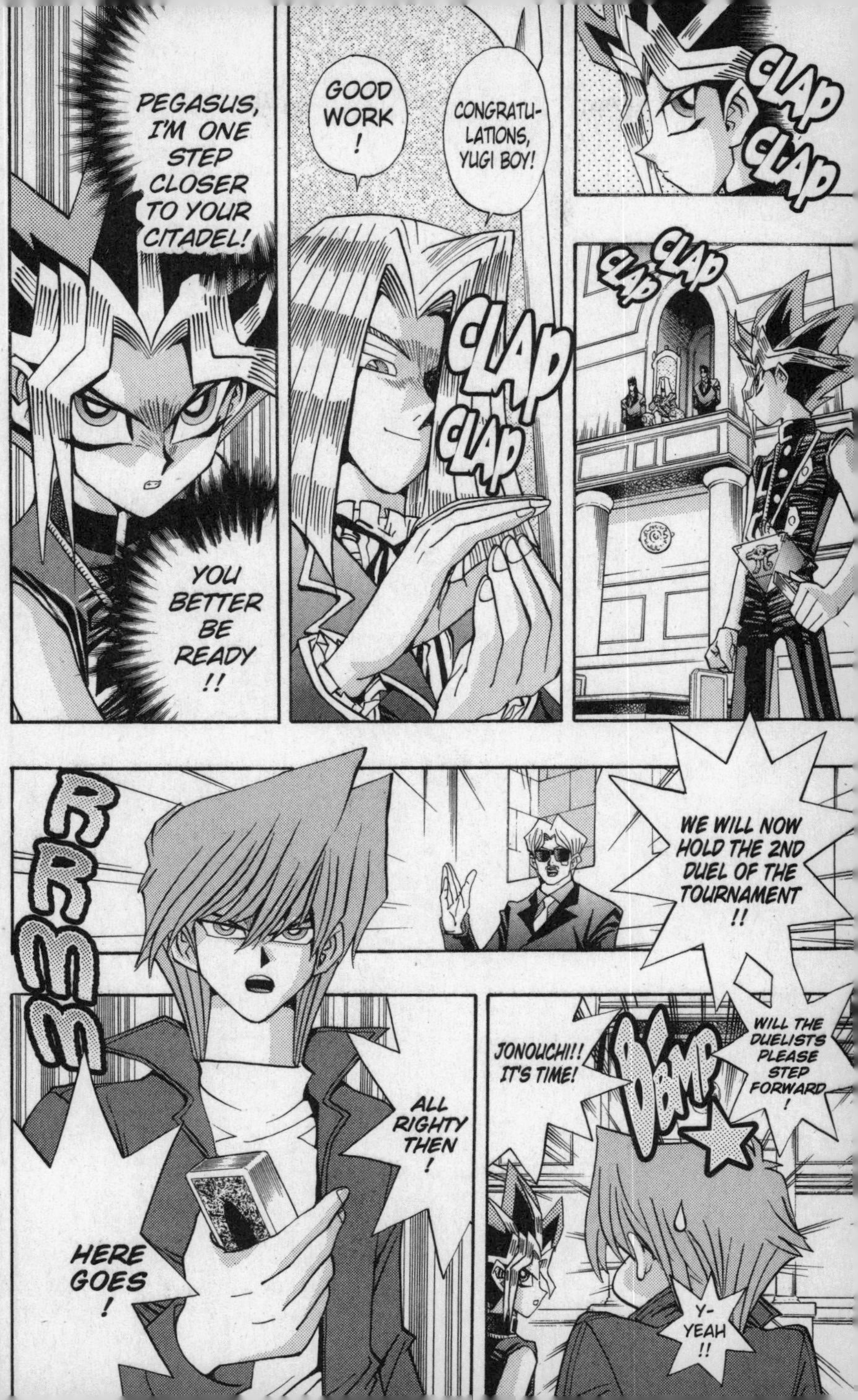
CLAP
CLAP
CLAP
CLAP
CONGRATULATIONS, YUGI BOY!
GOOD WORK!
CLAP
CLAP
PEGASUS, I'M ONE STEP CLOSER TO YOUR CITADEL!
YOU BETTER BE READY!!
WE WILL NOW HOLD THE 2ND DUEL OF THE TOURNAMENT!!
WILL THE DUELISTS PLEASE STEP FORWARD!
BAMP
JONOUCHI!! IT'S TIME!
Y-YEAH!!
RRMM
ALL RIGHTY THEN!
HERE GOES!

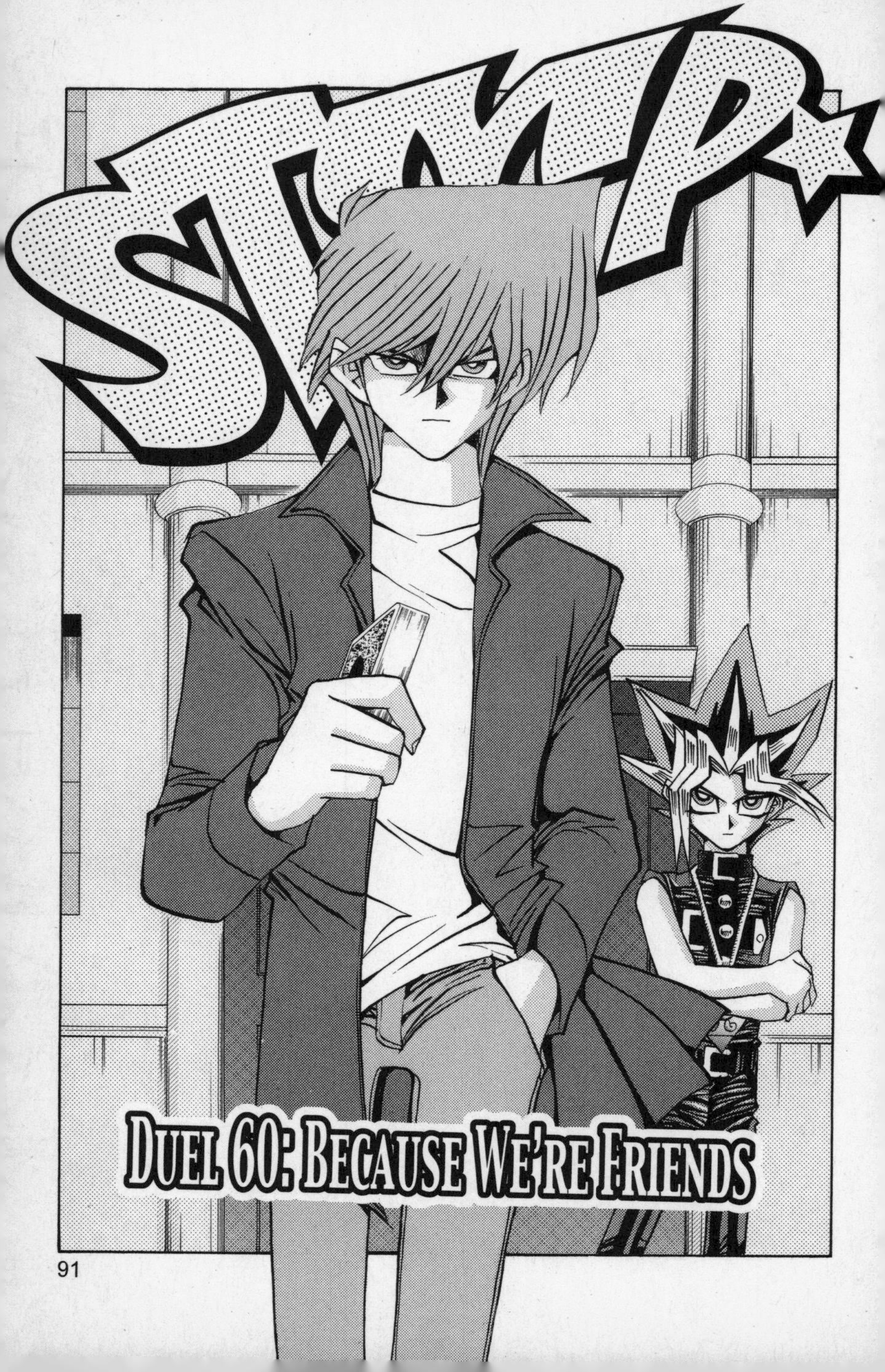

Duel 60: Because We're Friends

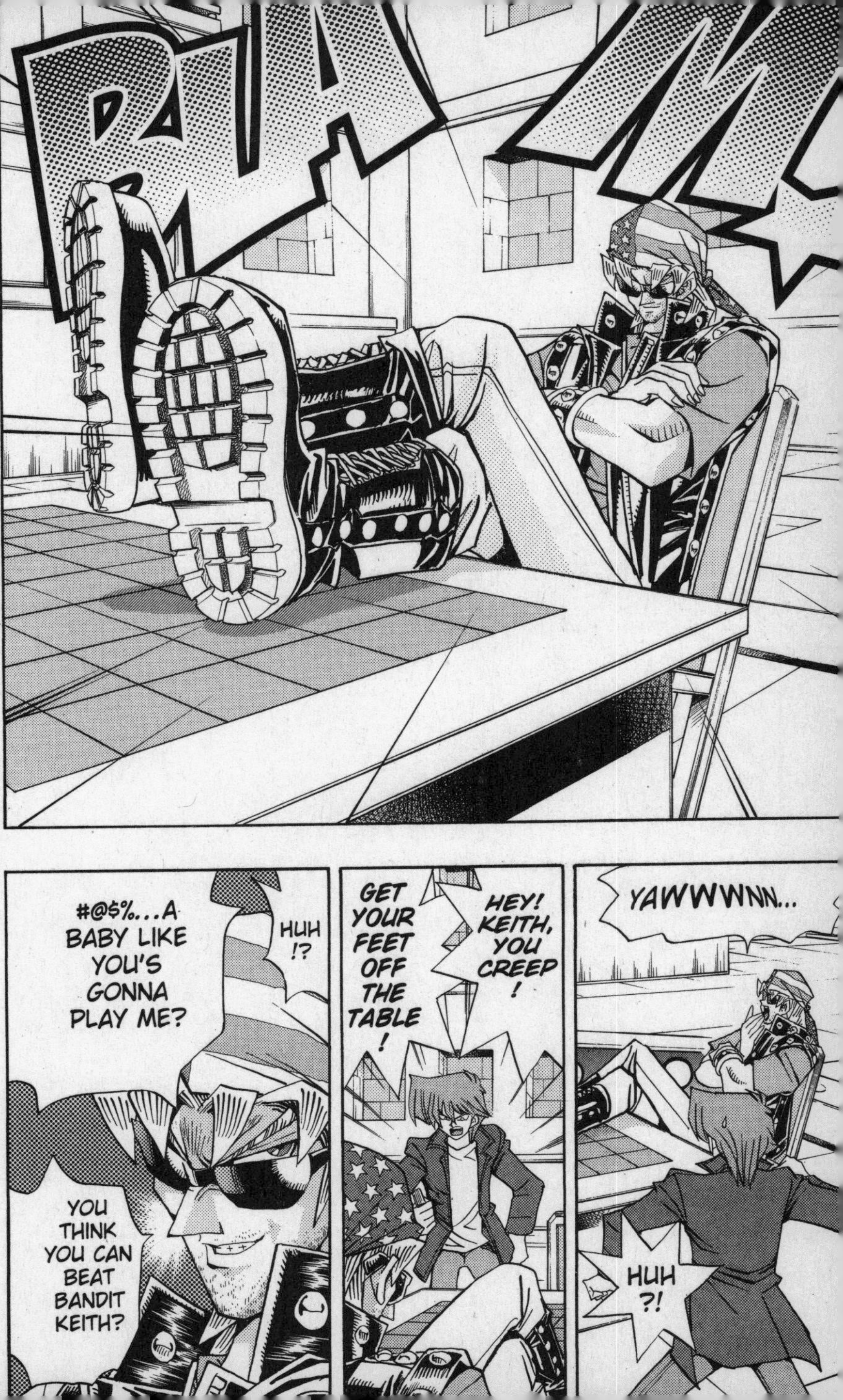
BAM
YAWWWNN...
HUH ?!
HEY! KEITH, YOU CREEP!
GET YOUR FEET OFF THE TABLE!
HUH !?
#@$%...A BABY LIKE YOU'S GONNA PLAY ME?
YOU THINK YOU CAN BEAT BANDIT KEITH?

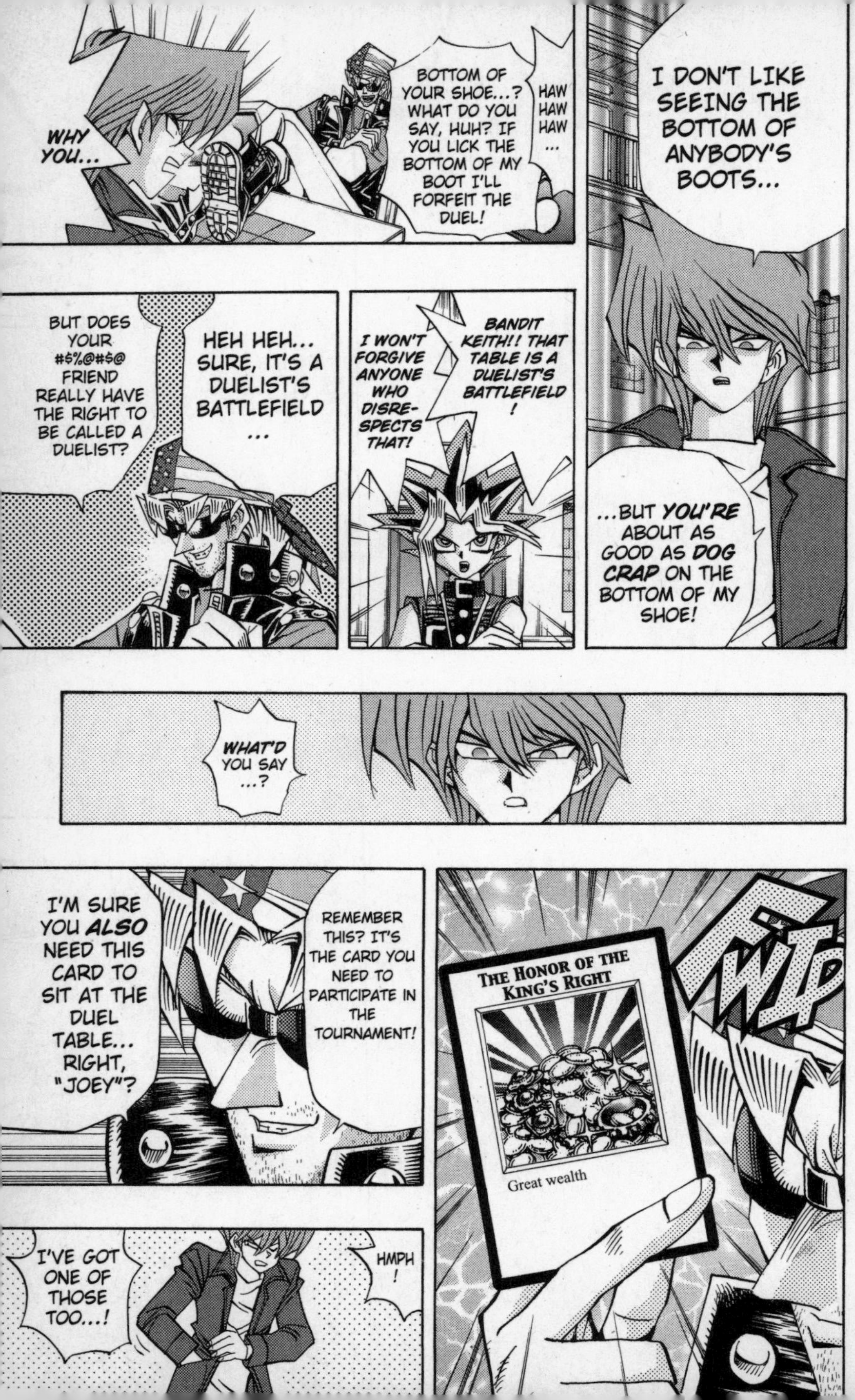
I DON'T LIKE SEEING THE BOTTOM OF ANYBODY'S BOOTS...
...BUT *YOU'RE* ABOUT AS GOOD AS *DOG CRAP* ON THE BOTTOM OF MY SHOE!
HAW HAW HAW ...
BOTTOM OF YOUR SHOE...? WHAT DO YOU SAY, HUH? IF YOU LICK THE BOTTOM OF MY BOOT I'LL FORFEIT THE DUEL!
WHY YOU...
BANDIT KEITH!! THAT TABLE IS A DUELIST'S BATTLEFIELD!
I WON'T FORGIVE ANYONE WHO DISRESPECTS THAT!
HEH HEH... SURE, IT'S A DUELIST'S BATTLEFIELD ...
BUT DOES YOUR #$%@#$@ FRIEND REALLY HAVE THE RIGHT TO BE CALLED A DUELIST?
WHAT'D YOU SAY ...?
THE HONOR OF THE KING'S RIGHT
Great wealth
REMEMBER THIS? IT'S THE CARD YOU NEED TO PARTICIPATE IN THE TOURNAMENT!
I'M SURE YOU *ALSO* NEED THIS CARD TO SIT AT THE DUEL TABLE... RIGHT, "JOEY"?
HMPH!
I'VE GOT ONE OF THOSE TOO...!

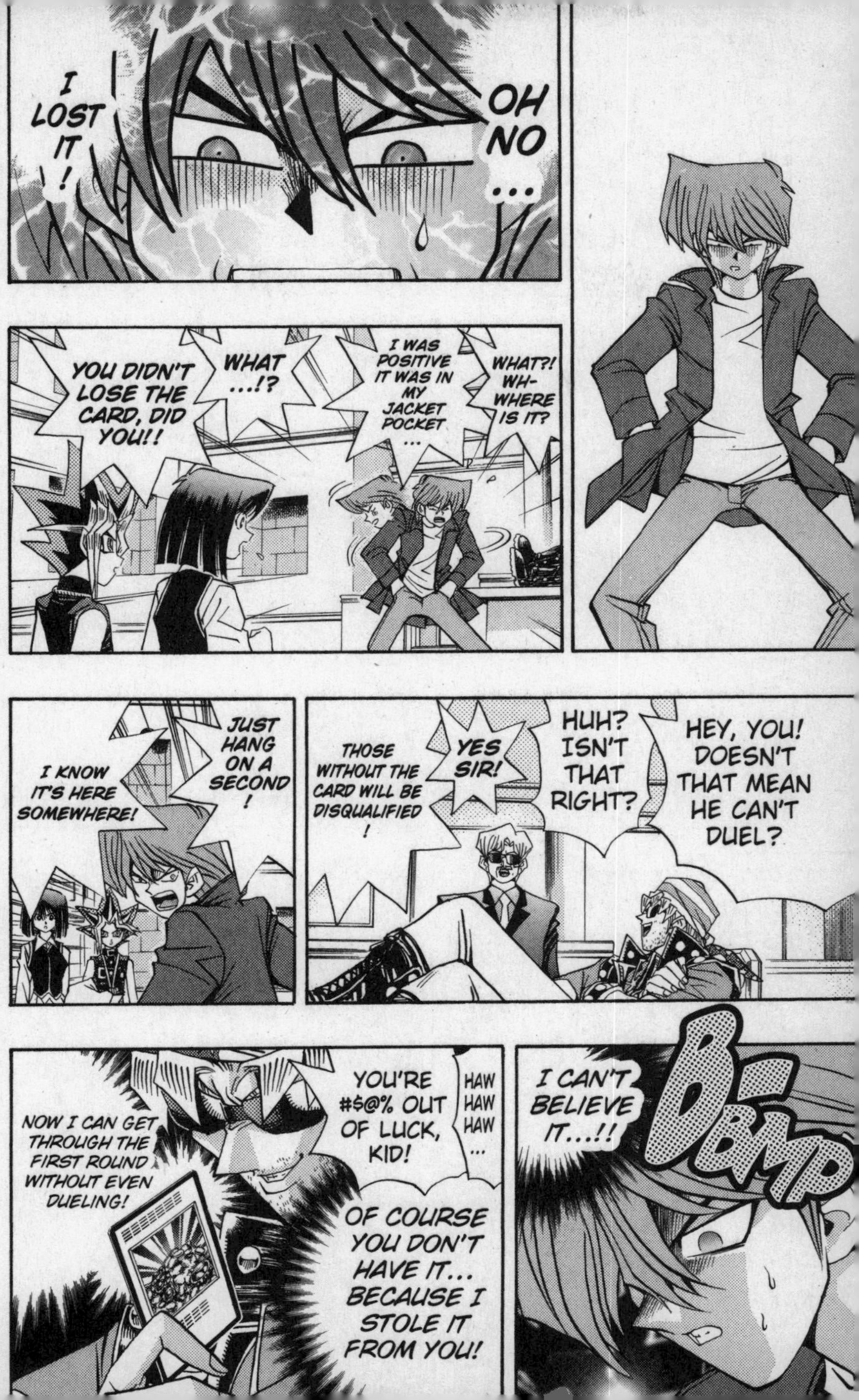
OH NO ...
I LOST IT !!
WHAT?! WH-WHERE IS IT?
I WAS POSITIVE IT WAS IN MY JACKET POCKET ...
WHAT ...!?
YOU DIDN'T LOSE THE CARD, DID YOU!!
HEY, YOU! DOESN'T THAT MEAN HE CAN'T DUEL?
HUH? ISN'T THAT RIGHT?
YES SIR!
THOSE WITHOUT THE CARD WILL BE DISQUALIFIED!
JUST HANG ON A SECOND!
I KNOW IT'S HERE SOMEWHERE!
BDMP
I CAN'T BELIEVE IT...!!
HAW HAW HAW ...
YOU'RE #$@%. OUT OF LUCK, KID!
NOW I CAN GET THROUGH THE FIRST ROUND WITHOUT EVEN DUELING!
OF COURSE YOU DON'T HAVE IT... BECAUSE I STOLE IT FROM YOU!

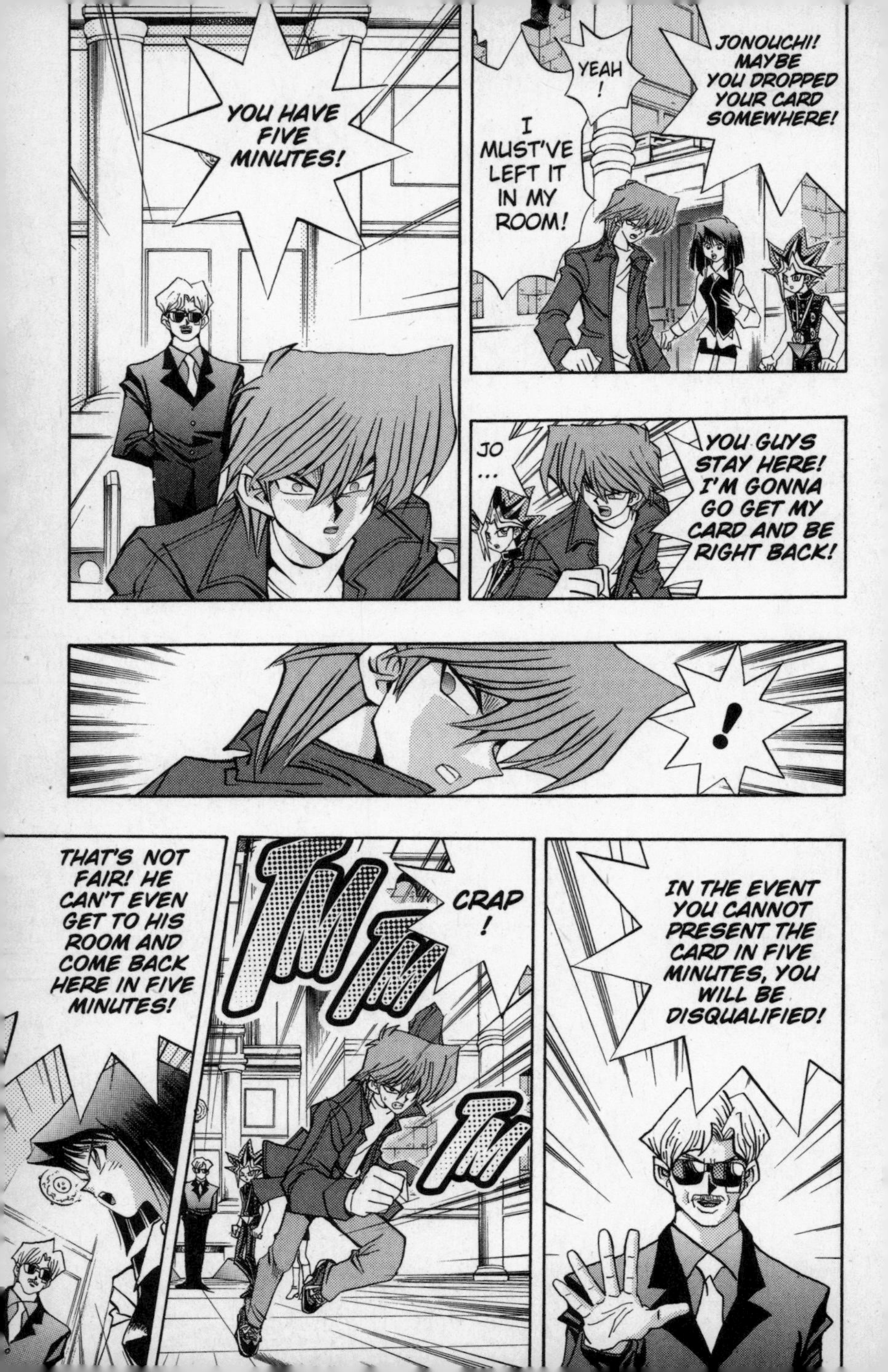
JONOUCHI! MAYBE YOU DROPPED YOUR CARD SOMEWHERE!
YEAH!
I MUST'VE LEFT IT IN MY ROOM!
YOU GUYS STAY HERE! I'M GONNA GO GET MY CARD AND BE RIGHT BACK!
JO...
YOU HAVE FIVE MINUTES!
!
IN THE EVENT YOU CANNOT PRESENT THE CARD IN FIVE MINUTES, YOU WILL BE DISQUALIFIED!
CRAP!
THAT'S NOT FAIR! HE CAN'T EVEN GET TO HIS ROOM AND COME BACK HERE IN FIVE MINUTES!

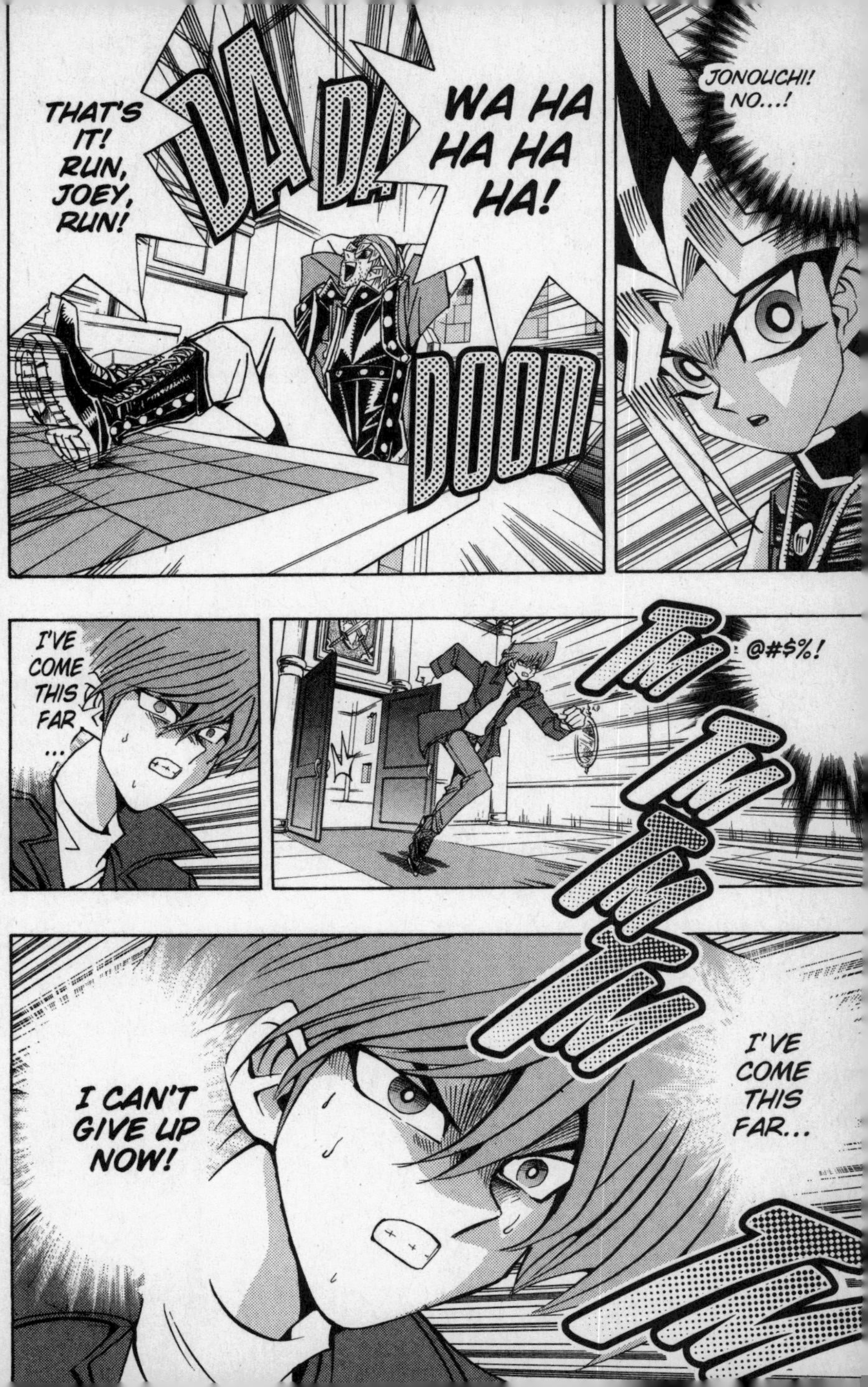

JONOUCHI! NO...!
WA HA HA HA HA!
DADA
THAT'S IT! RUN, JOEY, RUN!
DOOM
@#$%!
I'VE COME THIS FAR...
I'VE COME THIS FAR...
I CAN'T GIVE UP NOW!

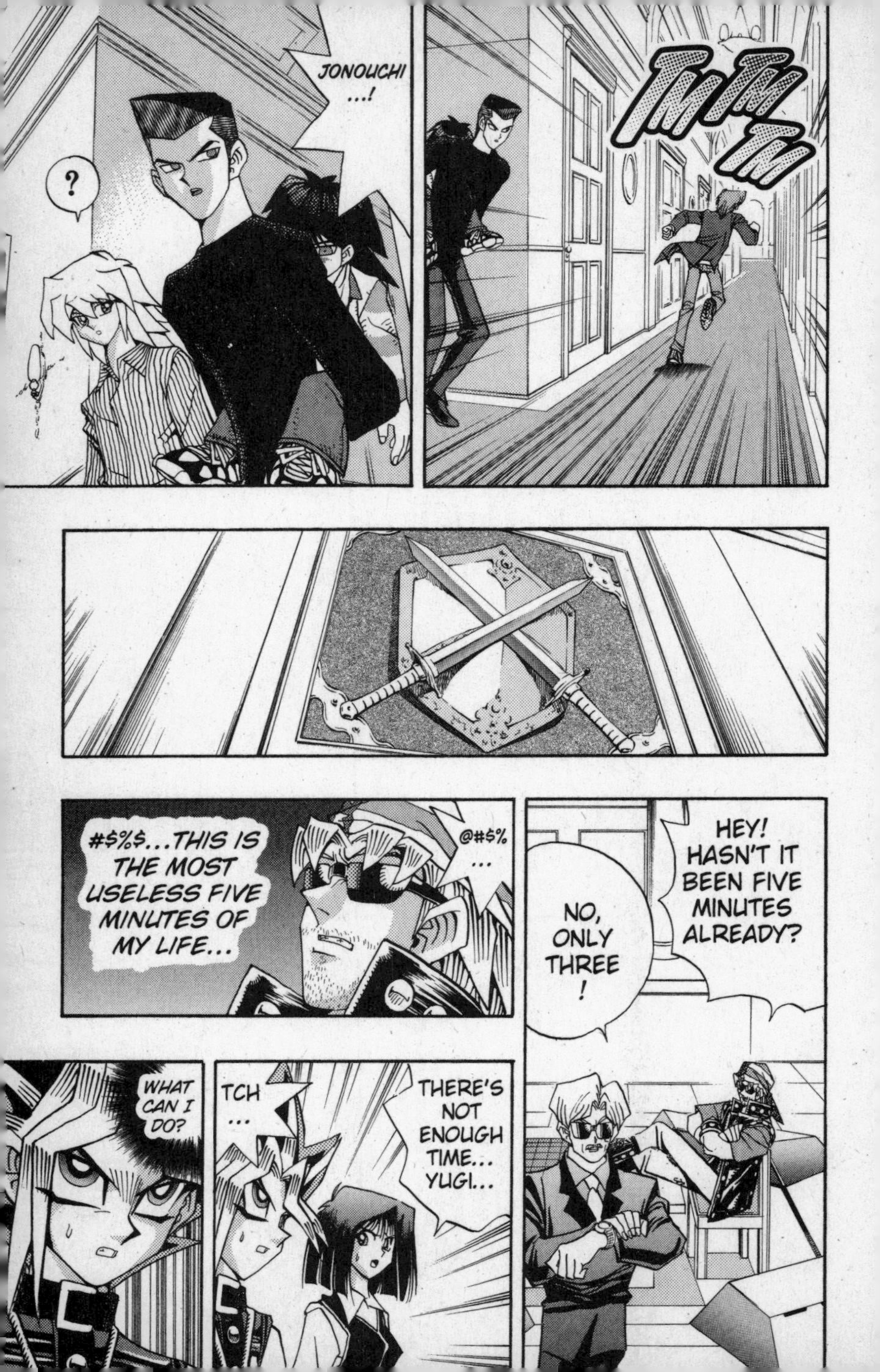
TM TM TM
JONOUCHI ...!
?
HEY! HASN'T IT BEEN FIVE MINUTES ALREADY?
NO, ONLY THREE !
@#$% ...
#$%$... THIS IS THE MOST USELESS FIVE MINUTES OF MY LIFE...
THERE'S NOT ENOUGH TIME... YUGI...
TCH ...
WHAT CAN I DO?

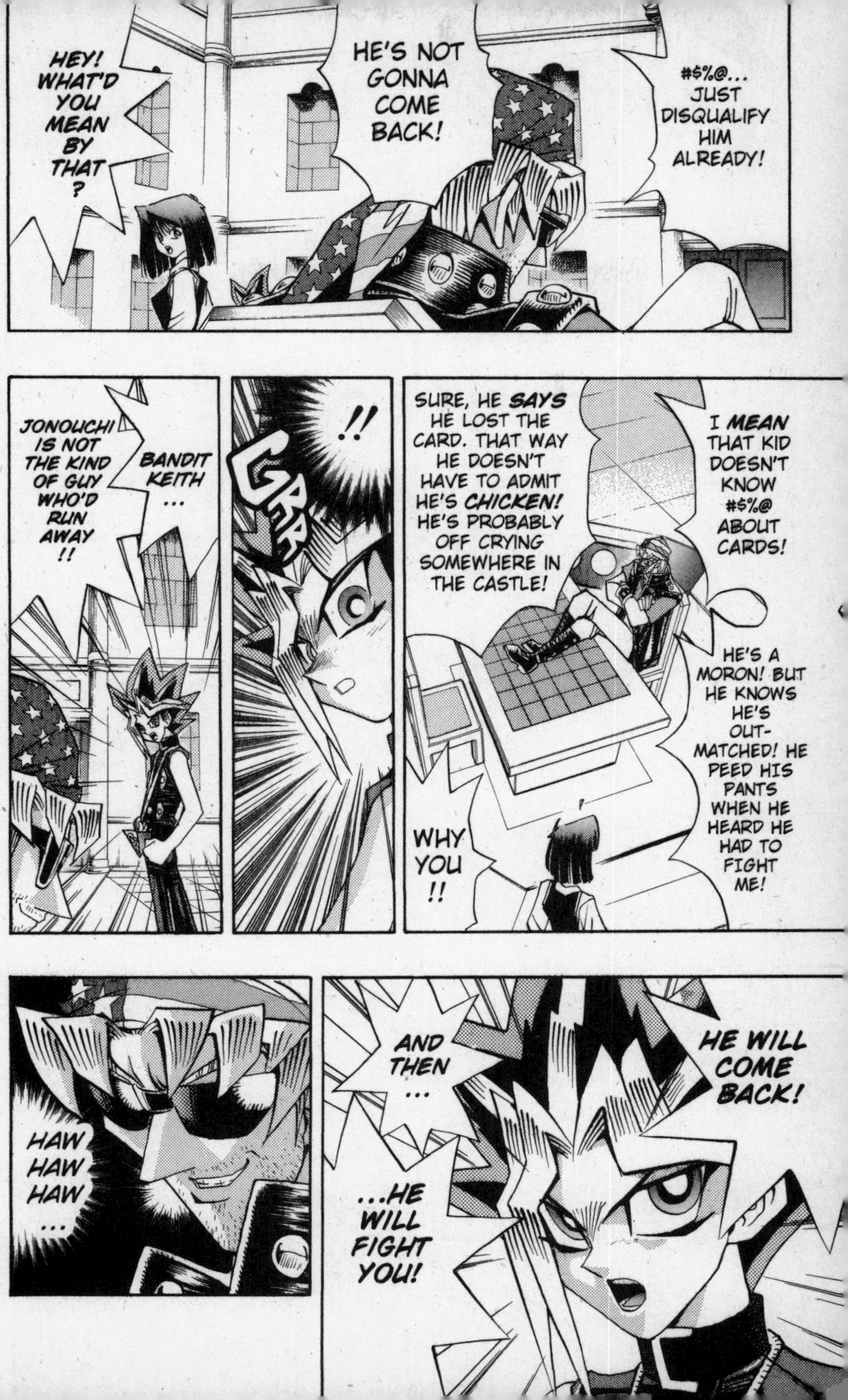
#$%@... JUST DISQUALIFY HIM ALREADY!
HE'S NOT GONNA COME BACK!
HEY! WHAT'D YOU MEAN BY THAT?
I MEAN THAT KID DOESN'T KNOW #$%@ ABOUT CARDS!
SURE, HE SAYS HE LOST THE CARD. THAT WAY HE DOESN'T HAVE TO ADMIT HE'S CHICKEN! HE'S PROBABLY OFF CRYING SOMEWHERE IN THE CASTLE!
HE'S A MORON! BUT HE KNOWS HE'S OUT-MATCHED! HE PEED HIS PANTS WHEN HE HEARD HE HAD TO FIGHT ME!
WHY YOU !!
!!
GRR
BANDIT KEITH ...
JONOUCHI IS NOT THE KIND OF GUY WHO'D RUN AWAY !!
HE WILL COME BACK!
AND THEN ...
...HE WILL FIGHT YOU!
HAW HAW HAW ...

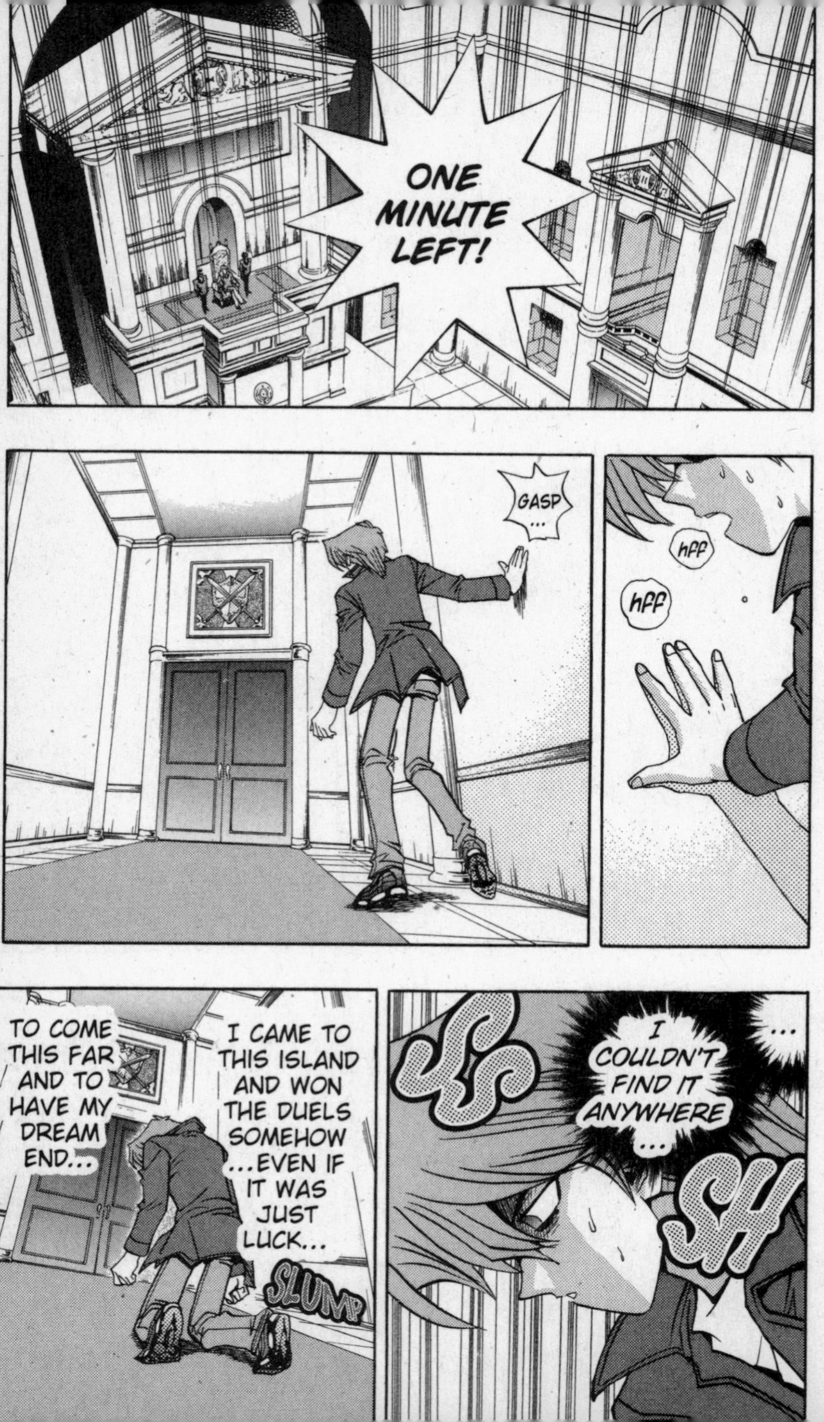
ONE MINUTE LEFT!
hff
hff
GASP...
...
I COULDN'T FIND IT ANYWHERE...
SH
US
I CAME TO THIS ISLAND AND WON THE DUELS SOMEHOW ...EVEN IF IT WAS JUST LUCK...
TO COME THIS FAR AND TO HAVE MY DREAM END...
SLUMP

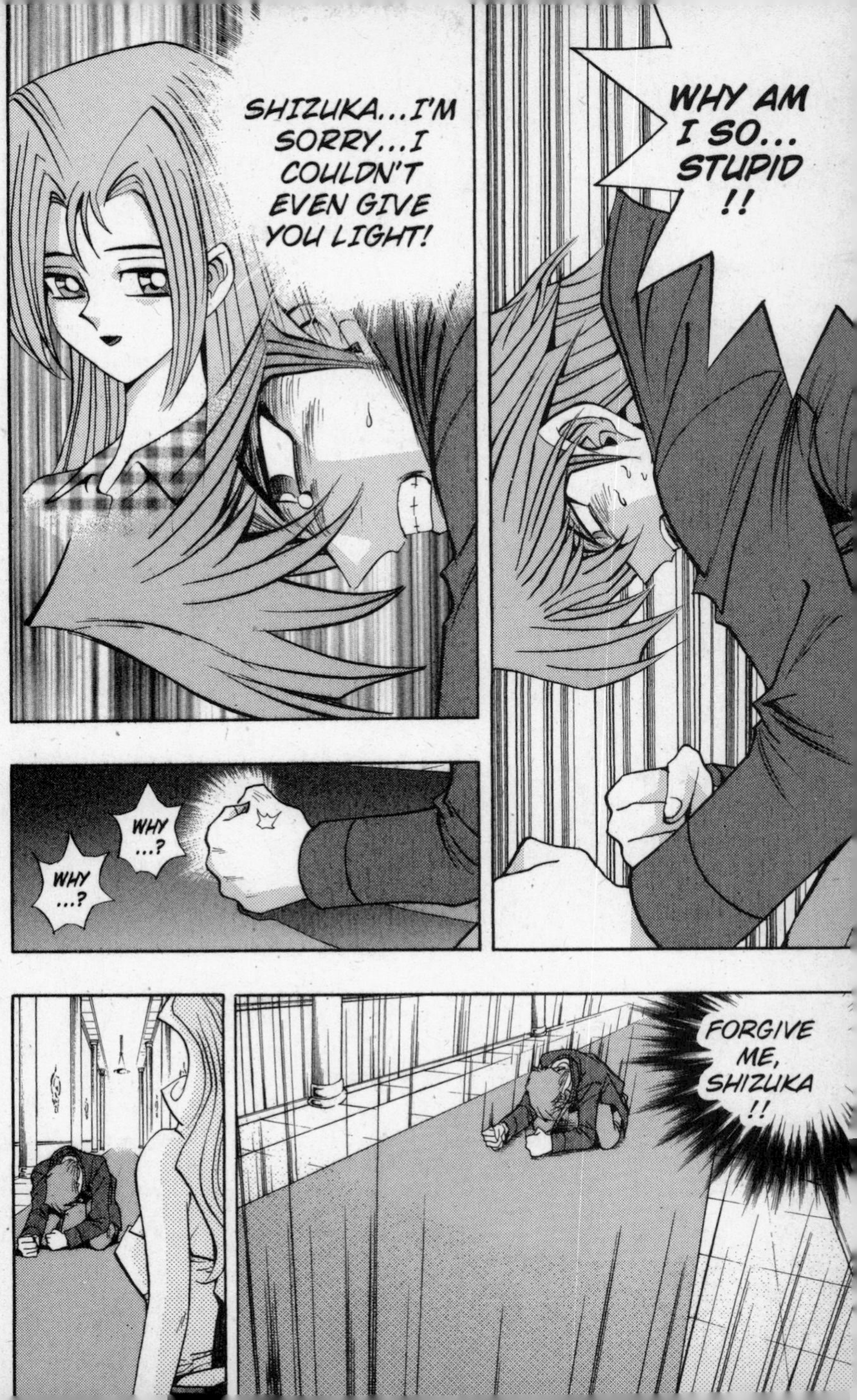
WHY AM I SO... STUPID !!
SHIZUKA...I'M SORRY...I COULDN'T EVEN GIVE YOU LIGHT!
WHY ...?
WHY ...?
FORGIVE ME, SHIZUKA !!

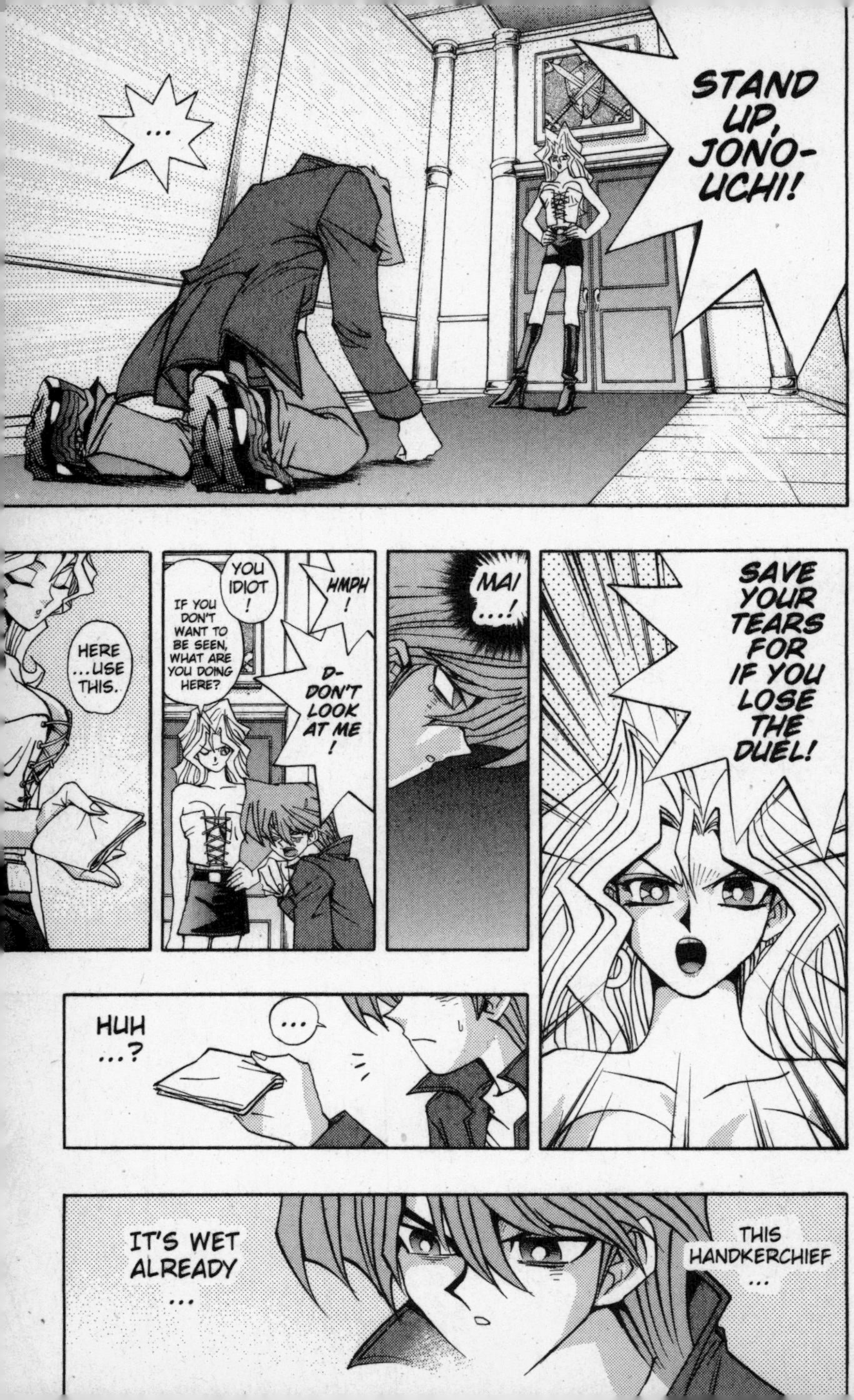
STAND UP, JONO-UCHI!
...
SAVE YOUR TEARS FOR IF YOU LOSE THE DUEL!
MAI ...!
HMPH!
D-DON'T LOOK AT ME!
YOU IDIOT!
IF YOU DON'T WANT TO BE SEEN, WHAT ARE YOU DOING HERE?
HERE ...USE THIS.
...
HUH ...?
THIS HANDKERCHIEF ...
IT'S WET ALREADY ...

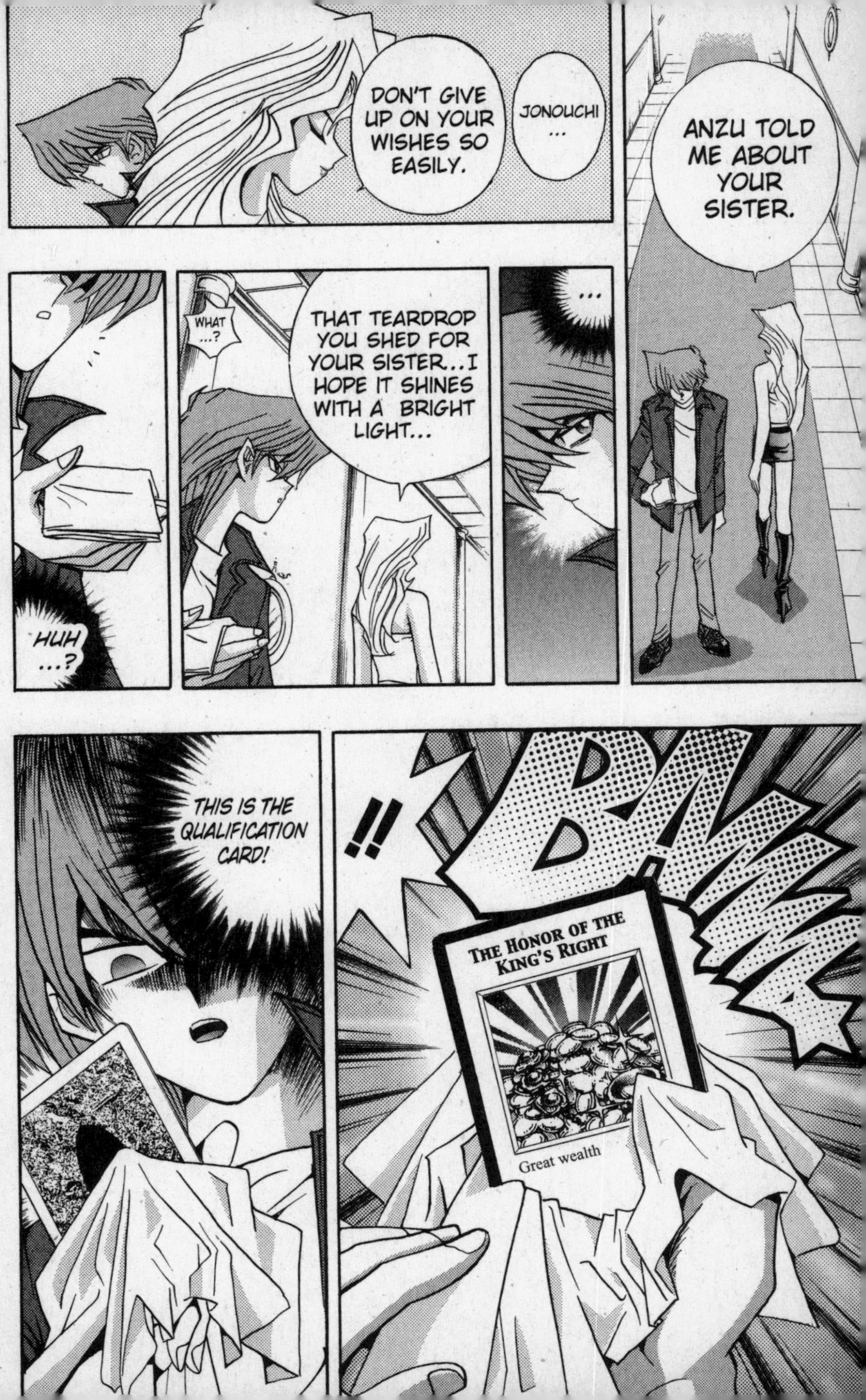
ANZU TOLD ME ABOUT YOUR SISTER.
JONOUCHI …
DON'T GIVE UP ON YOUR WISHES SO EASILY.
…
THAT TEARDROP YOU SHED FOR YOUR SISTER…I HOPE IT SHINES WITH A BRIGHT LIGHT…
WHAT …?
HUH …?
!!
THE HONOR OF THE KING'S RIGHT
Great wealth
THIS IS THE QUALIFICATION CARD!

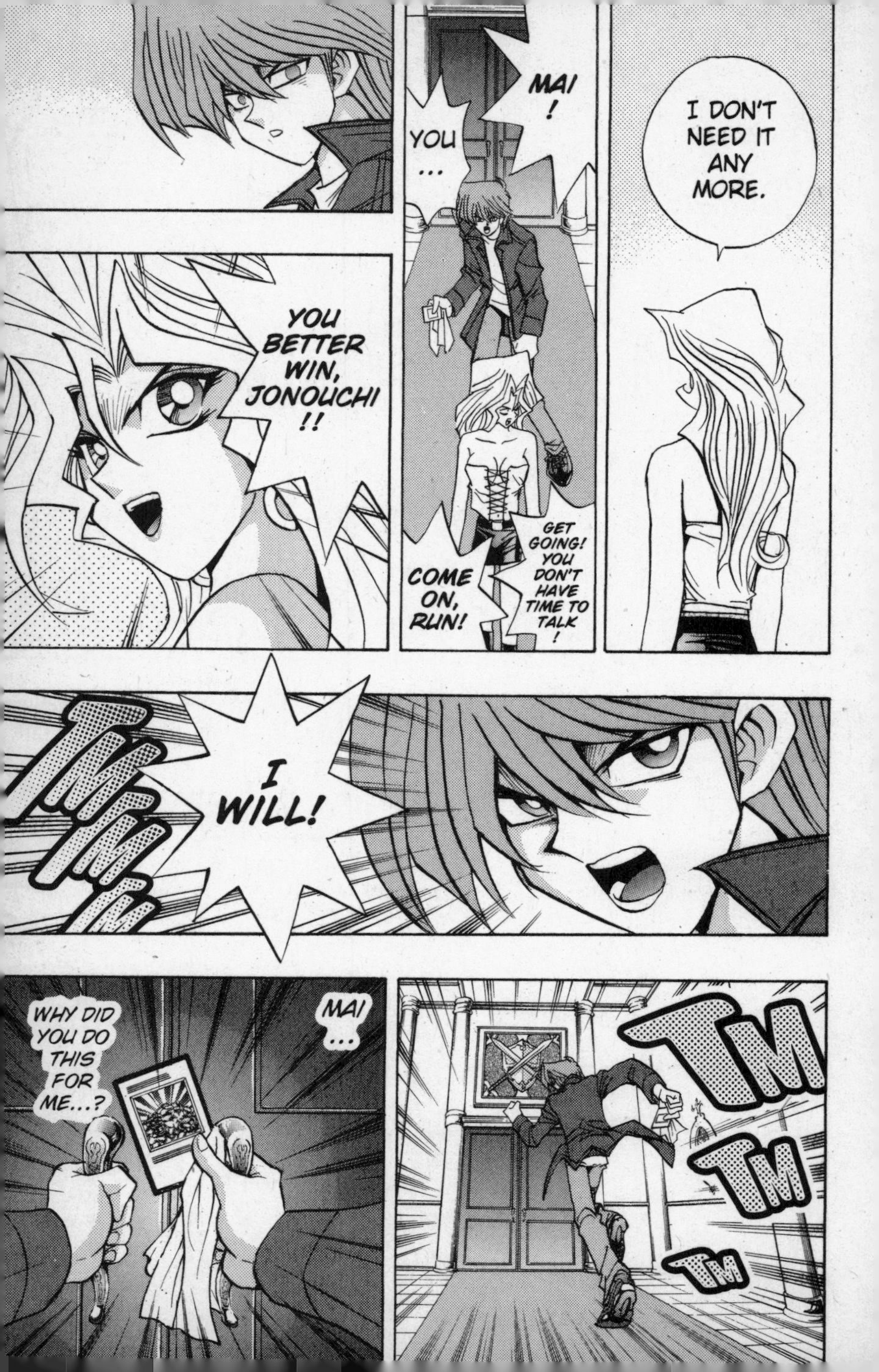
I DON'T NEED IT ANY MORE.
MAI!
YOU ...
GET GOING! YOU DON'T HAVE TIME TO TALK!
COME ON, RUN!
YOU BETTER WIN, JONOUCHI!!
I WILL!
TM
TM
TM
MAI ...
WHY DID YOU DO THIS FOR ME...?

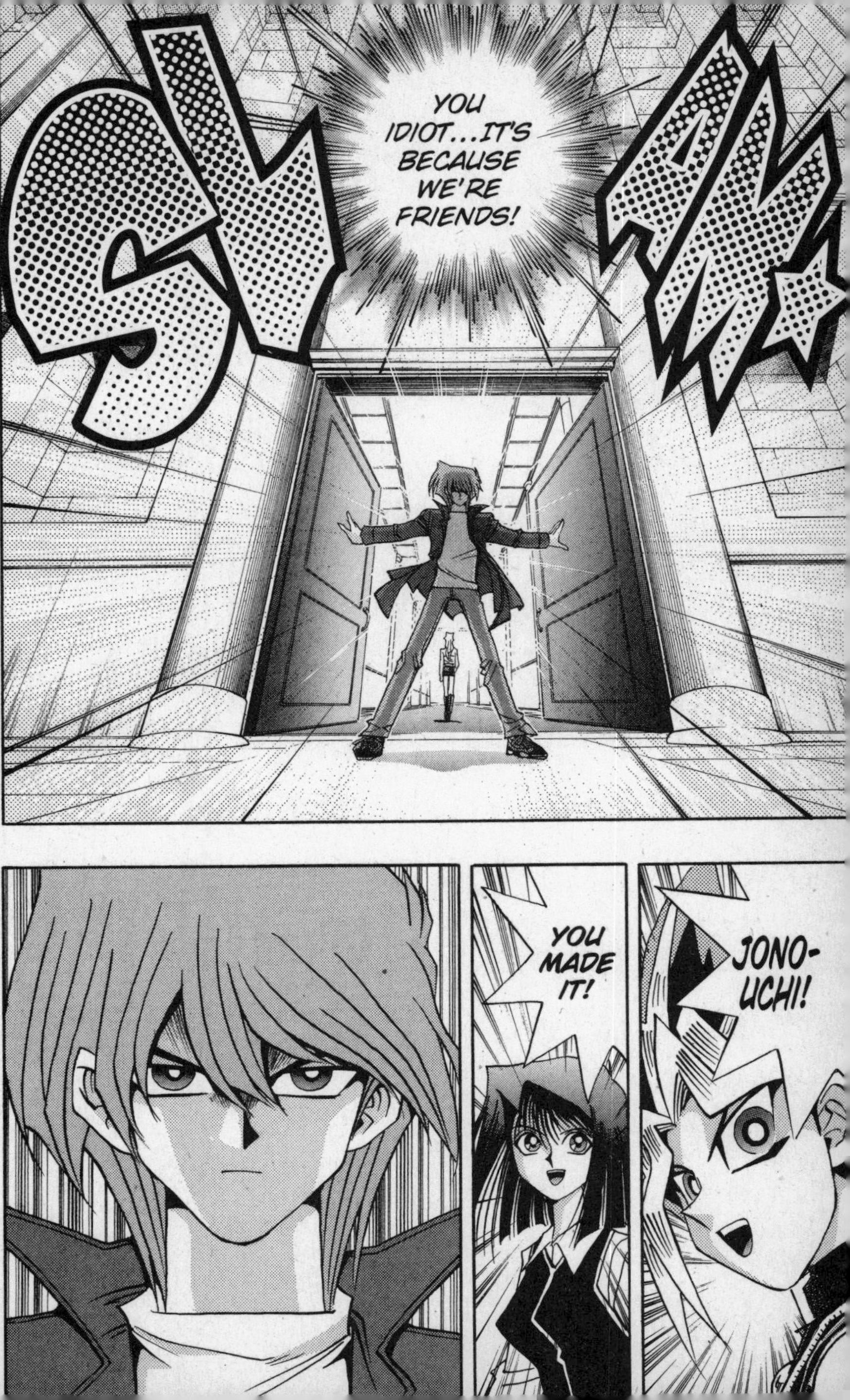
YOU IDIOT...IT'S BECAUSE WE'RE FRIENDS!
JONO-UCHI!
YOU MADE IT!

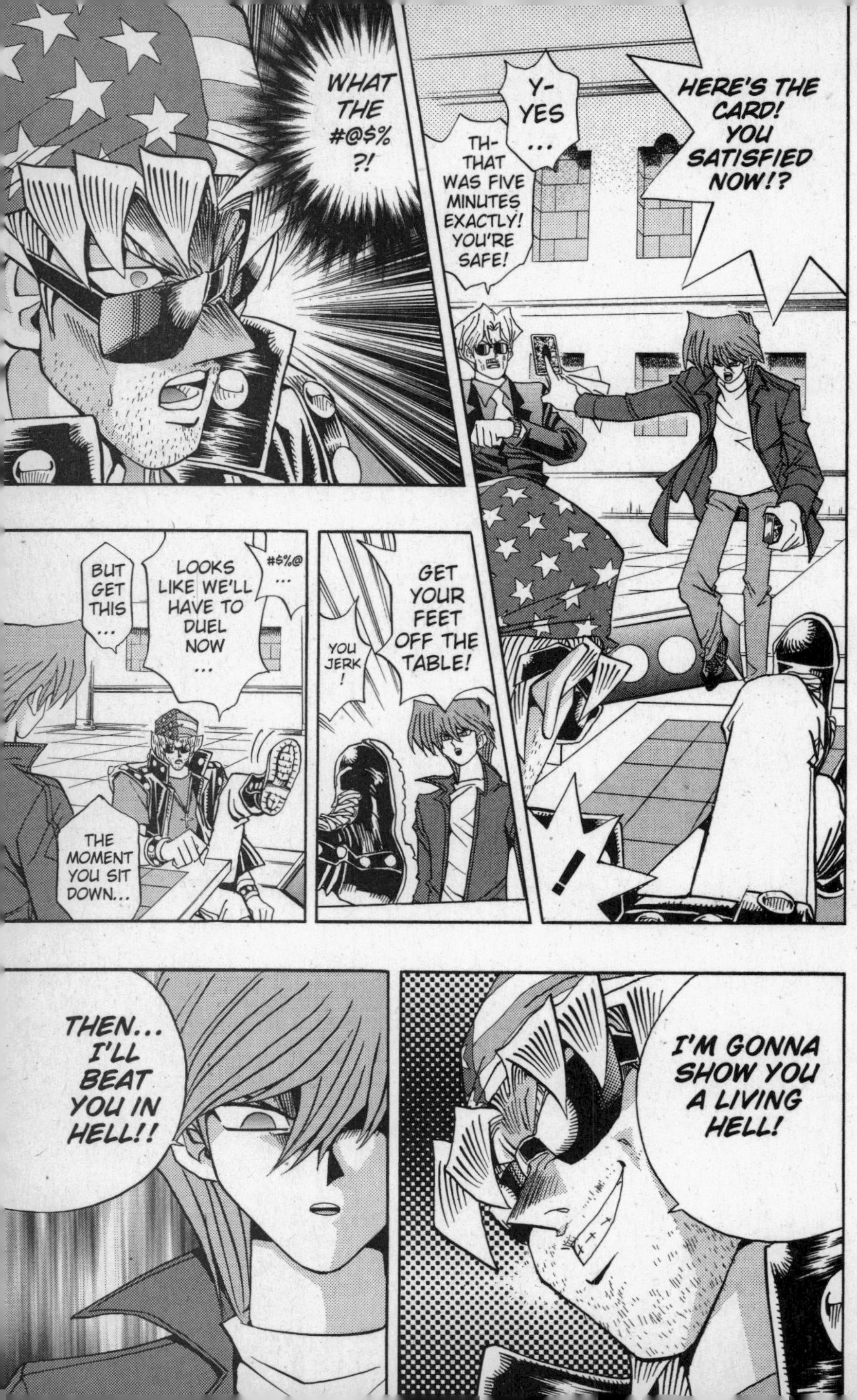
HERE'S THE CARD! YOU SATISFIED NOW!?
Y- YES...
TH- THAT WAS FIVE MINUTES EXACTLY! YOU'RE SAFE!
!
WHAT THE #@$% ?!
GET YOUR FEET OFF THE TABLE!
YOU JERK!
#$%@...
LOOKS LIKE WE'LL HAVE TO DUEL NOW...
BUT GET THIS...
THE MOMENT YOU SIT DOWN...
I'M GONNA SHOW YOU A LIVING HELL!
THEN... I'LL BEAT YOU IN HELL!!

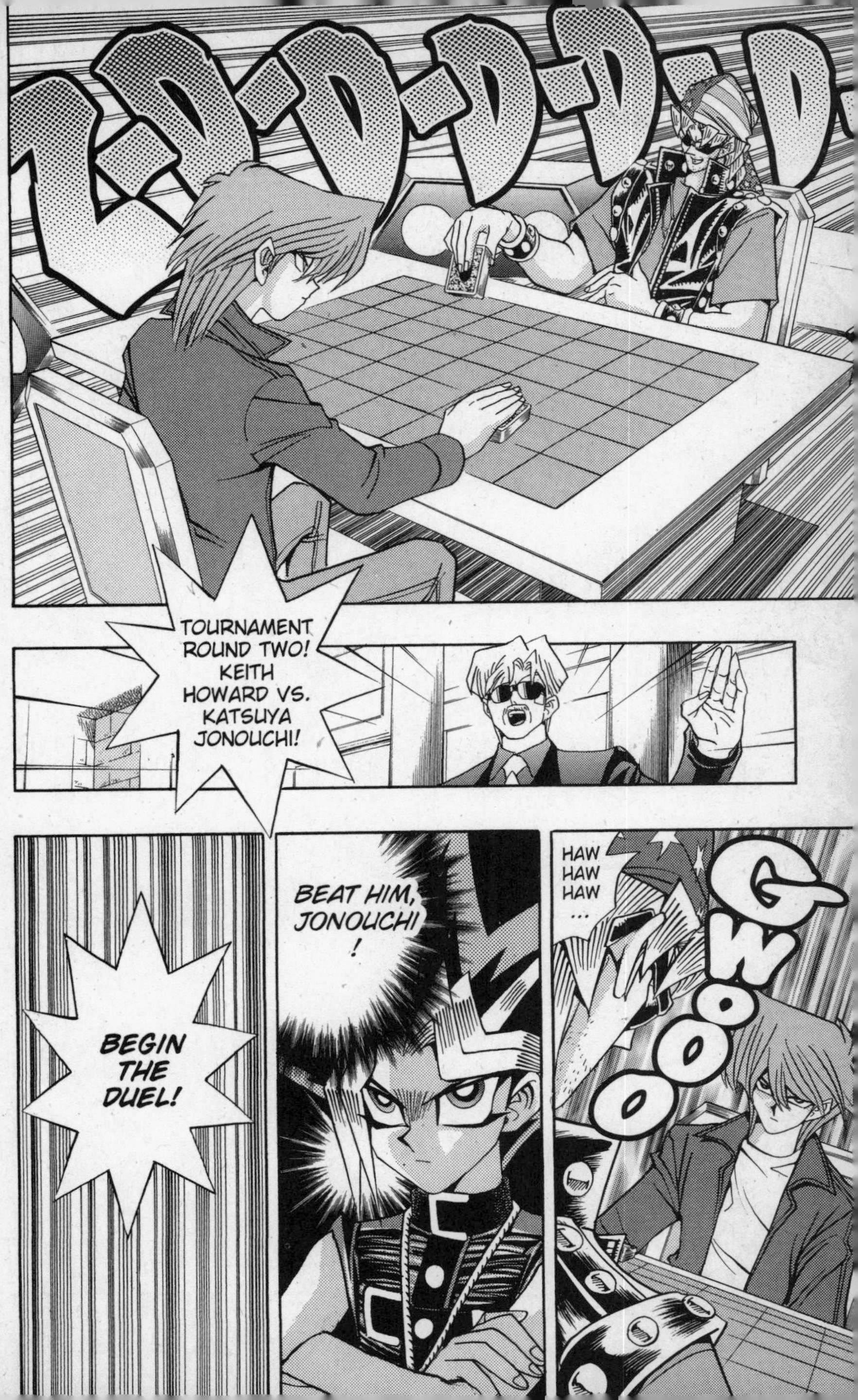
Z-D-D-D-D
TOURNAMENT ROUND TWO! KEITH HOWARD VS. KATSUYA JONOUCHI!
HAW HAW HAW ...
GWOOOO
BEAT HIM, JONOUCHI!
BEGIN THE DUEL!

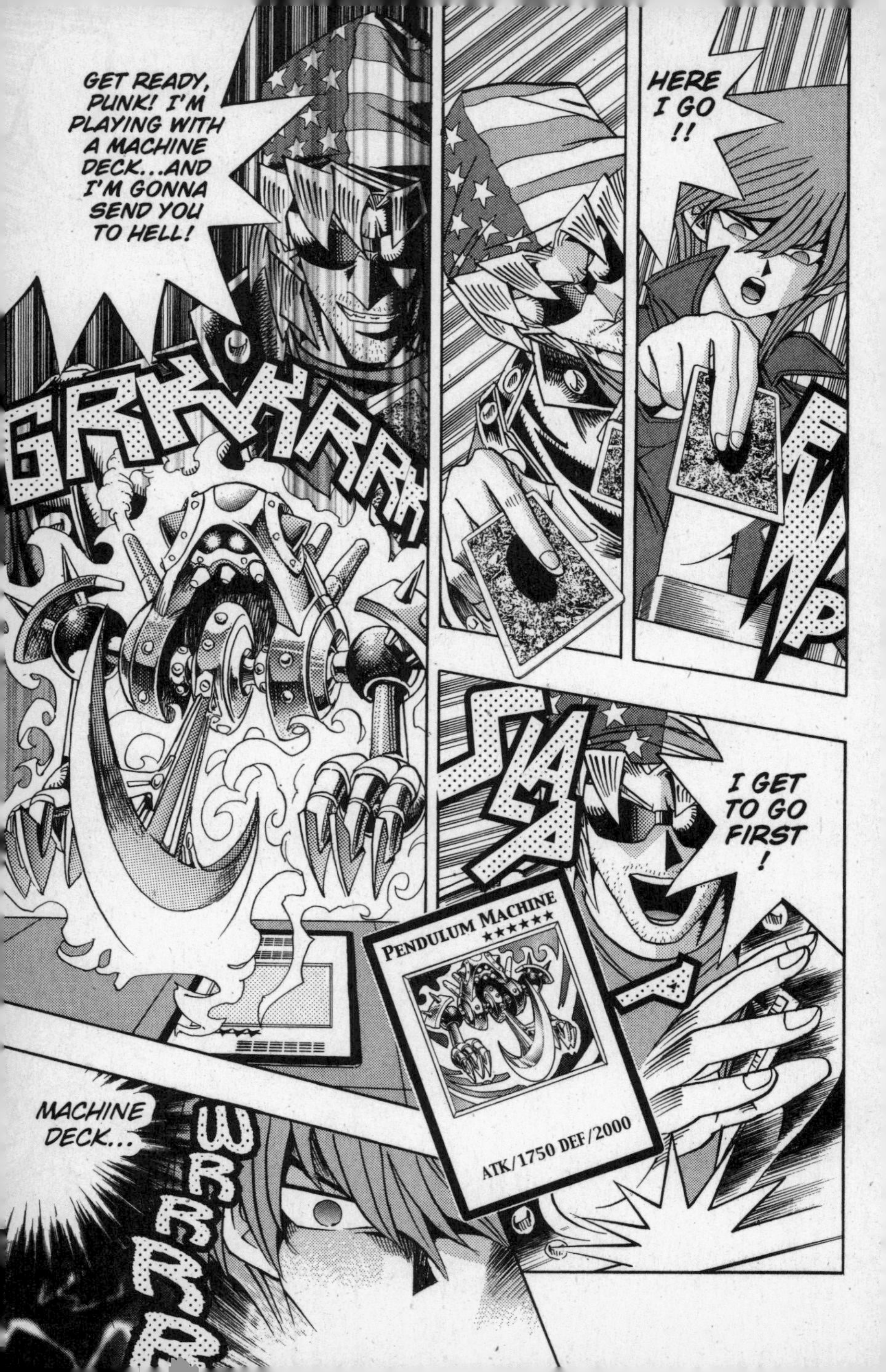
HERE I GO!!
I GET TO GO FIRST!
PENDULUM MACHINE
ATK/1750 DEF/2000
GET READY, PUNK! I'M PLAYING WITH A MACHINE DECK...AND I'M GONNA SEND YOU TO HELL!
MACHINE DECK...

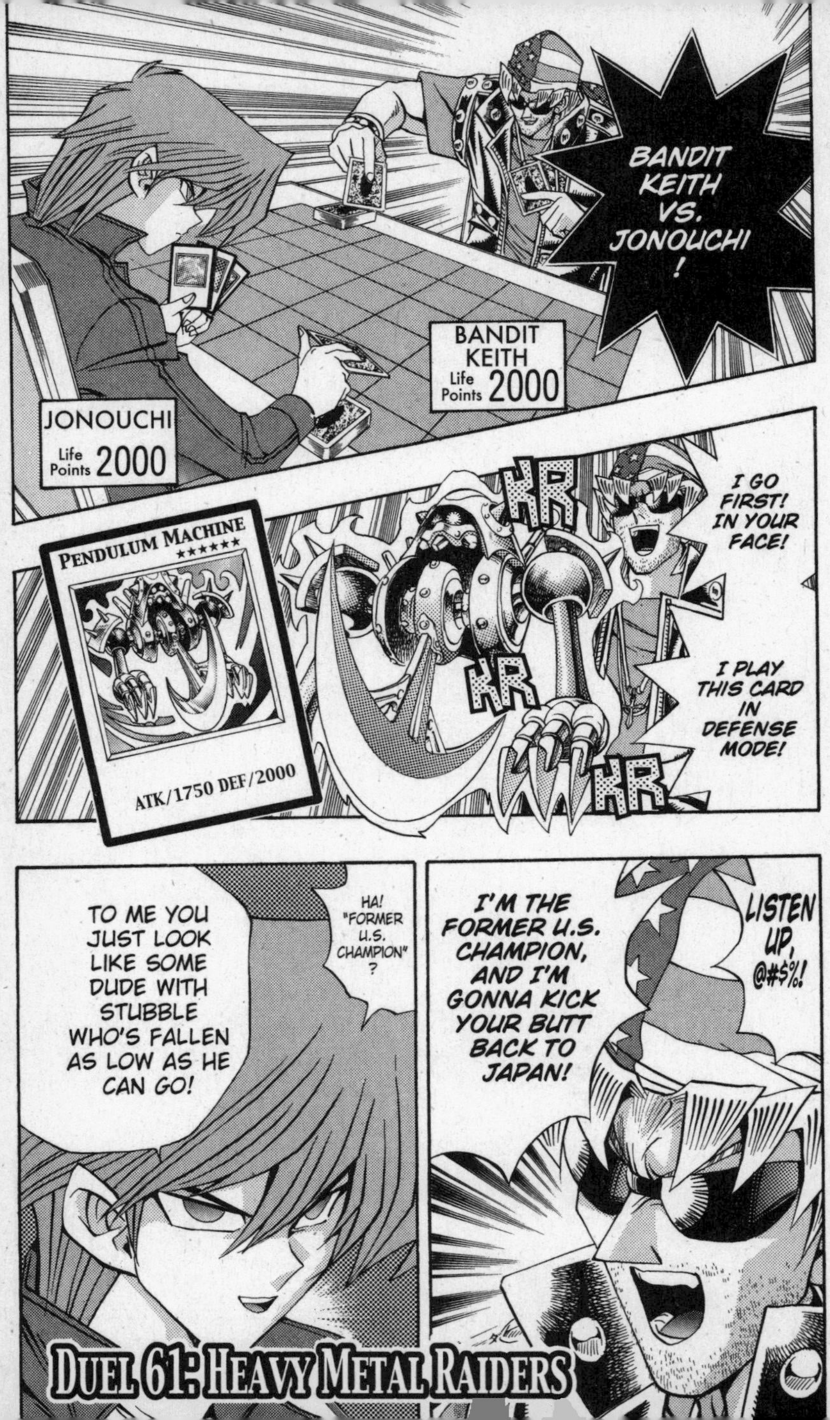
BANDIT KEITH VS. JONOUCHI!
BANDIT KEITH Life Points 2000
JONOUCHI Life Points 2000
I GO FIRST! IN YOUR FACE!
I PLAY THIS CARD IN DEFENSE MODE!
KR
KR
KR
PENDULUM MACHINE
ATK/1750 DEF/2000
LISTEN UP, @#$%!
I'M THE FORMER U.S. CHAMPION, AND I'M GONNA KICK YOUR BUTT BACK TO JAPAN!
HA! "FORMER U.S. CHAMPION"?
TO ME YOU JUST LOOK LIKE SOME DUDE WITH STUBBLE WHO'S FALLEN AS LOW AS HE CAN GO!
Duel 61: Heavy Metal Raiders

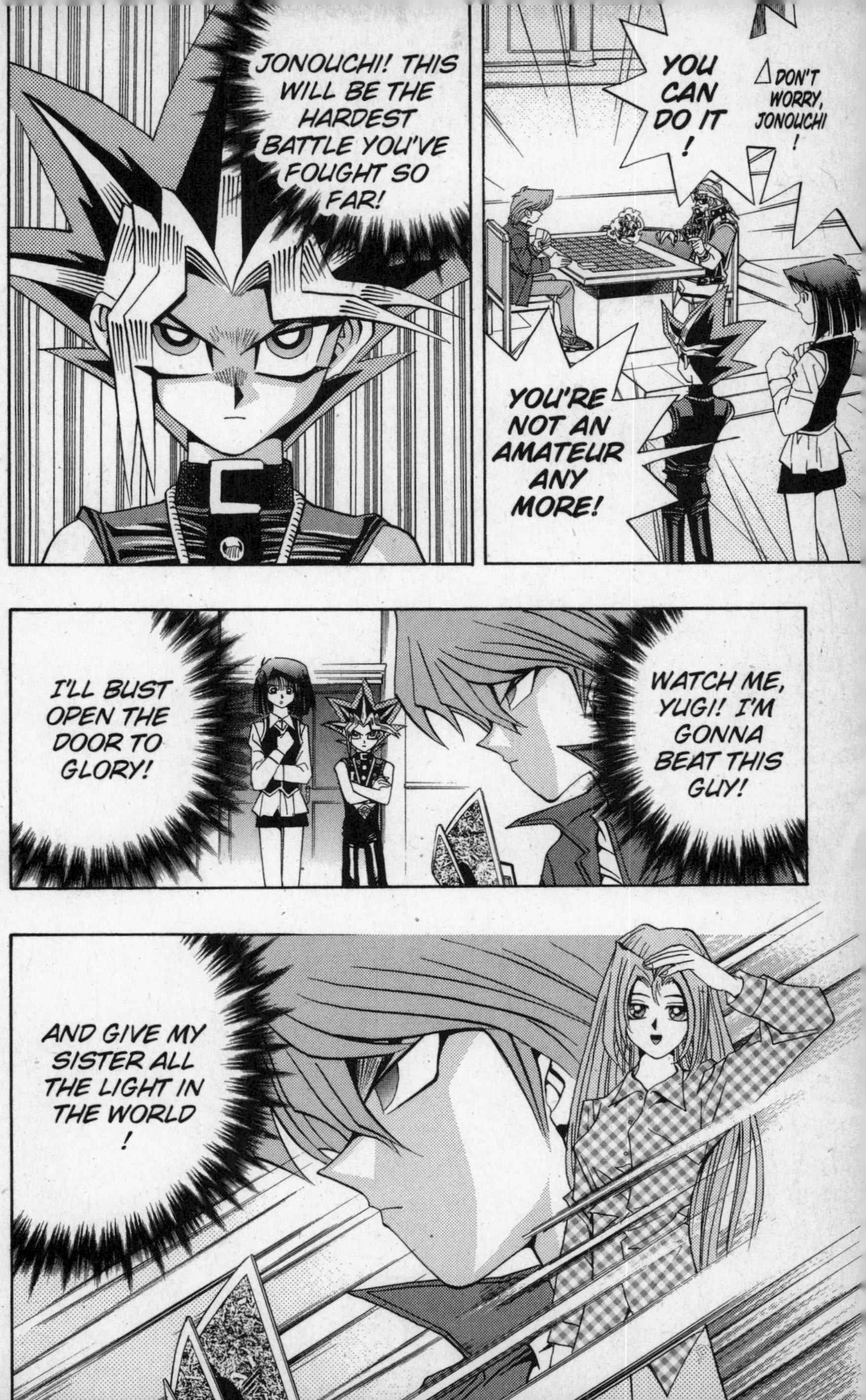
DON'T WORRY, JONOUCHI!
YOU CAN DO IT!
YOU'RE NOT AN AMATEUR ANY MORE!
JONOUCHI! THIS WILL BE THE HARDEST BATTLE YOU'VE FOUGHT SO FAR!
WATCH ME, YUGI! I'M GONNA BEAT THIS GUY!
I'LL BUST OPEN THE DOOR TO GLORY!
AND GIVE MY SISTER ALL THE LIGHT IN THE WORLD!

Duel 61: Heavy Metal Raiders

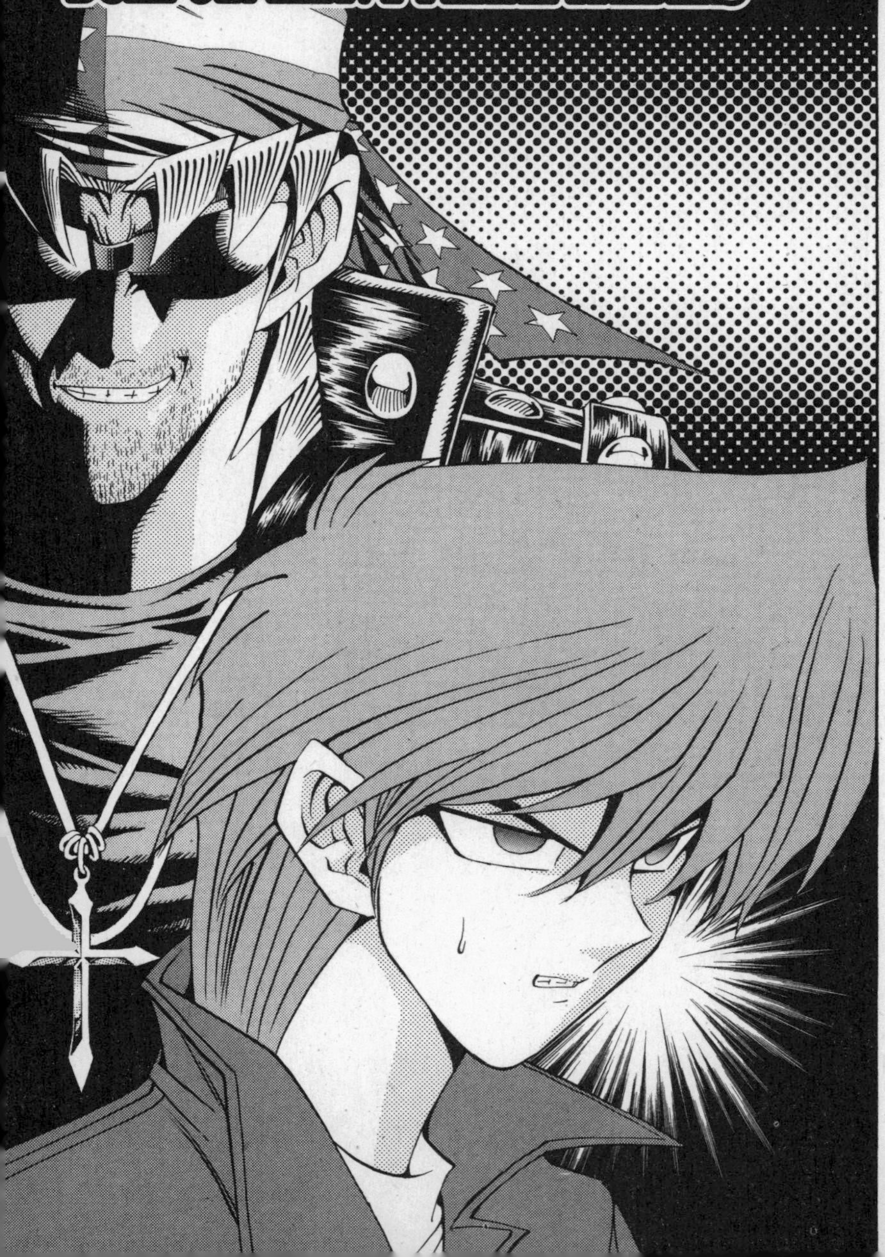

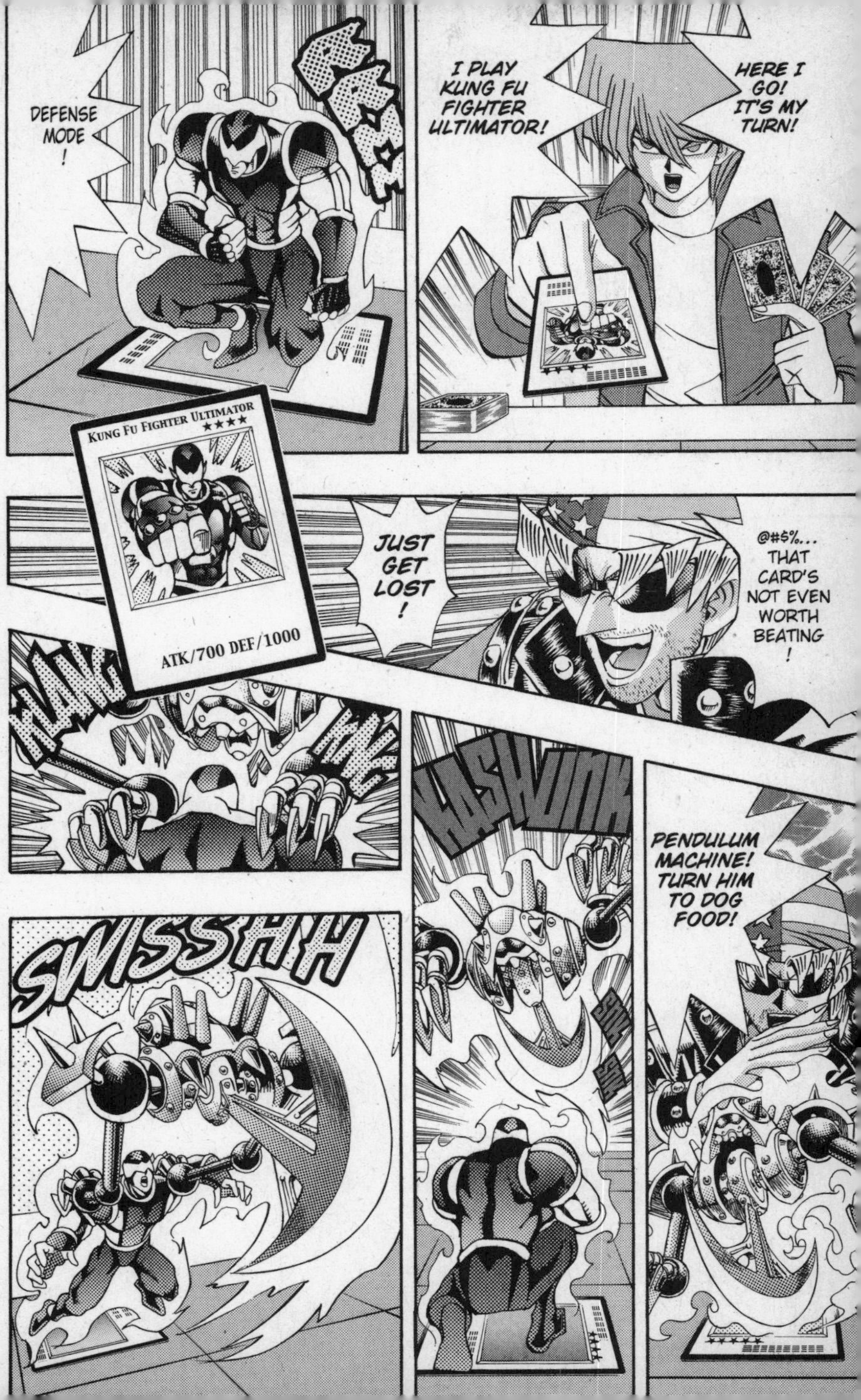
HERE I GO! IT'S MY TURN!
I PLAY KUNG FU FIGHTER ULTIMATOR!
DEFENSE MODE!
Kung Fu Fighter Ultimator ★★★★
ATK/700 DEF/1000
@#$%... THAT CARD'S NOT EVEN WORTH BEATING!
JUST GET LOST!
PENDULUM MACHINE! TURN HIM TO DOG FOOD!
SWISSHH

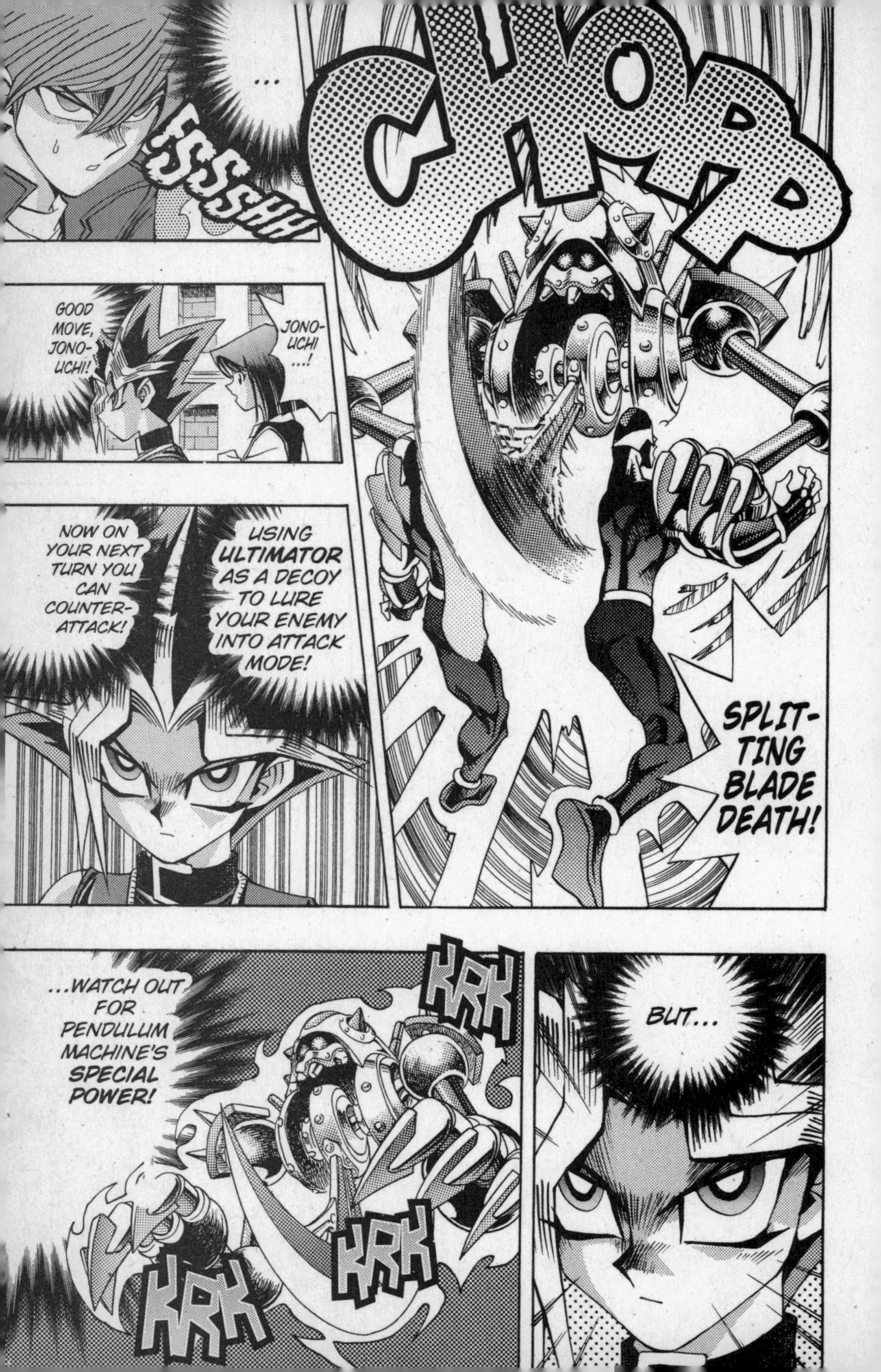
CHOP
SPLITTING BLADE DEATH!
...
FSSSHH
JONOUCHI...!
GOOD MOVE, JONOUCHI!
USING **ULTIMATOR** AS A DECOY TO LURE YOUR ENEMY INTO ATTACK MODE!
NOW ON YOUR NEXT TURN YOU CAN COUNTER-ATTACK!
BUT...
KRK
...WATCH OUT FOR **PENDULUM MACHINE'S SPECIAL POWER!**
KRK
KRK

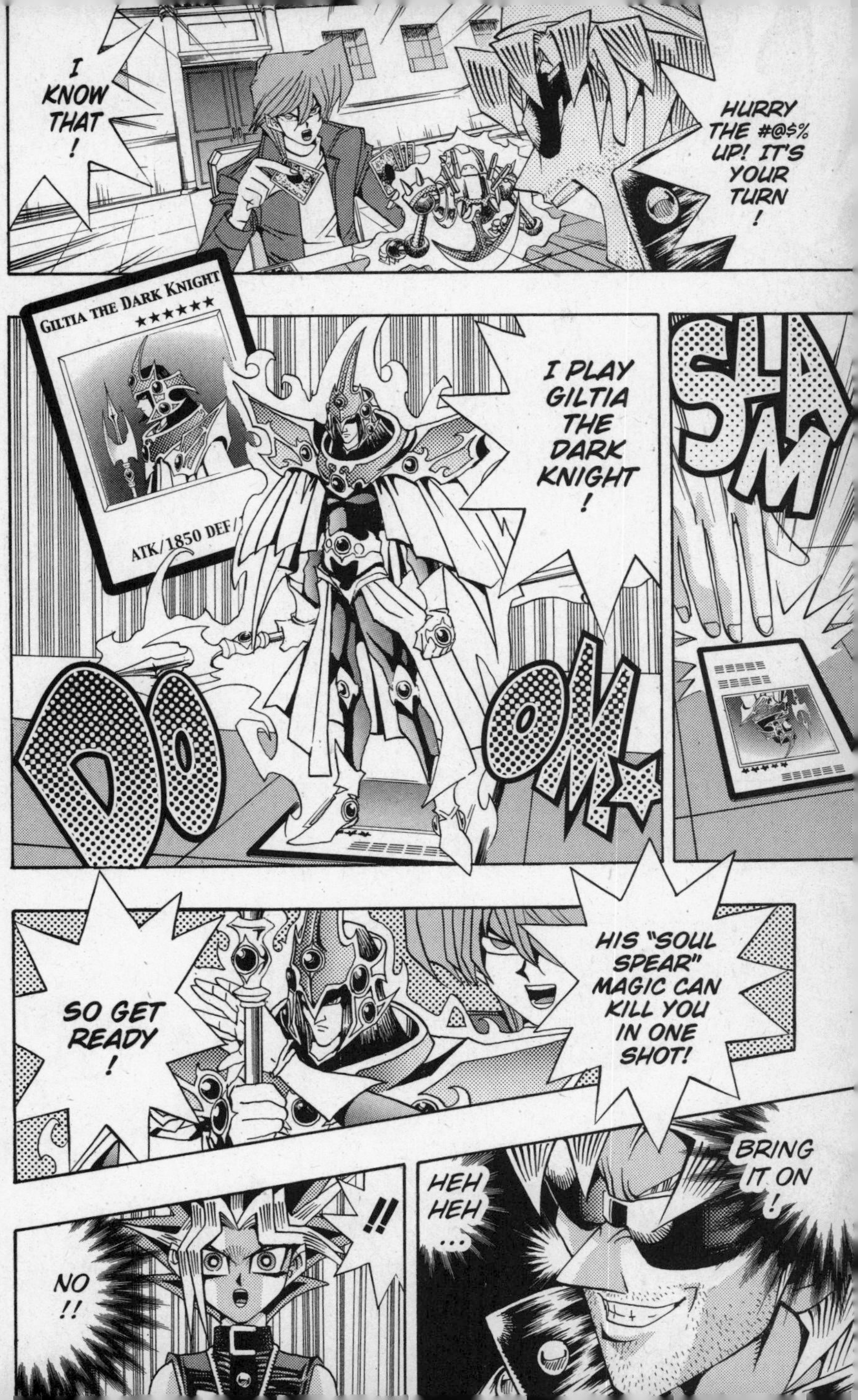
HURRY THE #@$% UP! IT'S YOUR TURN!
I KNOW THAT!
SLAM
I PLAY GILTIA THE DARK KNIGHT!
GILTIA THE DARK KNIGHT
ATK/1850 DEF/
DOOM
HIS "SOUL SPEAR" MAGIC CAN KILL YOU IN ONE SHOT!
SO GET READY!
BRING IT ON!
HEH HEH ...
!!
NO!!

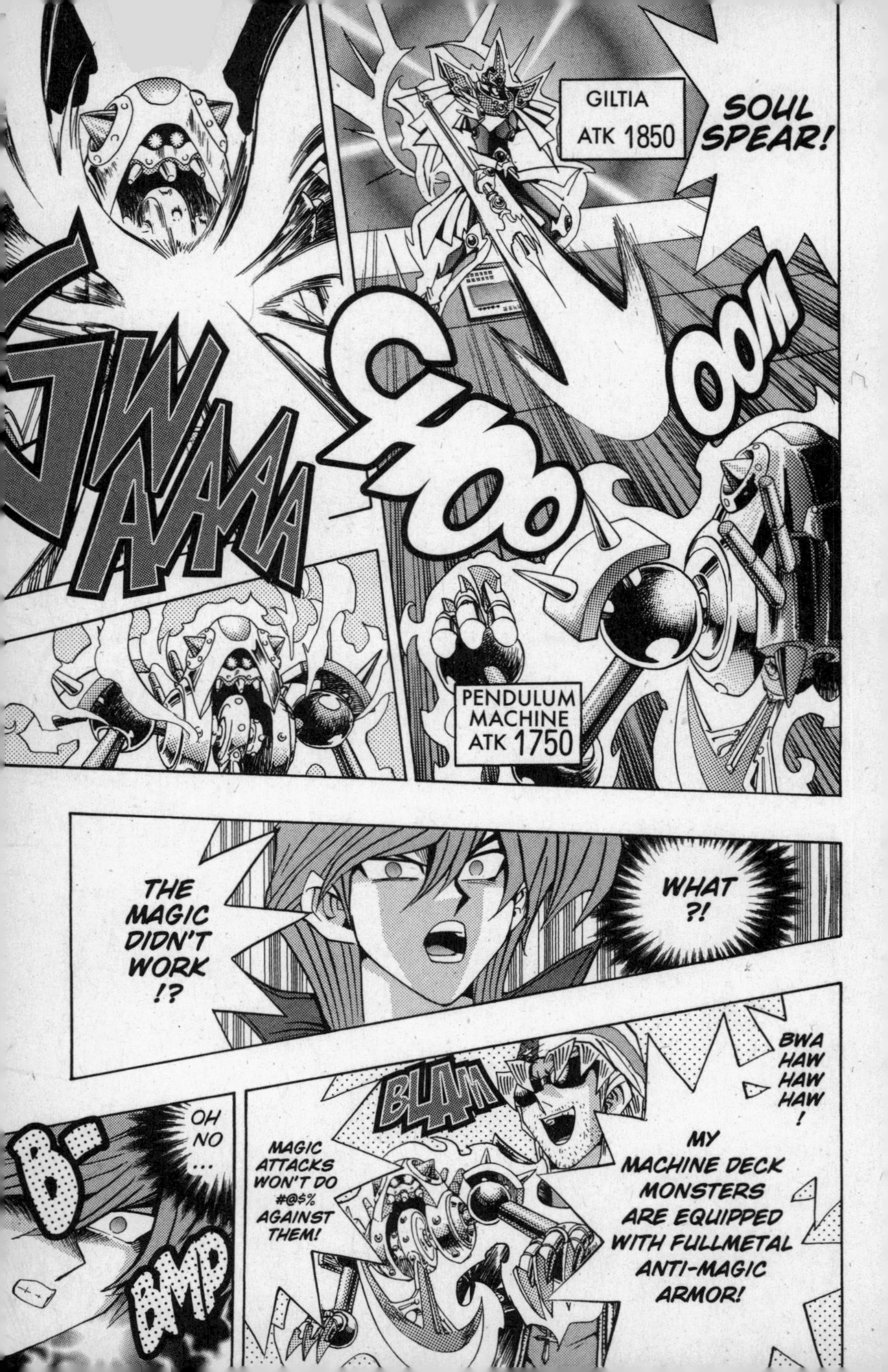
SOUL SPEAR!
GILTIA
ATK 1850
GOOOOOM
JWAAAA
PENDULUM MACHINE ATK 1750
WHAT ?!
THE MAGIC DIDN'T WORK !?
BWA HAW HAW HAW !
BLAM
MY MACHINE DECK MONSTERS ARE EQUIPPED WITH FULLMETAL ANTI-MAGIC ARMOR!
MAGIC ATTACKS WON'T DO #@$% AGAINST THEM!
OH NO ...
B
BMP

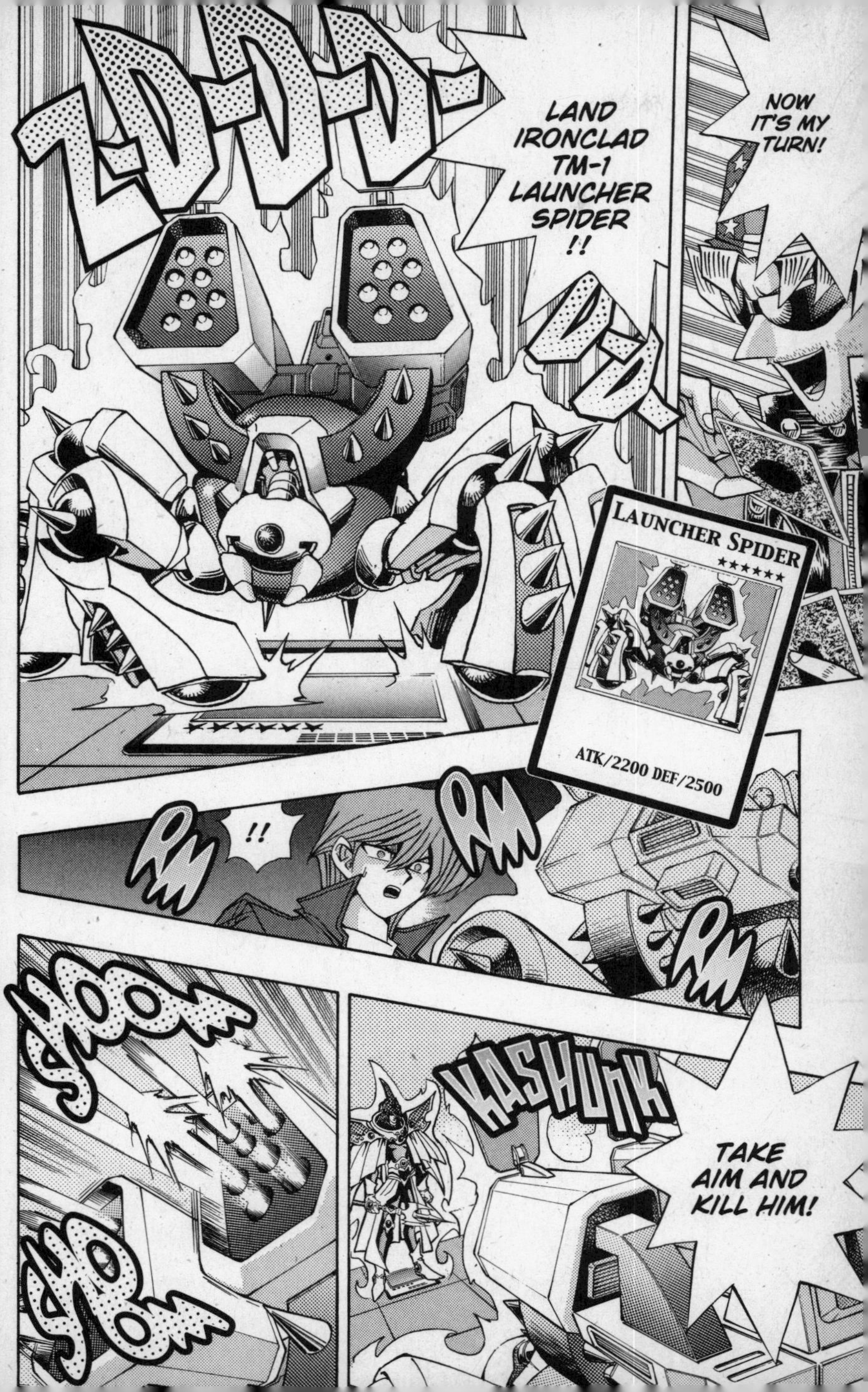
NOW IT'S MY TURN!
Z-D-D-D-
LAND IRONCLAD TM-1 LAUNCHER SPIDER !!
LAUNCHER SPIDER
ATK/2200 DEF/2500
RM
!!
RM
RM
KASHUNK
TAKE AIM AND KILL HIM!

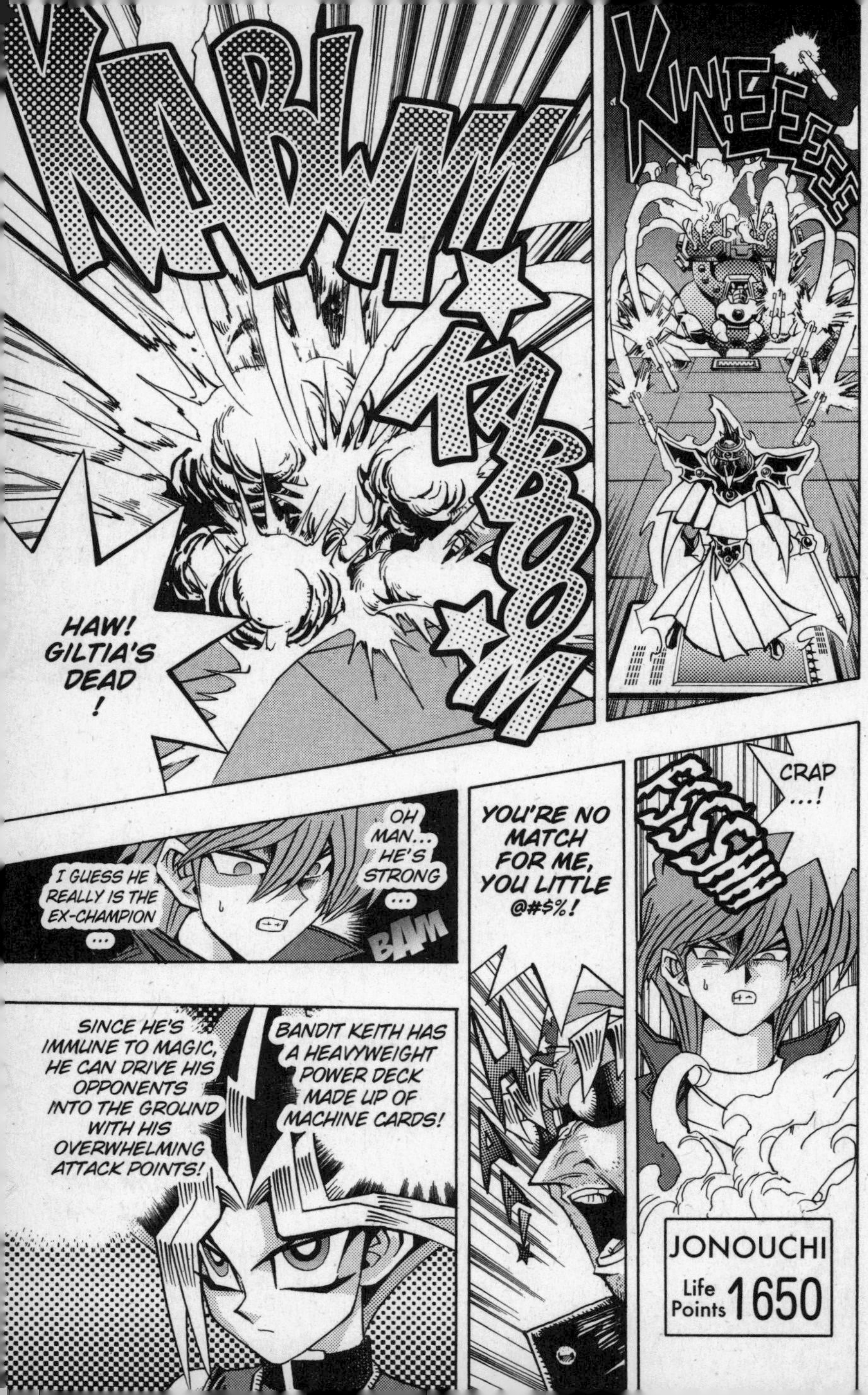

KIWEEEEEE
KABLAM
KABOOM
HAW! GILTIA'S DEAD!
CRAP...!
JONOUCHI
Life Points 1650
YOU'RE NO MATCH FOR ME, YOU LITTLE @#$%!
OH MAN... HE'S STRONG...
I GUESS HE REALLY IS THE EX-CHAMPION...
BAM
BANDIT KEITH HAS A HEAVYWEIGHT POWER DECK MADE UP OF MACHINE CARDS!
SINCE HE'S IMMUNE TO MAGIC, HE CAN DRIVE HIS OPPONENTS INTO THE GROUND WITH HIS OVERWHELMING ATTACK POINTS!

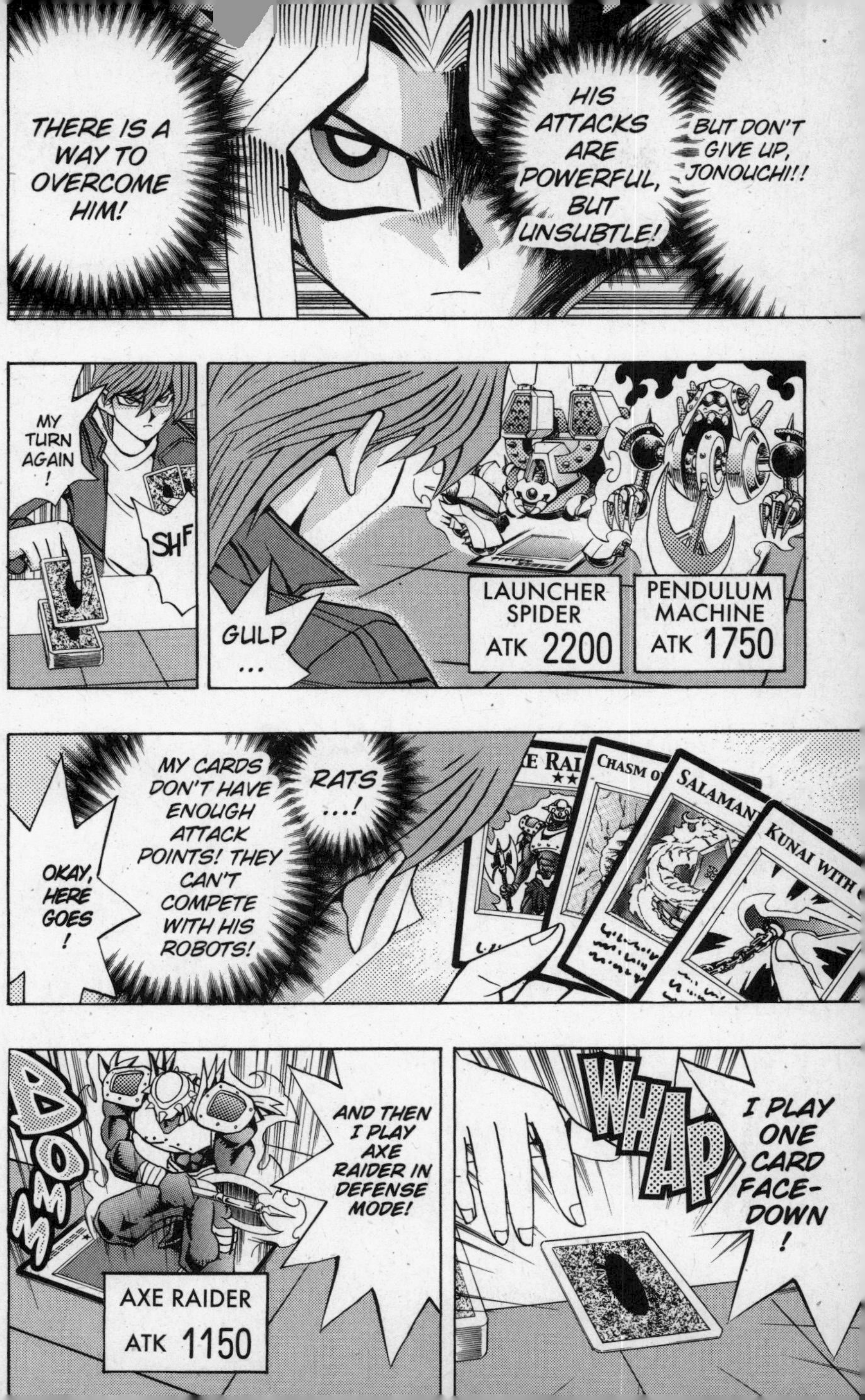
BUT DON'T GIVE UP, JONOUCHI!!
HIS ATTACKS ARE POWERFUL, BUT UNSUBTLE!
THERE IS A WAY TO OVERCOME HIM!
PENDULUM MACHINE ATK 1750
LAUNCHER SPIDER ATK 2200
GULP ...
MY TURN AGAIN!
SHF
RATS ...!
MY CARDS DON'T HAVE ENOUGH ATTACK POINTS! THEY CAN'T COMPETE WITH HIS ROBOTS!
OKAY, HERE GOES!
WHAP
I PLAY ONE CARD FACE-DOWN!
AND THEN I PLAY AXE RAIDER IN DEFENSE MODE!
BOOM
AXE RAIDER ATK 1150

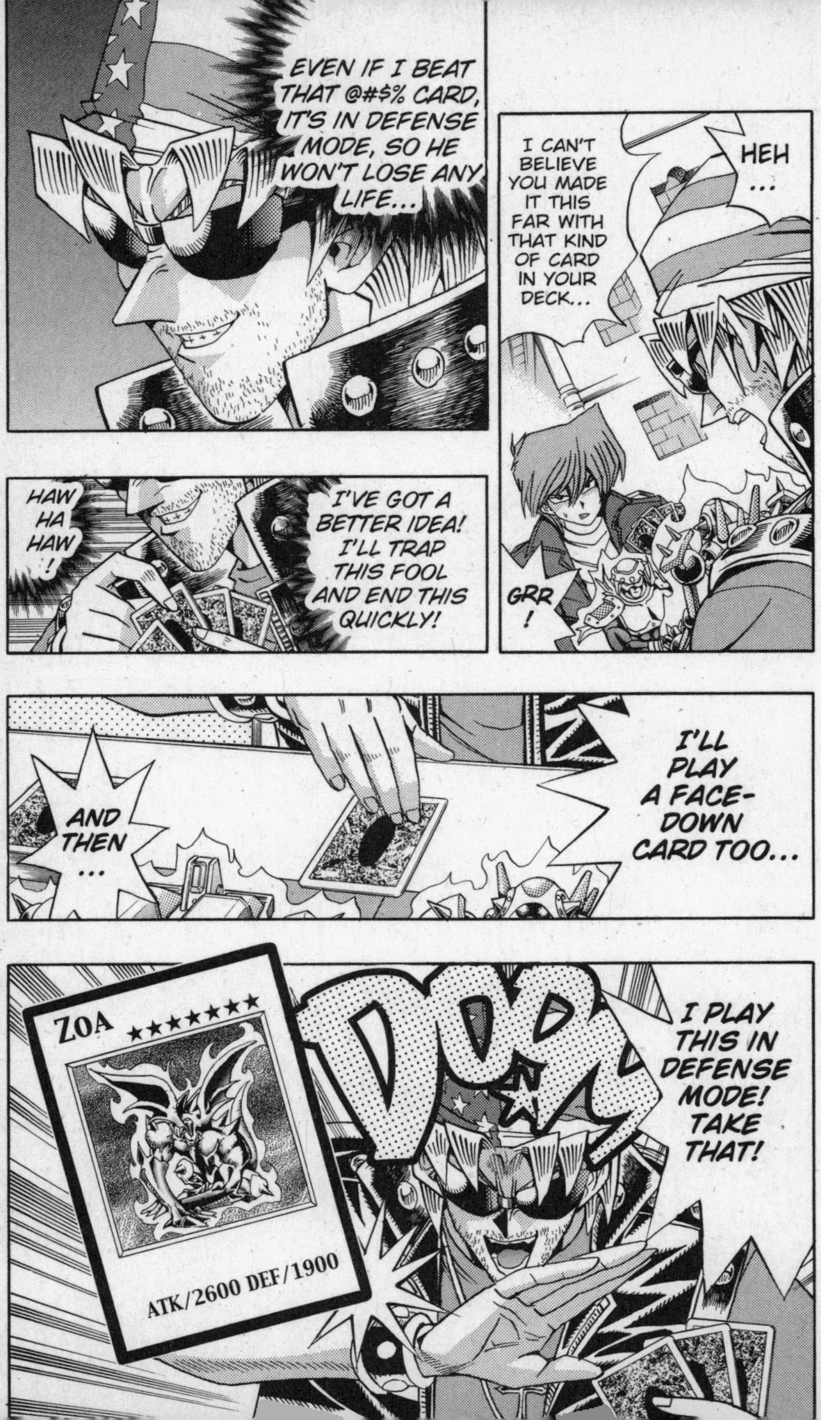
HEH ...
I CAN'T BELIEVE YOU MADE IT THIS FAR WITH THAT KIND OF CARD IN YOUR DECK...
GRR !
EVEN IF I BEAT THAT @#$% CARD, IT'S IN DEFENSE MODE, SO HE WON'T LOSE ANY LIFE...
I'VE GOT A BETTER IDEA! I'LL TRAP THIS FOOL AND END THIS QUICKLY!
HAW HA HAW !
I'LL PLAY A FACE-DOWN CARD TOO...
AND THEN ...
I PLAY THIS IN DEFENSE MODE! TAKE THAT!
ZOA
ATK/2600 DEF/1900

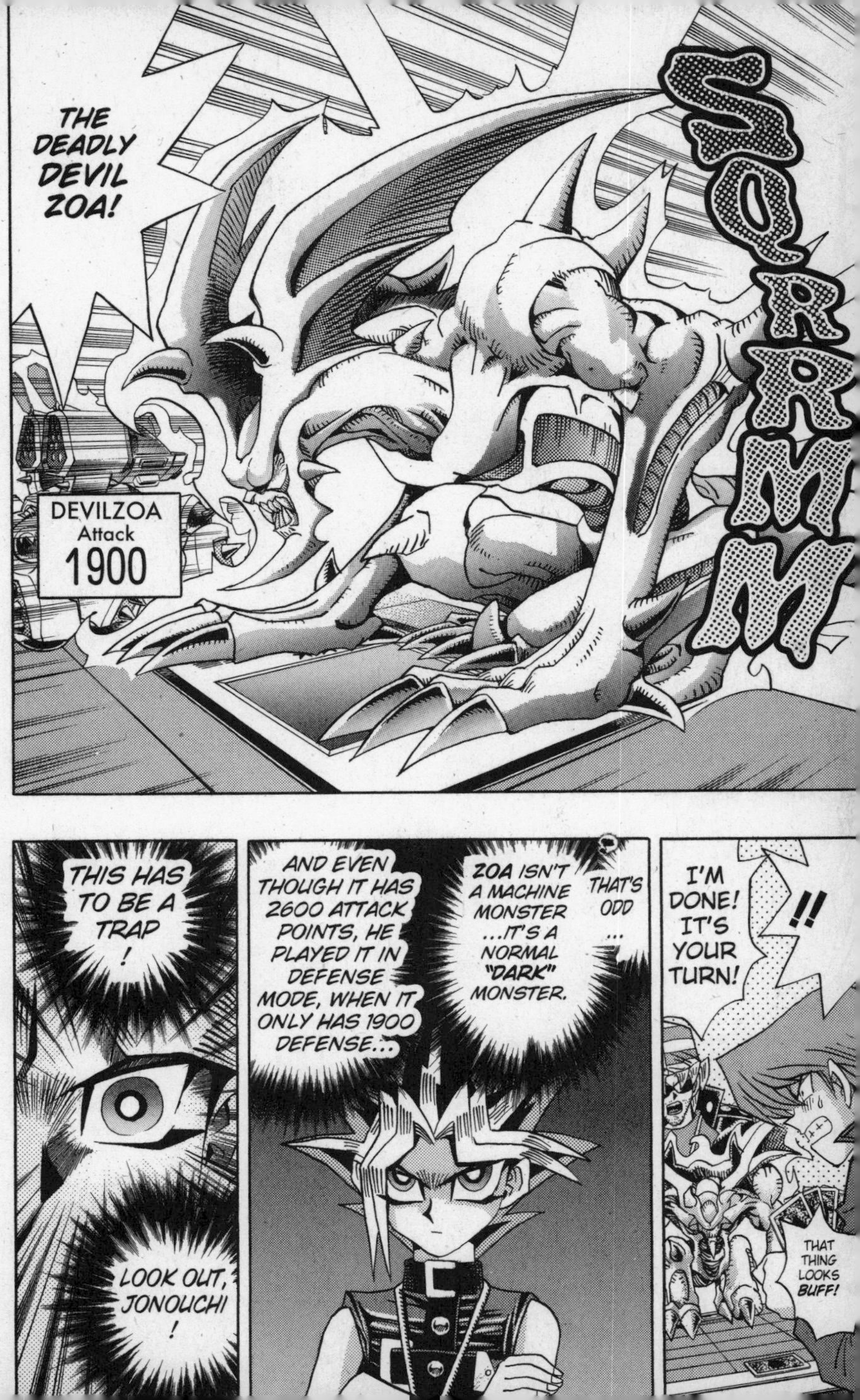
SQRMM
THE DEADLY DEVIL ZOA!
DEVILZOA Attack 1900
I'M DONE! IT'S YOUR TURN!
!!
THAT THING LOOKS BUFF!
THAT'S ODD ...
ZOA ISN'T A MACHINE MONSTER ...IT'S A NORMAL "DARK" MONSTER.
AND EVEN THOUGH IT HAS 2600 ATTACK POINTS, HE PLAYED IT IN DEFENSE MODE, WHEN IT ONLY HAS 1900 DEFENSE...
THIS HAS TO BE A TRAP!
LOOK OUT, JONOUCHI!

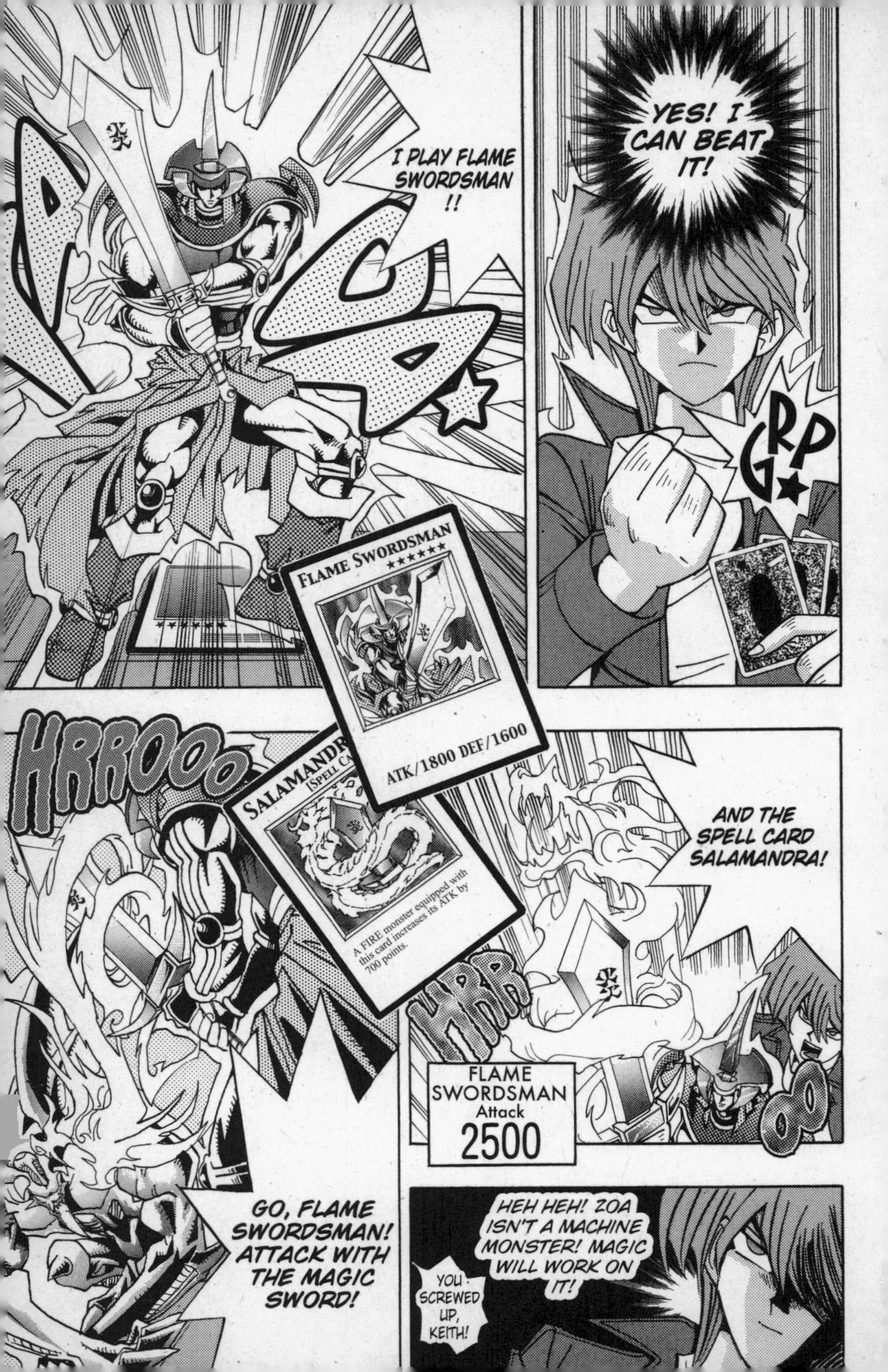

YES! I CAN BEAT IT!
GRP
I PLAY FLAME SWORDSMAN !!
FLAME SWORDSMAN
ATK/1800 DEF/1600
AND THE SPELL CARD SALAMANDRA!
HRR
FLAME SWORDSMAN Attack 2500
GOO
HEH HEH! ZOA ISN'T A MACHINE MONSTER! MAGIC WILL WORK ON IT!
YOU SCREWED UP, KEITH!
HRROOO
A FIRE monster equipped with this card increases its ATK by 700 points.
GO, FLAME SWORDSMAN! ATTACK WITH THE MAGIC SWORD!

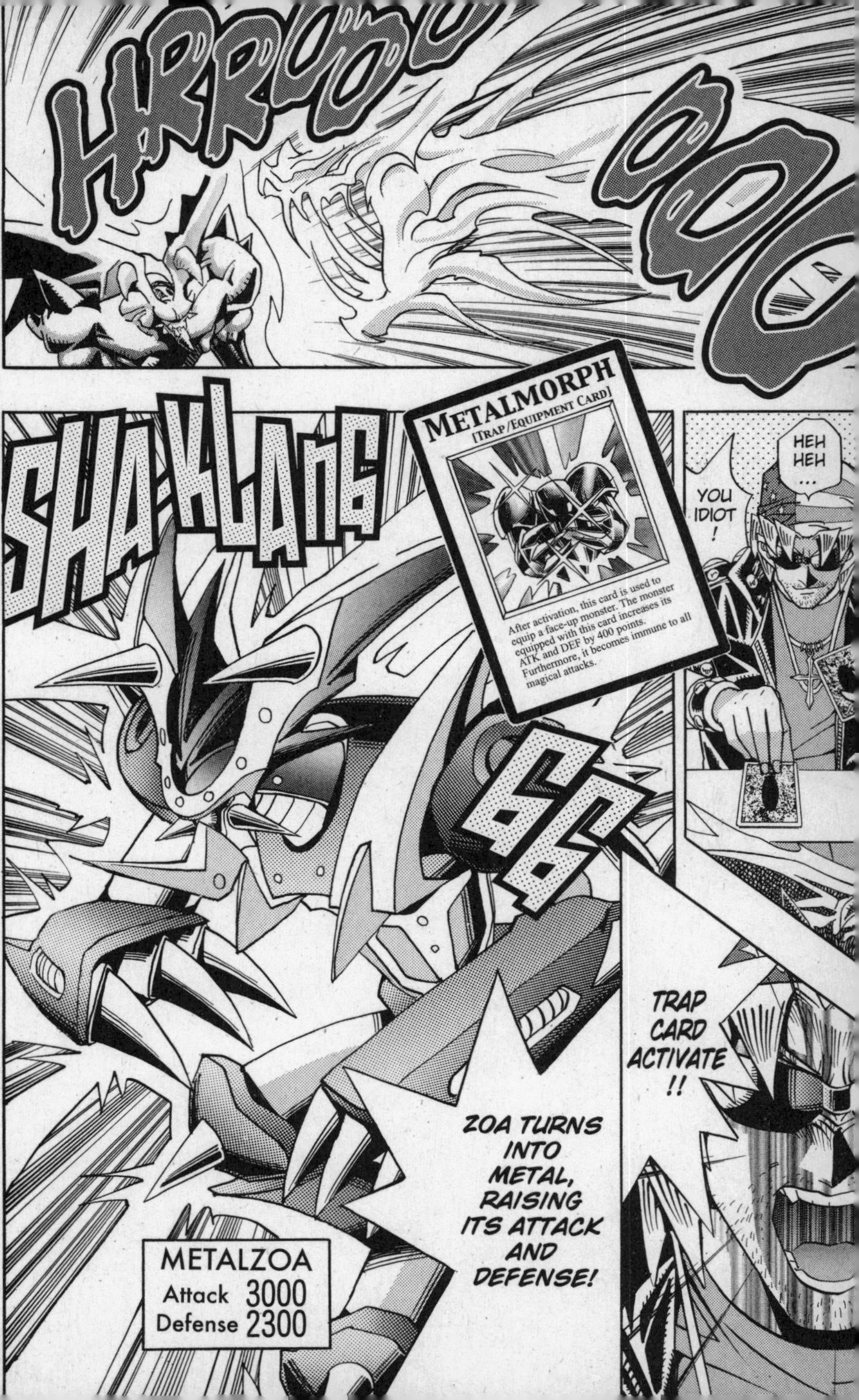
HEH HEH ...
YOU IDIOT !
METALMORPH
[TRAP/EQUIPMENT CARD]
After activation, this card is used to equip a face-up monster. The monster equipped with this card increases its ATK and DEF by 400 points. Furthermore, it becomes immune to all magical attacks.
SHAKLANG
TRAP CARD ACTIVATE !!
ZOA TURNS INTO METAL, RAISING ITS ATTACK AND DEFENSE!
METALZOA
Attack 3000
Defense 2300

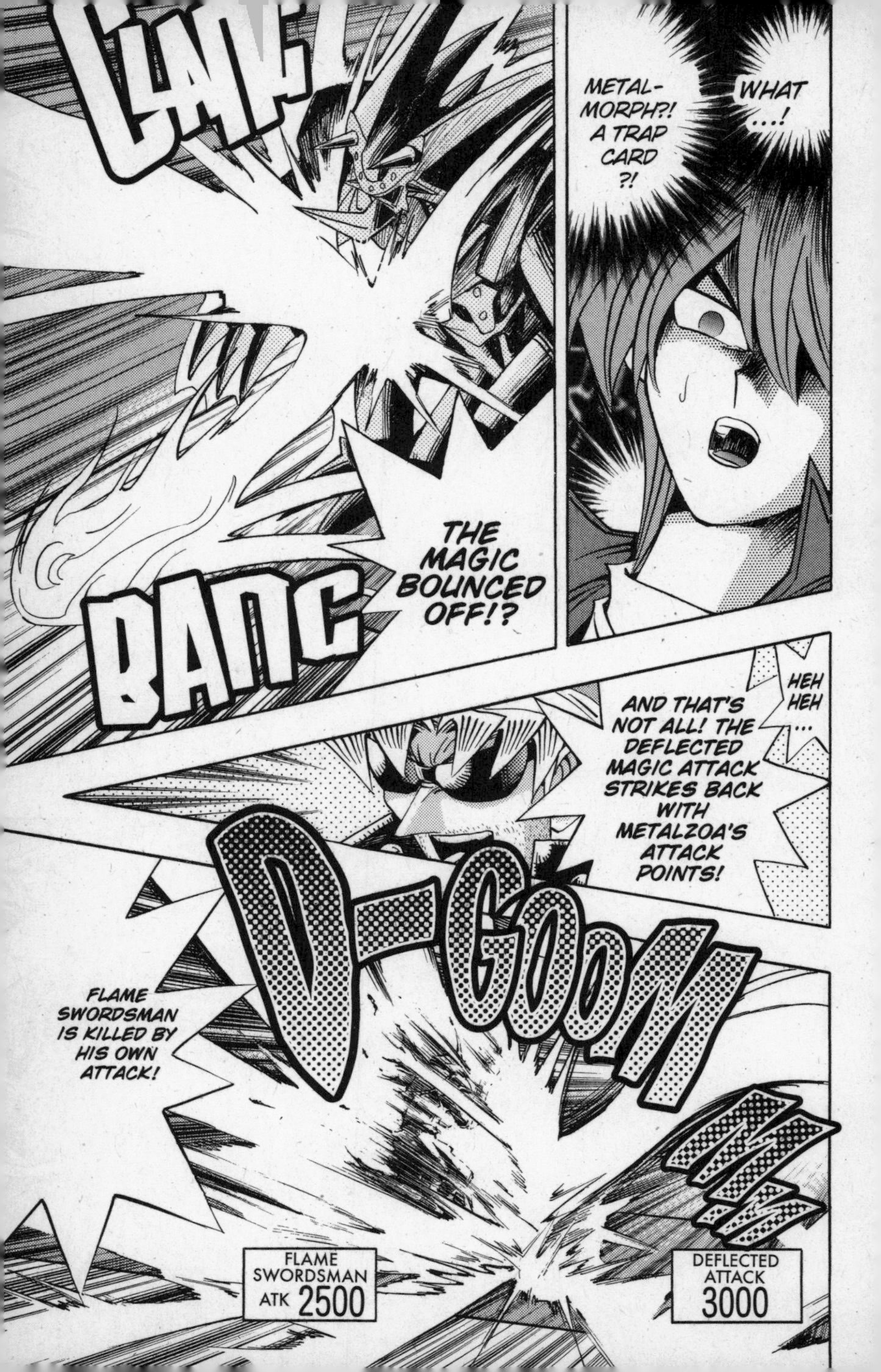
WHAT ...!
METAL-MORPH?! A TRAP CARD ?!
CLAK!
THE MAGIC BOUNCED OFF!?
BANC
HEH HEH ...
AND THAT'S NOT ALL! THE DEFLECTED MAGIC ATTACK STRIKES BACK WITH METALZOA'S ATTACK POINTS!
D-GOOM
FLAME SWORDSMAN IS KILLED BY HIS OWN ATTACK!
DEFLECTED ATTACK 3000
FLAME SWORDSMAN ATK 2500

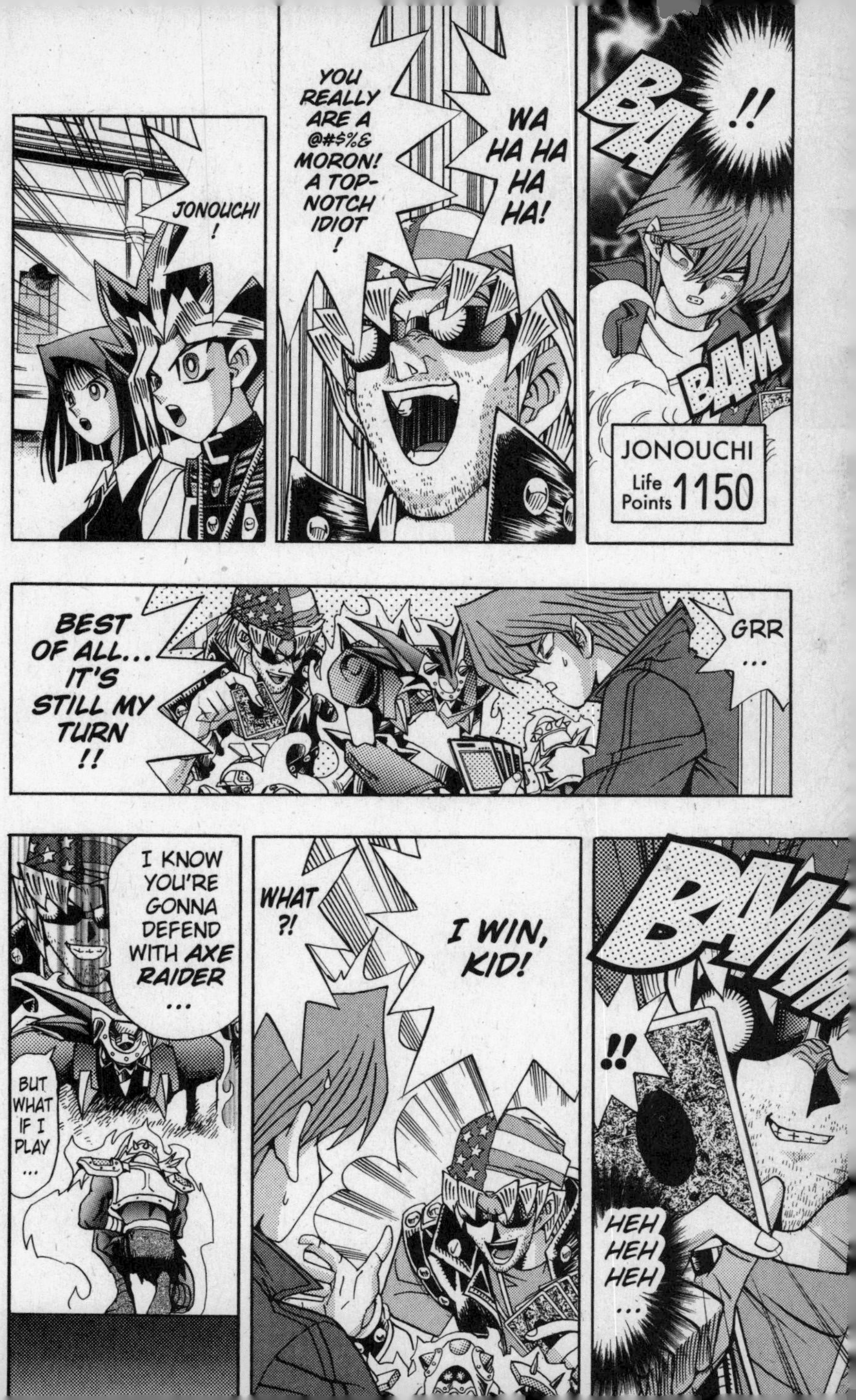
BA !!
BAM
JONOUCHI Life Points 1150
WA HA HA HA HA!
YOU REALLY ARE A @#$%& MORON! A TOP-NOTCH IDIOT!
JONOUCHI!
GRR...
BEST OF ALL... IT'S STILL MY TURN!!
BAM
!!
HEH HEH HEH...
I WIN, KID!
WHAT?!
I KNOW YOU'RE GONNA DEFEND WITH AXE RAIDER...
BUT WHAT IF I PLAY...

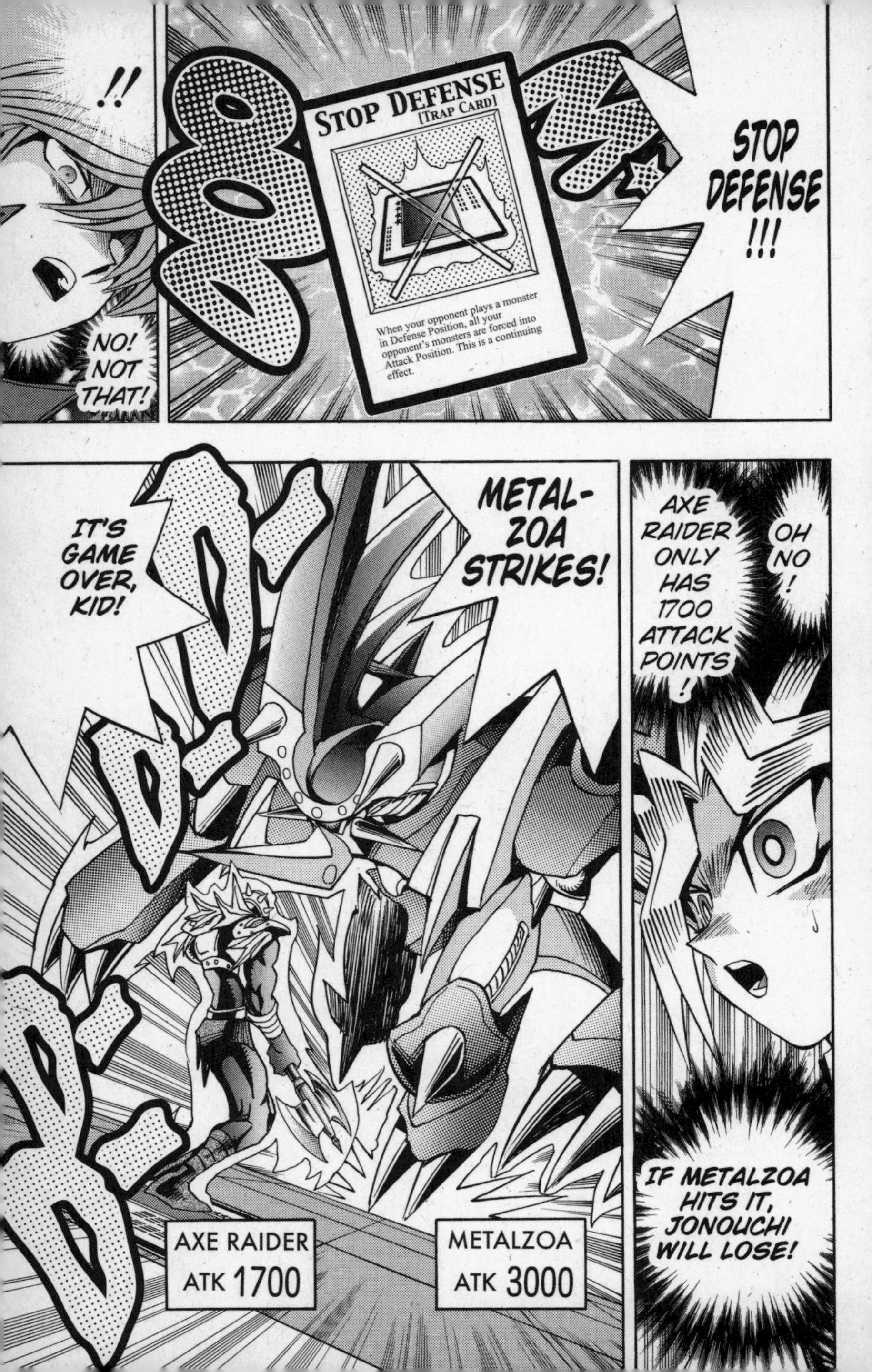
STOP DEFENSE !!!
STOP DEFENSE [TRAP CARD]
When your opponent plays a monster in Defense Position, all your opponent's monsters are forced into Attack Position. This is a continuing effect.
!!
NO! NOT THAT!
OH NO!
AXE RAIDER ONLY HAS 1700 ATTACK POINTS!
IF METALZOA HITS IT, JONOUCHI WILL LOSE!
METAL-ZOA STRIKES!
IT'S GAME OVER, KID!
METALZOA ATK 3000
AXE RAIDER ATK 1700

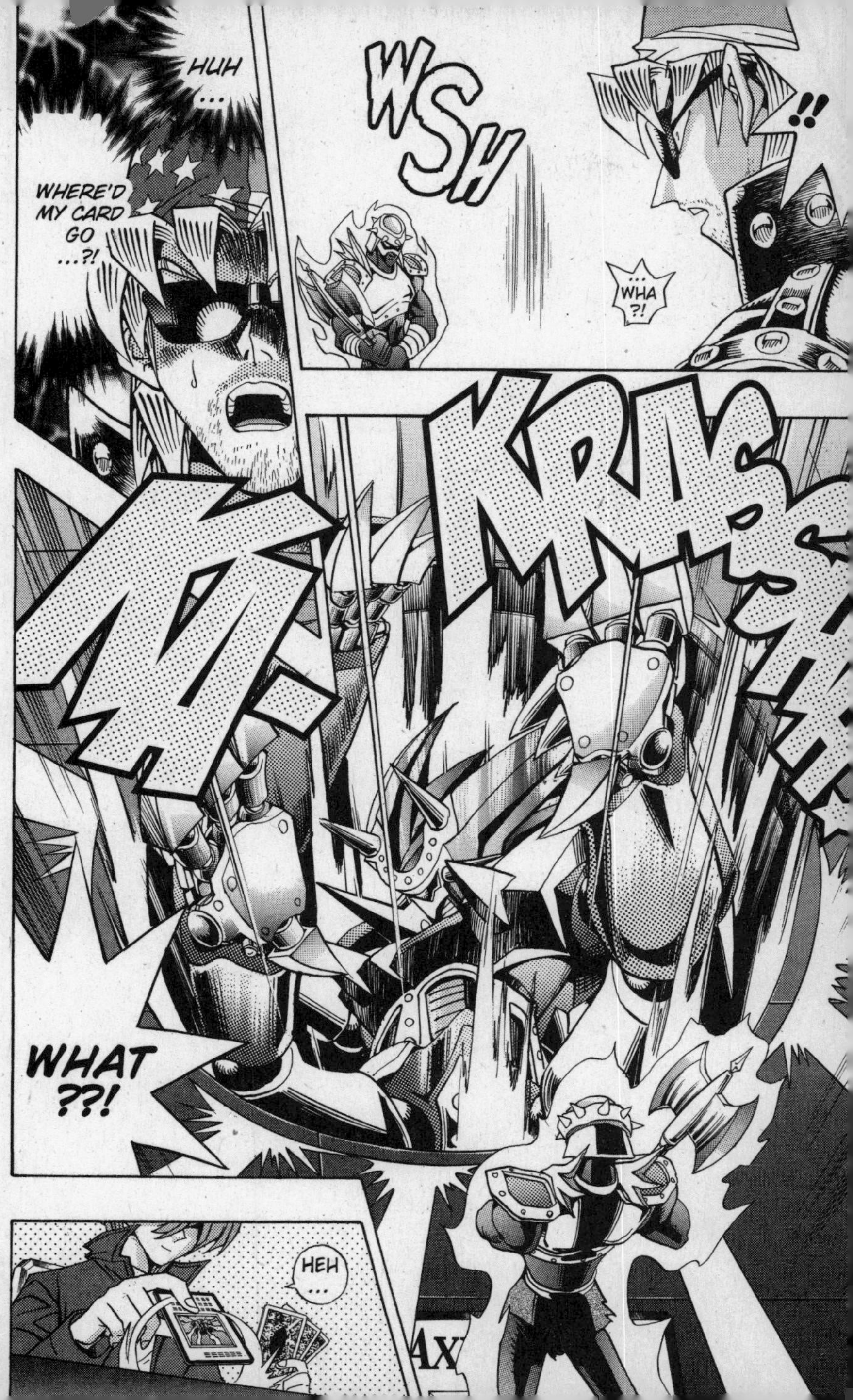
!!
...WHA?!
WSH
HUH...
WHERE'D MY CARD GO ...?!
WHAT ??!
HEH ...

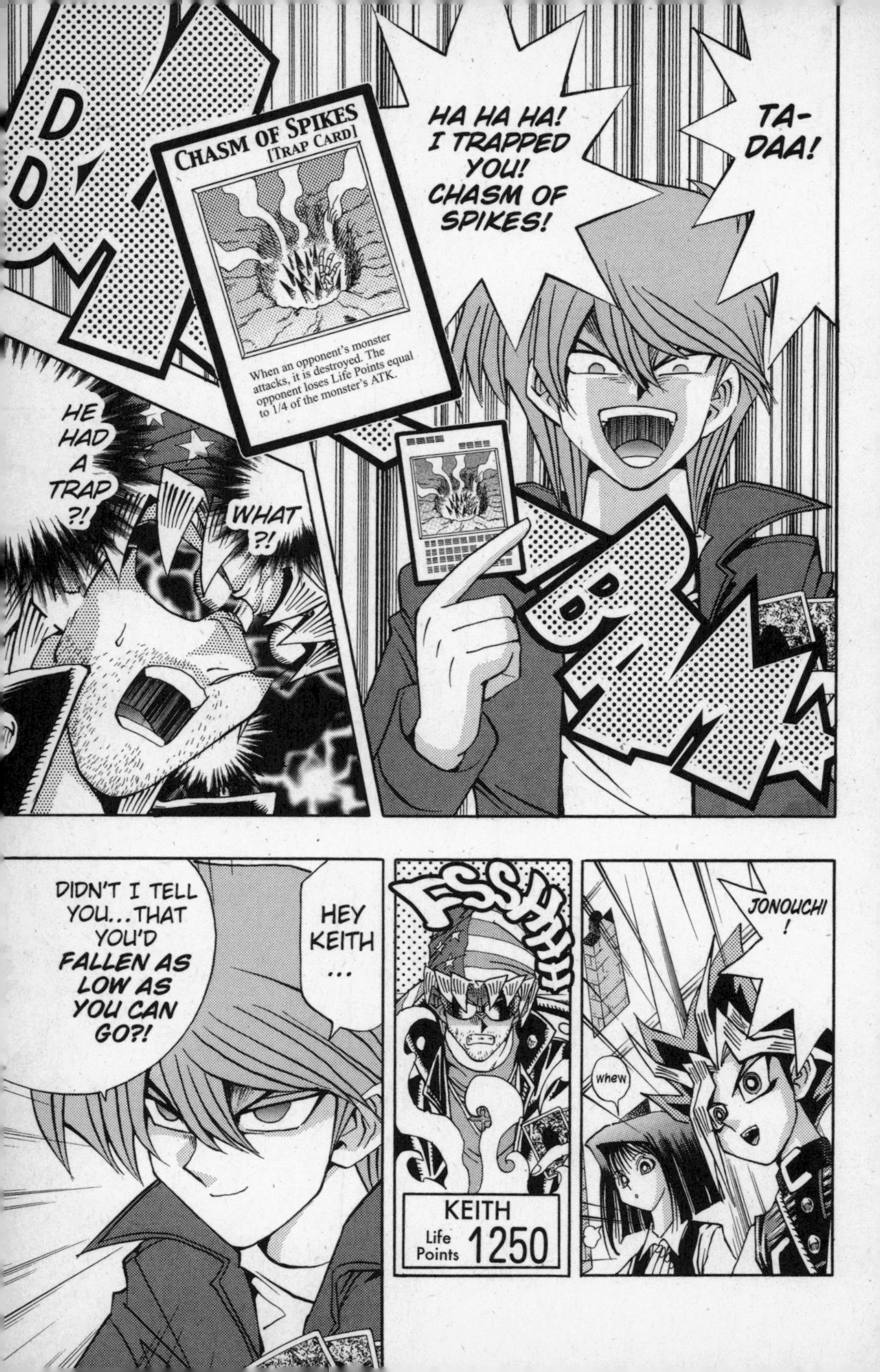
TA-DAA!
HA HA HA! I TRAPPED YOU! CHASM OF SPIKES!
CHASM OF SPIKES
[TRAP CARD]
When an opponent's monster attacks, it is destroyed. The opponent loses Life Points equal to 1/4 of the monster's ATK.
D
D
WHAT ?!
HE HAD A TRAP ?!
JONOUCHI !
whew
KEITH
Life Points 1250
HEY KEITH ...
DIDN'T I TELL YOU...THAT YOU'D FALLEN AS LOW AS YOU CAN GO?!

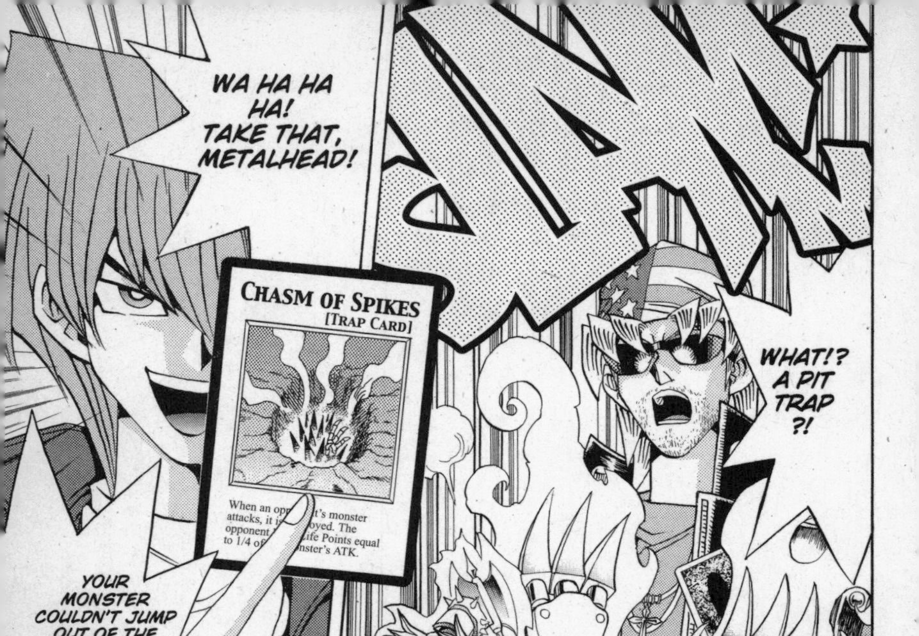
WHAT!? A PIT TRAP ?!
WA HA HA HA! TAKE THAT, METALHEAD!
CHASM OF SPIKES
[TRAP CARD]
YOUR MONSTER COULDN'T JUMP OUT OF THE WAY! THE BIGGER THEY COME, THE HARDER THEY FALL!
FSSSSHH
GRR RR ...
YOU #$@% GOT ME ...

Duel 62: Rise of the Machines

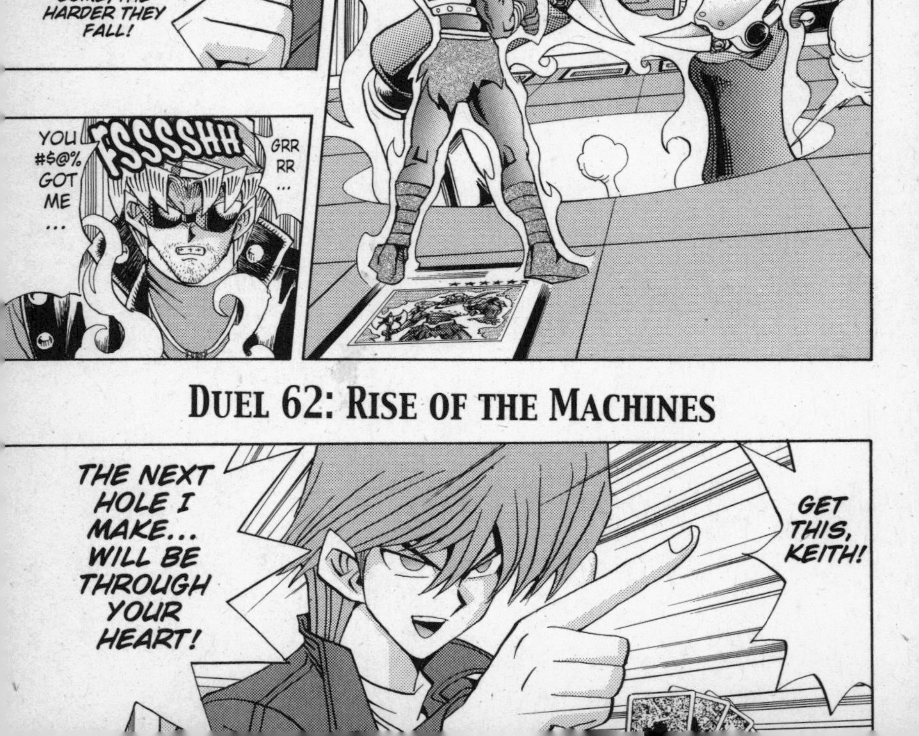
GET THIS, KEITH!
THE NEXT HOLE I MAKE... WILL BE THROUGH YOUR HEART!

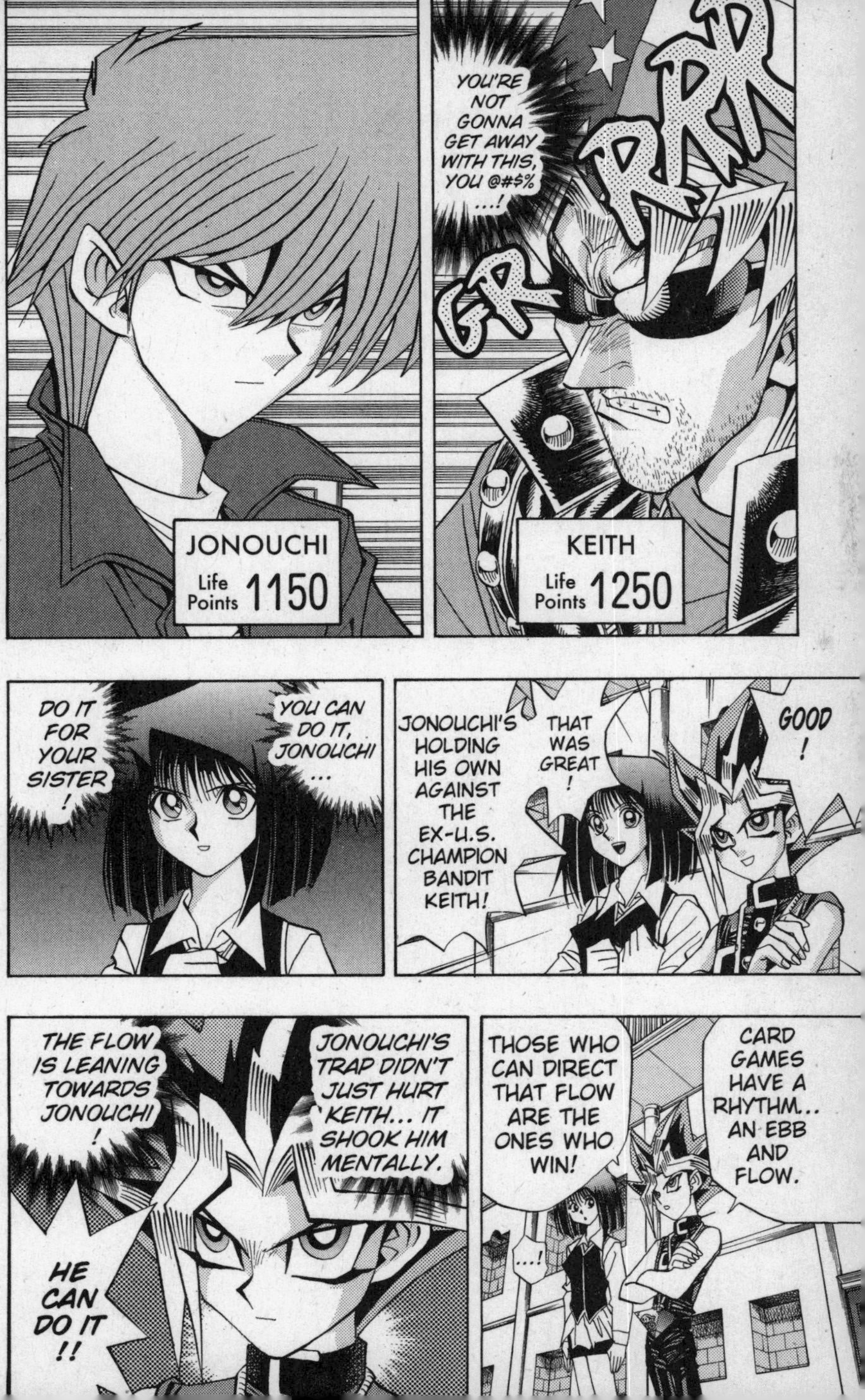
YOU'RE NOT GONNA GET AWAY WITH THIS, YOU @#$% ...!
GRRRR
KEITH Life Points 1250
JONOUCHI Life Points 1150
GOOD!
THAT WAS GREAT!
JONOUCHI'S HOLDING HIS OWN AGAINST THE EX-U.S. CHAMPION BANDIT KEITH!
YOU CAN DO IT, JONOUCHI...
DO IT FOR YOUR SISTER!
CARD GAMES HAVE A RHYTHM... AN EBB AND FLOW.
THOSE WHO CAN DIRECT THAT FLOW ARE THE ONES WHO WIN!
...!
JONOUCHI'S TRAP DIDN'T JUST HURT KEITH... IT SHOOK HIM MENTALLY.
THE FLOW IS LEANING TOWARDS JONOUCHI!
HE CAN DO IT!!

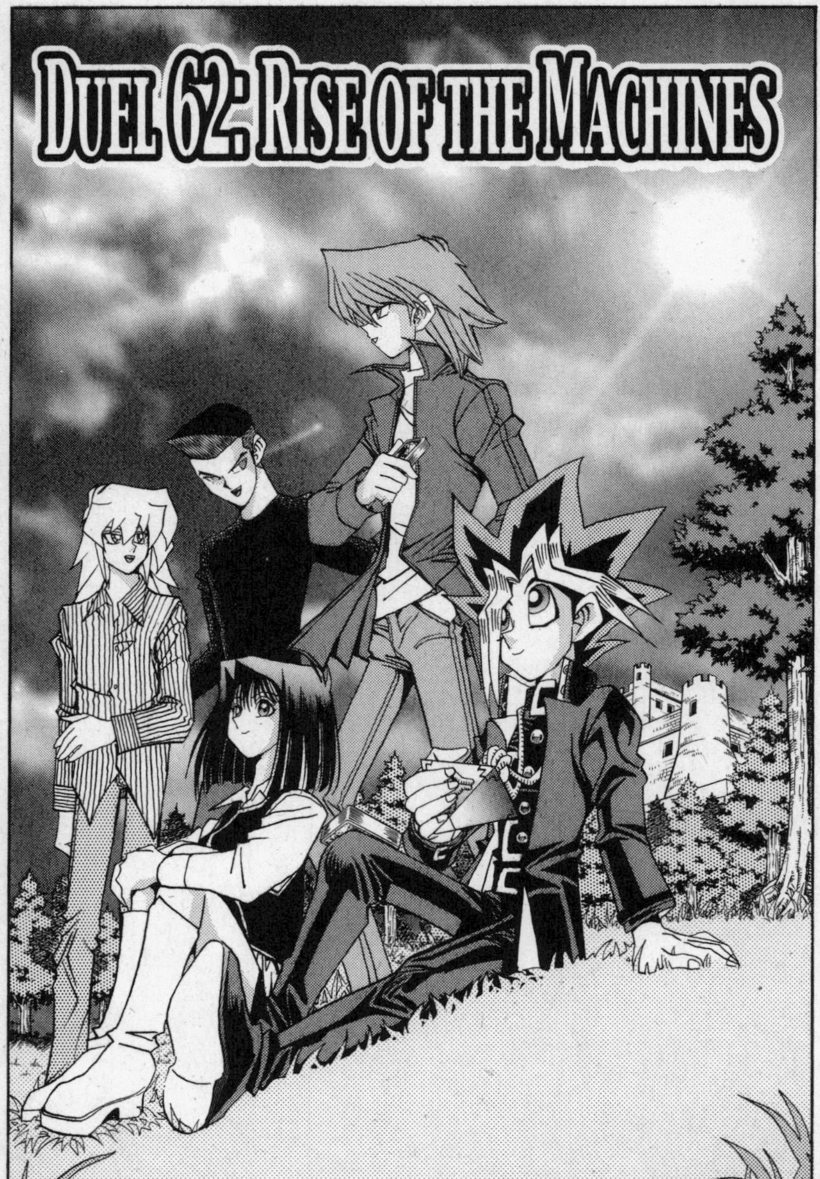
DUEL 62: RISE OF THE MACHINES

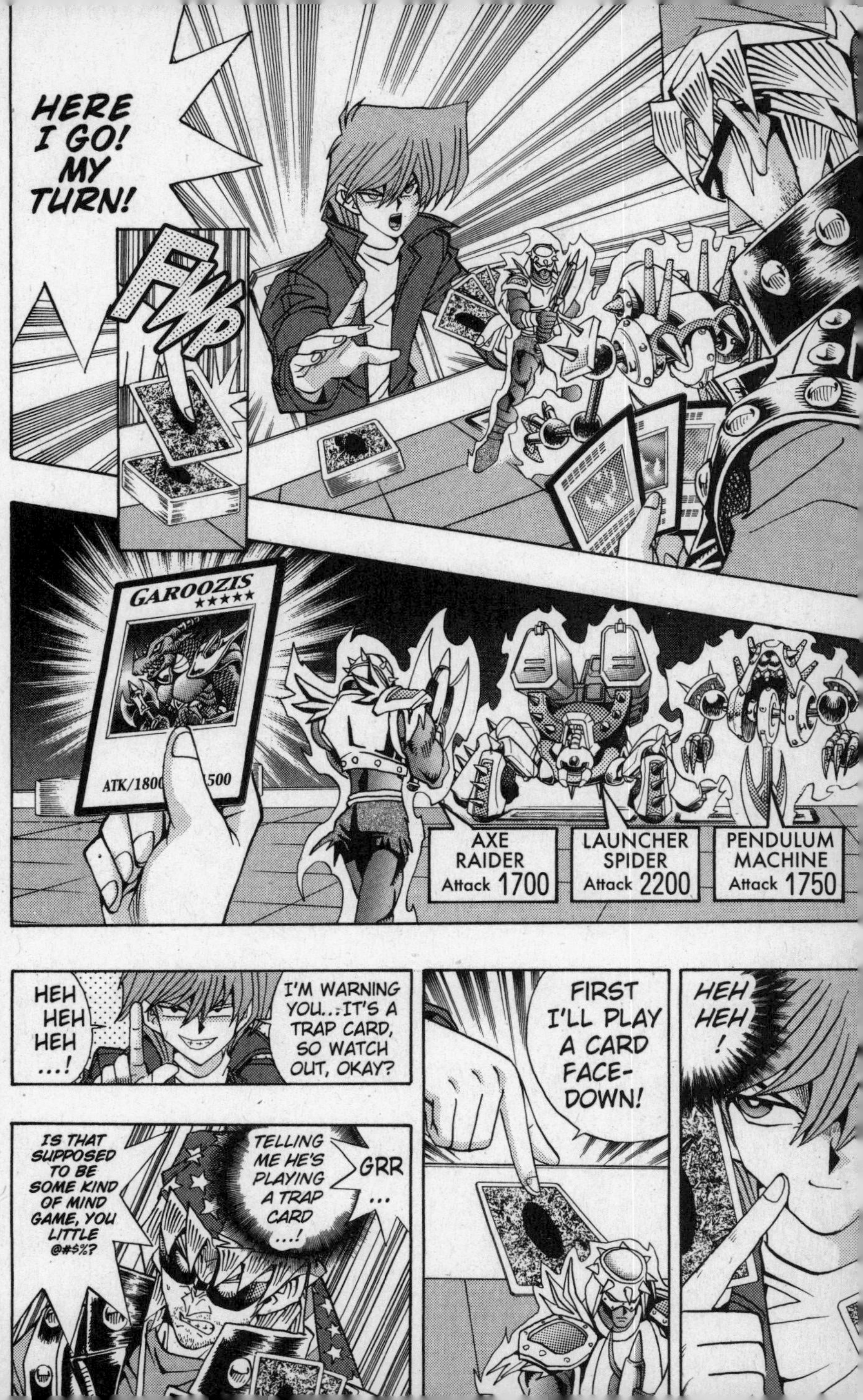
HERE I GO! MY TURN!
FWIP
GAROOZIS
ATK/1800
1500
PENDULUM MACHINE Attack 1750
LAUNCHER SPIDER Attack 2200
AXE RAIDER Attack 1700
HEH HEH !
FIRST I'LL PLAY A CARD FACE-DOWN!
I'M WARNING YOU...IT'S A TRAP CARD, SO WATCH OUT, OKAY?
HEH HEH HEH ...!
GRR ...
TELLING ME HE'S PLAYING A TRAP CARD ...!
IS THAT SUPPOSED TO BE SOME KIND OF MIND GAME, YOU LITTLE @#$%?

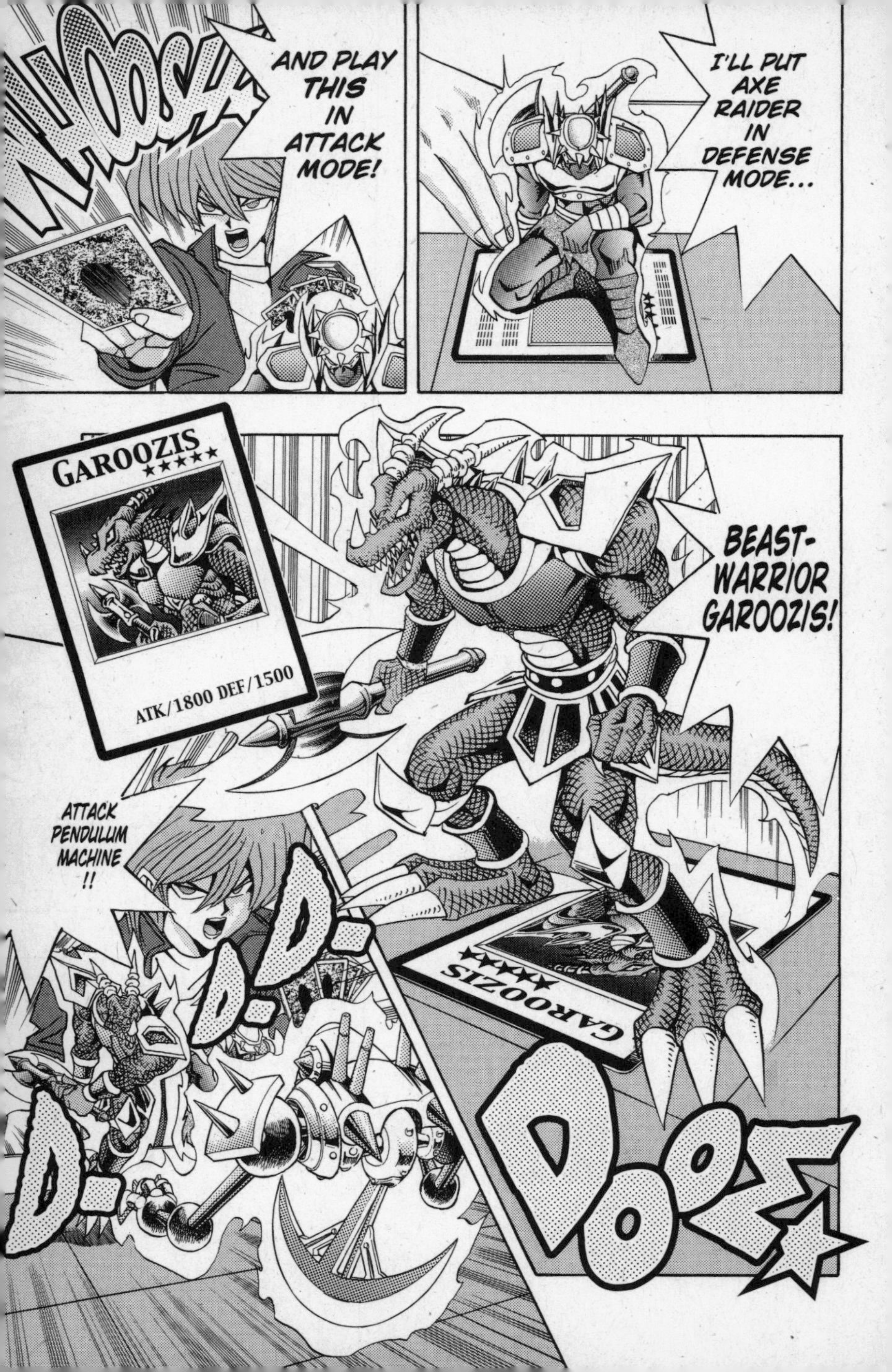
I'LL PUT AXE RAIDER IN DEFENSE MODE...
WHOOSH
AND PLAY THIS IN ATTACK MODE!
BEAST-WARRIOR GAROOZIS!
GAROOZIS
ATK/1800 DEF/1500
GAROOZIS
ATTACK PENDULUM MACHINE !!
DOOF
D-D-D

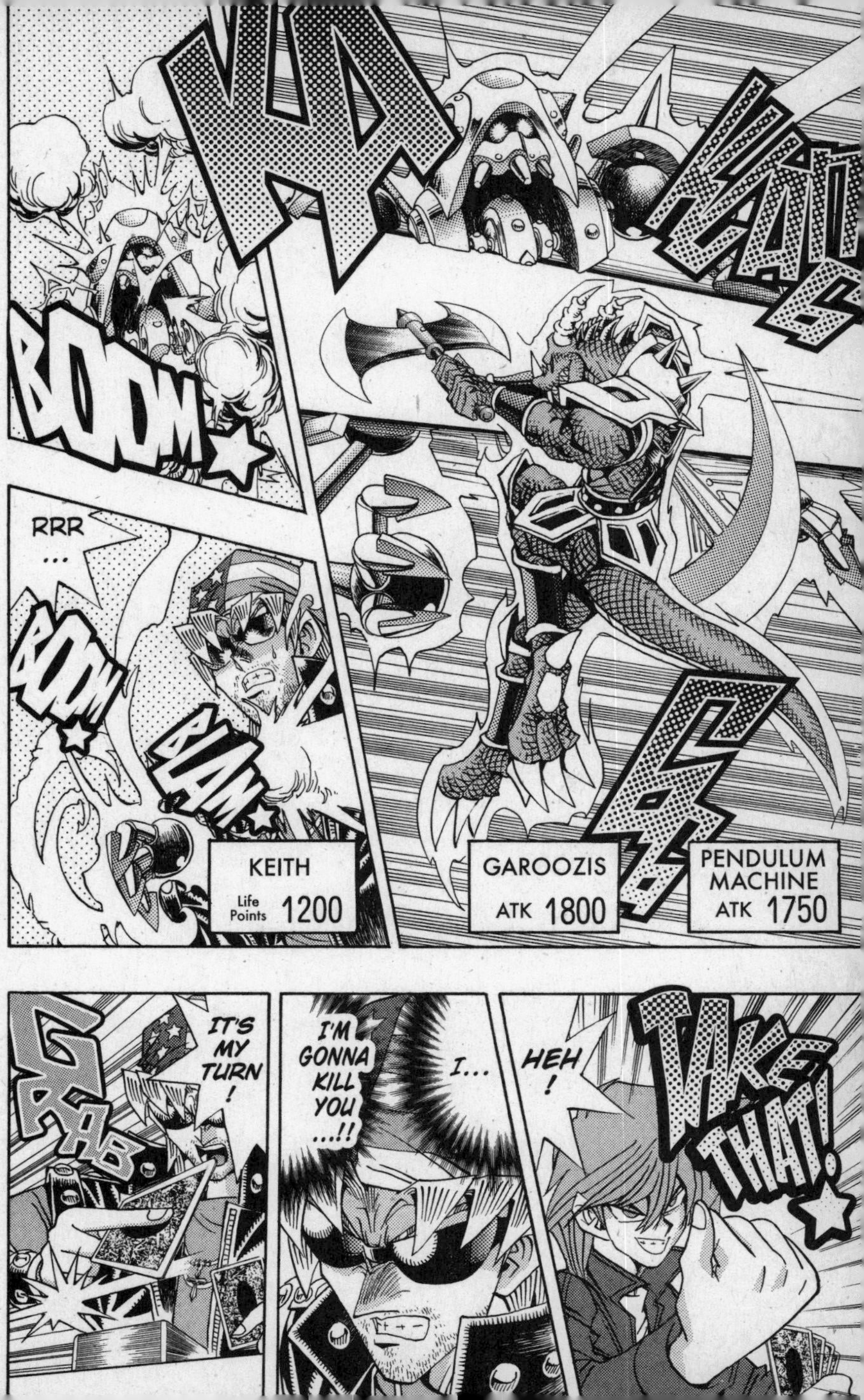
PENDULUM MACHINE ATK 1750
GAROOZIS ATK 1800
BOOM
RRR ...
BOOM
BLAM
KEITH Life Points 1200
TAKE THAT!
HEH!
I...
I'M GONNA KILL YOU ...!!
IT'S MY TURN!
GRAB

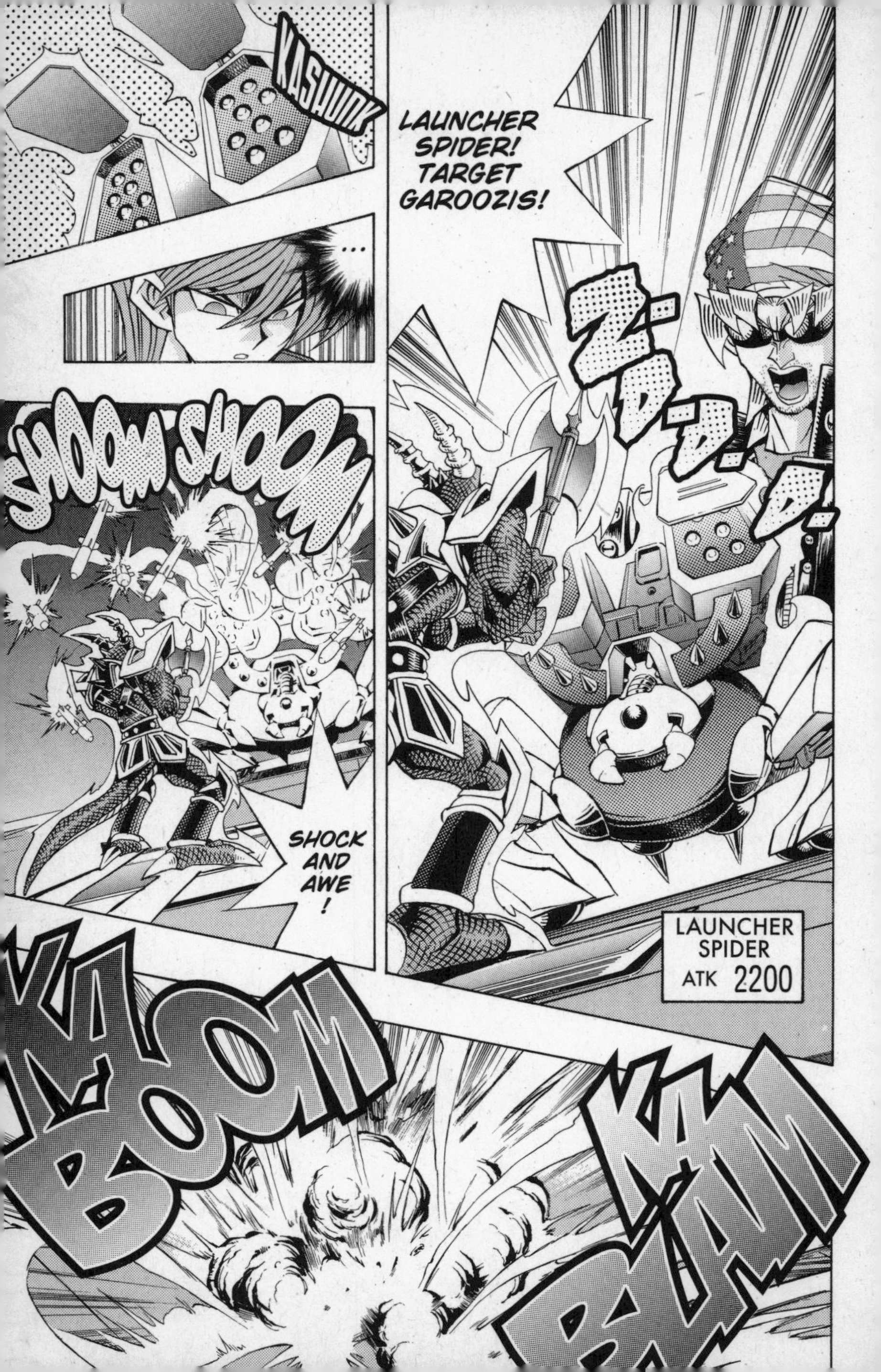
LAUNCHER SPIDER! TARGET GAROOZIS!
Z-D-D-D!
LAUNCHER SPIDER ATK 2200
KASHUNK
...
SHOOM SHOOM
SHOCK AND AWE!
KA-BAM
KA-BOOM

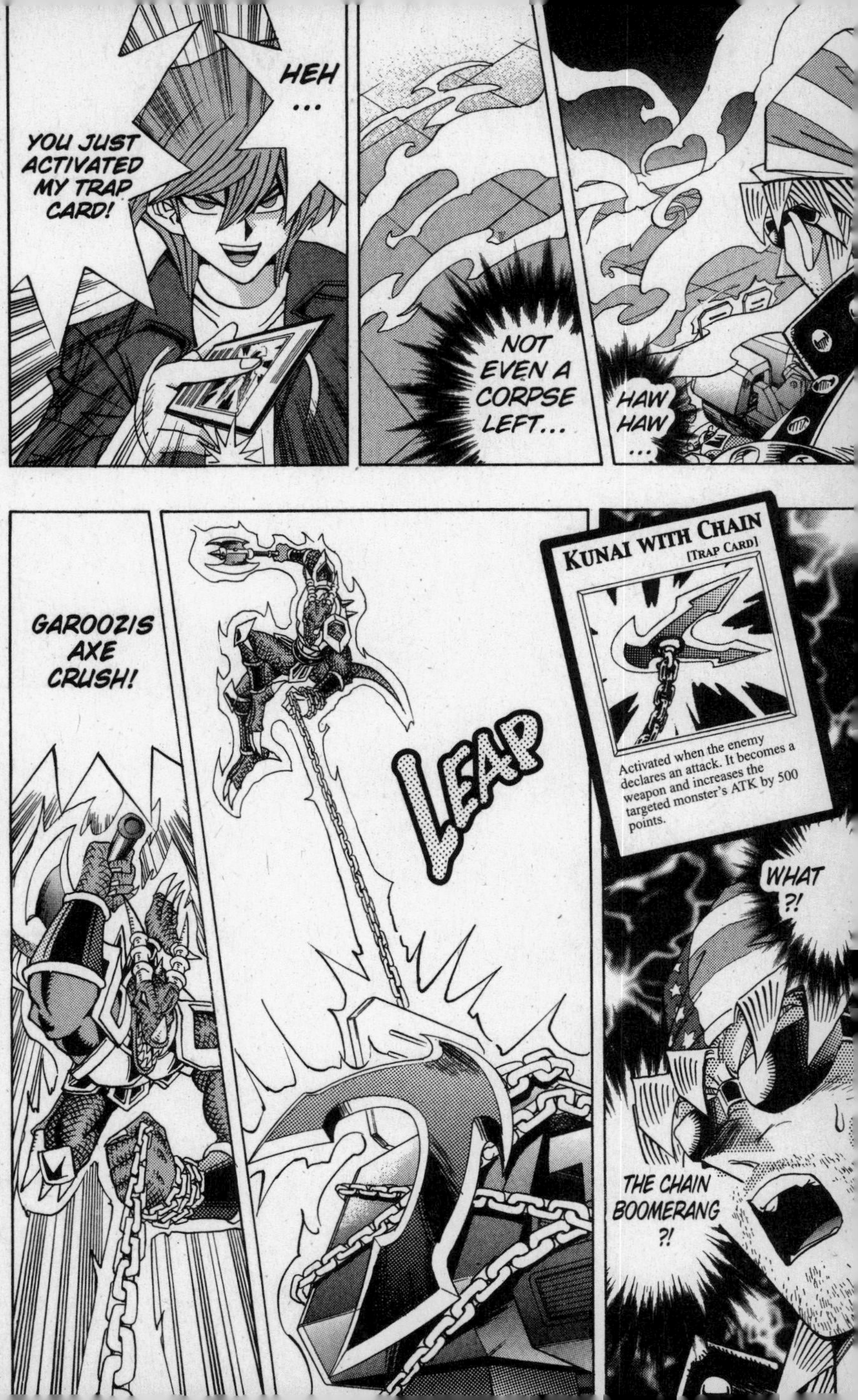
HAW HAW ...
NOT EVEN A CORPSE LEFT...
HEH ...
YOU JUST ACTIVATED MY TRAP CARD!
KUNAI WITH CHAIN
[TRAP CARD]
Activated when the enemy declares an attack. It becomes a weapon and increases the targeted monster's ATK by 500 points.
WHAT ?!
THE CHAIN BOOMERANG ?!
LEAP
GAROOZIS AXE CRUSH!

READ THIS WAY

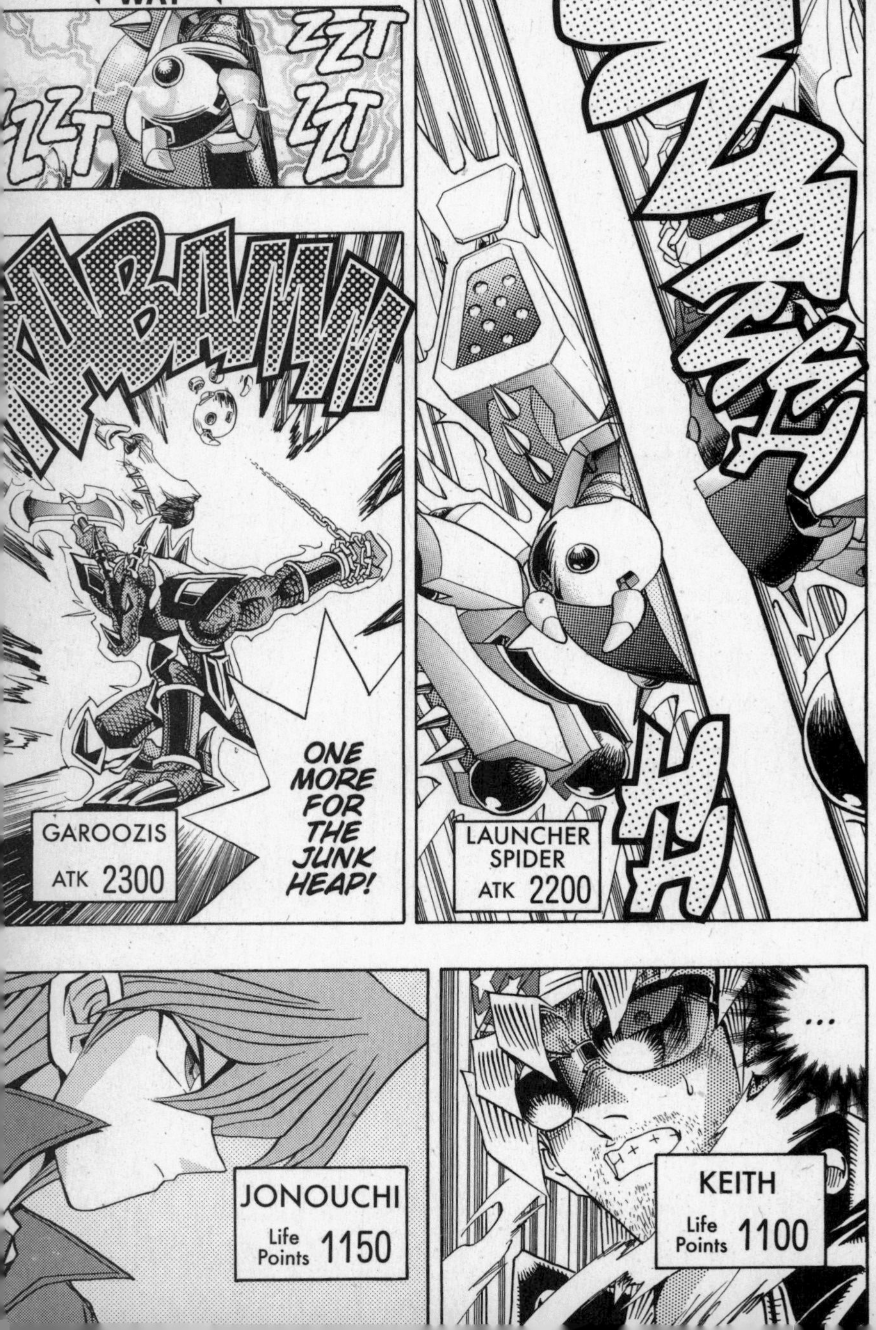
LAUNCHER SPIDER
ATK 2200
ZZZT
ZZZT
ZZZT
ONE MORE FOR THE JUNK HEAP!
GAROOZIS
ATK 2300
...
KEITH
Life Points 1100
JONOUCHI
Life Points 1150

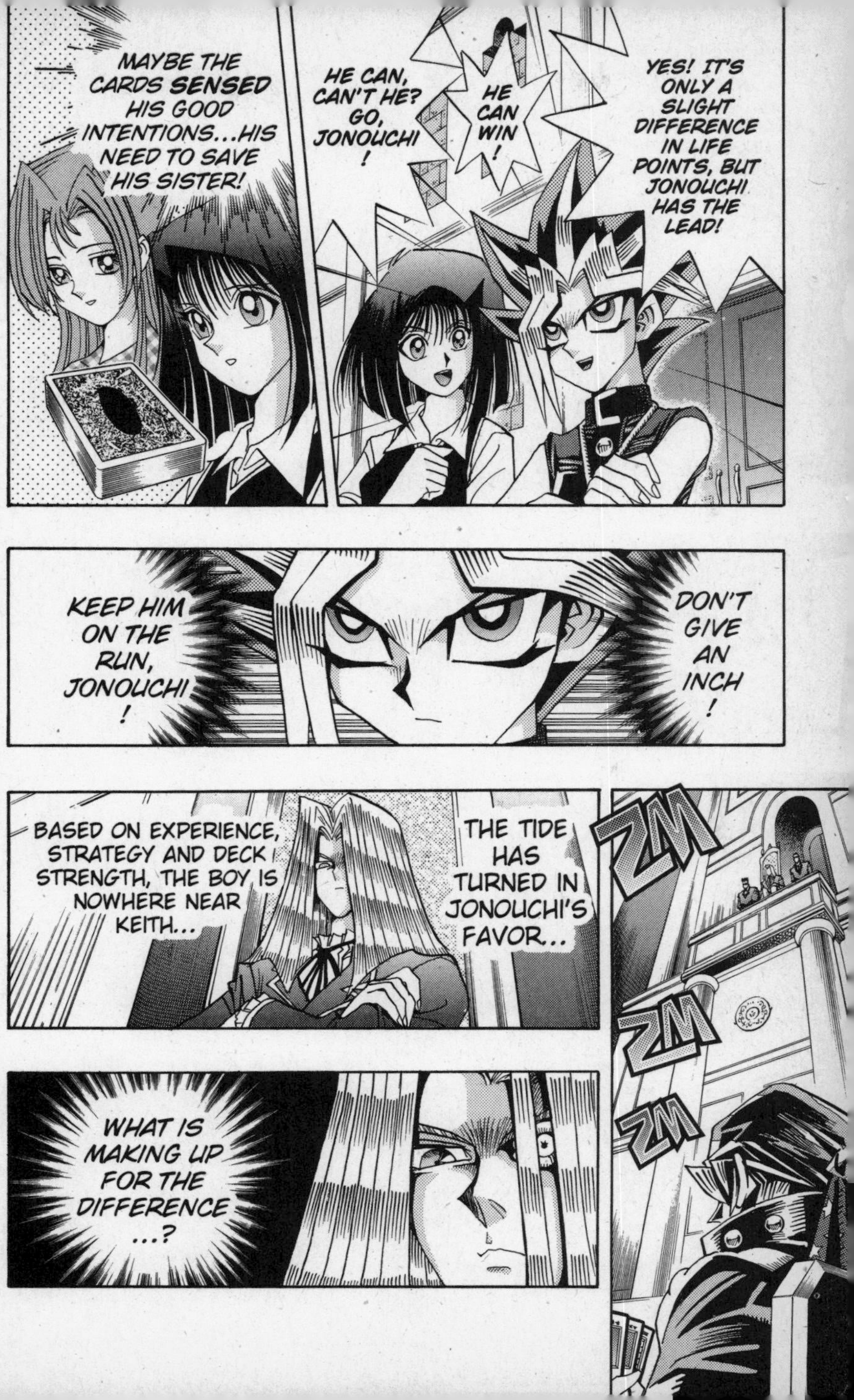
YES! IT'S ONLY A SLIGHT DIFFERENCE IN LIFE POINTS, BUT JONOUCHI HAS THE LEAD!
HE CAN WIN!
HE CAN, CAN'T HE? GO, JONOUCHI!
MAYBE THE CARDS SENSED HIS GOOD INTENTIONS...HIS NEED TO SAVE HIS SISTER!
DON'T GIVE AN INCH!
KEEP HIM ON THE RUN, JONOUCHI!
ZM
ZM
ZM
THE TIDE HAS TURNED IN JONOUCHI'S FAVOR...
BASED ON EXPERIENCE, STRATEGY AND DECK STRENGTH, THE BOY IS NOWHERE NEAR KEITH...
WHAT IS MAKING UP FOR THE DIFFERENCE ...?

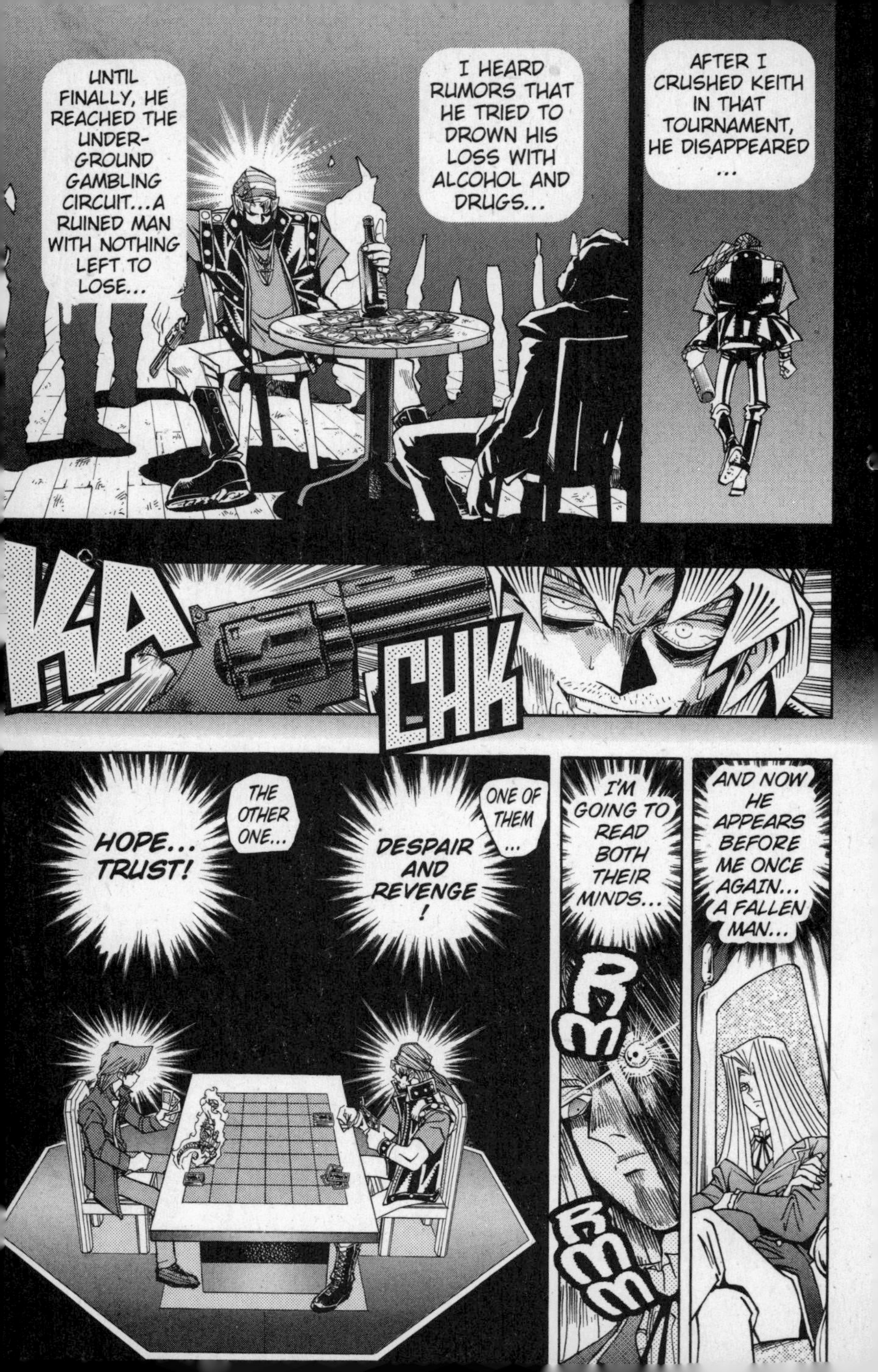
AFTER I CRUSHED KEITH IN THAT TOURNAMENT, HE DISAPPEARED...
I HEARD RUMORS THAT HE TRIED TO DROWN HIS LOSS WITH ALCOHOL AND DRUGS...
UNTIL FINALLY, HE REACHED THE UNDER-GROUND GAMBLING CIRCUIT...A RUINED MAN WITH NOTHING LEFT TO LOSE...
KA
CHK
AND NOW HE APPEARS BEFORE ME ONCE AGAIN... A FALLEN MAN...
I'M GOING TO READ BOTH THEIR MINDS...
RMM
RMM
ONE OF THEM...
DESPAIR AND REVENGE!
THE OTHER ONE...
HOPE... TRUST!

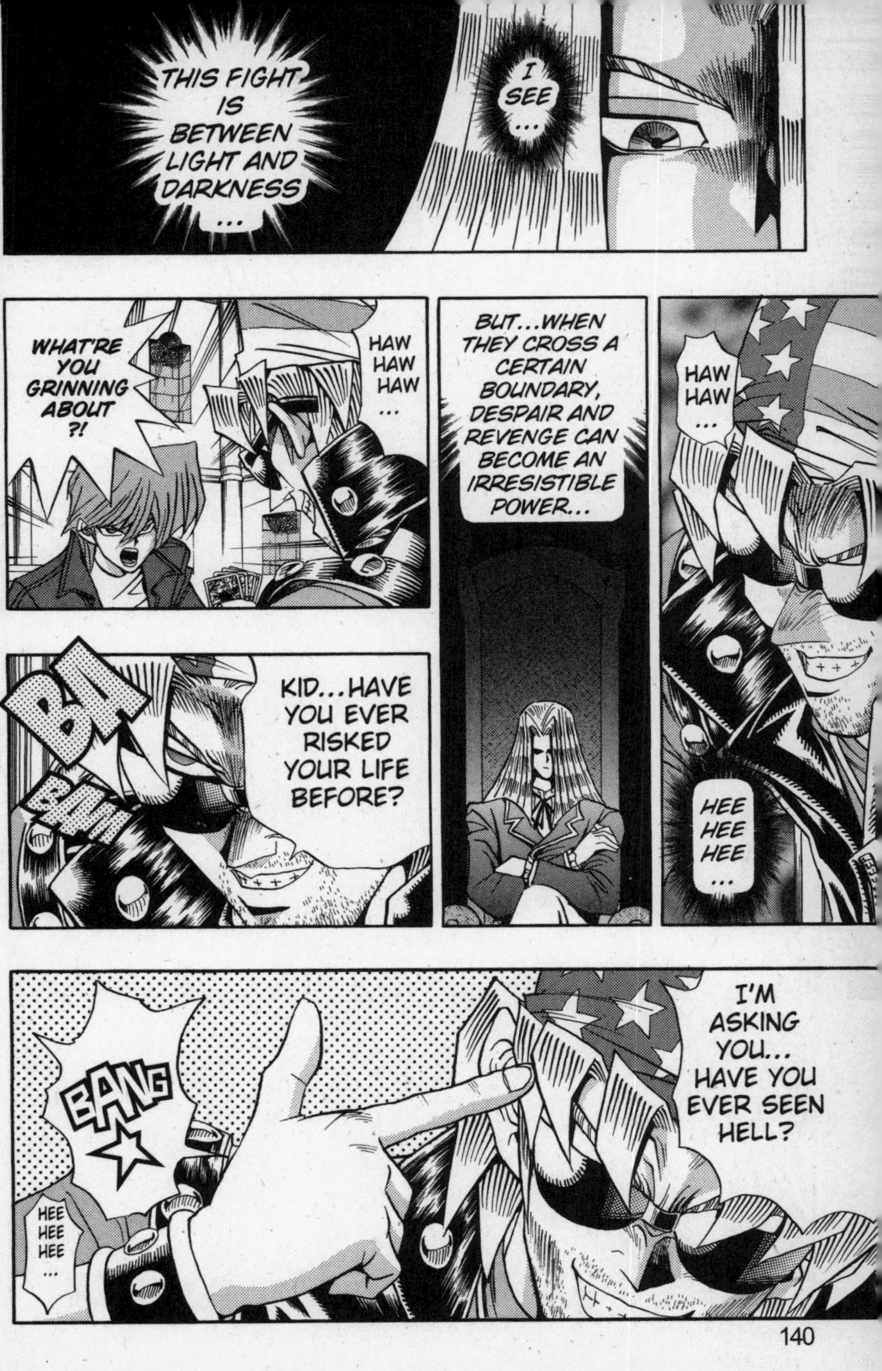
I SEE...
THIS FIGHT IS BETWEEN LIGHT AND DARKNESS...
HAW HAW...
HEE HEE HEE...
BUT...WHEN THEY CROSS A CERTAIN BOUNDARY, DESPAIR AND REVENGE CAN BECOME AN IRRESISTIBLE POWER...
HAW HAW HAW...
WHAT'RE YOU GRINNING ABOUT?!
KID...HAVE YOU EVER RISKED YOUR LIFE BEFORE?
BA
BAM
I'M ASKING YOU... HAVE YOU EVER SEEN HELL?
BANG
HEE HEE HEE...

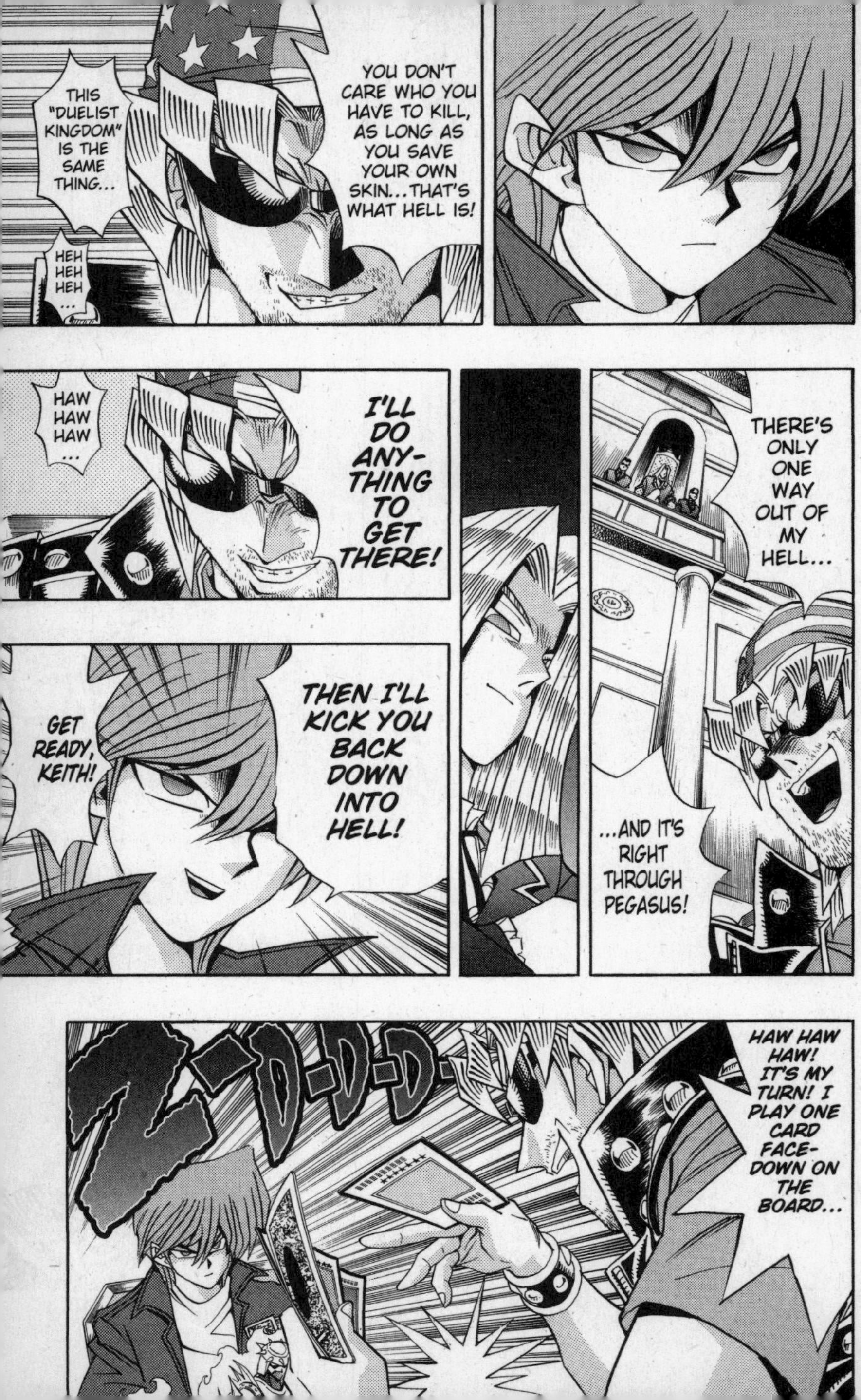
YOU DON'T CARE WHO YOU HAVE TO KILL, AS LONG AS YOU SAVE YOUR OWN SKIN...THAT'S WHAT HELL IS!
THIS "DUELIST KINGDOM" IS THE SAME THING...
HEH HEH HEH ...
THERE'S ONLY ONE WAY OUT OF MY HELL...
...AND IT'S RIGHT THROUGH PEGASUS!
I'LL DO ANYTHING TO GET THERE!
HAW HAW HAW ...
THEN I'LL KICK YOU BACK DOWN INTO HELL!
GET READY, KEITH!
HAW HAW HAW! IT'S MY TURN! I PLAY ONE CARD FACE-DOWN ON THE BOARD...

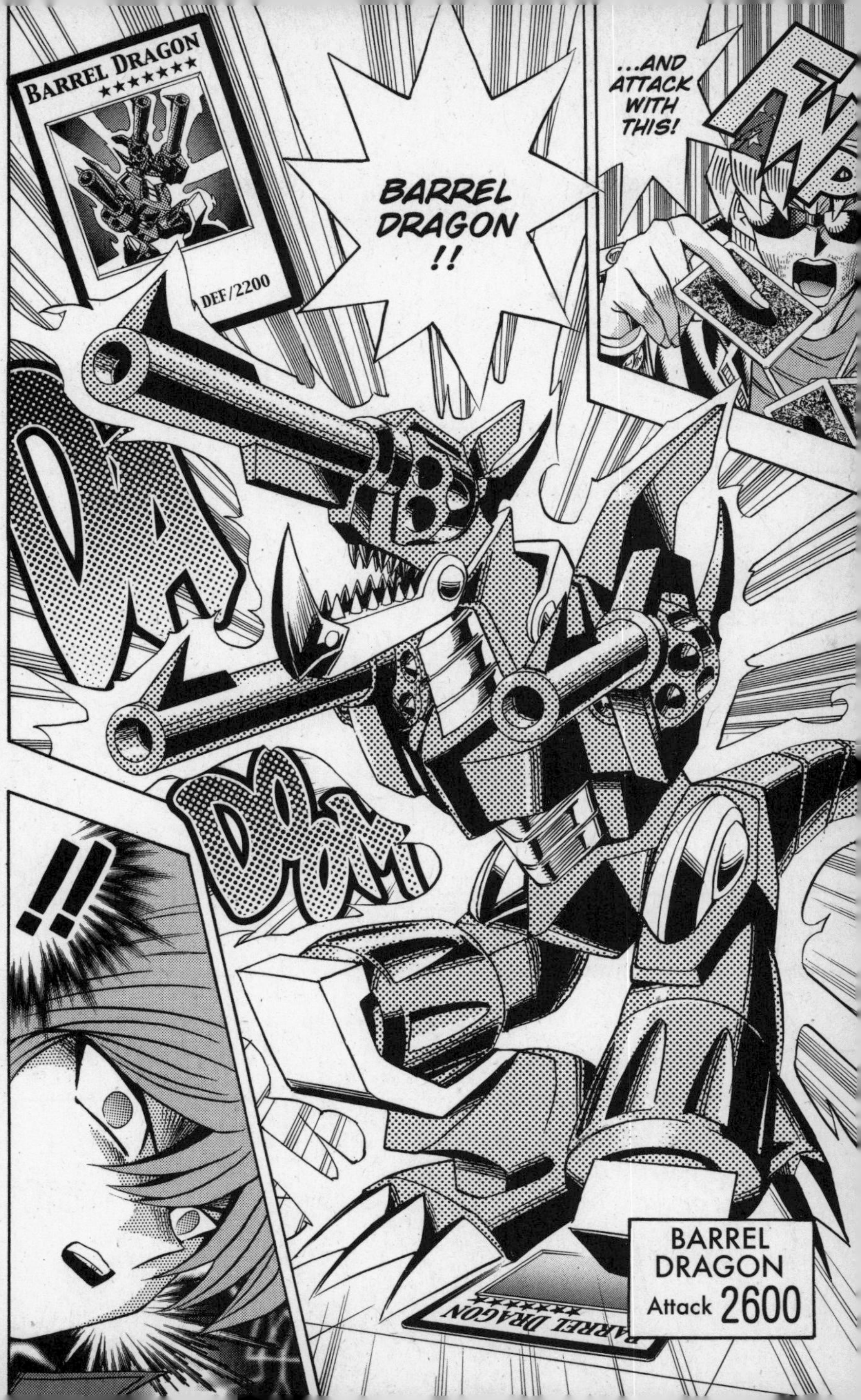
...AND ATTACK WITH THIS!
BARREL DRAGON
DEF/2200
BARREL DRAGON !!
DOOM
BARREL DRAGON Attack 2600
!!

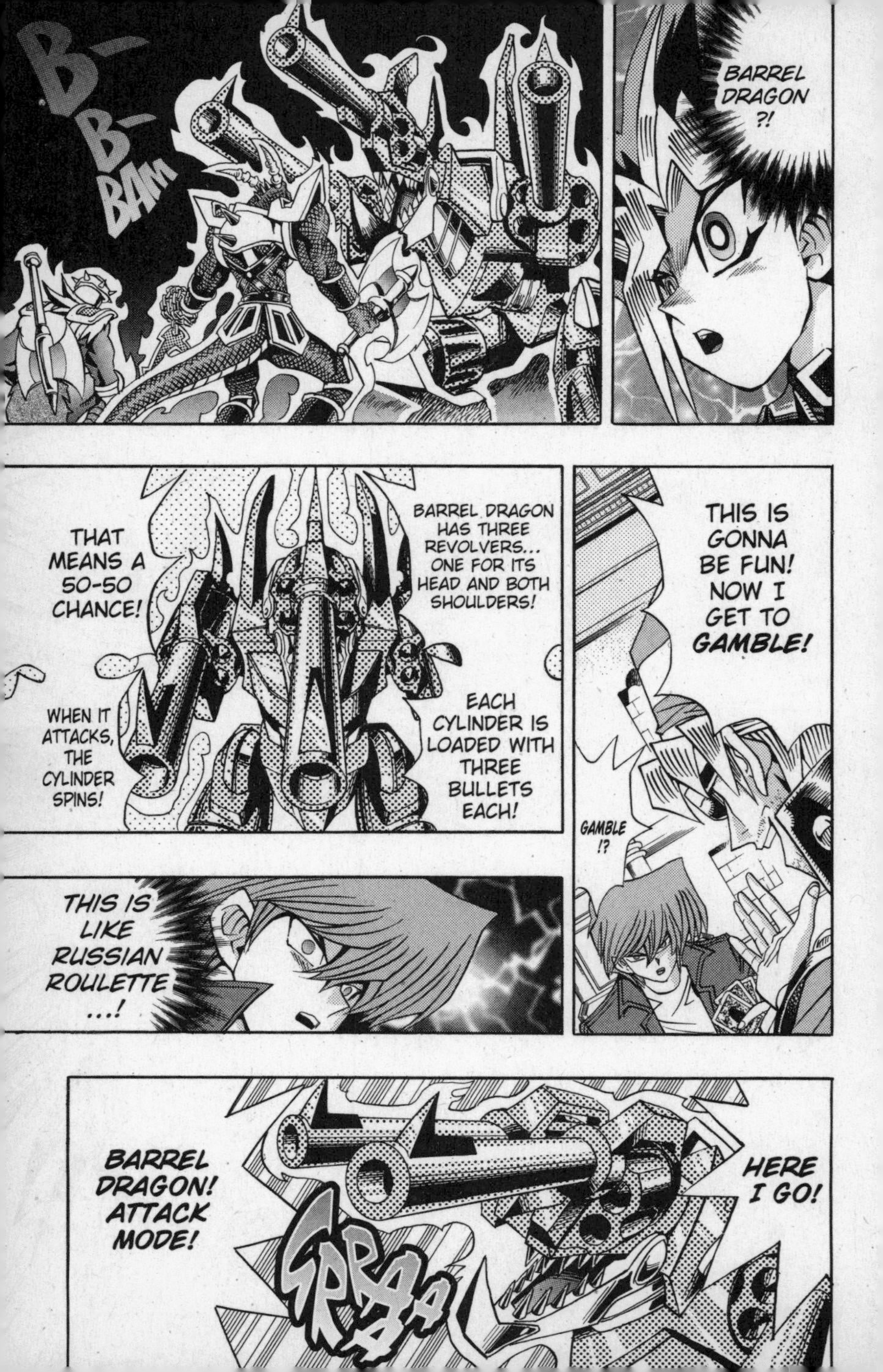
BARREL DRAGON ?!
B-B-BAM
THIS IS GONNA BE FUN! NOW I GET TO GAMBLE!
GAMBLE !?
BARREL DRAGON HAS THREE REVOLVERS... ONE FOR ITS HEAD AND BOTH SHOULDERS!
THAT MEANS A 50-50 CHANCE!
EACH CYLINDER IS LOADED WITH THREE BULLETS EACH!
WHEN IT ATTACKS, THE CYLINDER SPINS!
THIS IS LIKE RUSSIAN ROULETTE ...!
HERE I GO!
BARREL DRAGON! ATTACK MODE!

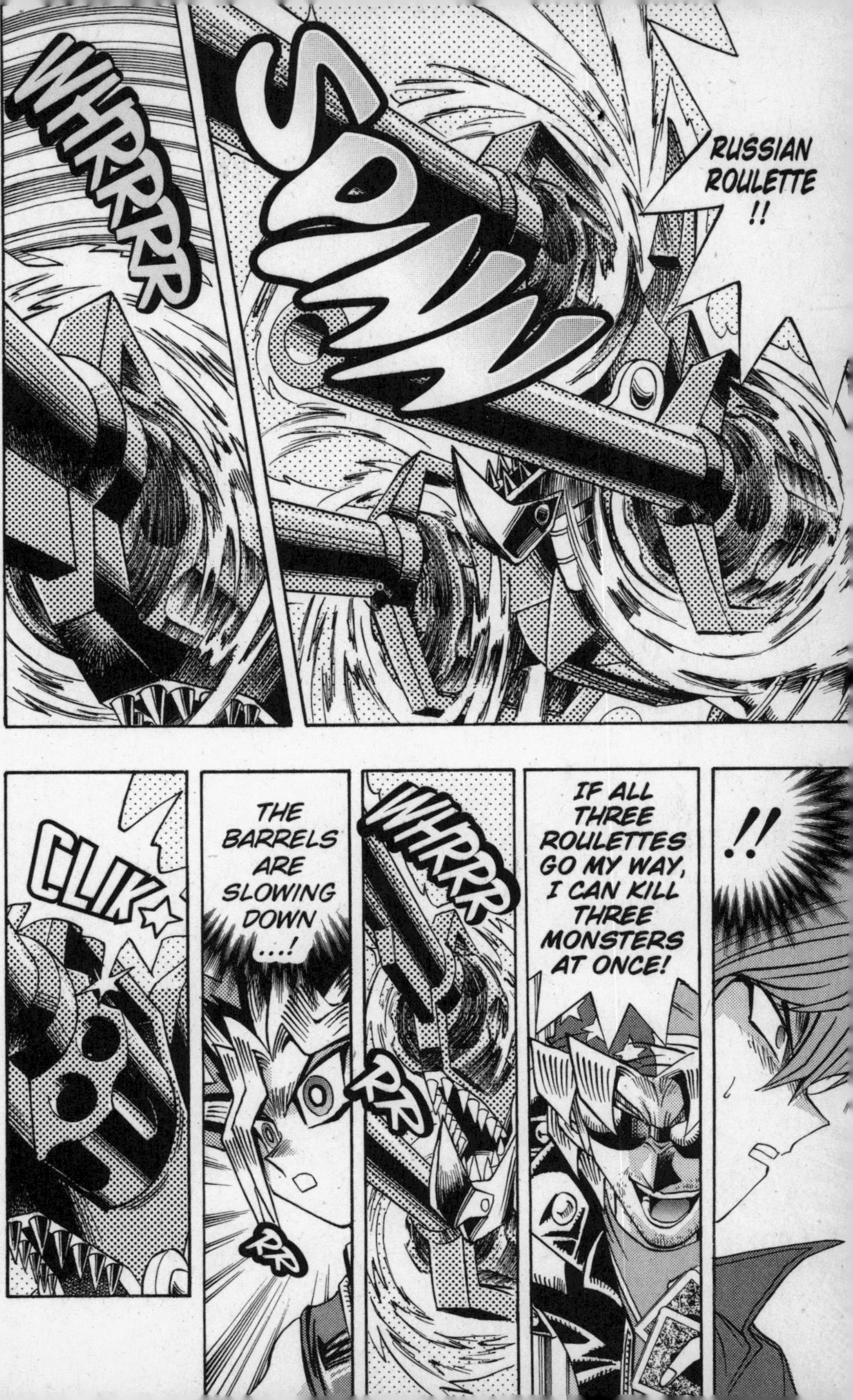
RUSSIAN ROULETTE !!
SPIN
WHRRRR
!!
IF ALL THREE ROULETTES GO MY WAY, I CAN KILL THREE MONSTERS AT ONCE!
WHRRR
RR
THE BARRELS ARE SLOWING DOWN ...!
RR
CLIK

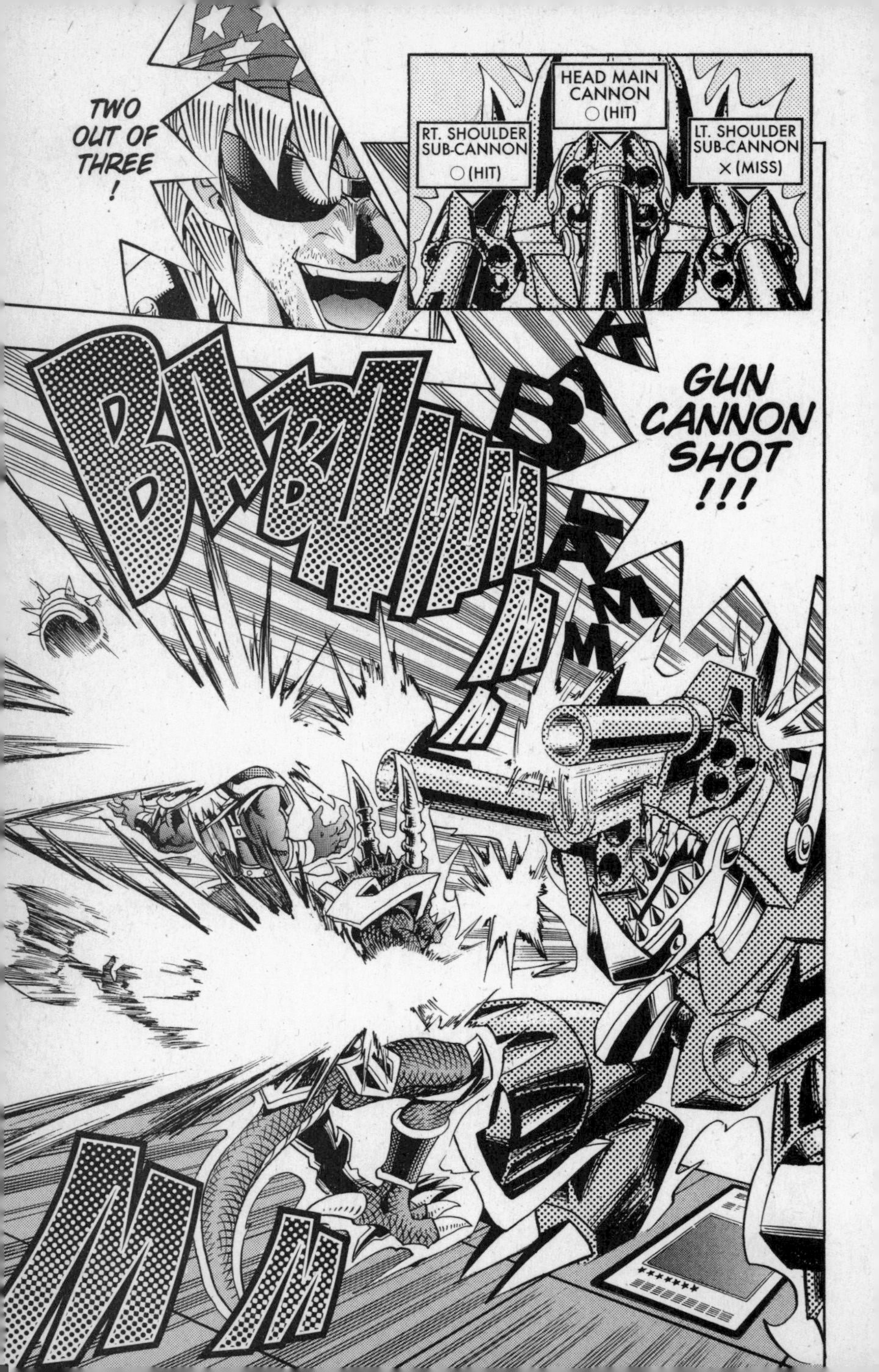
HEAD MAIN CANNON ○ (HIT)
LT. SHOULDER SUB-CANNON × (MISS)
RT. SHOULDER SUB-CANNON ○ (HIT)
TWO OUT OF THREE !
GUN CANNON SHOT !!!

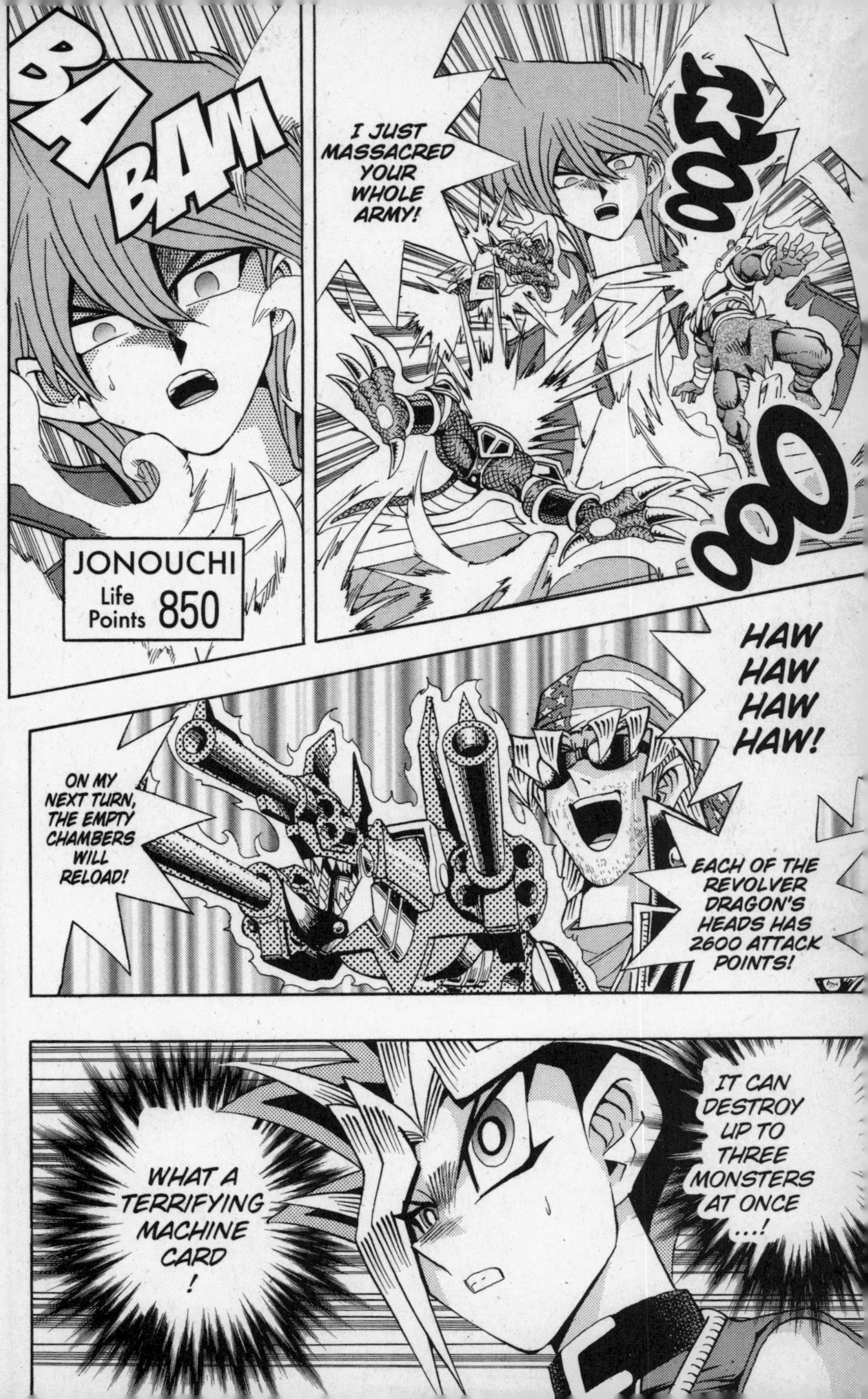
I JUST MASSACRED YOUR WHOLE ARMY!
BA BAM
JONOUCHI
Life Points 850
HAW HAW HAW HAW!
EACH OF THE REVOLVER DRAGON'S HEADS HAS 2600 ATTACK POINTS!
ON MY NEXT TURN, THE EMPTY CHAMBERS WILL RELOAD!
IT CAN DESTROY UP TO THREE MONSTERS AT ONCE ...!
WHAT A TERRIFYING MACHINE CARD !

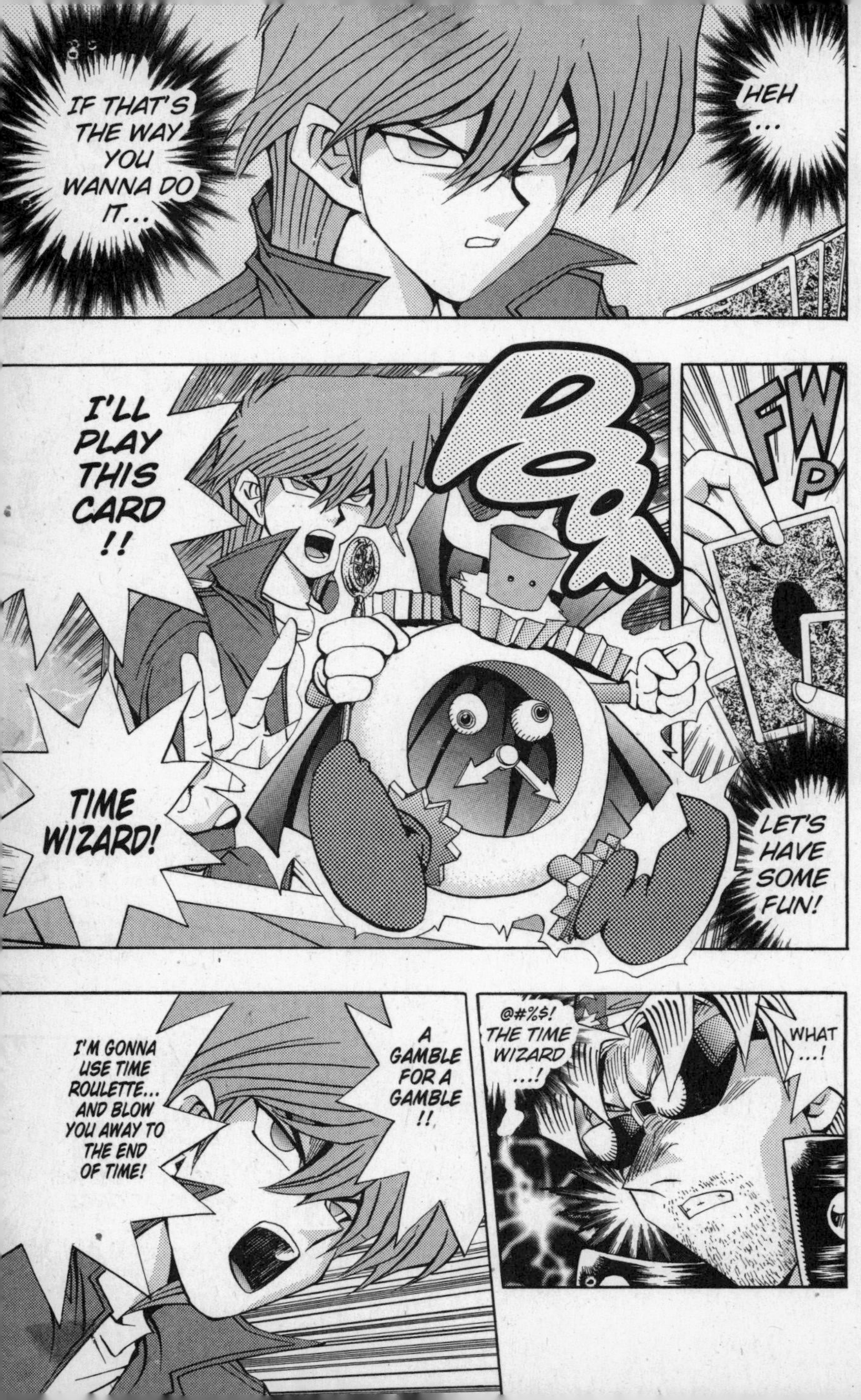
HEH ...
IF THAT'S THE WAY YOU WANNA DO IT...
FWP
POP
I'LL PLAY THIS CARD !!
TIME WIZARD!
LET'S HAVE SOME FUN!
WHAT ...!
@#%$! THE TIME WIZARD ...!
A GAMBLE FOR A GAMBLE !!
I'M GONNA USE TIME ROULETTE... AND BLOW YOU AWAY TO THE END OF TIME!

Duel 63: Betting to Win!

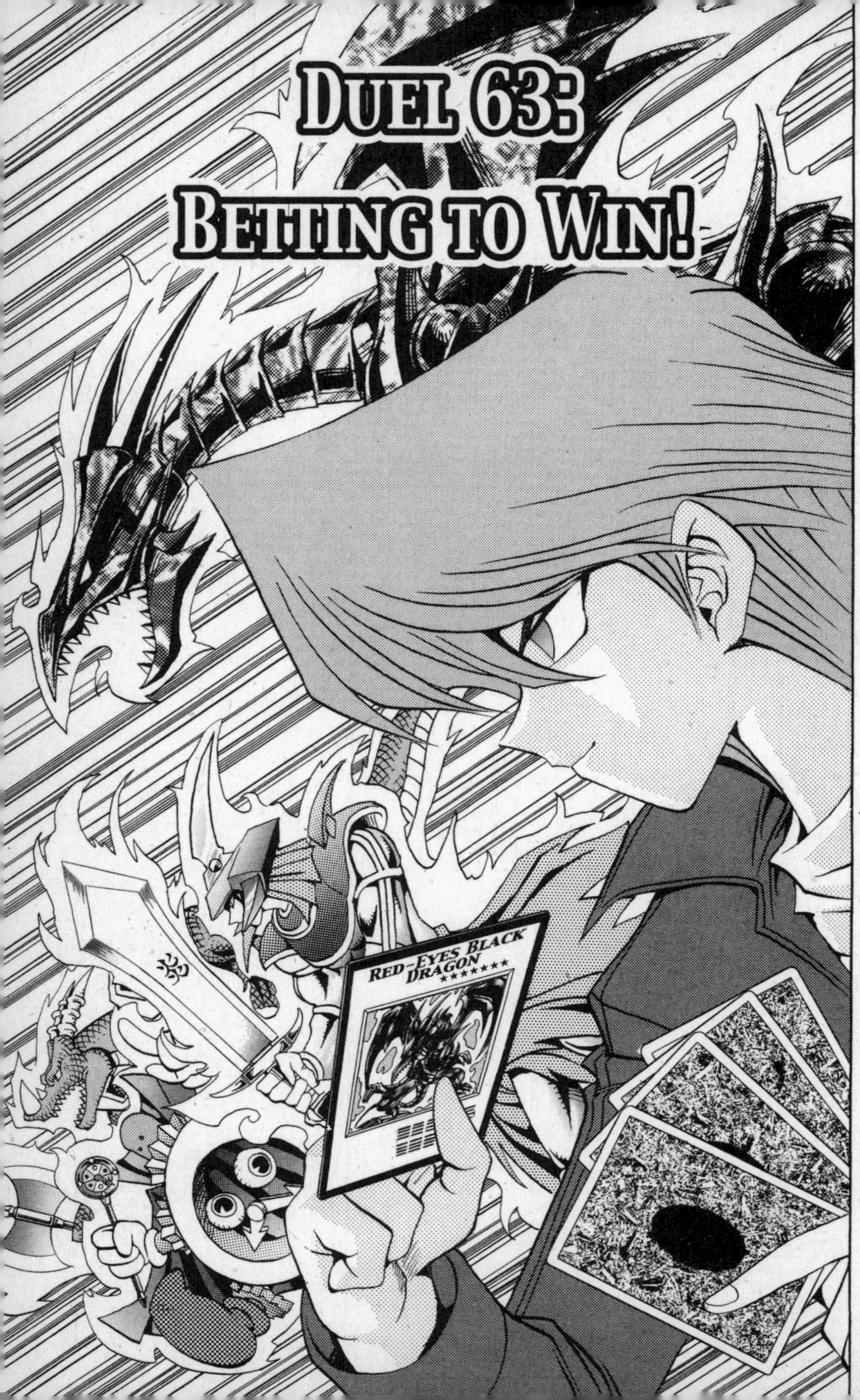
RED-EYES BLACK DRAGON

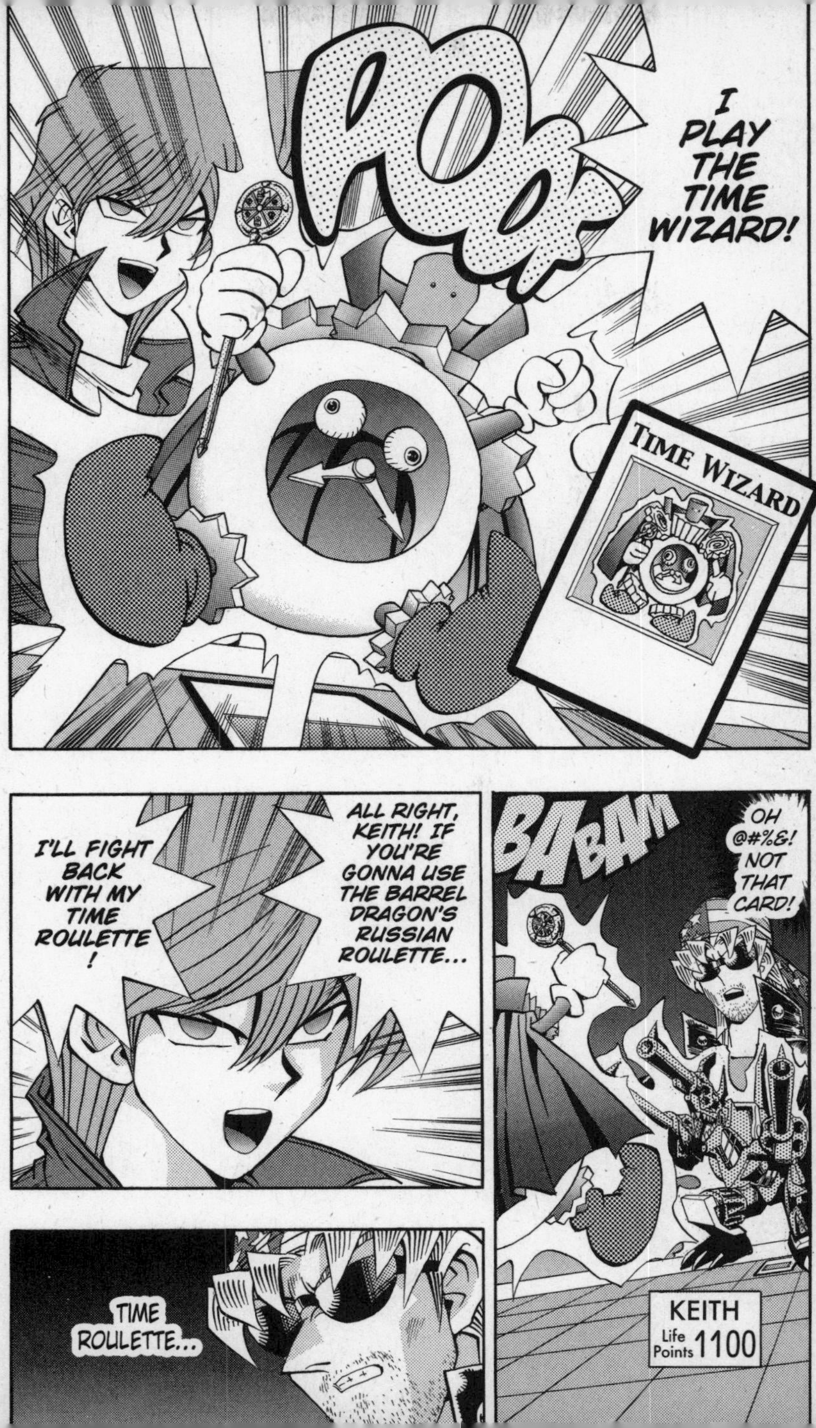
POW
I PLAY THE TIME WIZARD!
TIME WIZARD
BABAM
OH @#%&! NOT THAT CARD!
KEITH
Life Points 1100
ALL RIGHT, KEITH! IF YOU'RE GONNA USE THE BARREL DRAGON'S RUSSIAN ROULETTE...
I'LL FIGHT BACK WITH MY TIME ROULETTE!
TIME ROULETTE...

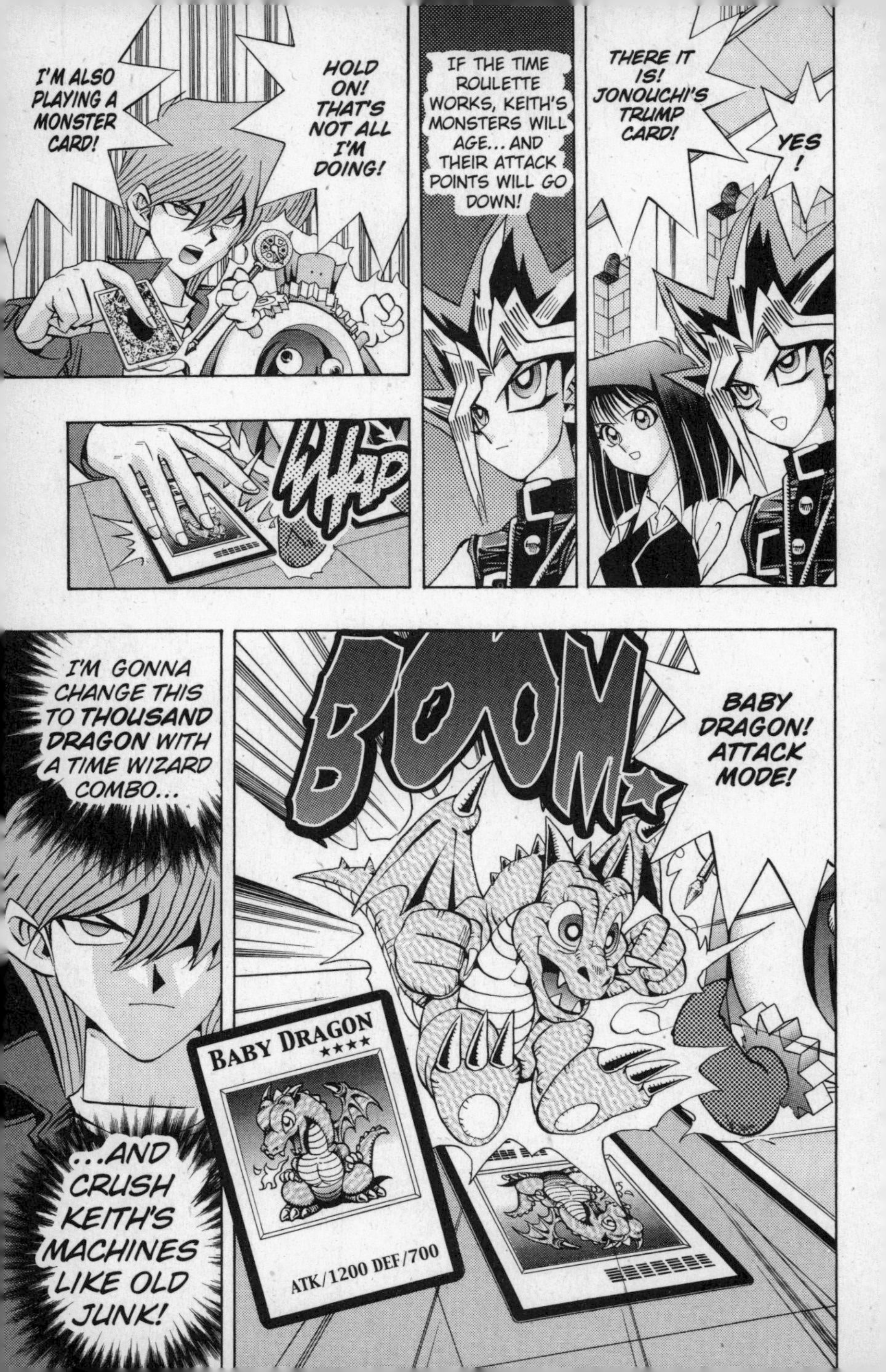
THERE IT IS! JONOUCHI'S TRUMP CARD!
YES!
IF THE TIME ROULETTE WORKS, KEITH'S MONSTERS WILL AGE... AND THEIR ATTACK POINTS WILL GO DOWN!
HOLD ON! THAT'S NOT ALL I'M DOING!
I'M ALSO PLAYING A MONSTER CARD!
WHAP
BOOM
BABY DRAGON! ATTACK MODE!
BABY DRAGON ★★★★
ATK/1200 DEF/700
I'M GONNA CHANGE THIS TO THOUSAND DRAGON WITH A TIME WIZARD COMBO...
...AND CRUSH KEITH'S MACHINES LIKE OLD JUNK!

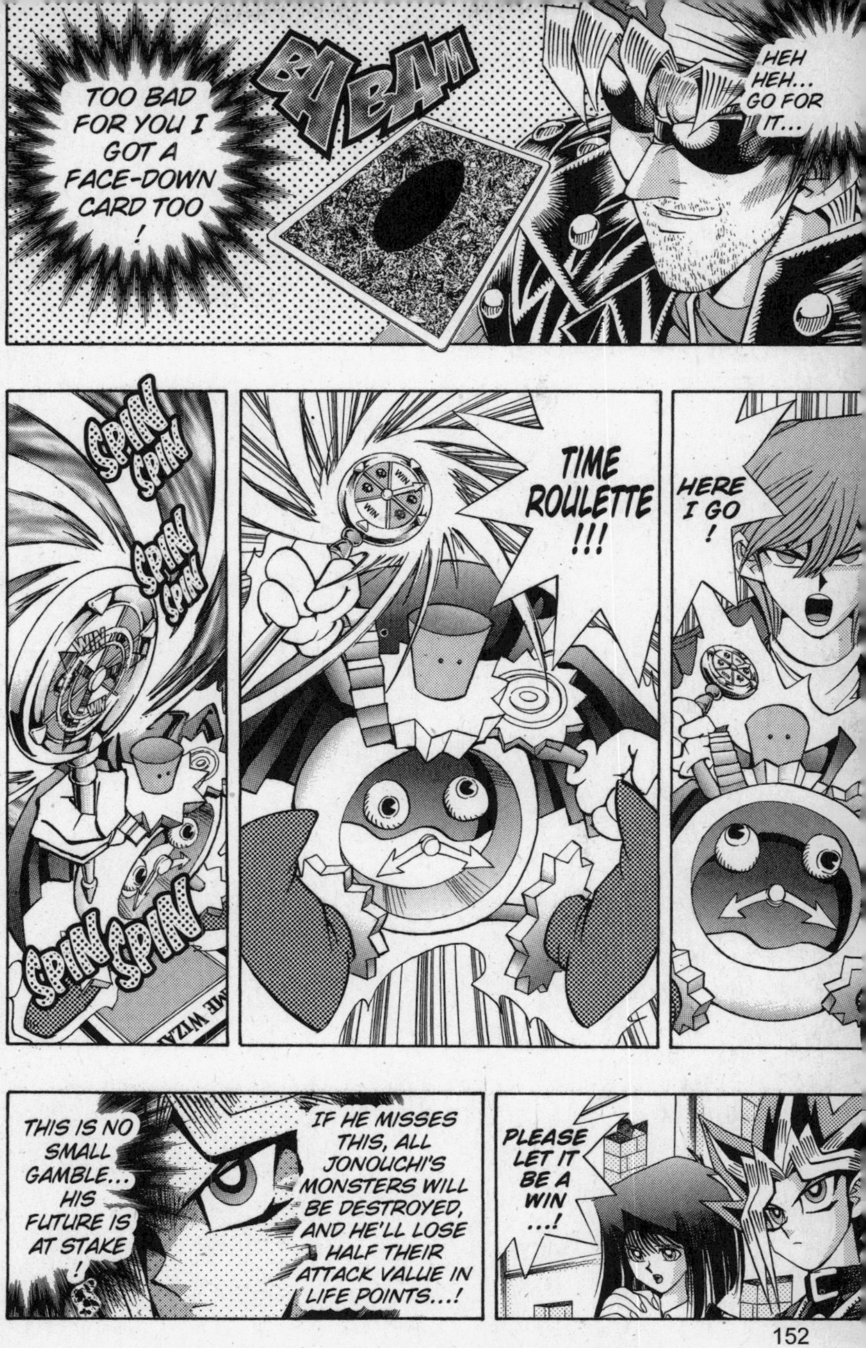
HEH HEH... GO FOR IT...
BA BAM
TOO BAD FOR YOU I GOT A FACE-DOWN CARD TOO!
HERE I GO!
TIME ROULETTE!!!
SPIN SPIN
SPIN SPIN
SPIN SPIN
PLEASE LET IT BE A WIN...!
IF HE MISSES THIS, ALL JONOUCHI'S MONSTERS WILL BE DESTROYED, AND HE'LL LOSE HALF THEIR ATTACK VALUE IN LIFE POINTS...!
THIS IS NO SMALL GAMBLE... HIS FUTURE IS AT STAKE!

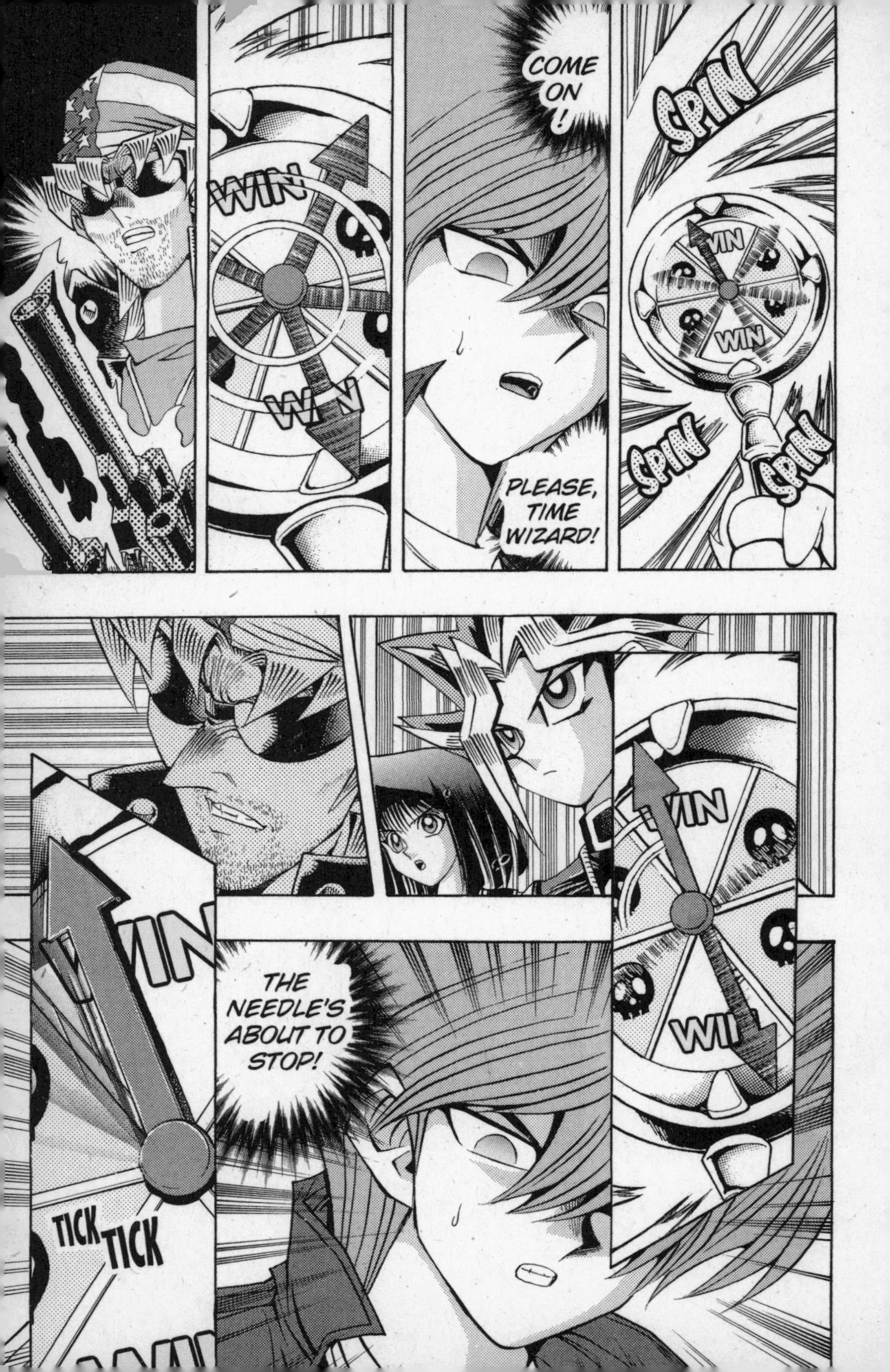
SPIN
WIN
WIN
SPIN
SPIN
COME ON!
PLEASE, TIME WIZARD!
WIN
WIN
THE NEEDLE'S ABOUT TO STOP!
TICK
TICK

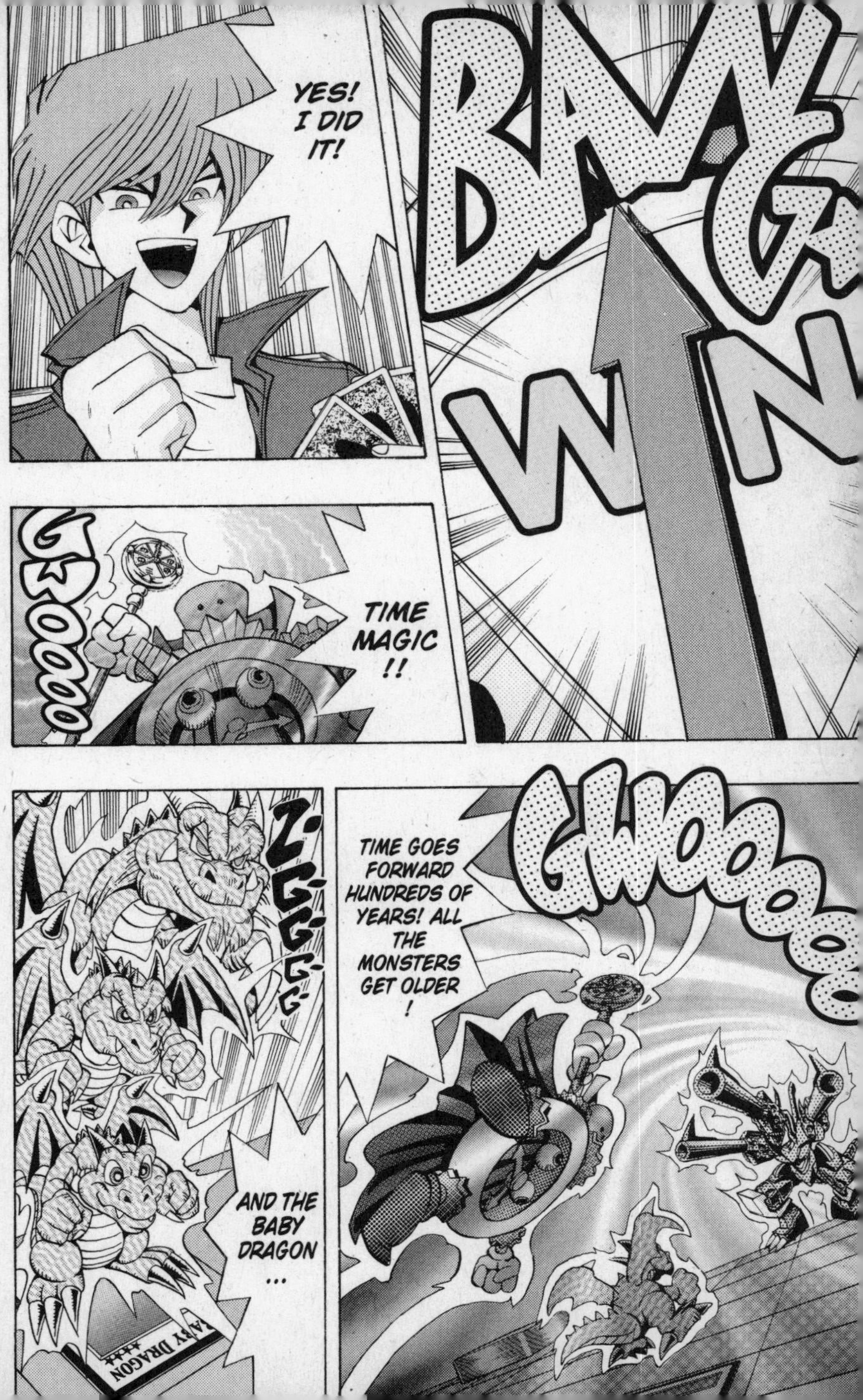
YES! I DID IT!
TIME MAGIC !!
TIME GOES FORWARD HUNDREDS OF YEARS! ALL THE MONSTERS GET OLDER !
AND THE BABY DRAGON ...

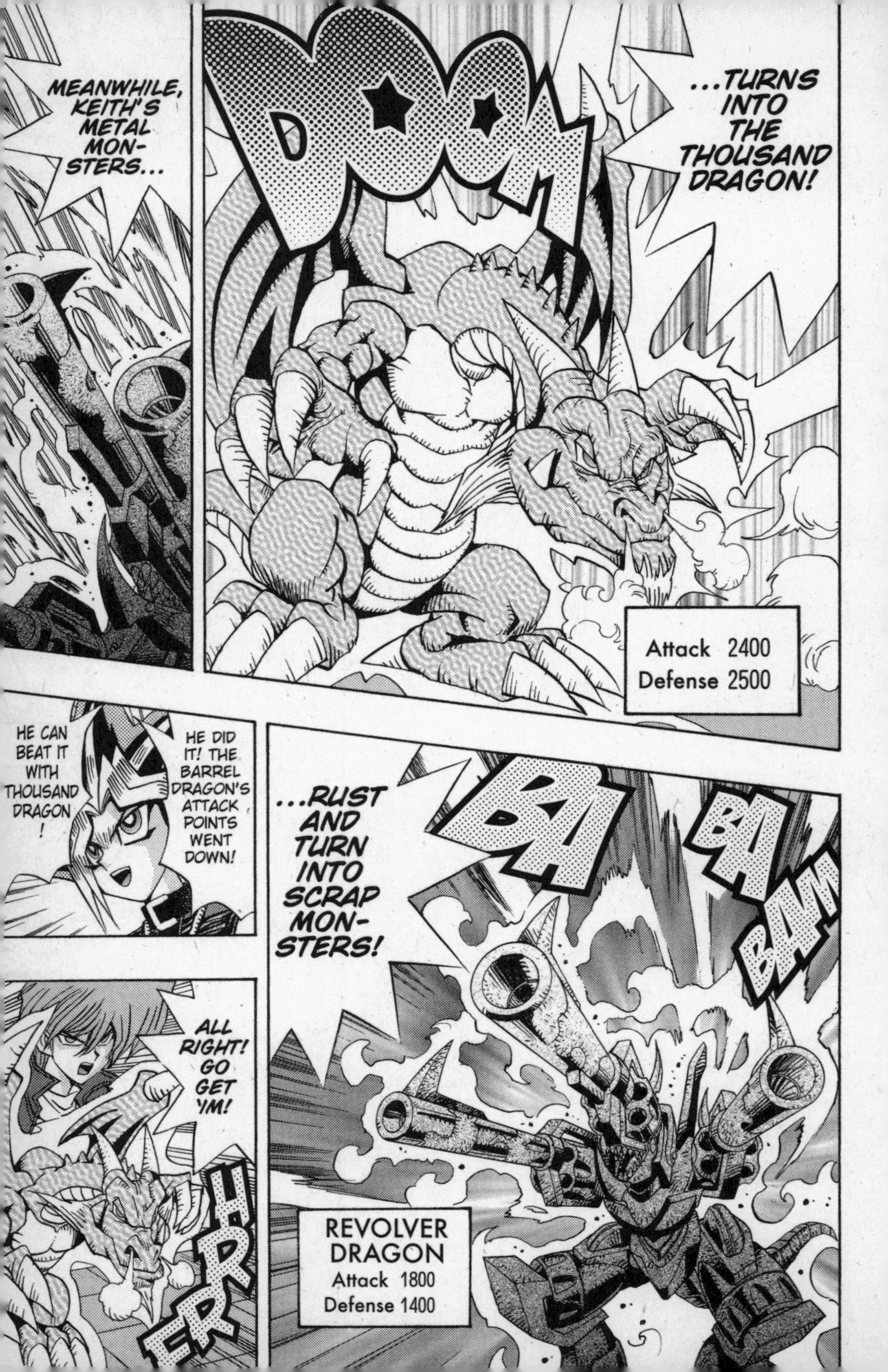
DOOM
...TURNS INTO THE THOUSAND DRAGON!
Attack 2400
Defense 2500
MEANWHILE, KEITH'S METAL MON-STERS...
...RUST AND TURN INTO SCRAP MON-STERS!
BA
BA
BAM
REVOLVER DRAGON
Attack 1800
Defense 1400
HE DID IT! THE BARREL DRAGON'S ATTACK POINTS WENT DOWN!
HE CAN BEAT IT WITH THOUSAND DRAGON!
ALL RIGHT! GO GET 'YM!
HRR

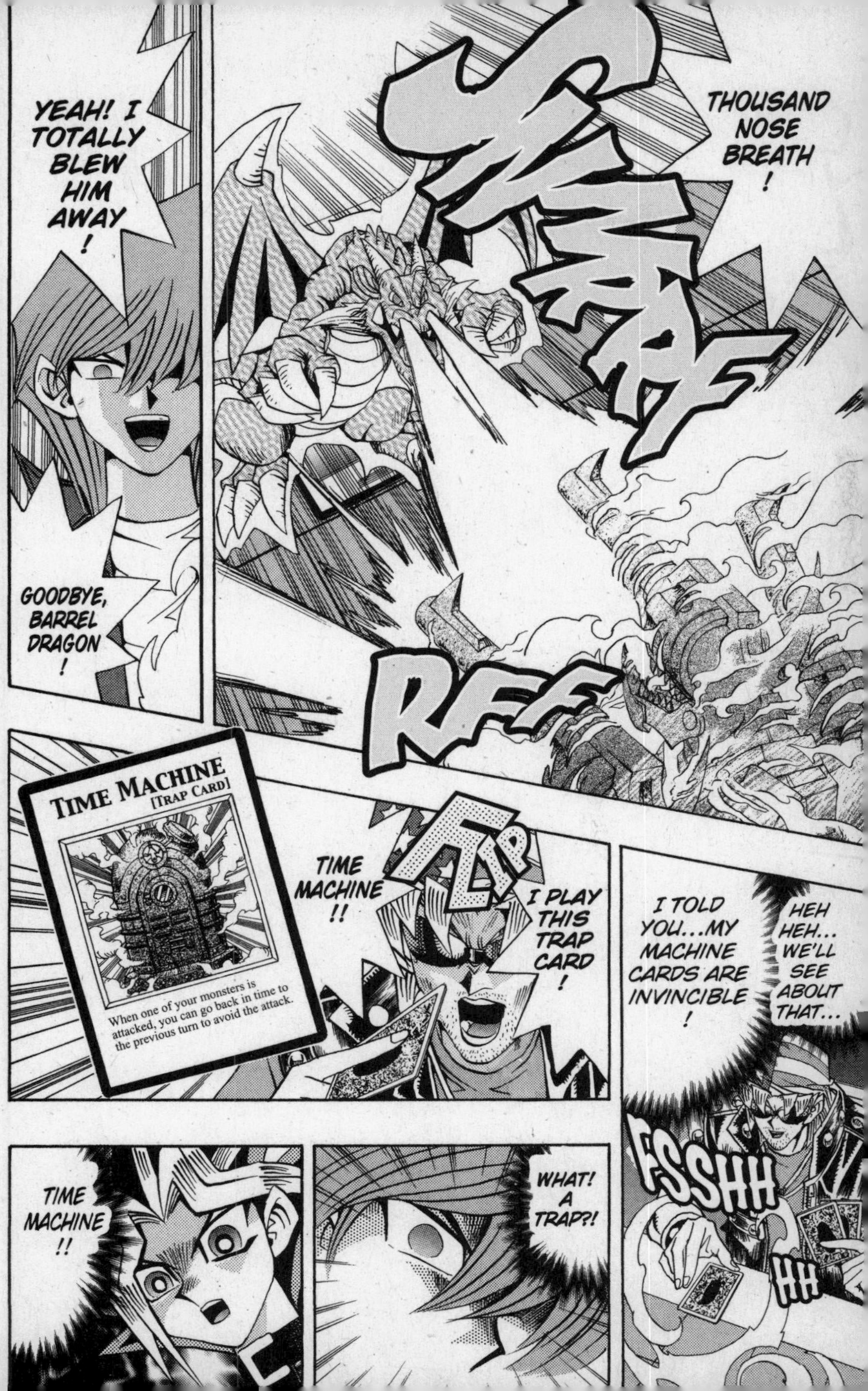
THOUSAND NOSE BREATH!
YEAH! I TOTALLY BLEW HIM AWAY!
GOODBYE, BARREL DRAGON!
HEH HEH... WE'LL SEE ABOUT THAT...
I TOLD YOU...MY MACHINE CARDS ARE INVINCIBLE!
FSSHH
HH
I PLAY THIS TRAP CARD!
TIME MACHINE!!
TIME MACHINE
[TRAP CARD]
When one of your monsters is attacked, you can go back in time to the previous turn to avoid the attack.
WHAT! A TRAP?!
TIME MACHINE!!

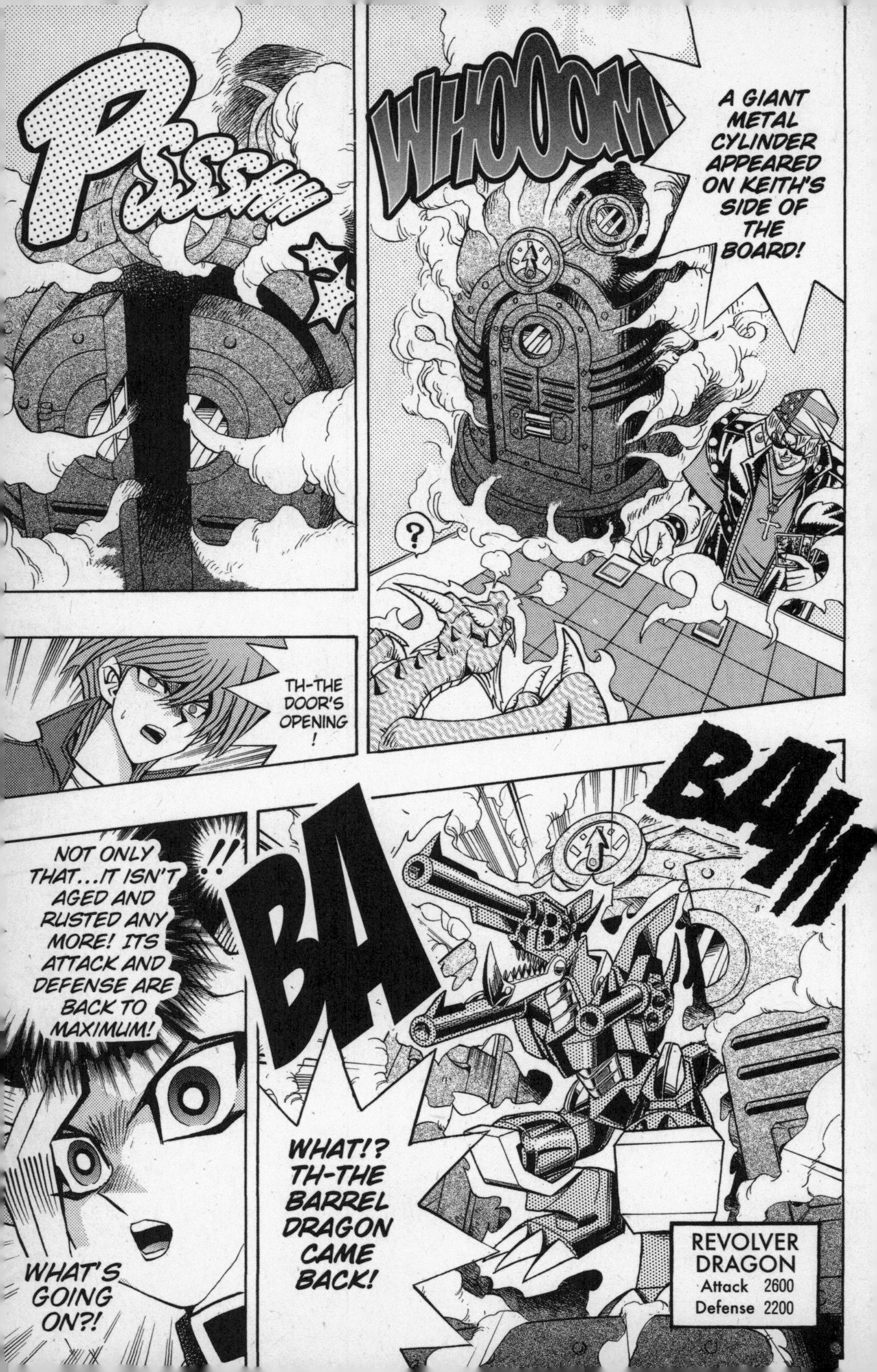
WHOOOM
A GIANT METAL CYLINDER APPEARED ON KEITH'S SIDE OF THE BOARD!
?
PSSSH
TH-THE DOOR'S OPENING!
BAM
BA
WHAT!? TH-THE BARREL DRAGON CAME BACK!
REVOLVER DRAGON
Attack 2600
Defense 2200
!!
NOT ONLY THAT...IT ISN'T AGED AND RUSTED ANY MORE! ITS ATTACK AND DEFENSE ARE BACK TO MAXIMUM!
WHAT'S GOING ON?!

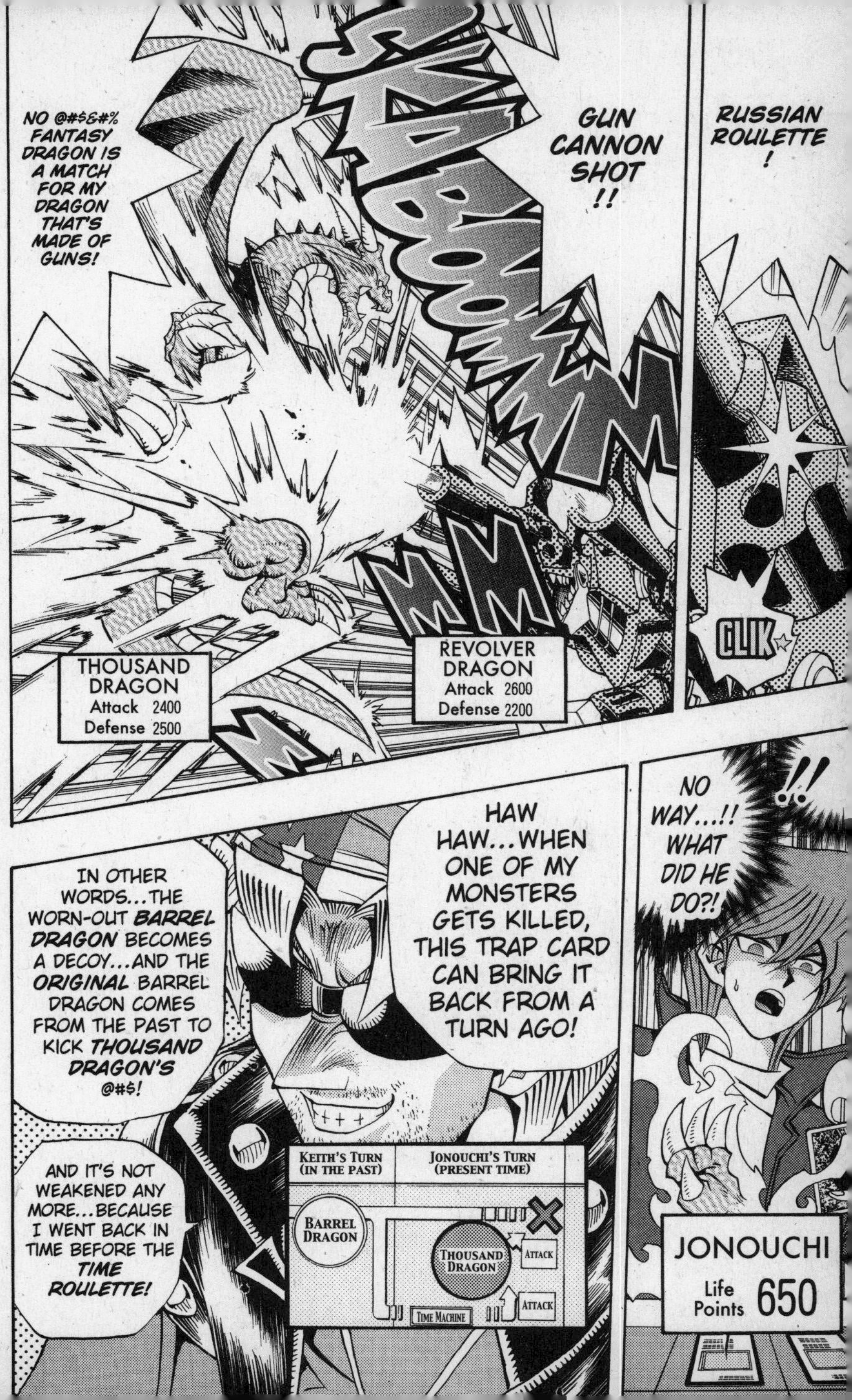

RUSSIAN ROULETTE!
CLIK
GUN CANNON SHOT!!
NO @#$&#% FANTASY DRAGON IS A MATCH FOR MY DRAGON THAT'S MADE OF GUNS!
REVOLVER DRAGON Attack 2600 Defense 2200
THOUSAND DRAGON Attack 2400 Defense 2500
!!
NO WAY...!! WHAT DID HE DO?!
JONOUCHI Life Points 650
HAW HAW...WHEN ONE OF MY MONSTERS GETS KILLED, THIS TRAP CARD CAN BRING IT BACK FROM A TURN AGO!
IN OTHER WORDS...THE WORN-OUT ***BARREL DRAGON*** BECOMES A DECOY...AND THE ***ORIGINAL*** BARREL DRAGON COMES FROM THE PAST TO KICK ***THOUSAND DRAGON'S*** @#$!
AND IT'S NOT WEAKENED ANY MORE...BECAUSE I WENT BACK IN TIME BEFORE THE ***TIME ROULETTE!***
KEITH'S TURN (IN THE PAST)
JONOUCHI'S TURN (PRESENT TIME)
BARREL DRAGON
THOUSAND DRAGON
ATTACK
ATTACK
TIME MACHINE

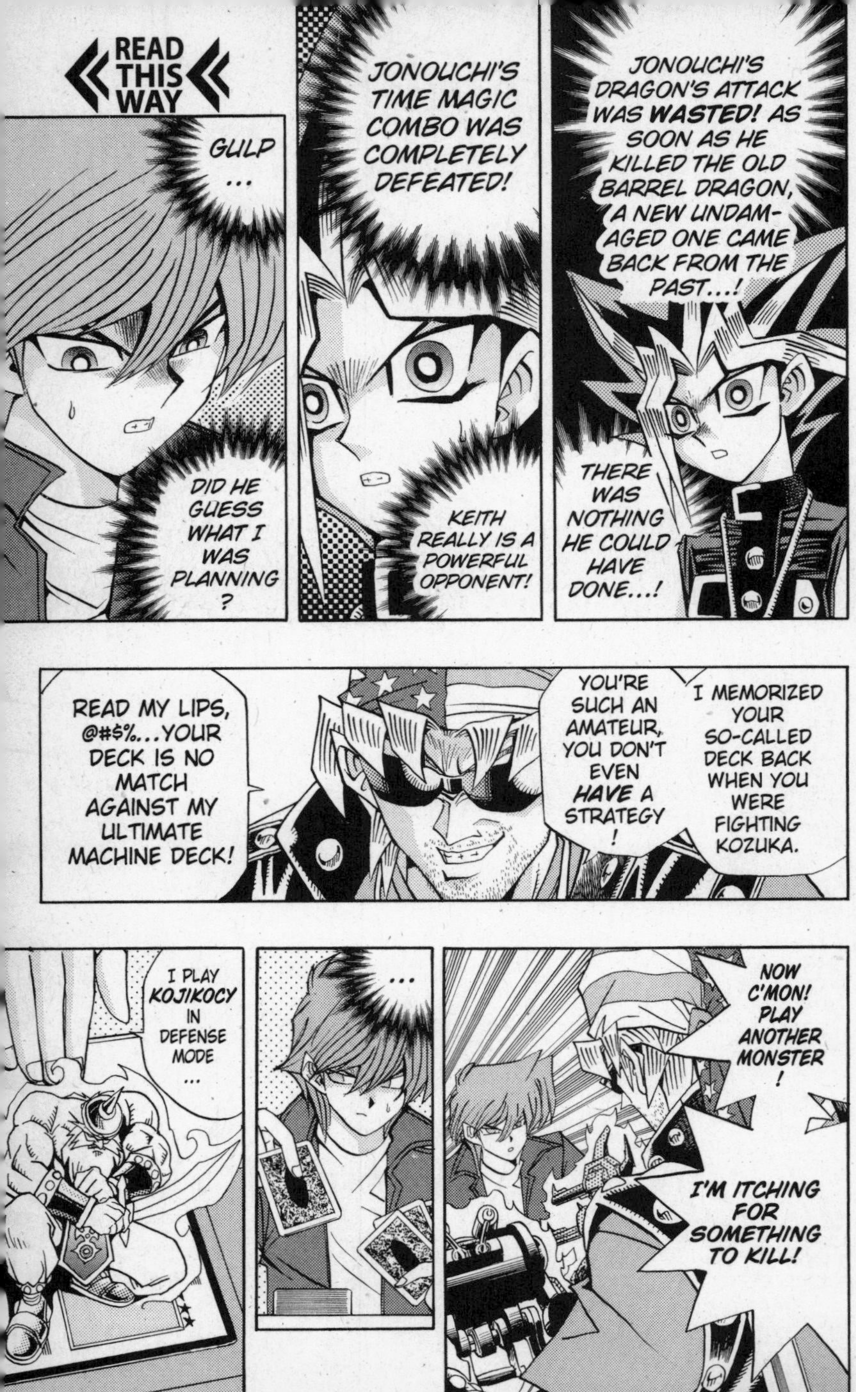
READ THIS WAY
JONOUCHI'S DRAGON'S ATTACK WAS WASTED! AS SOON AS HE KILLED THE OLD BARREL DRAGON, A NEW UNDAM-AGED ONE CAME BACK FROM THE PAST...!
THERE WAS NOTHING HE COULD HAVE DONE...!
JONOUCHI'S TIME MAGIC COMBO WAS COMPLETELY DEFEATED!
KEITH REALLY IS A POWERFUL OPPONENT!
GULP ...
DID HE GUESS WHAT I WAS PLANNING ?
I MEMORIZED YOUR SO-CALLED DECK BACK WHEN YOU WERE FIGHTING KOZUKA.
YOU'RE SUCH AN AMATEUR, YOU DON'T EVEN HAVE A STRATEGY !
READ MY LIPS, @#$%...YOUR DECK IS NO MATCH AGAINST MY ULTIMATE MACHINE DECK!
NOW C'MON! PLAY ANOTHER MONSTER !
I'M ITCHING FOR SOMETHING TO KILL!
...
I PLAY KOJIKOCY IN DEFENSE MODE ...

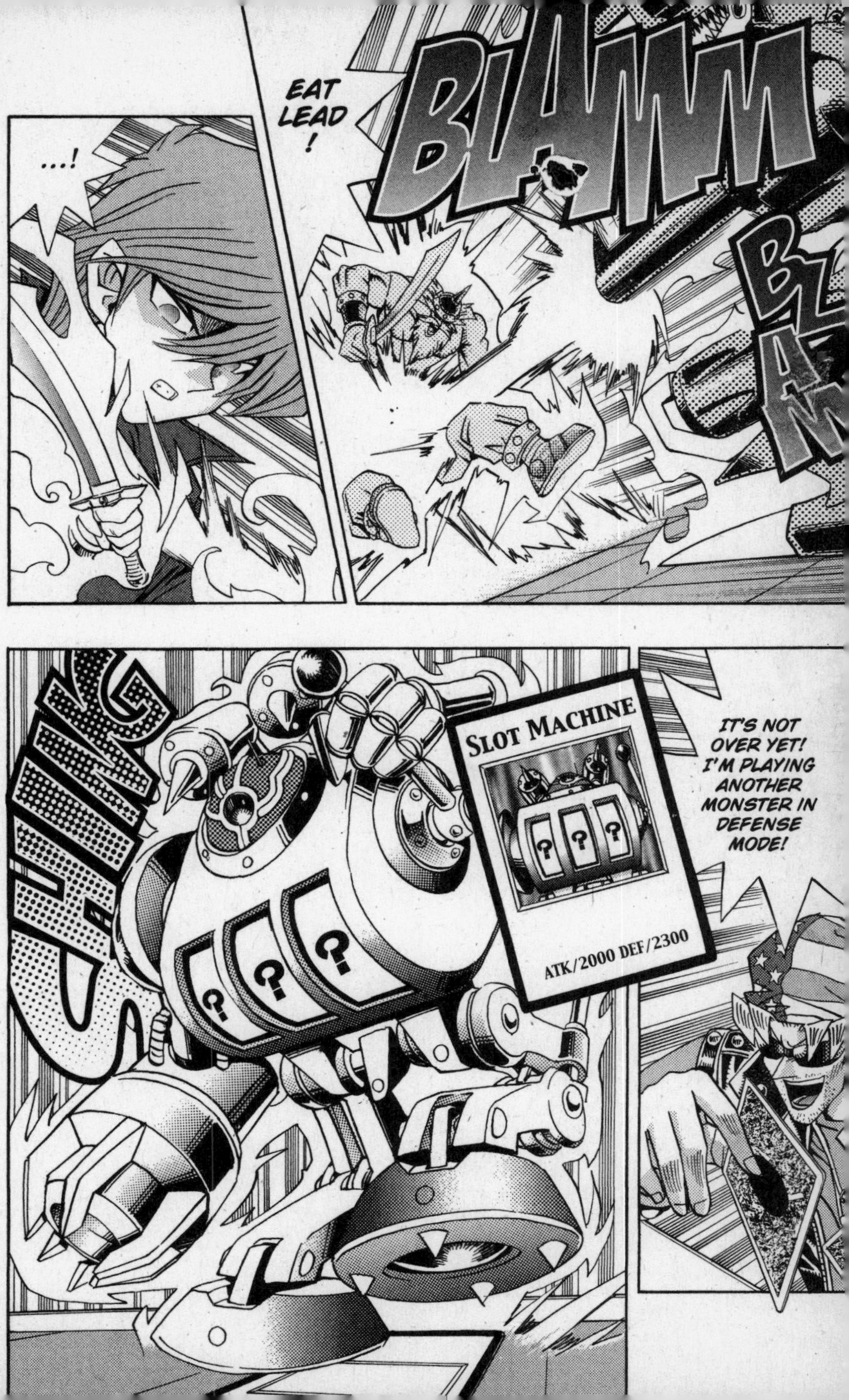
EAT LEAD!
BLAMM
...!
IT'S NOT OVER YET! I'M PLAYING ANOTHER MONSTER IN DEFENSE MODE!
SLOT MACHINE
ATK/2000 DEF/2300
CHING

READ THIS WAY

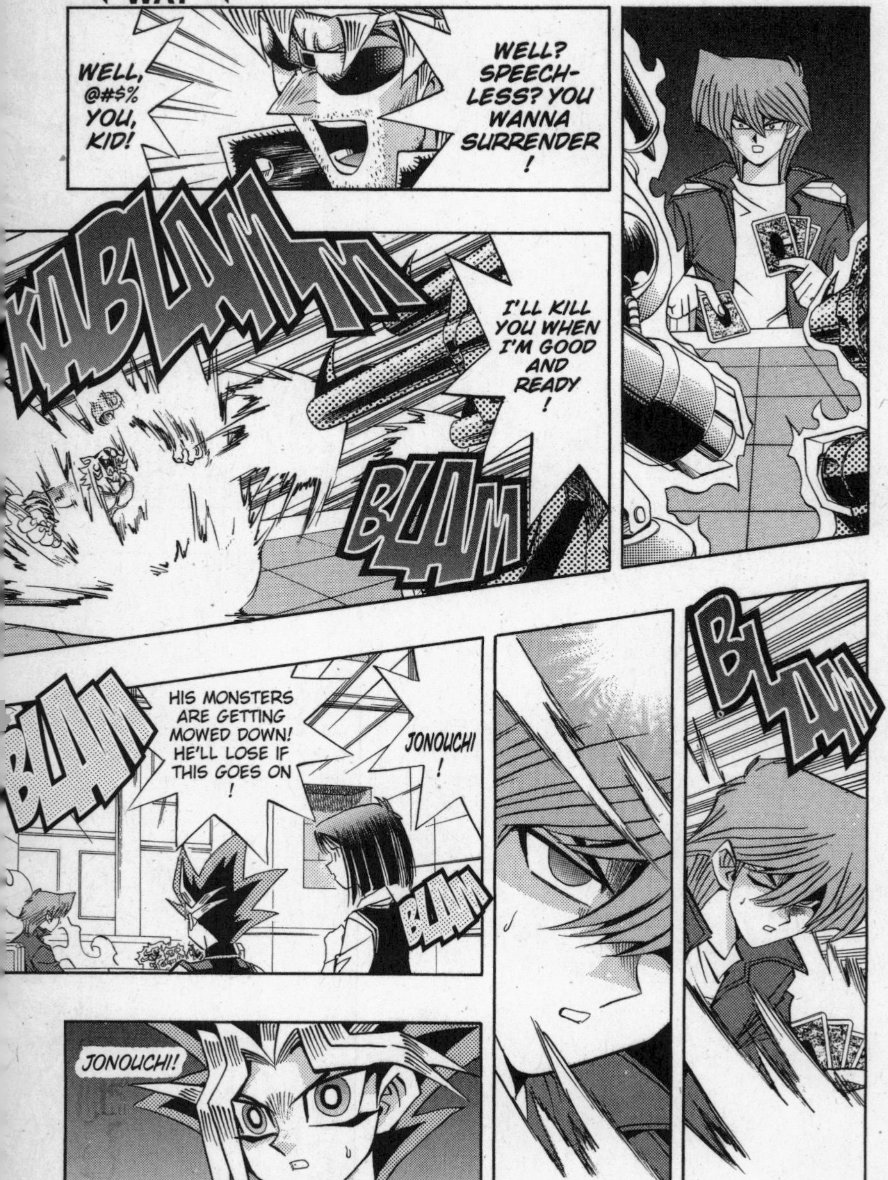
WELL? SPEECH-LESS? YOU WANNA SURRENDER!
WELL, @#$% YOU, KID!
I'LL KILL YOU WHEN I'M GOOD AND READY!
KABLAMM
BLAM
BLAM
JONOUCHI!
HIS MONSTERS ARE GETTING MOWED DOWN! HE'LL LOSE IF THIS GOES ON!
BLAM
BLAM
JONOUCHI!

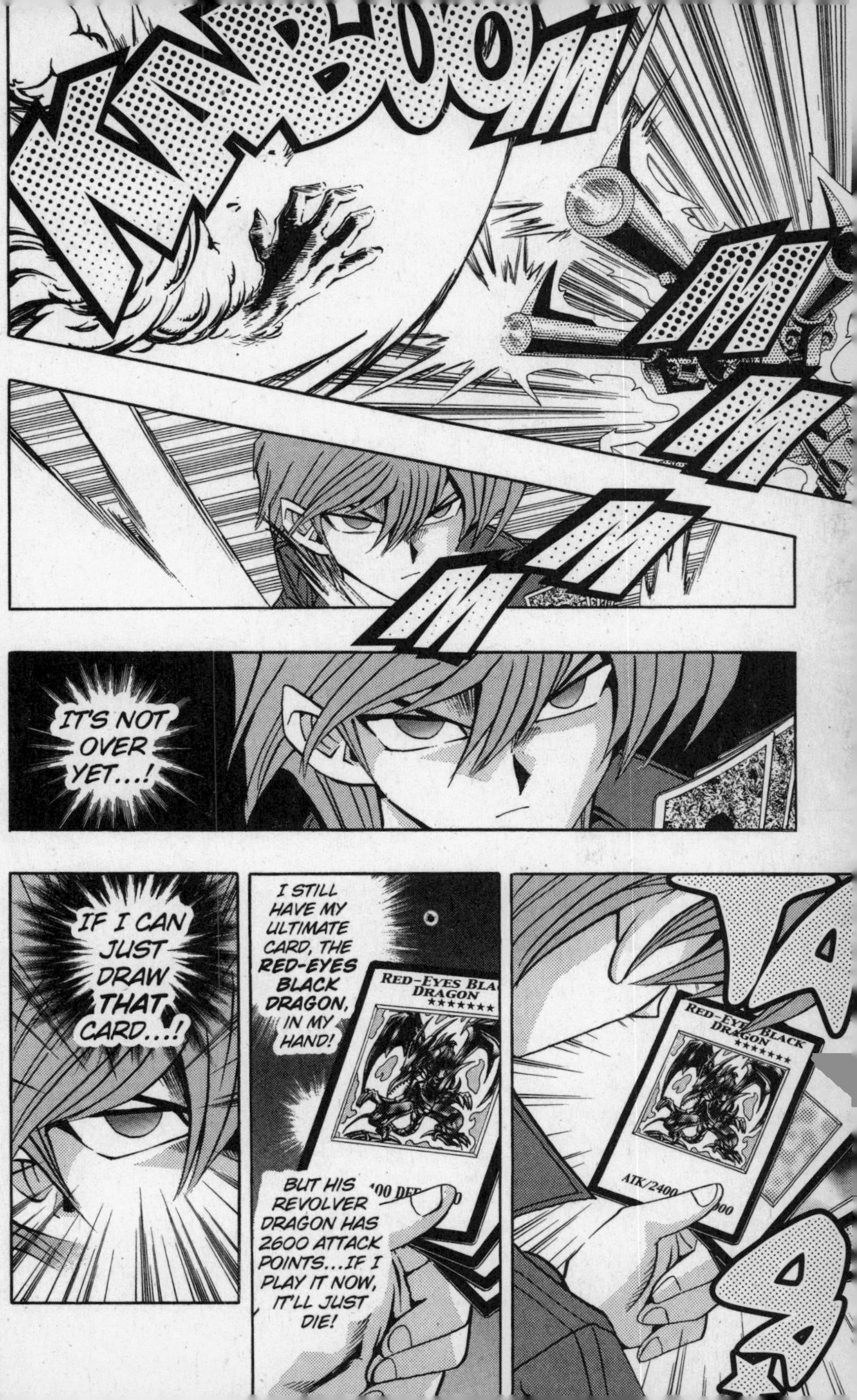
IT'S NOT OVER YET...!
I STILL HAVE MY ULTIMATE CARD, THE RED-EYES BLACK DRAGON, IN MY HAND!
BUT HIS REVOLVER DRAGON HAS 2600 ATTACK POINTS...IF I PLAY IT NOW, IT'LL JUST DIE!
IF I CAN JUST DRAW THAT CARD...!

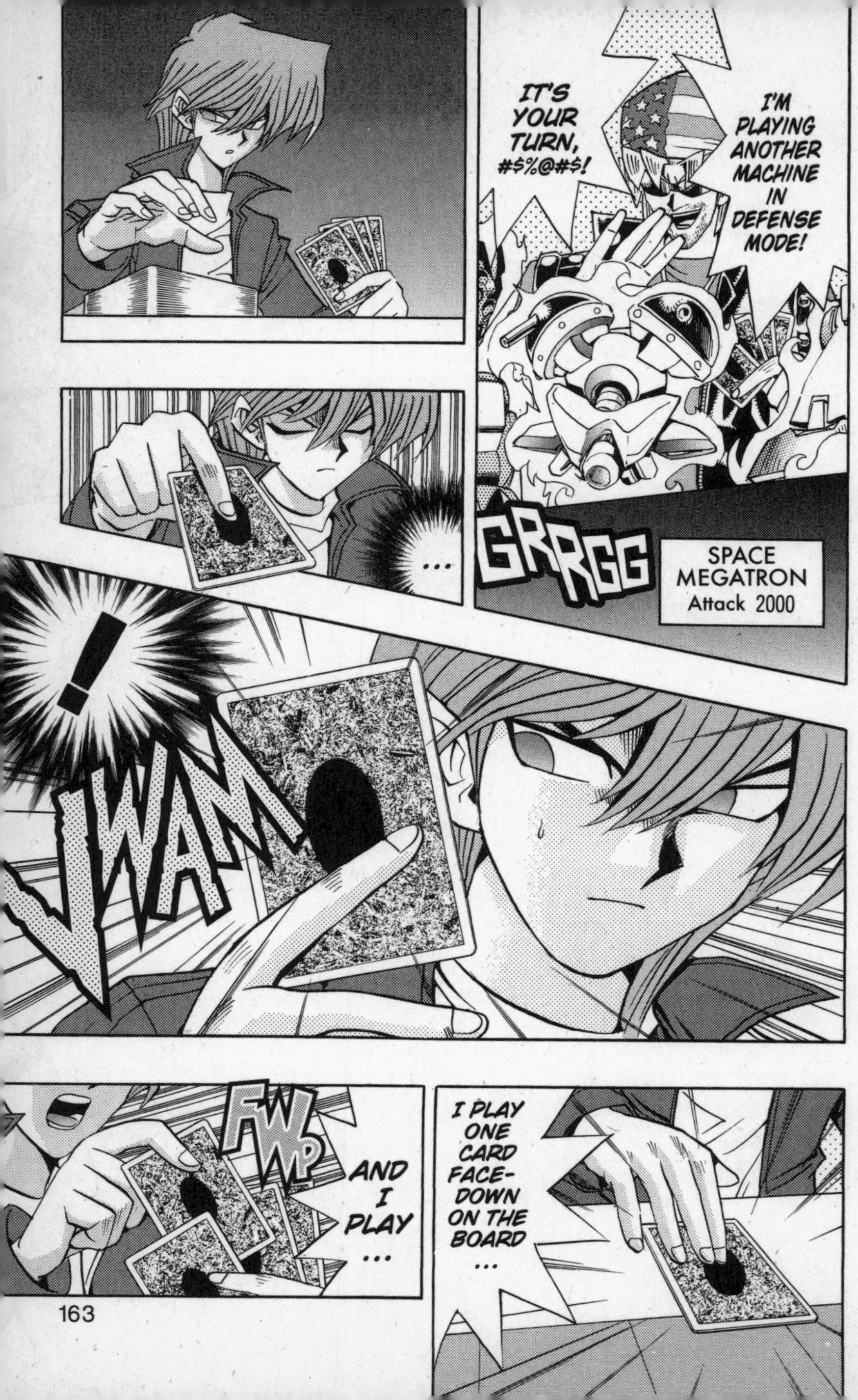
I'M PLAYING ANOTHER MACHINE IN DEFENSE MODE!
IT'S YOUR TURN, #$%@#$!
GRRGG
SPACE MEGATRON
Attack 2000
...
!
WAM
I PLAY ONE CARD FACE-DOWN ON THE BOARD ...
FWP
AND I PLAY ...

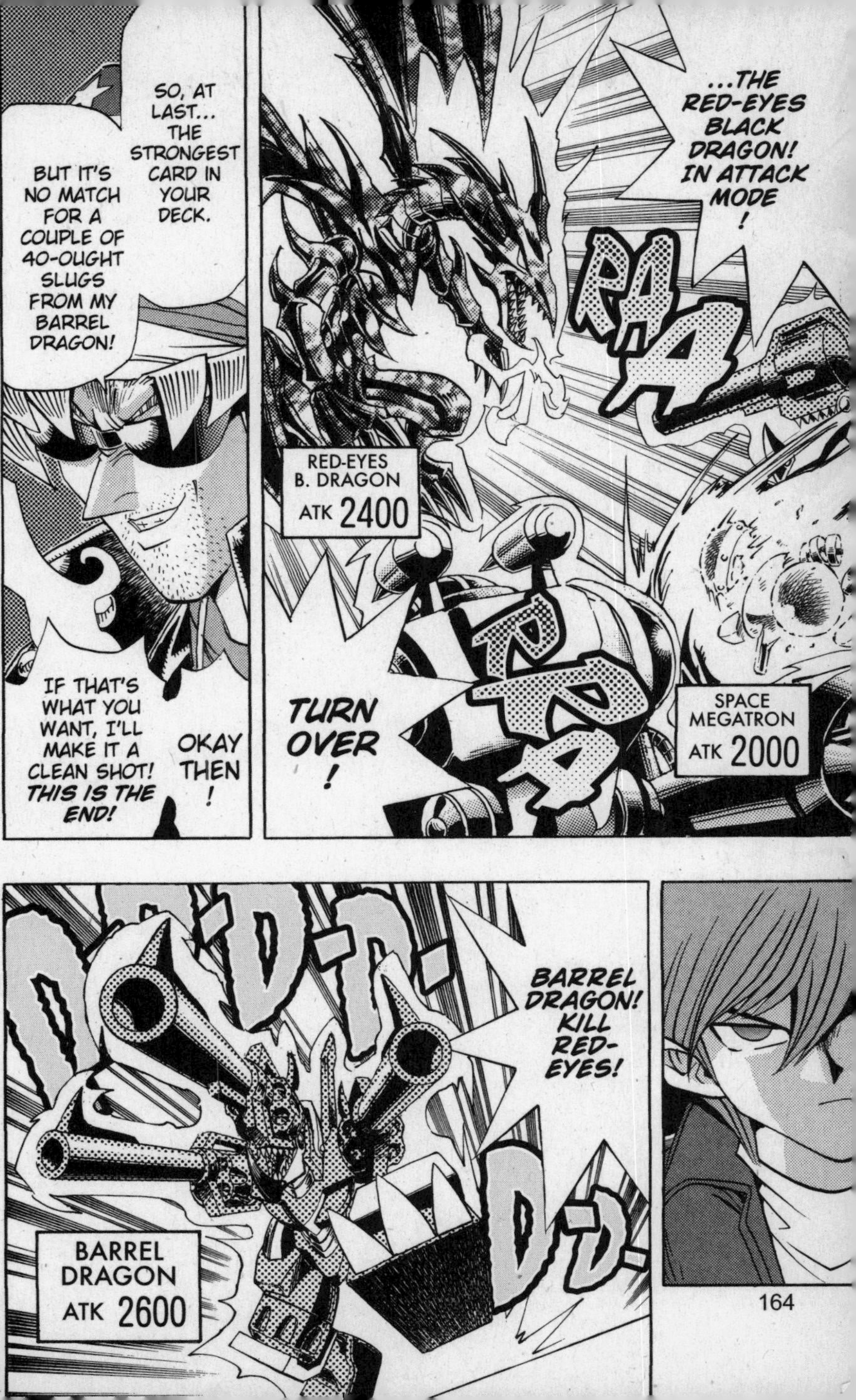
...THE RED-EYES BLACK DRAGON! IN ATTACK MODE!
RED-EYES B. DRAGON ATK 2400
SPACE MEGATRON ATK 2000
TURN OVER!
SO, AT LAST... THE STRONGEST CARD IN YOUR DECK.
BUT IT'S NO MATCH FOR A COUPLE OF 40-OUGHT SLUGS FROM MY BARREL DRAGON!
OKAY THEN!
IF THAT'S WHAT YOU WANT, I'LL MAKE IT A CLEAN SHOT! *THIS IS THE END!*
BARREL DRAGON! KILL RED-EYES!
BARREL DRAGON ATK 2600

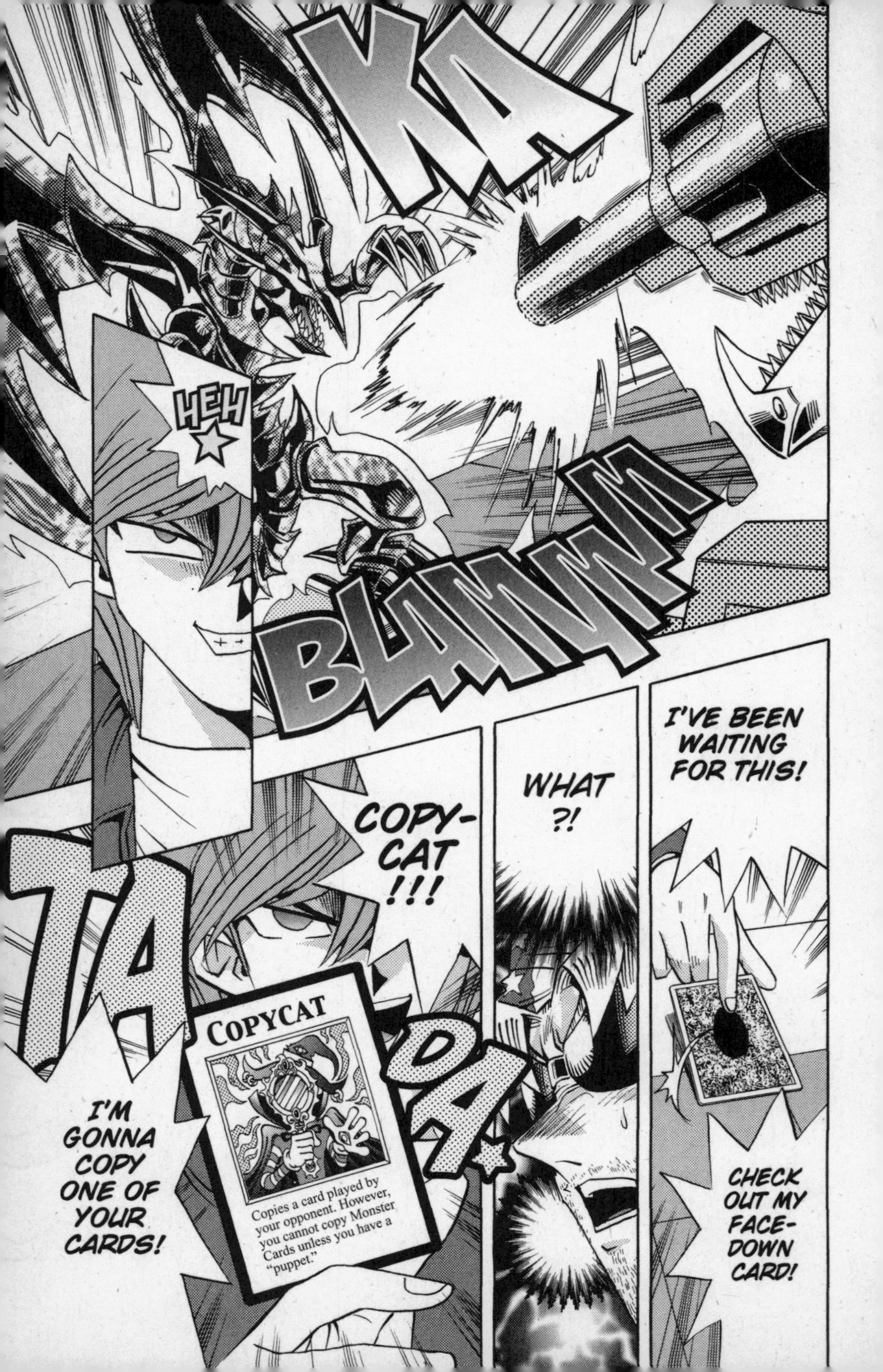
KA
BLAMM!
HEH ★
I'VE BEEN WAITING FOR THIS!
CHECK OUT MY FACE-DOWN CARD!
WHAT ?!
COPY-CAT !!!
TA DA ★
COPYCAT
Copies a card played by your opponent. However, you cannot copy Monster Cards unless you have a "puppet."
I'M GONNA COPY ONE OF YOUR CARDS!

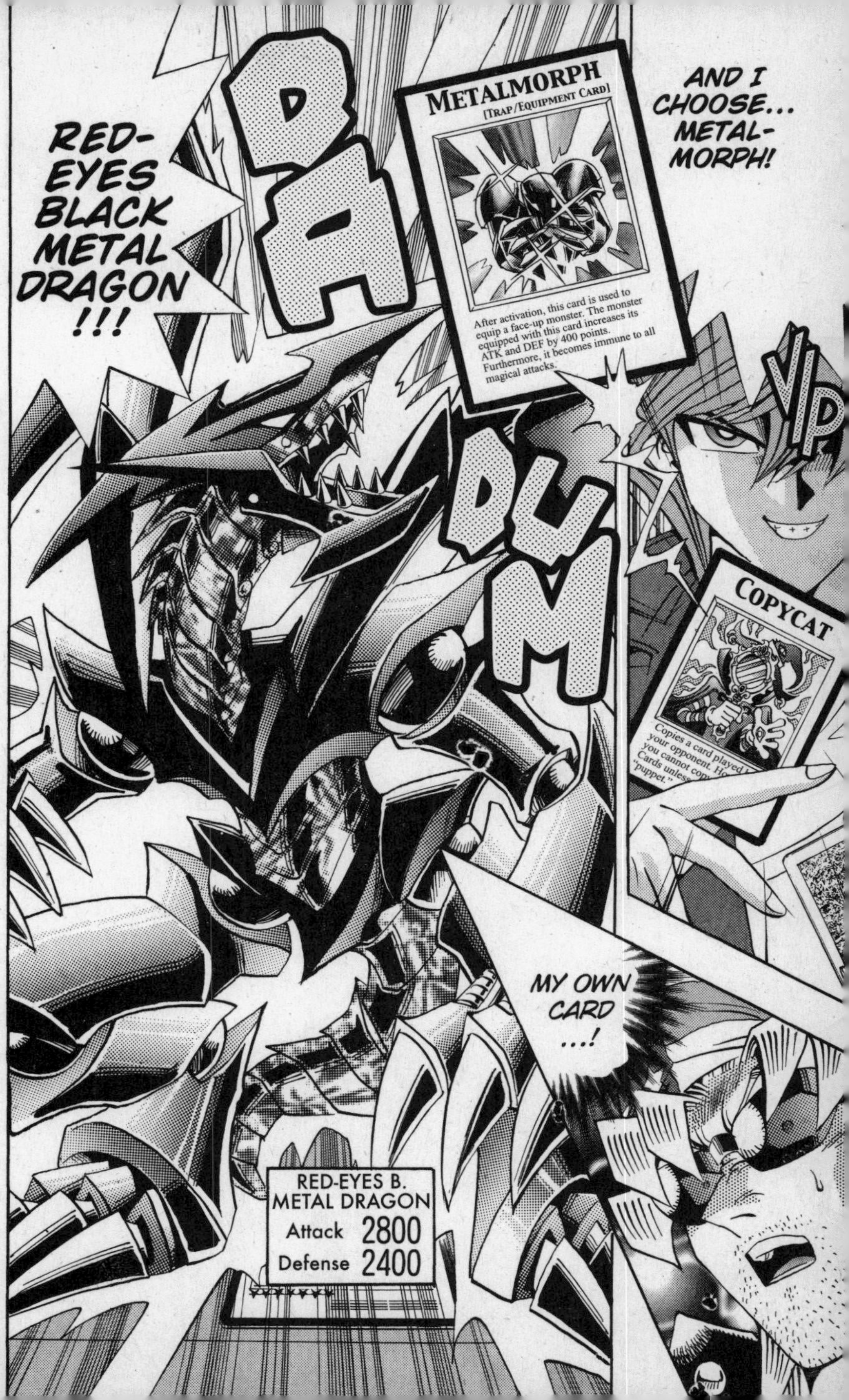
AND I CHOOSE... METAL-MORPH!
VIP
COPYCAT
Copies a card played
your opponent. Ho
Cards unless
"puppet."
MY OWN CARD ...!
DA
METALMORPH
[TRAP/EQUIPMENT CARD]
After activation, this card is used to equip a face-up monster. The monster equipped with this card increases its ATK and DEF by 400 points. Furthermore, it becomes immune to all magical attacks.
RED-EYES BLACK METAL DRAGON !!!
DUM
RED-EYES B. METAL DRAGON
Attack 2800
Defense 2400

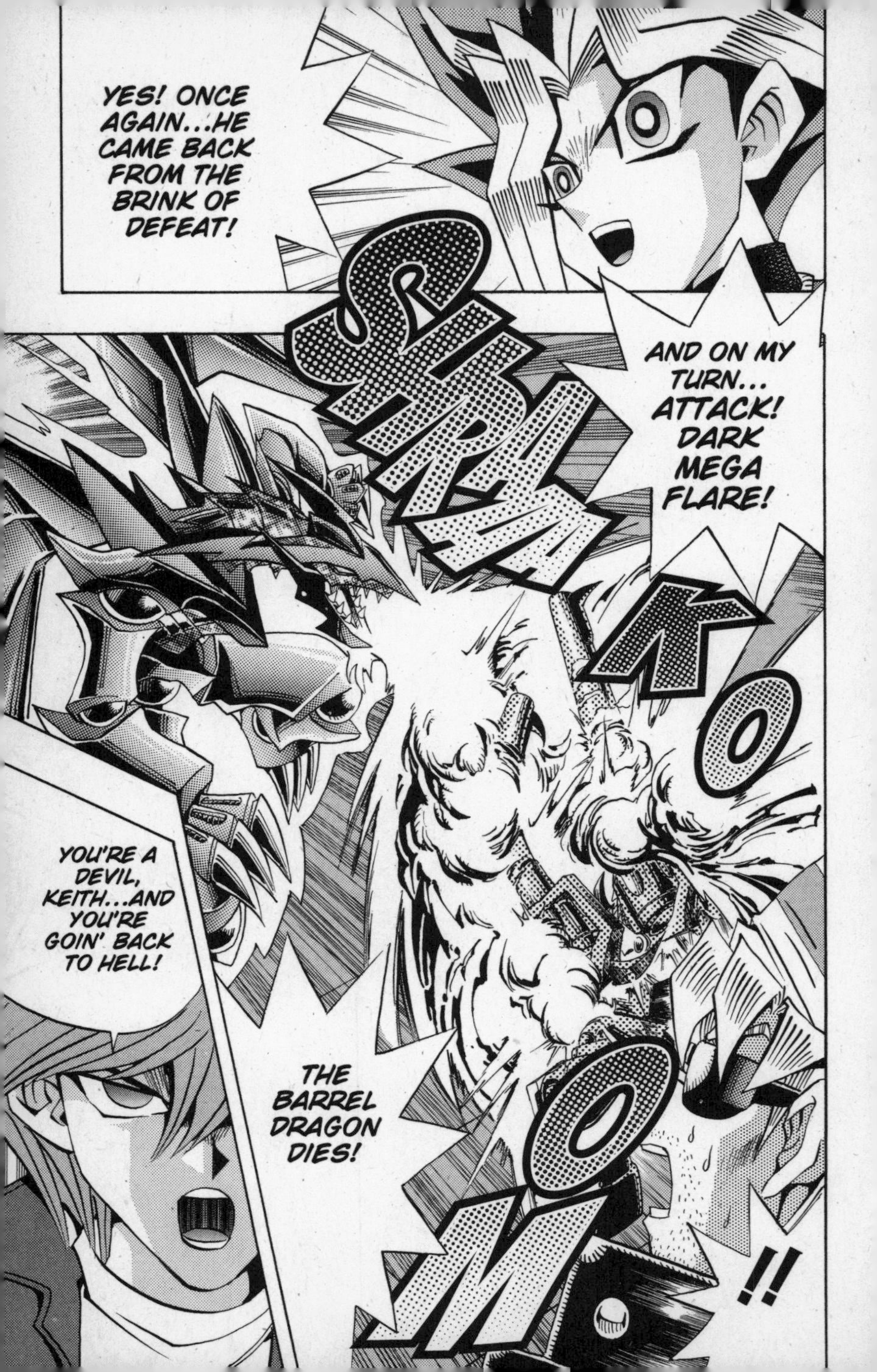
YES! ONCE AGAIN...HE CAME BACK FROM THE BRINK OF DEFEAT!
AND ON MY TURN... ATTACK! DARK MEGA FLARE!
THE BARREL DRAGON DIES!
YOU'RE A DEVIL, KEITH...AND YOU'RE GOIN' BACK TO HELL!

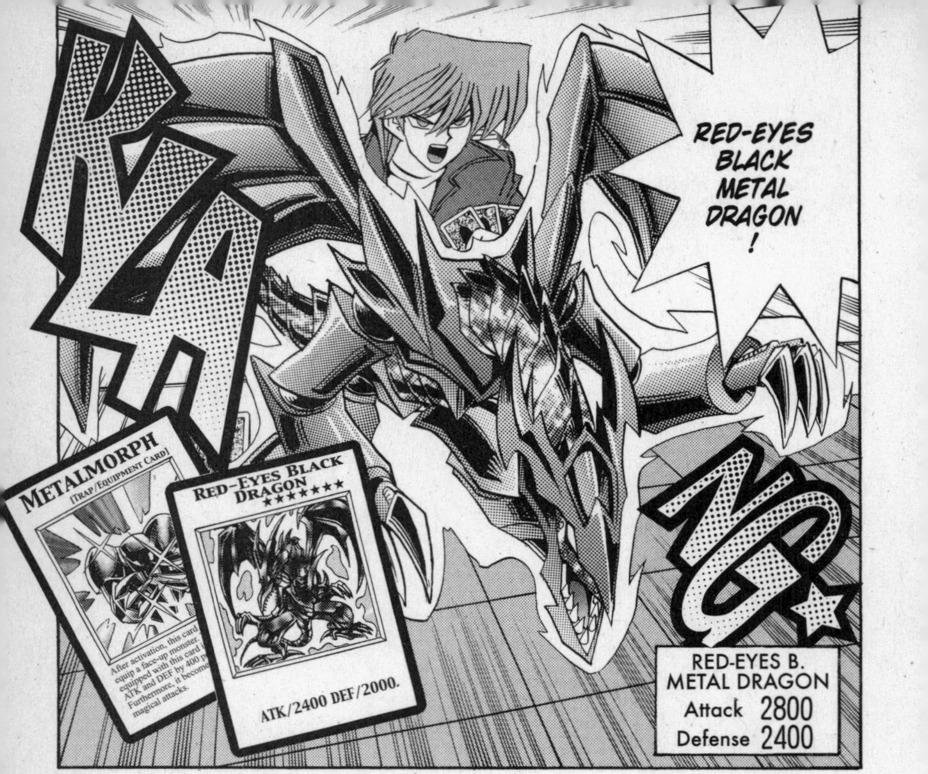
RED-EYES BLACK METAL DRAGON !
KA
NG
RED-EYES B. METAL DRAGON
Attack 2800
Defense 2400
RED-EYES BLACK DRAGON
ATK/2400 DEF/2000.
METALMORPH
[TRAP/EQUIPMENT CARD]

DUEL 64: THE FINAL TURN!

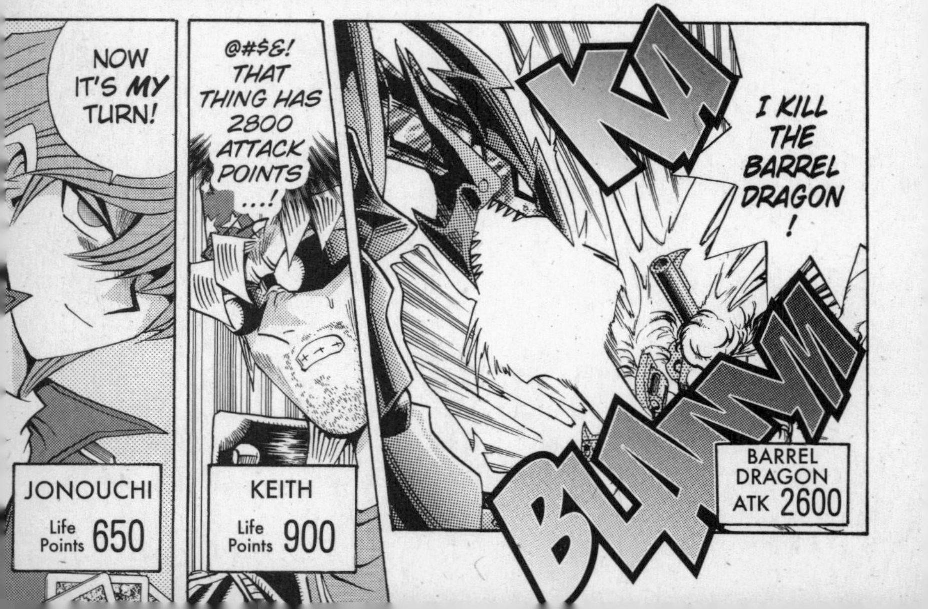
I KILL THE BARREL DRAGON !
KA
BLAMM
BARREL DRAGON
ATK 2600
@#$&! THAT THING HAS 2800 ATTACK POINTS ...!
KEITH
Life Points 900
NOW IT'S *MY* TURN!
JONOUCHI
Life Points 650

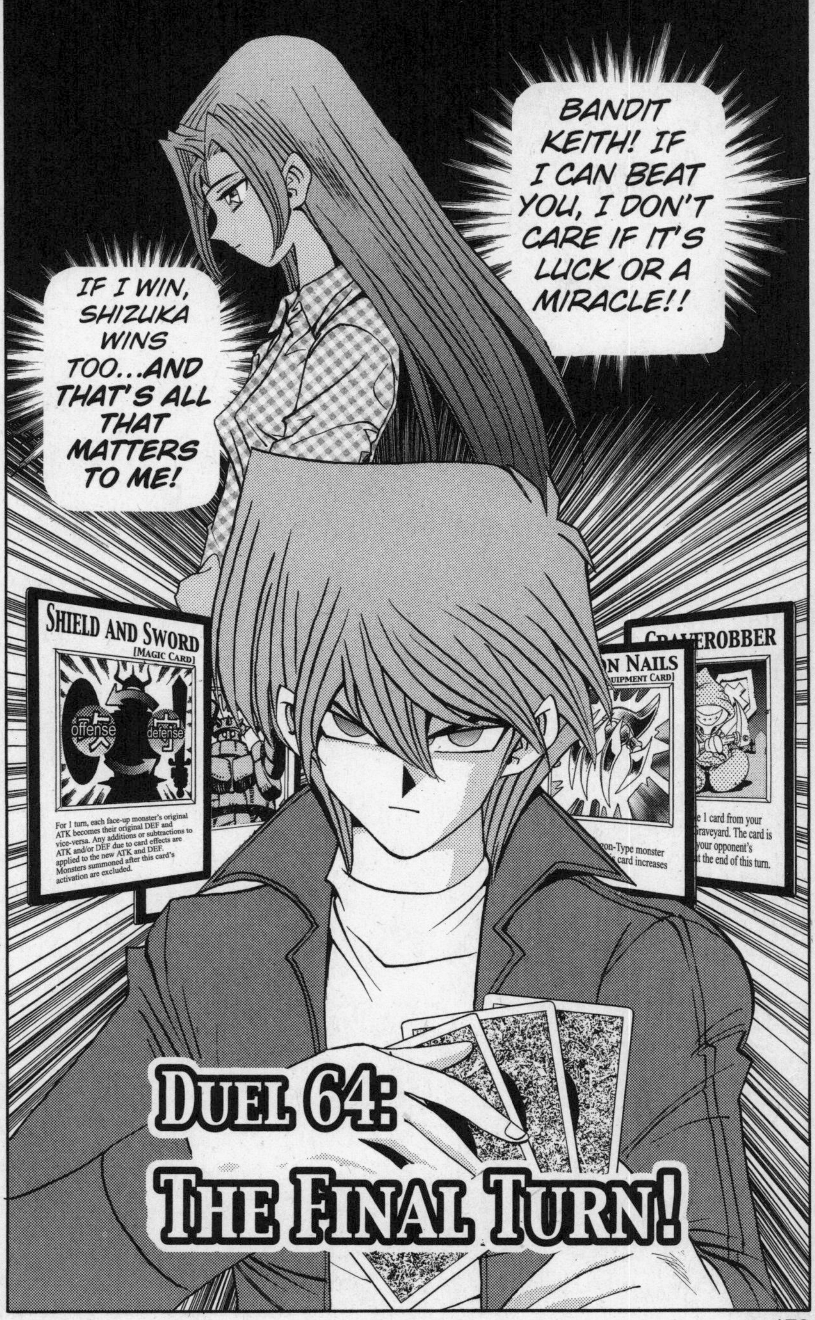
BANDIT KEITH! IF I CAN BEAT YOU, I DON'T CARE IF IT'S LUCK OR A MIRACLE!!
IF I WIN, SHIZUKA WINS TOO...AND THAT'S ALL THAT MATTERS TO ME!
SHIELD AND SWORD
[MAGIC CARD]
offense
defense
For 1 turn, each face-up monster's original ATK becomes their original DEF and vice-versa. Any additions or subtractions to ATK and/or DEF due to card effects are applied to the new ATK and DEF. Monsters summoned after this card's activation are excluded.
DUEL 64:
THE FINAL TURN!

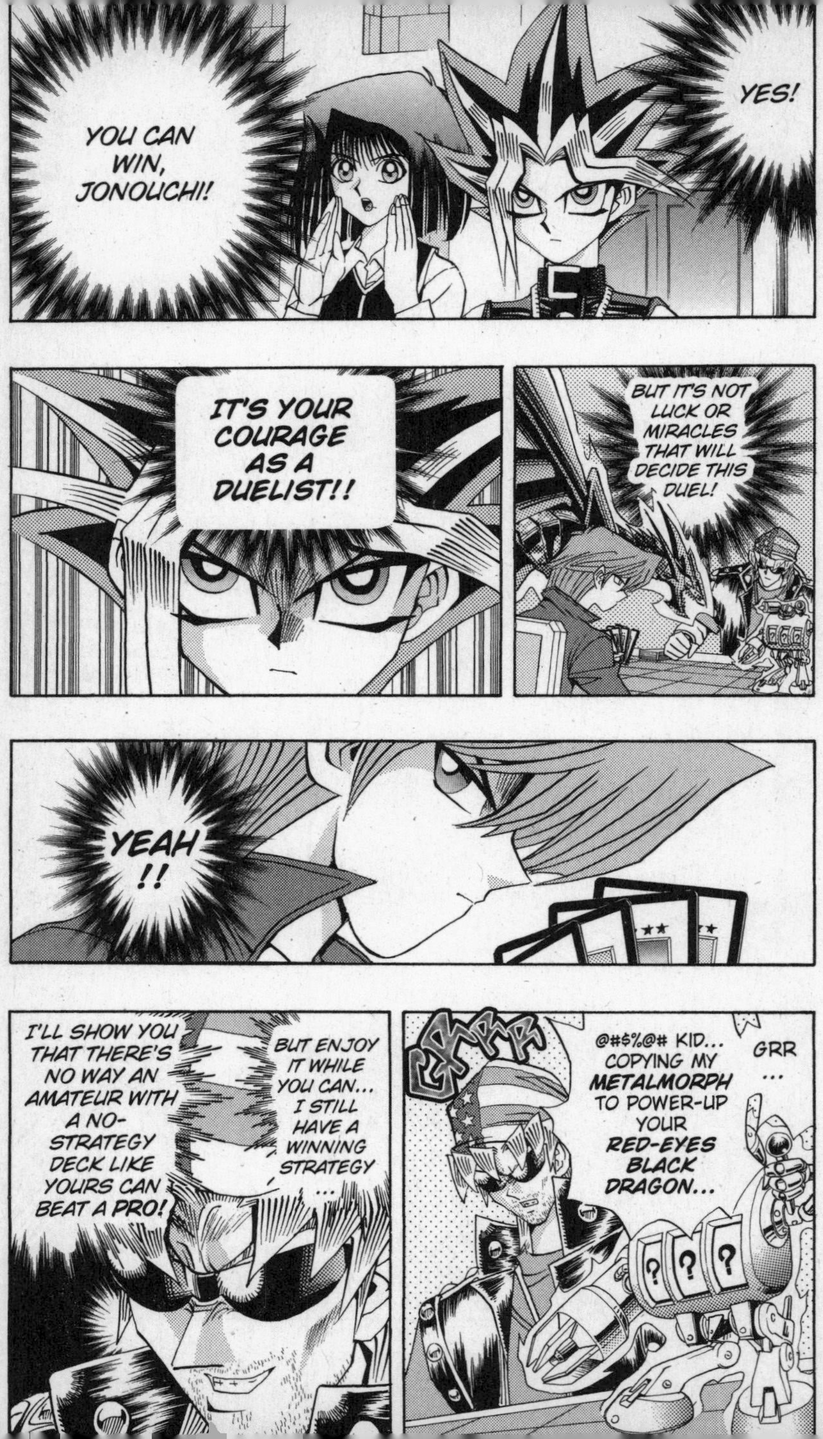
YES!
YOU CAN WIN, JONOUCHI!
BUT IT'S NOT LUCK OR MIRACLES THAT WILL DECIDE THIS DUEL!
IT'S YOUR COURAGE AS A DUELIST!!
YEAH!!
GRR...
@#$%@# KID... COPYING MY METALMORPH TO POWER-UP YOUR RED-EYES BLACK DRAGON...
BUT ENJOY IT WHILE YOU CAN... I STILL HAVE A WINNING STRATEGY...
I'LL SHOW YOU THAT THERE'S NO WAY AN AMATEUR WITH A NO-STRATEGY DECK LIKE YOURS CAN BEAT A PRO!

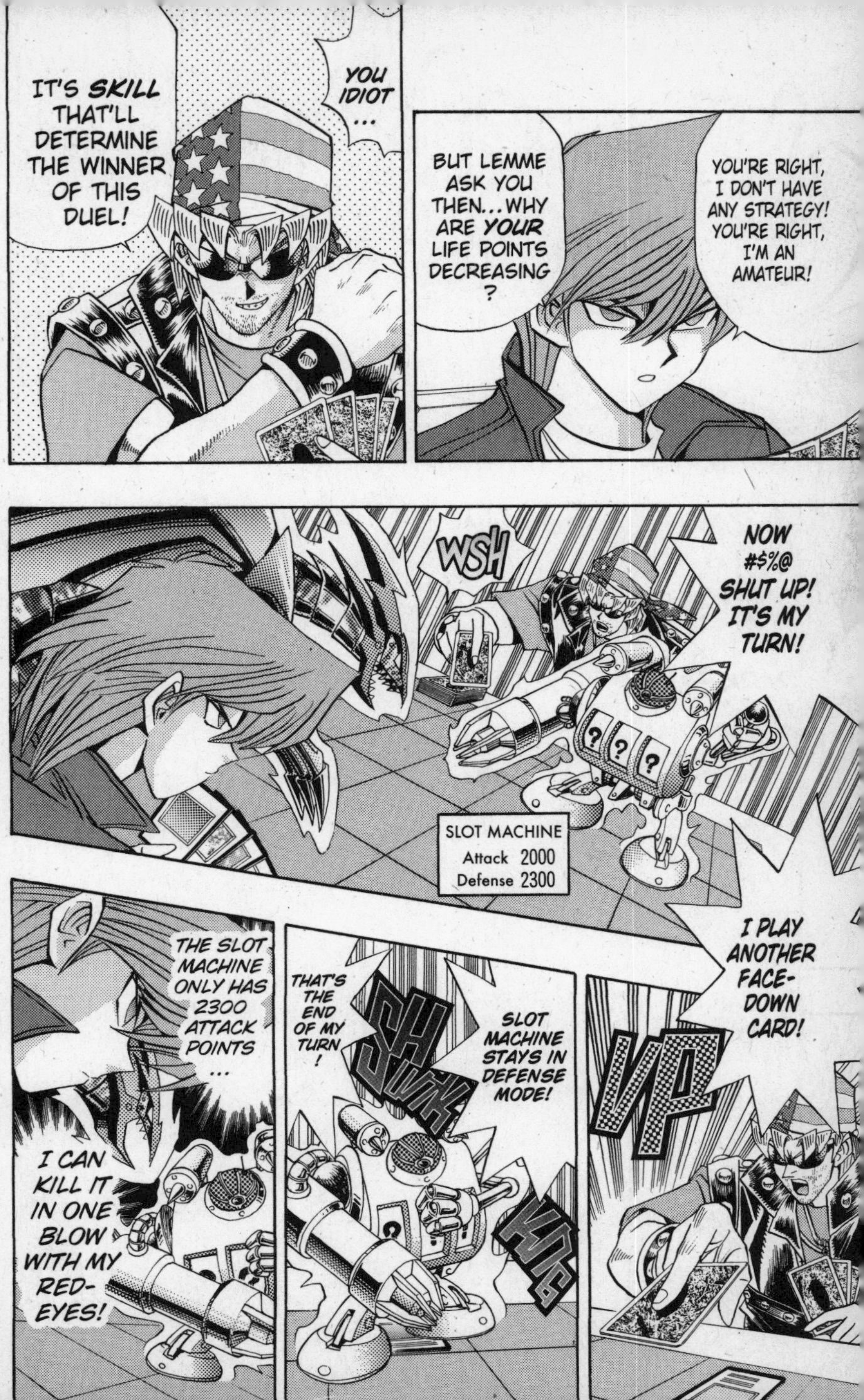
YOU'RE RIGHT, I DON'T HAVE ANY STRATEGY! YOU'RE RIGHT, I'M AN AMATEUR!
BUT LEMME ASK YOU THEN...WHY ARE *YOUR* LIFE POINTS DECREASING?
YOU IDIOT...
IT'S *SKILL* THAT'LL DETERMINE THE WINNER OF THIS DUEL!
NOW #$%@ SHUT UP! IT'S MY TURN!
WSH
SLOT MACHINE
Attack 2000
Defense 2300
I PLAY ANOTHER FACE-DOWN CARD!
SLOT MACHINE STAYS IN DEFENSE MODE!
THAT'S THE END OF MY TURN!
THE SLOT MACHINE ONLY HAS 2300 ATTACK POINTS...
I CAN KILL IT IN ONE BLOW WITH MY RED-EYES!

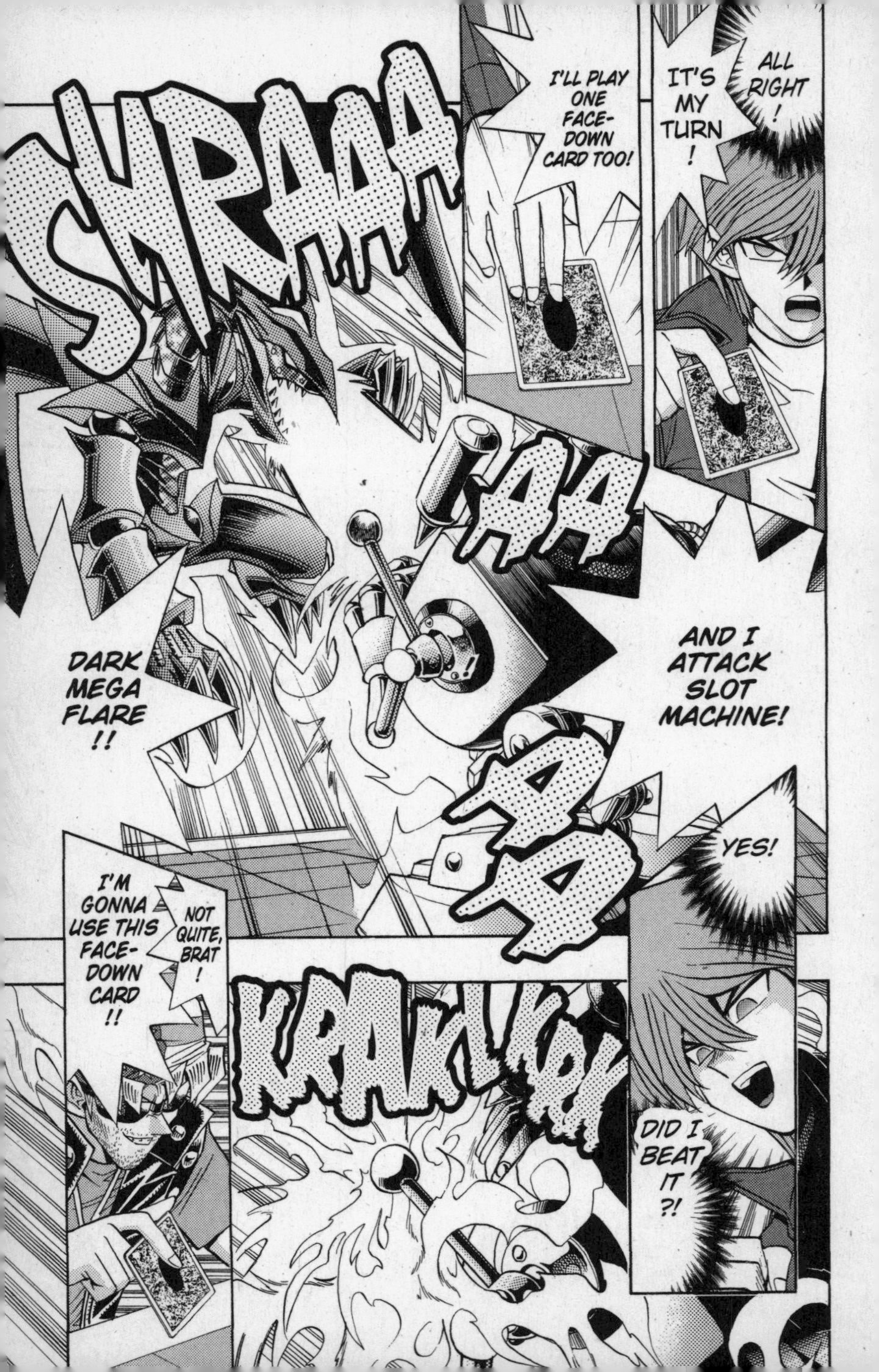
ALL RIGHT!
IT'S MY TURN!
I'LL PLAY ONE FACE-DOWN CARD TOO!
SHRAAA
AND I ATTACK SLOT MACHINE!
DARK MEGA FLARE!!
YES!
DID I BEAT IT?!
NOT QUITE, BRAT!
I'M GONNA USE THIS FACE-DOWN CARD!!

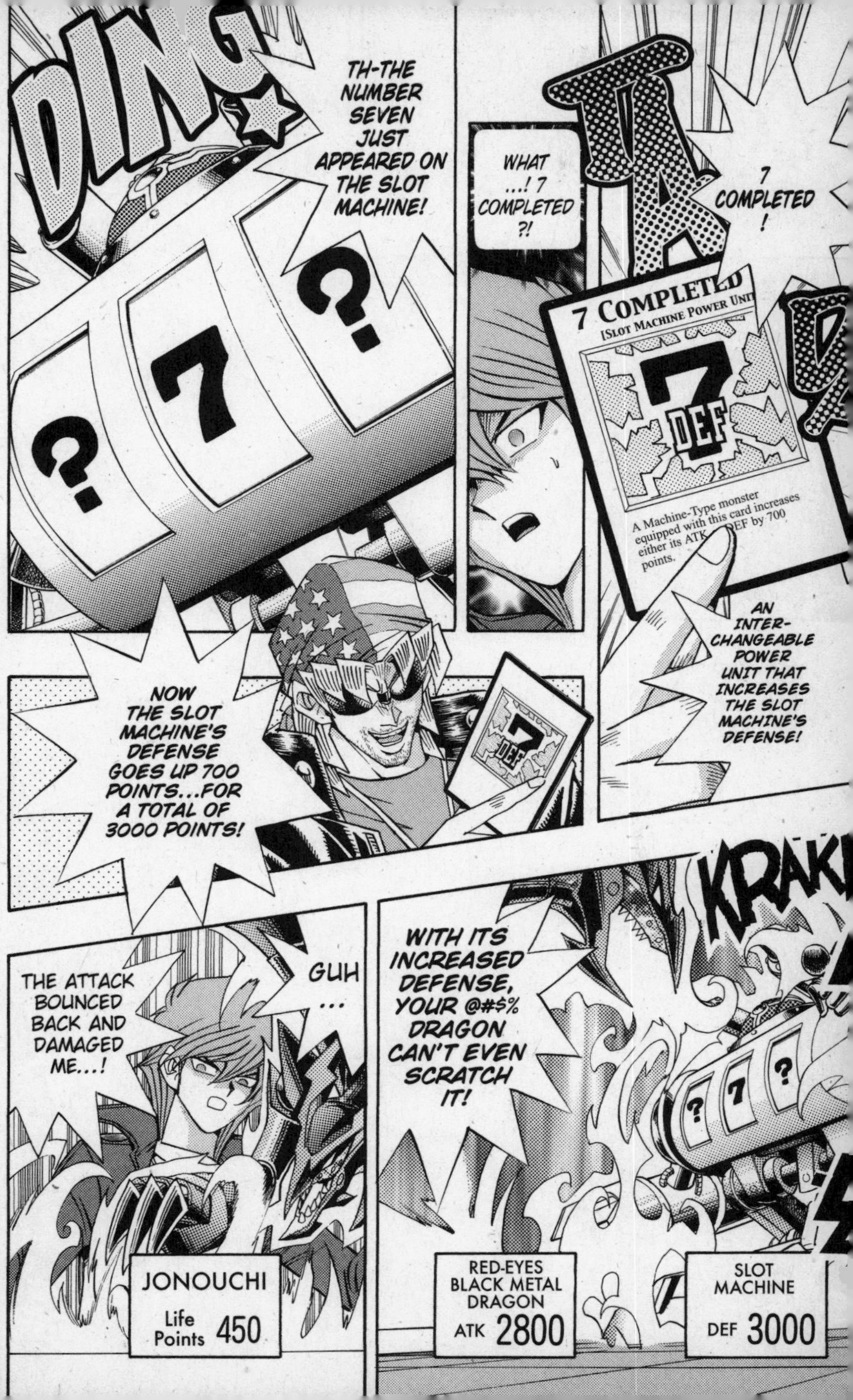
7 COMPLETED!
7 COMPLETED
[SLOT MACHINE POWER UNIT]
7
DEF
A Machine-Type monster equipped with this card increases either its ATK DEF by 700 points.
AN INTER-CHANGEABLE POWER UNIT THAT INCREASES THE SLOT MACHINE'S DEFENSE!
WHAT ...! 7 COMPLETED ?!
TH-THE NUMBER SEVEN JUST APPEARED ON THE SLOT MACHINE!
DING
? 7 ?
NOW THE SLOT MACHINE'S DEFENSE GOES UP 700 POINTS...FOR A TOTAL OF 3000 POINTS!
KRAK
WITH ITS INCREASED DEFENSE, YOUR @#$% DRAGON CAN'T EVEN SCRATCH IT!
SLOT MACHINE DEF 3000
RED-EYES BLACK METAL DRAGON ATK 2800
GUH ...
THE ATTACK BOUNCED BACK AND DAMAGED ME...!
JONOUCHI Life Points 450

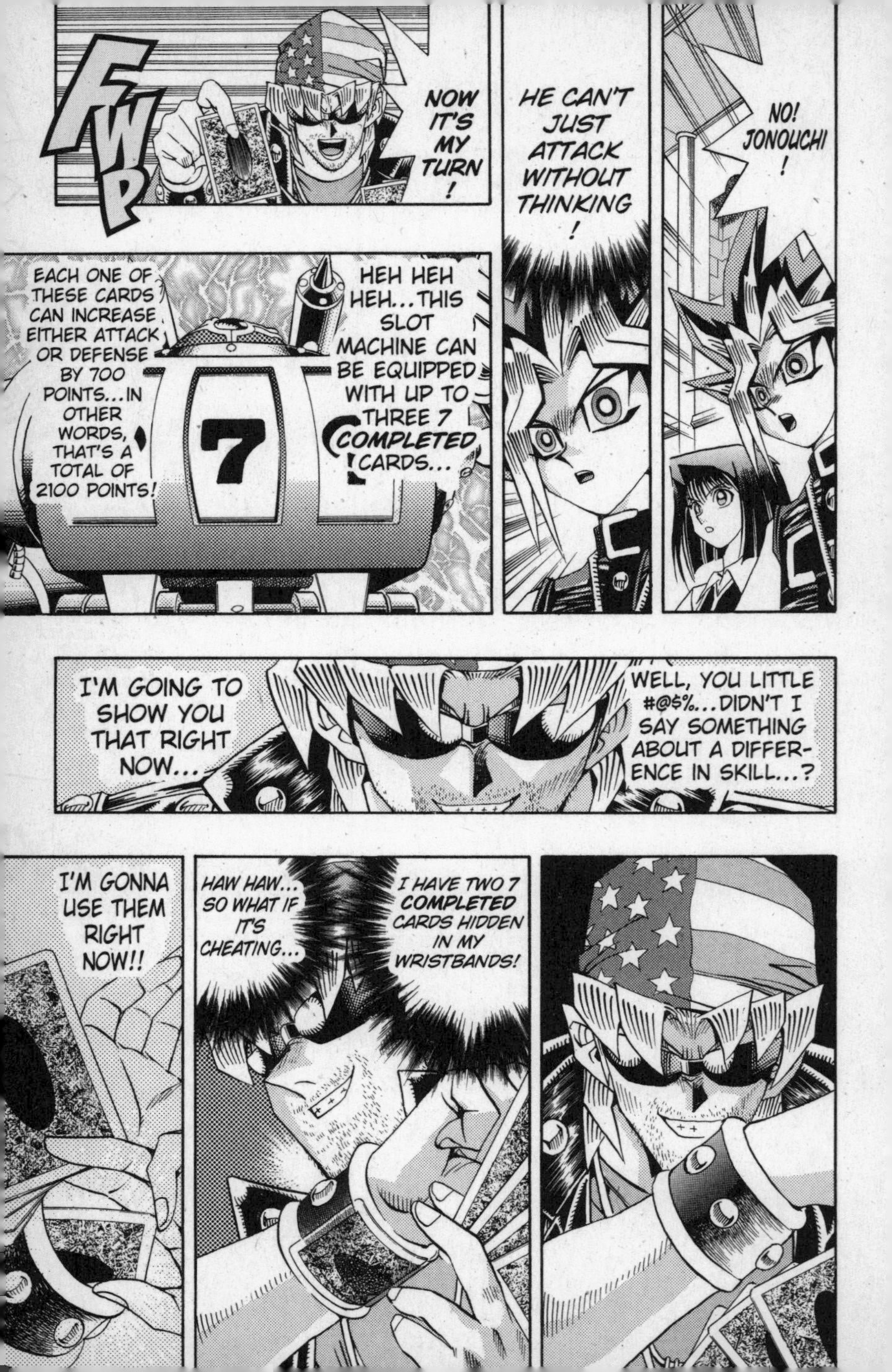
NO! JONOUCHI!
HE CAN'T JUST ATTACK WITHOUT THINKING!
NOW IT'S MY TURN!
FWP
HEH HEH HEH...THIS SLOT MACHINE CAN BE EQUIPPED WITH UP TO THREE 7 COMPLETED CARDS...
EACH ONE OF THESE CARDS CAN INCREASE EITHER ATTACK OR DEFENSE BY 700 POINTS...IN OTHER WORDS, THAT'S A TOTAL OF 2100 POINTS!
WELL, YOU LITTLE #@$%...DIDN'T I SAY SOMETHING ABOUT A DIFFERENCE IN SKILL...?
I'M GOING TO SHOW YOU THAT RIGHT NOW...
I HAVE TWO 7 COMPLETED CARDS HIDDEN IN MY WRISTBANDS!
HAW HAW... SO WHAT IF IT'S CHEATING...
I'M GONNA USE THEM RIGHT NOW!!

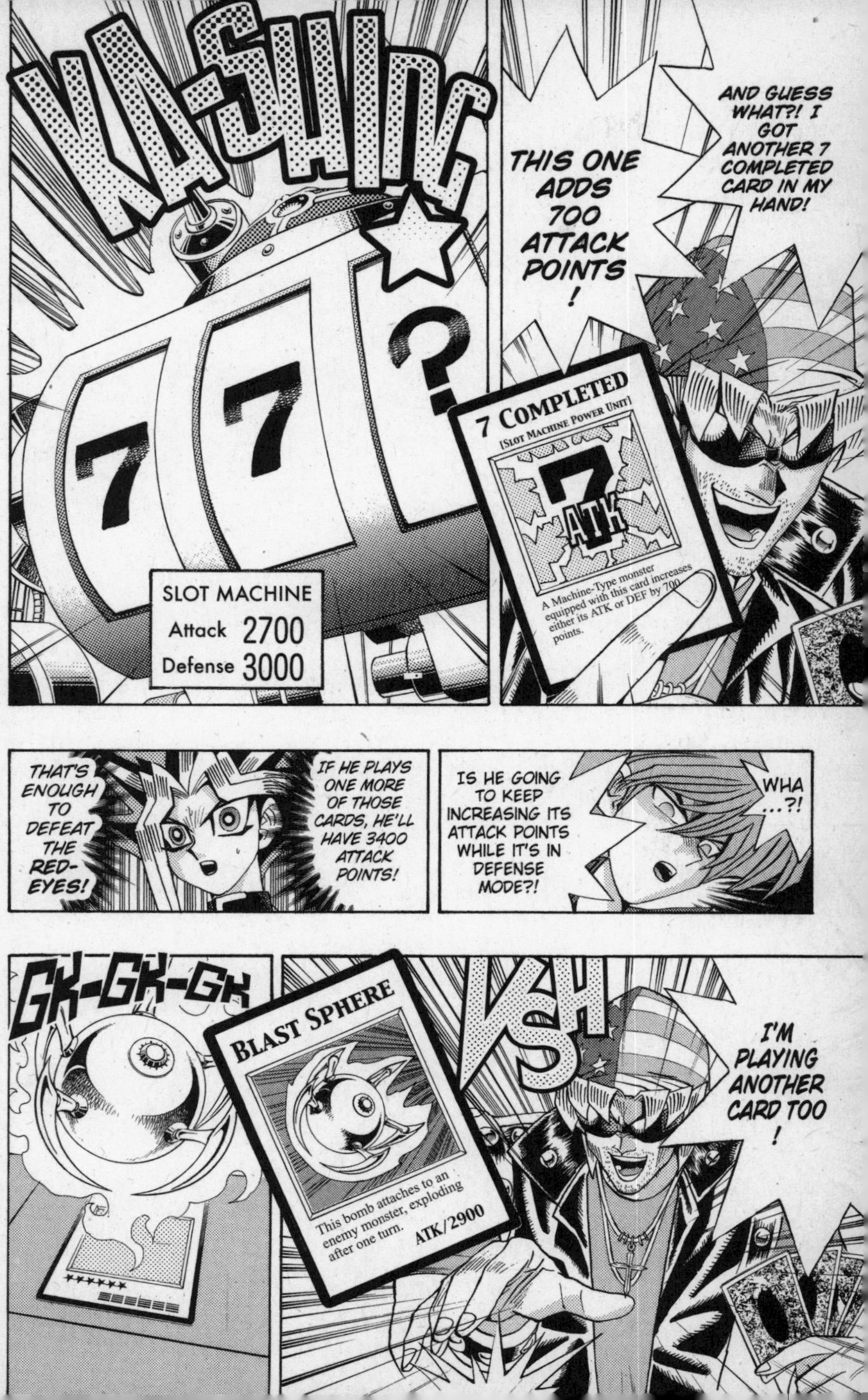
AND GUESS WHAT?! I GOT ANOTHER 7 COMPLETED CARD IN MY HAND!
THIS ONE ADDS 700 ATTACK POINTS!
7 COMPLETED
[SLOT MACHINE POWER UNIT]
ATK
A Machine-Type monster equipped with this card increases either its ATK or DEF by 700 points.
KA-SHING
7 7 ?
SLOT MACHINE
Attack 2700
Defense 3000
WHA...?!
IS HE GOING TO KEEP INCREASING ITS ATTACK POINTS WHILE IT'S IN DEFENSE MODE?!
IF HE PLAYS ONE MORE OF THOSE CARDS, HE'LL HAVE 3400 ATTACK POINTS!
THAT'S ENOUGH TO DEFEAT THE RED-EYES!
VSH
I'M PLAYING ANOTHER CARD TOO!
BLAST SPHERE
This bomb attaches to an enemy monster, exploding after one turn.
ATK/2900
GK-GK-GK

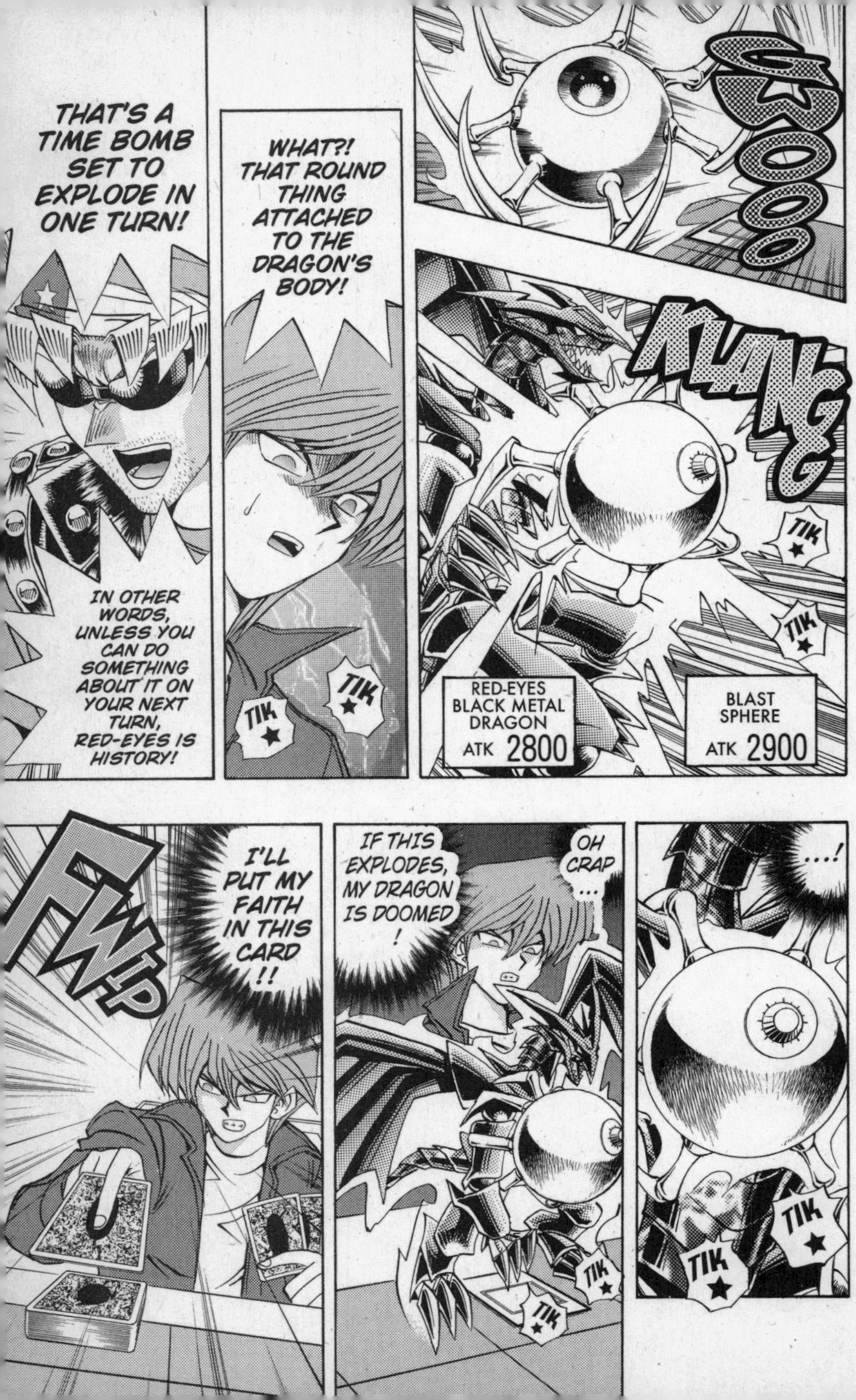
GOOOO
KLANG
TIK ★
TIK ★
RED-EYES BLACK METAL DRAGON ATK 2800
BLAST SPHERE ATK 2900
WHAT?! THAT ROUND THING ATTACHED TO THE DRAGON'S BODY!
TIK ★
TIK ★
THAT'S A TIME BOMB SET TO EXPLODE IN ONE TURN!
IN OTHER WORDS, UNLESS YOU CAN DO SOMETHING ABOUT IT ON YOUR NEXT TURN, RED-EYES IS HISTORY!
...!
TIK ★
TIK ★
OH CRAP ...
IF THIS EXPLODES, MY DRAGON IS DOOMED!
TIK ★
TIK ★
FWIP
I'LL PUT MY FAITH IN THIS CARD!!

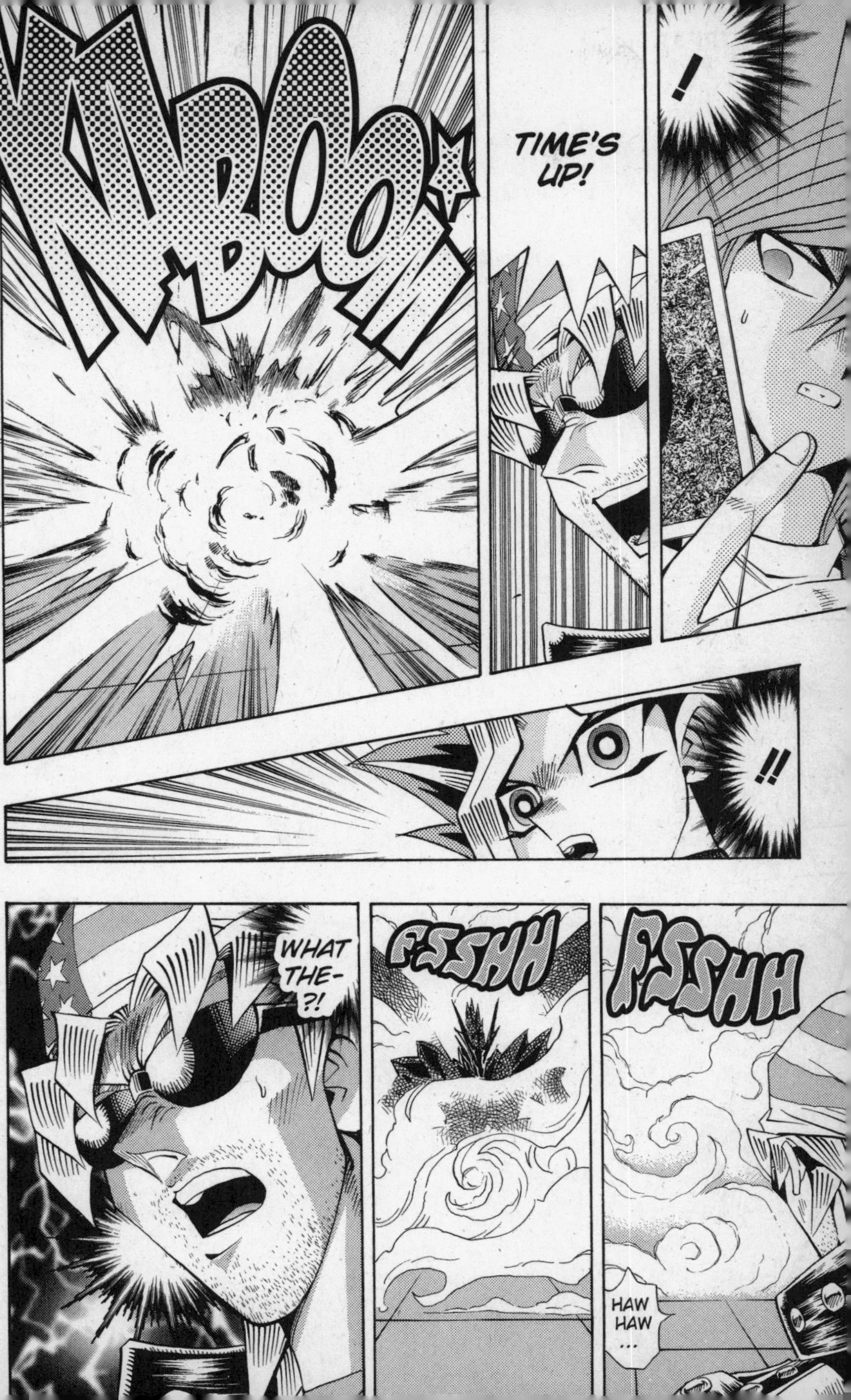
!
TIME'S UP!
KABOOM
!!
FSSHH
HAW HAW ...
FSSHH
WHAT THE-?!

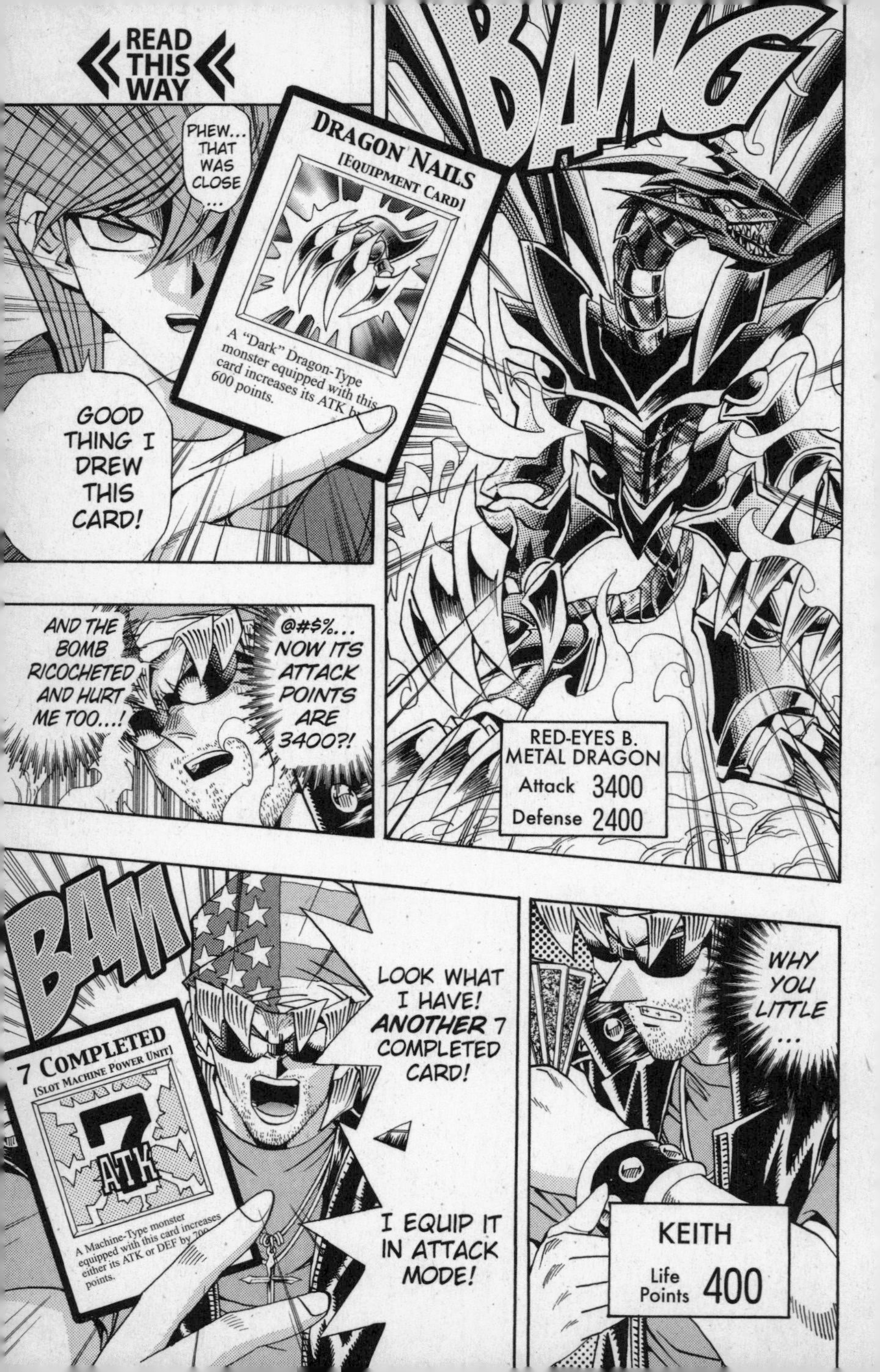
READ THIS WAY
BANG
RED-EYES B. METAL DRAGON
Attack 3400
Defense 2400
PHEW... THAT WAS CLOSE ...
DRAGON NAILS
[EQUIPMENT CARD]
A "Dark" Dragon-Type monster equipped with this card increases its ATK b
600 points.
GOOD THING I DREW THIS CARD!
@#$%... NOW ITS ATTACK POINTS ARE 3400?!
AND THE BOMB RICOCHETED AND HURT ME TOO...!
WHY YOU LITTLE ...
KEITH
Life Points 400
LOOK WHAT I HAVE! ANOTHER 7 COMPLETED CARD!
I EQUIP IT IN ATTACK MODE!
BAM
7 COMPLETED
[SLOT MACHINE POWER UNIT]
7
ATK
A Machine-Type monster equipped with this card increases either its ATK or DEF by 70
points.

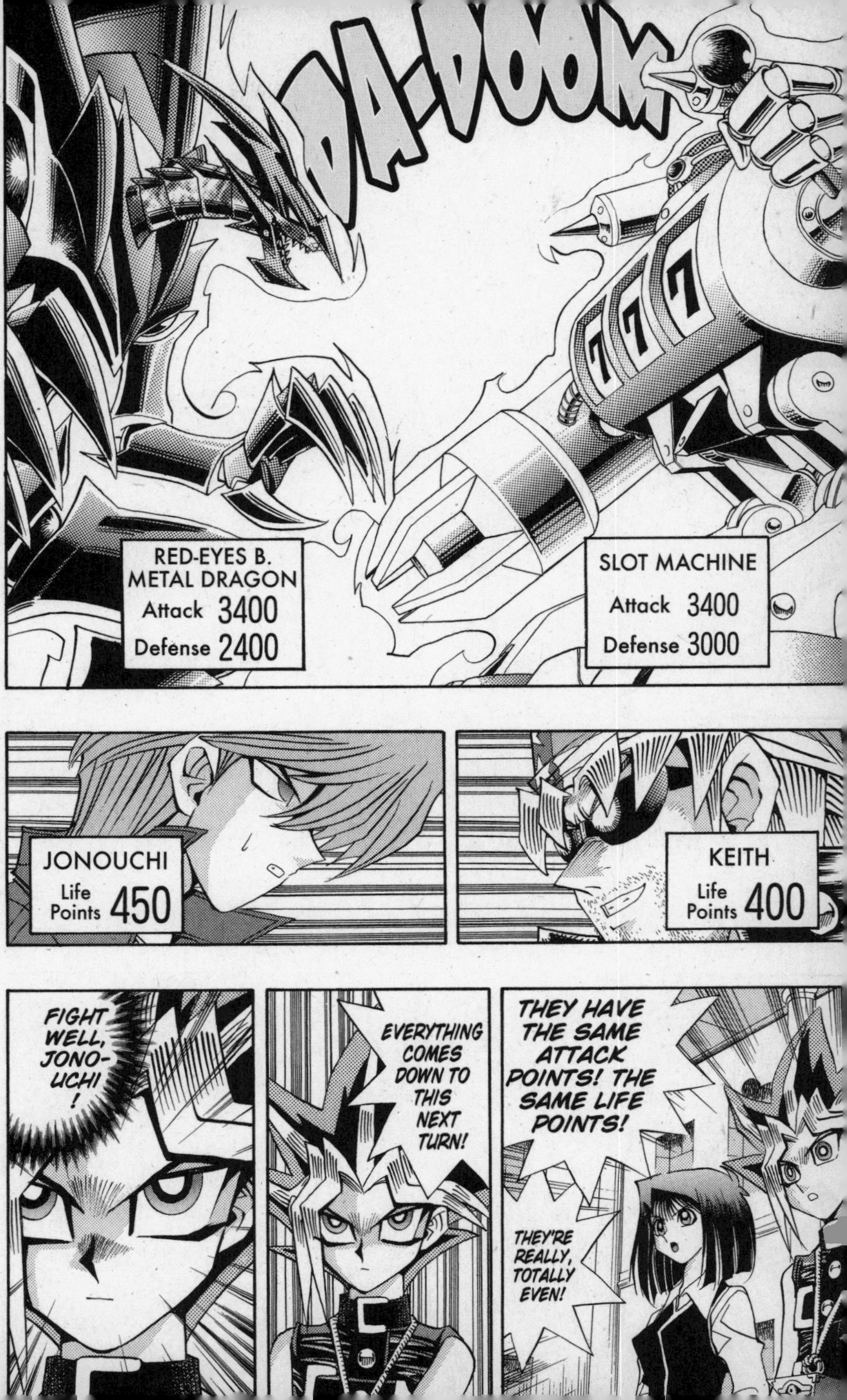
DA-DOOM
SLOT MACHINE
Attack 3400
Defense 3000
RED-EYES B. METAL DRAGON
Attack 3400
Defense 2400
KEITH
Life Points 400
JONOUCHI
Life Points 450
THEY HAVE THE SAME ATTACK POINTS! THE SAME LIFE POINTS!
THEY'RE REALLY, TOTALLY EVEN!
EVERYTHING COMES DOWN TO THIS NEXT TURN!
FIGHT WELL, JONOUCHI!

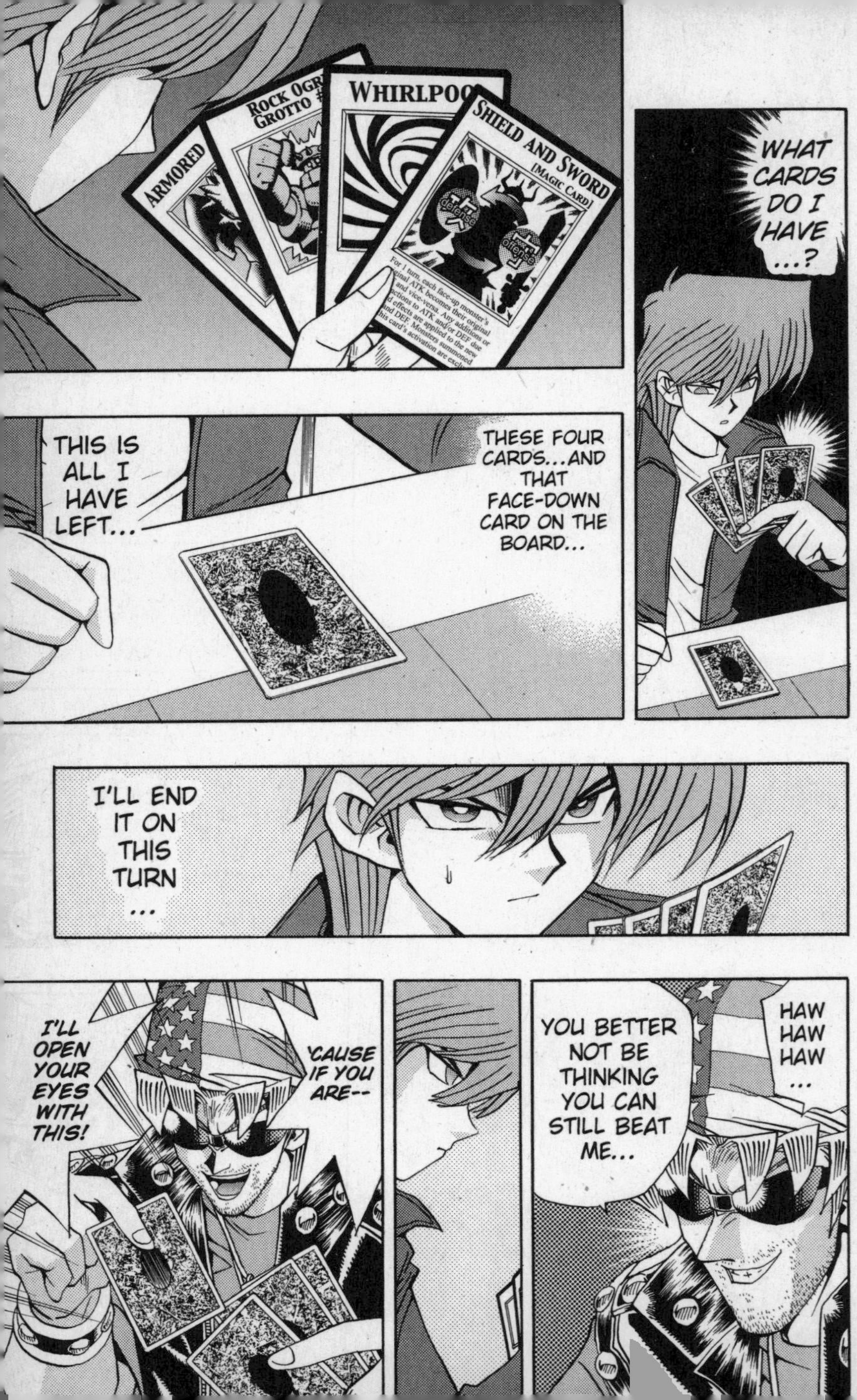
WHAT CARDS DO I HAVE ...?
ARMORED
WHIRLPOO
SHIELD AND SWORD
[MAGIC CARD]
THESE FOUR CARDS...AND THAT FACE-DOWN CARD ON THE BOARD...
THIS IS ALL I HAVE LEFT...
I'LL END IT ON THIS TURN ...
HAW HAW HAW ...
YOU BETTER NOT BE THINKING YOU CAN STILL BEAT ME...
'CAUSE IF YOU ARE--
I'LL OPEN YOUR EYES WITH THIS!

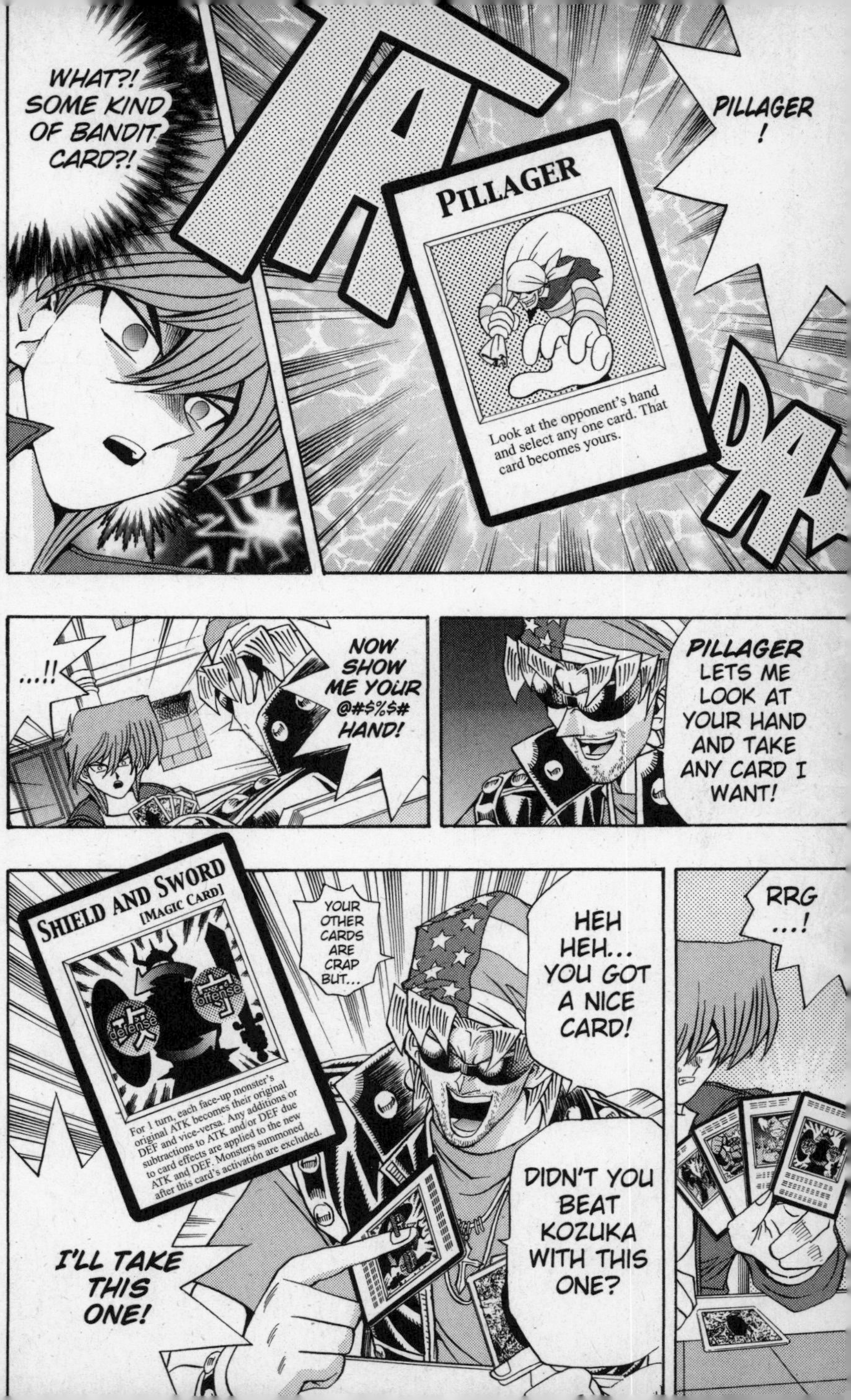
PILLAGER!
PILLAGER
Look at the opponent's hand and select any one card. That card becomes yours.
TA DA
WHAT?! SOME KIND OF BANDIT CARD?!
PILLAGER LETS ME LOOK AT YOUR HAND AND TAKE ANY CARD I WANT!
NOW SHOW ME YOUR @#$%$# HAND!
...!!
RRG ...!
HEH HEH... YOU GOT A NICE CARD!
YOUR OTHER CARDS ARE CRAP BUT...
SHIELD AND SWORD [MAGIC CARD]
offense
defense
For 1 turn, each face-up monster's original ATK becomes their original DEF and vice-versa. Any additions or subtractions to ATK and/or DEF due to card effects are applied to the new ATK and DEF. Monsters summoned after this card's activation are excluded.
DIDN'T YOU BEAT KOZUKA WITH THIS ONE?
I'LL TAKE THIS ONE!

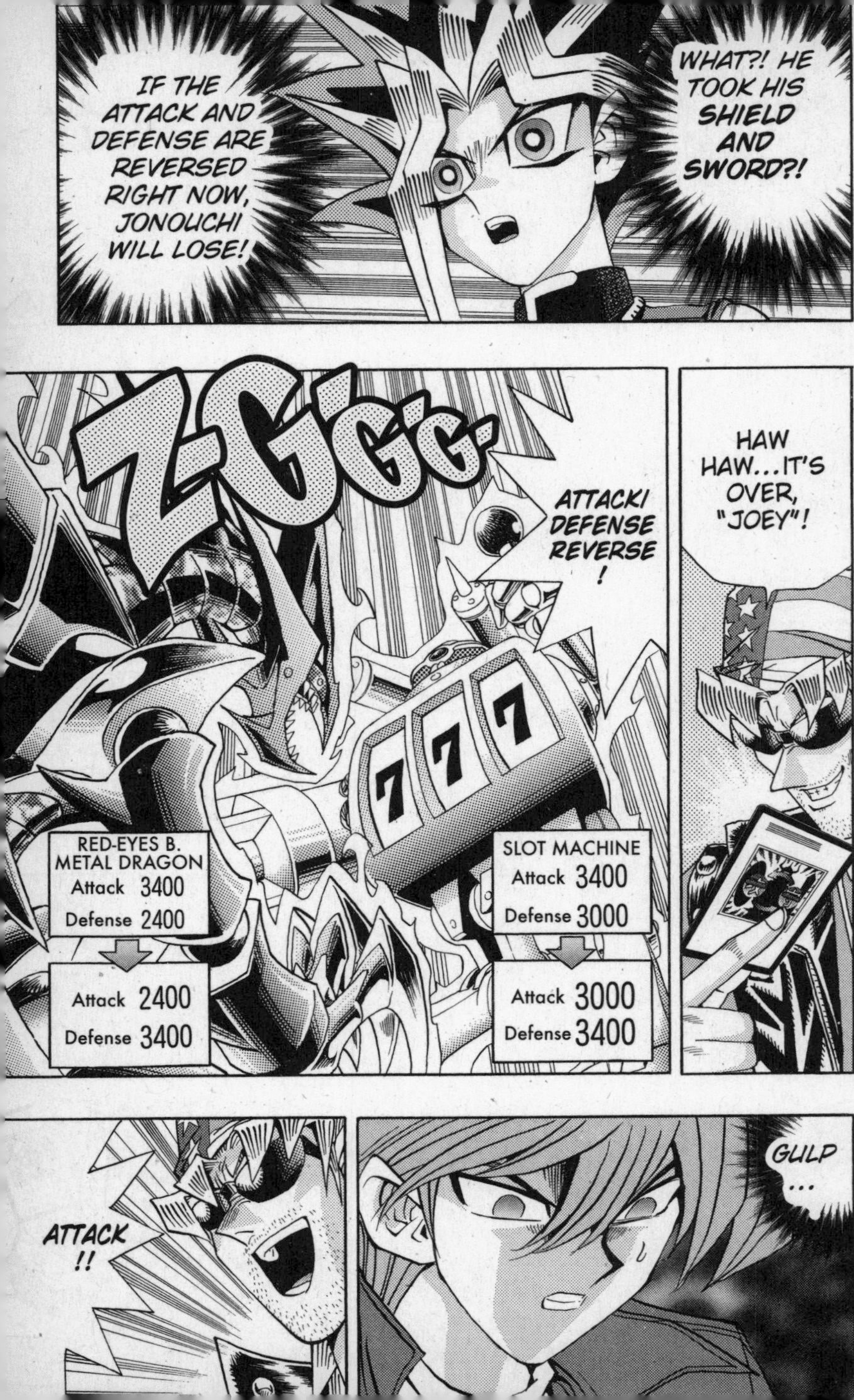
WHAT?! HE TOOK HIS SHIELD AND SWORD?!
IF THE ATTACK AND DEFENSE ARE REVERSED RIGHT NOW, JONOUCHI WILL LOSE!
HAW HAW...IT'S OVER, "JOEY"!
Z-G'G'G
ATTACK/ DEFENSE REVERSE !
SLOT MACHINE
Attack 3400
Defense 3000
Attack 3000
Defense 3400
RED-EYES B. METAL DRAGON
Attack 3400
Defense 2400
Attack 2400
Defense 3400
GULP ...
ATTACK !!

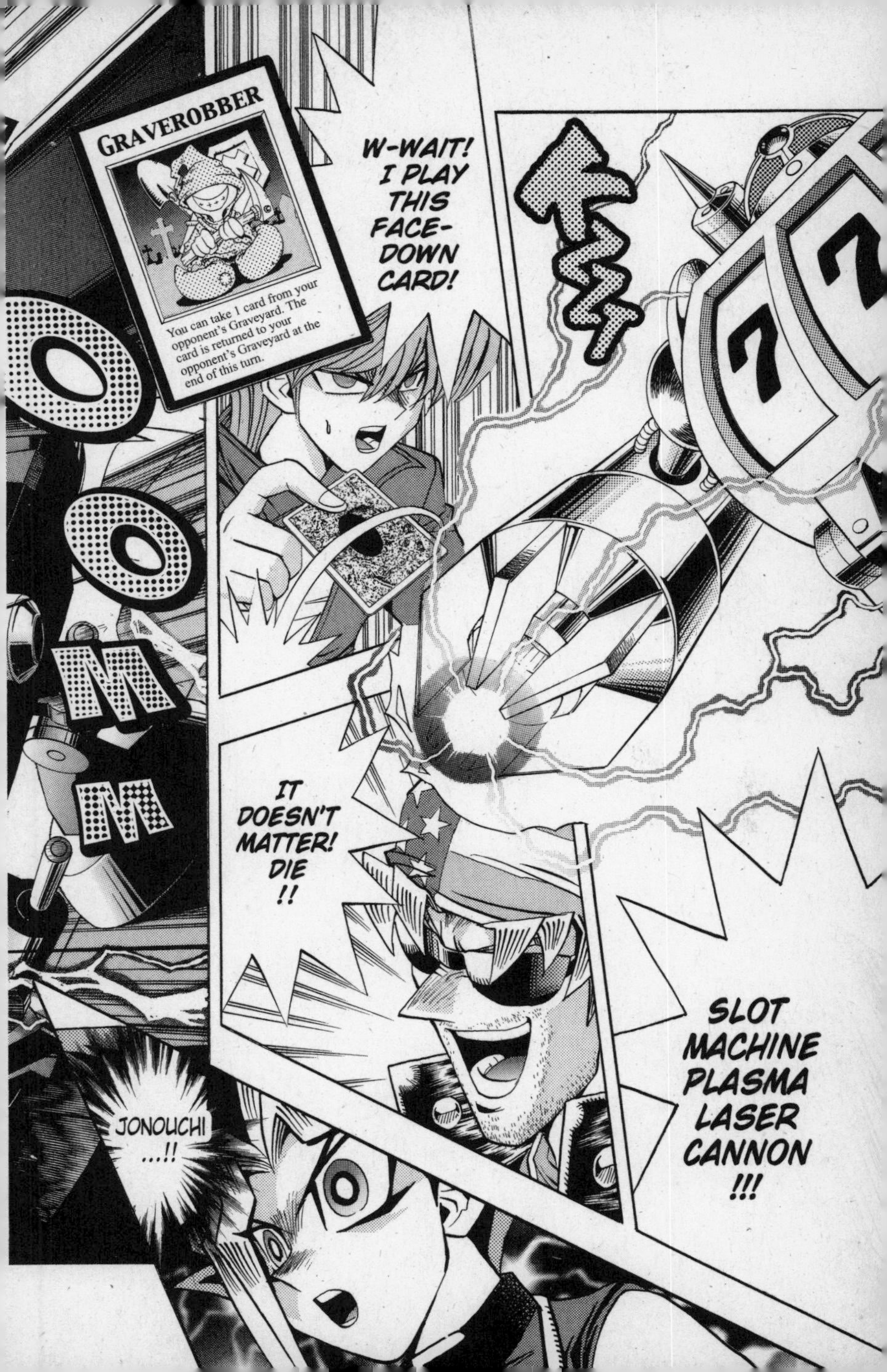
W-WAIT! I PLAY THIS FACE-DOWN CARD!
SLOT MACHINE PLASMA LASER CANNON!!!
IT DOESN'T MATTER! DIE!!
GRAVEROBBER
You can take 1 card from your opponent's Graveyard. The card is returned to your opponent's Graveyard at the end of this turn.
JONOUCHI ...!!

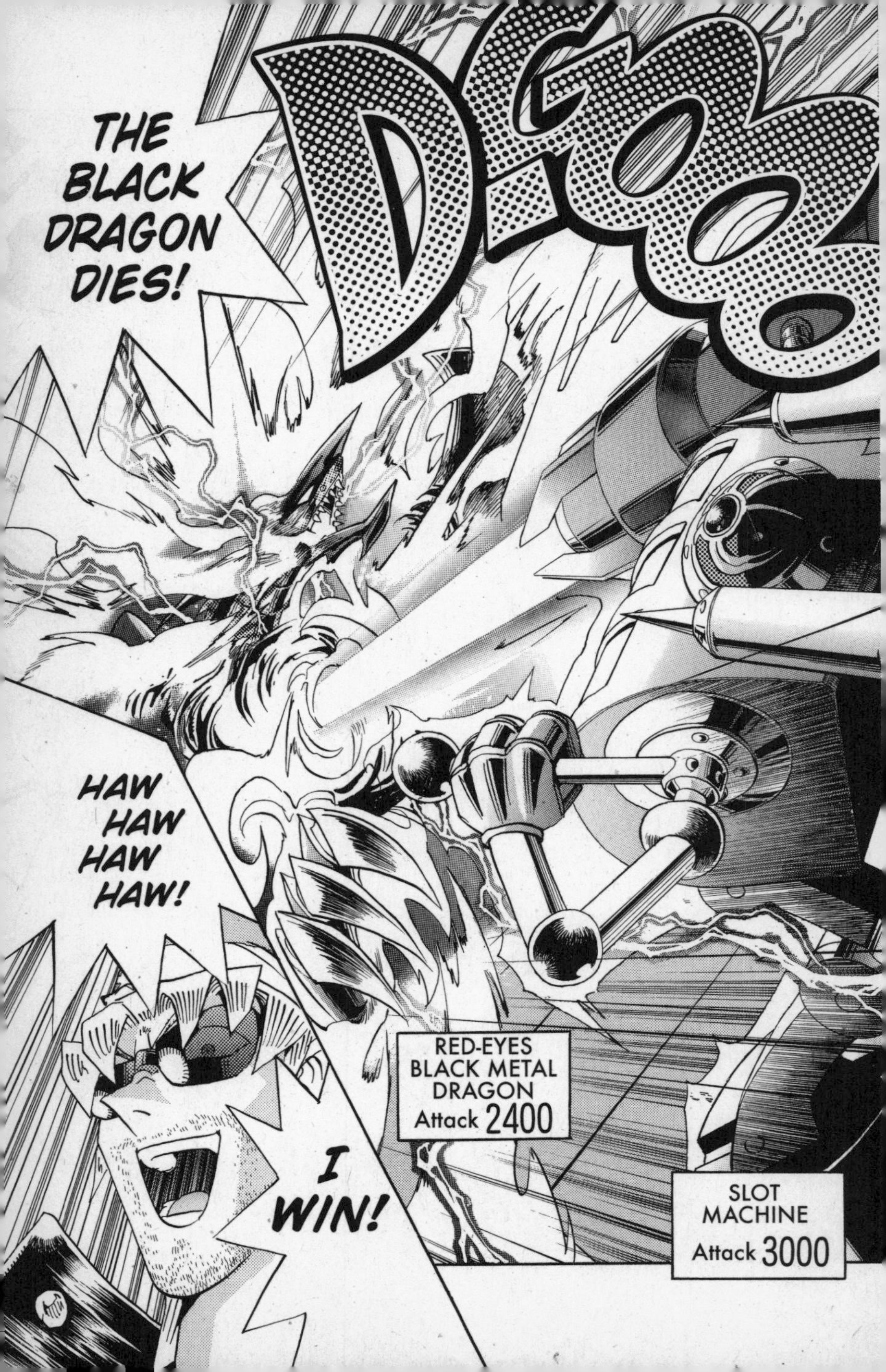
THE BLACK DRAGON DIES!
HAW HAW HAW HAW!
RED-EYES BLACK METAL DRAGON Attack 2400
SLOT MACHINE Attack 3000
I WIN!

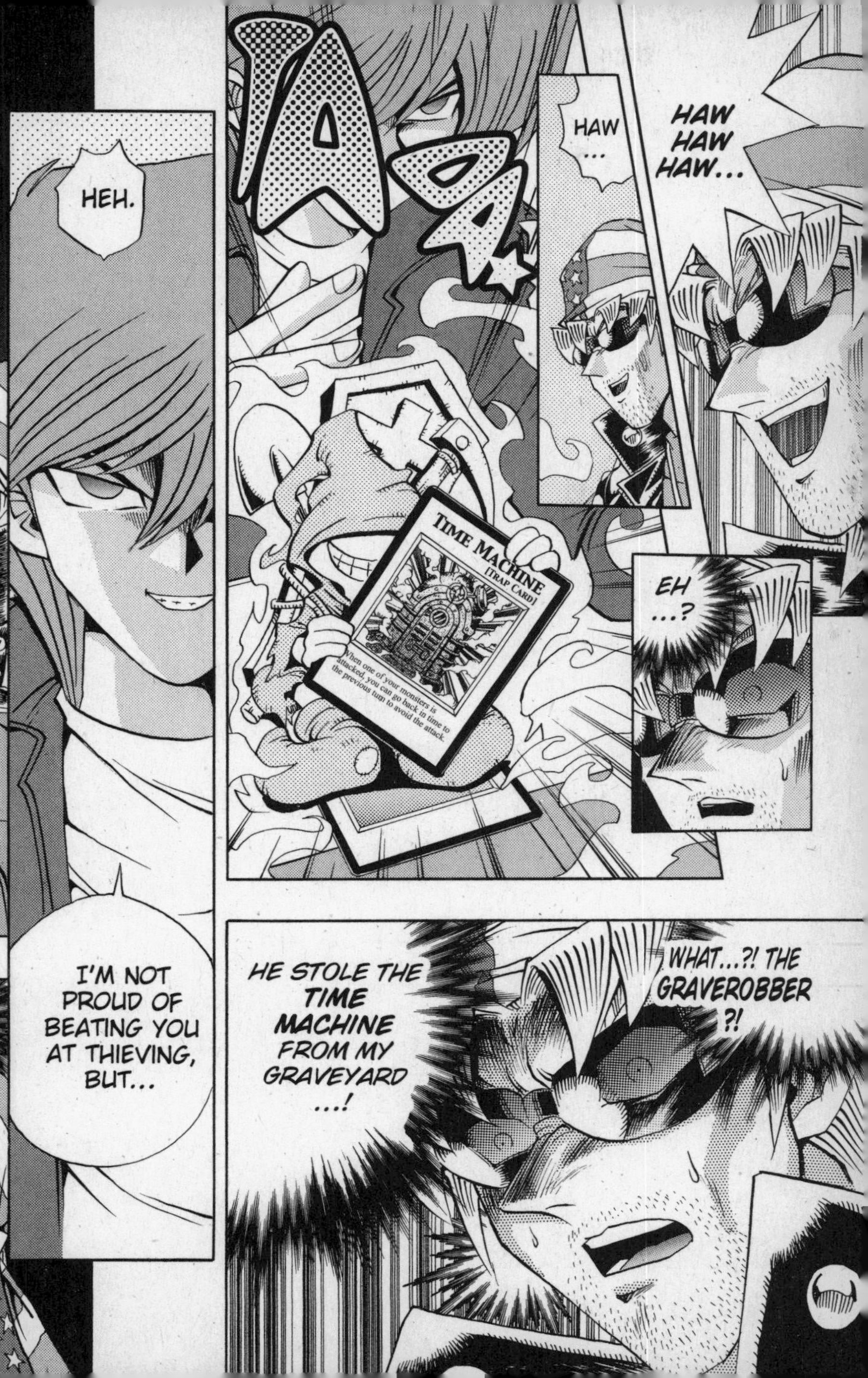
HAW HAW HAW...
HAW ...
TIME MACHINE
[TRAP CARD]
When one of your monsters is attacked, you can go back in time to the previous turn to avoid the attack.
EH ...?
WHAT...?! THE GRAVEROBBER ?!
HE STOLE THE TIME MACHINE FROM MY GRAVEYARD ...!
HEH.
I'M NOT PROUD OF BEATING YOU AT THIEVING, BUT...

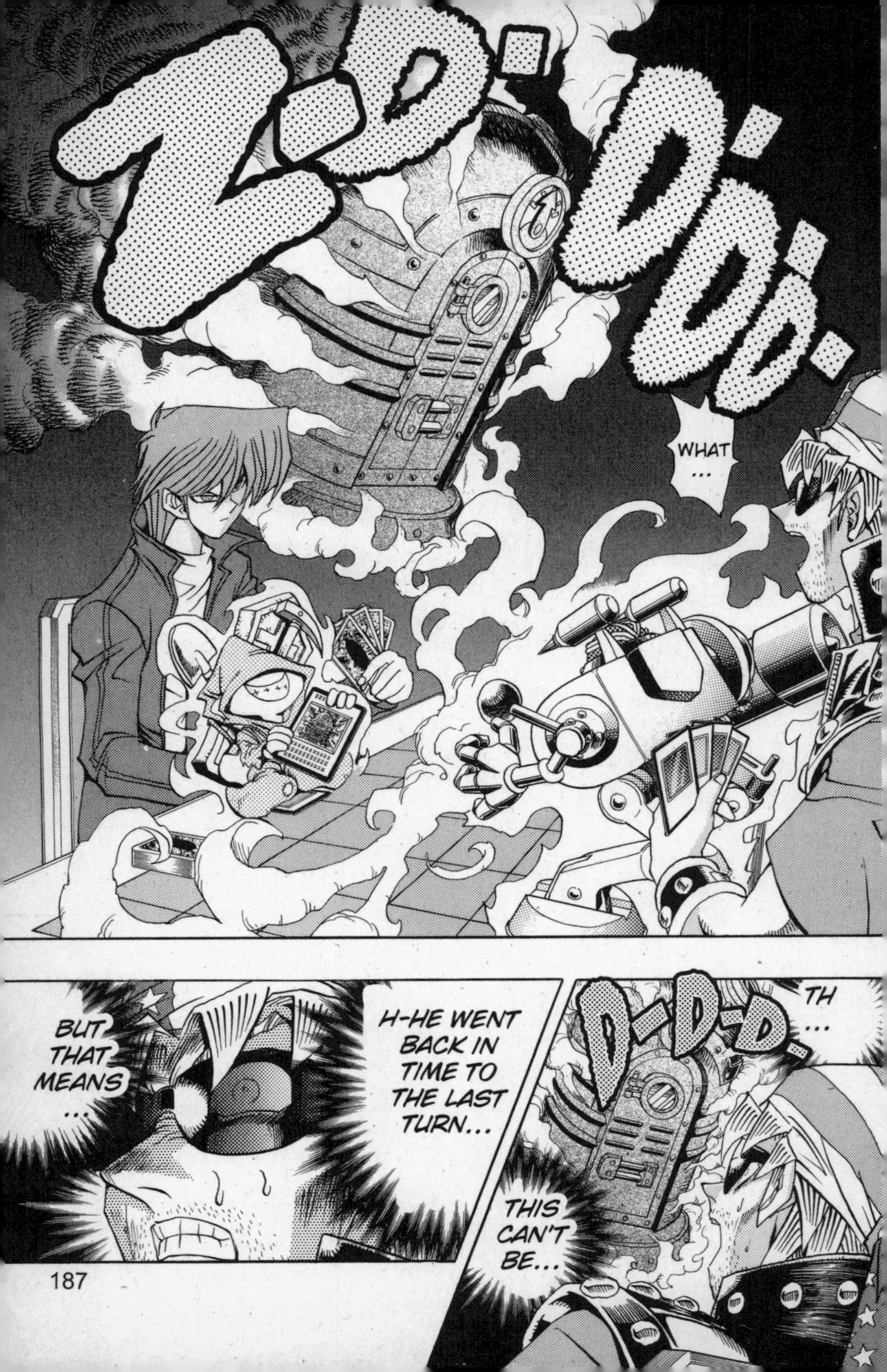
Z-D-D-D-D
WHAT...
TH...
D-D-D
THIS CAN'T BE...
H-HE WENT BACK IN TIME TO THE LAST TURN...
BUT THAT MEANS...

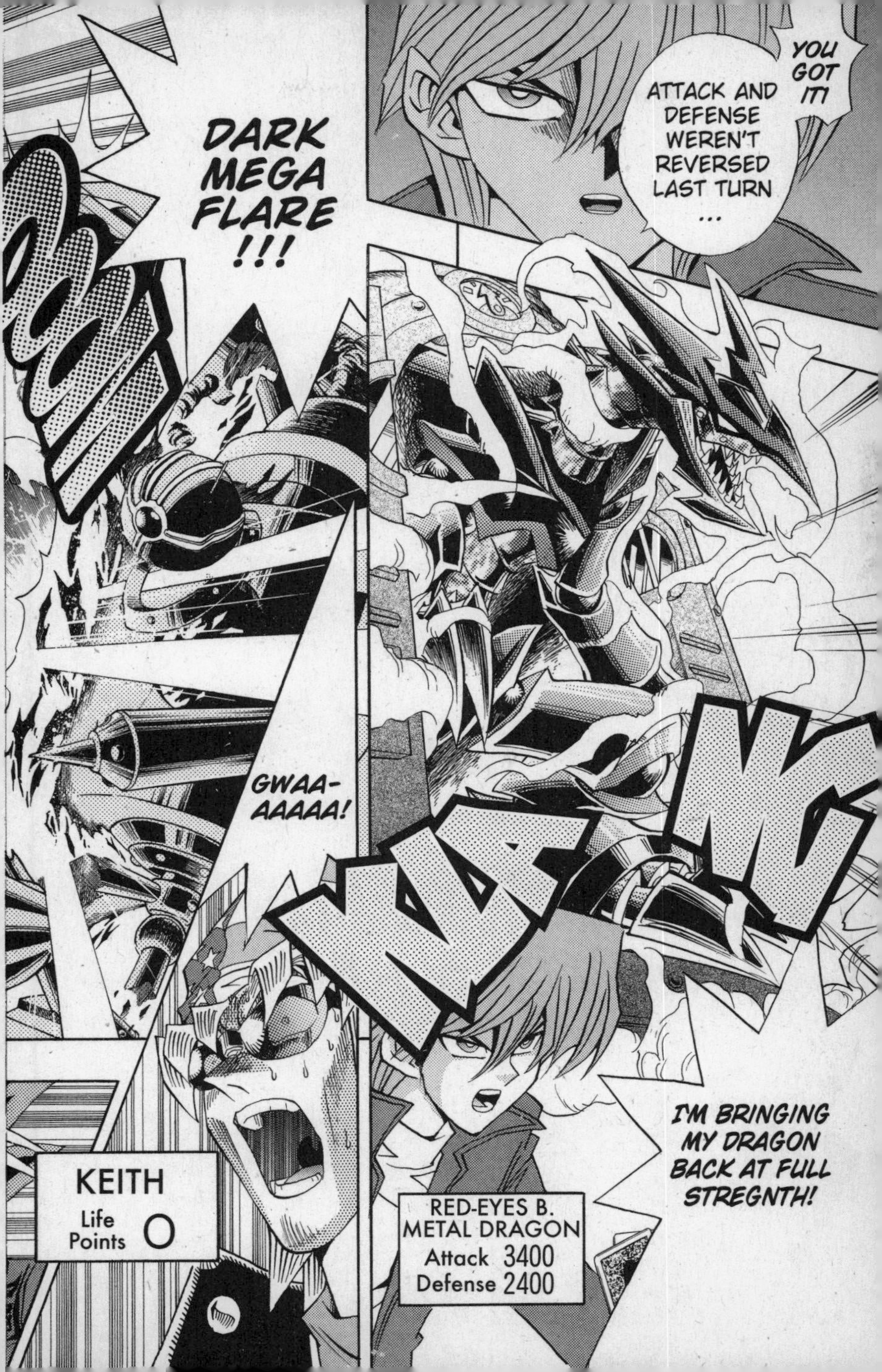
YOU GOT IT!
ATTACK AND DEFENSE WEREN'T REVERSED LAST TURN ...
I'M BRINGING MY DRAGON BACK AT FULL STREGNTH!
RED-EYES B. METAL DRAGON Attack 3400 Defense 2400
DARK MEGA FLARE !!!
GWAA-AAAAA!
KEITH Life Points 0

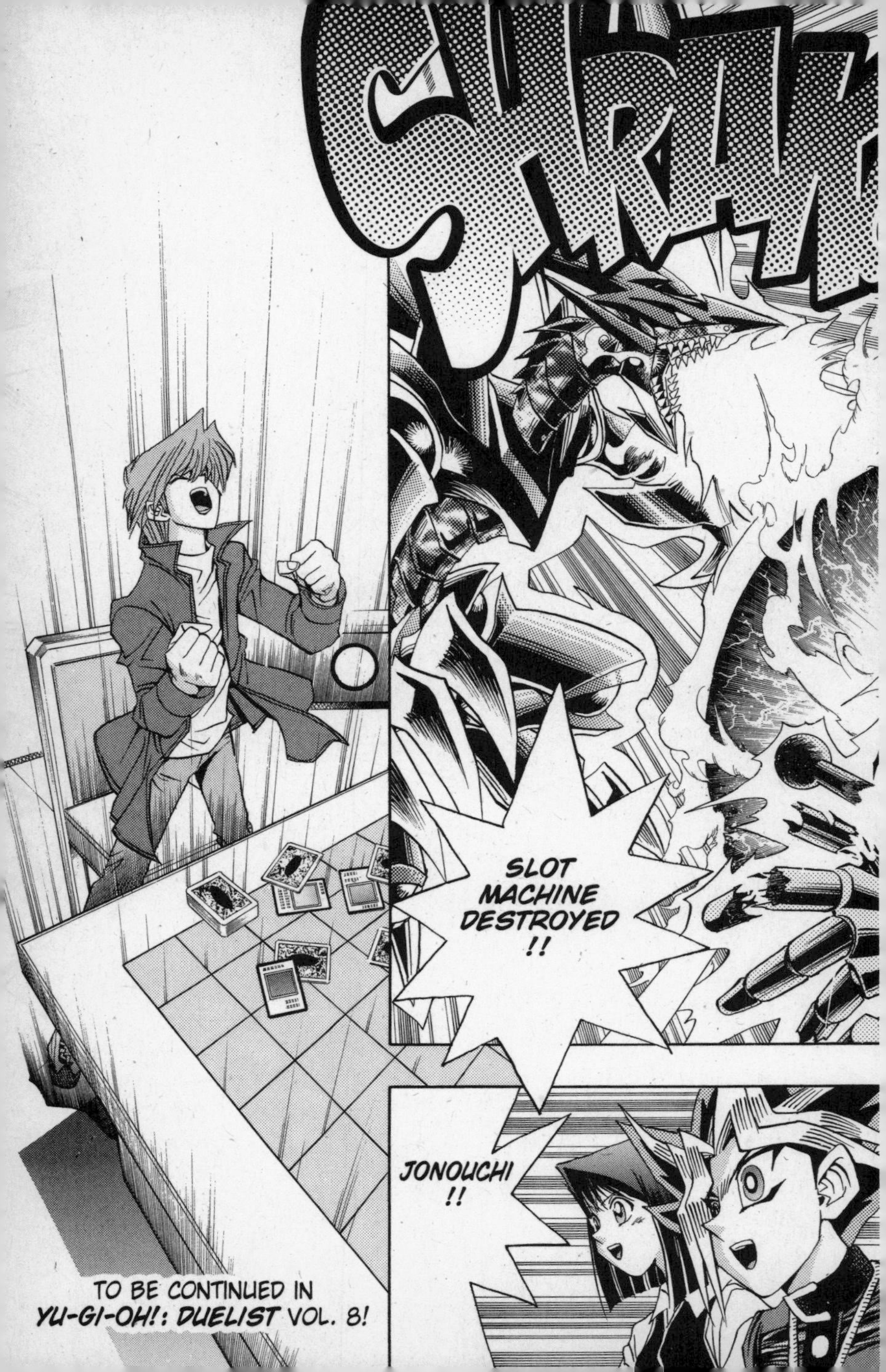
CHRA
SLOT MACHINE DESTROYED !!
JONOUCHI !!
TO BE CONTINUED IN
YU-GI-OH!: DUELIST VOL. 8!

MASTER OF THE CARDS

The "Duel Monsters" card game first appeared in volume two of the original **Yu-Gi-Oh!** graphic novel series, but it's in **Yu-Gi-Oh!: Duelist** (originally printed in Japan as volumes 8-31 of **Yu-Gi-Oh!**) that it gets really important. As many fans know, some of the card names are different between the English and Japanese versions. In case you play the game, or you're interested in playing, here's a rundown of some of the cards in this graphic novel. Some cards only appear in the **Yu-Gi-Oh!** video games, not in the actual collectible card game.

FIRST APPEARANCE IN THIS VOLUME	JAPANESE CARD NAME	ENGLISH CARD NAME
p.8	*Harpie Lady*	Harpy Lady
p.8	*Ankoku Kishi Gaia* (Dark Knight Gaia)	Gaia the Fierce Knight
P.8	*Ginmaku no Mirror Wall* (Mirror Wall of the Silver Screen)	Mirror Wall
p.8	*Cyber Bondage*	Cyber Bondage (NOTE: Not a real game card. Called "Cyber Shield" in the video games.)
p.9	*Demon no Shôkan* (Demon Summoning)	Summoned Skull
p.19	*Harpy no Hanebôki* (Harpy's Feather Brush)	Harpy's Feather Duster
p.20	*Rokubôsei no Jubaku* (Binding Curse of the Hexagram)	Spellbinding Circle

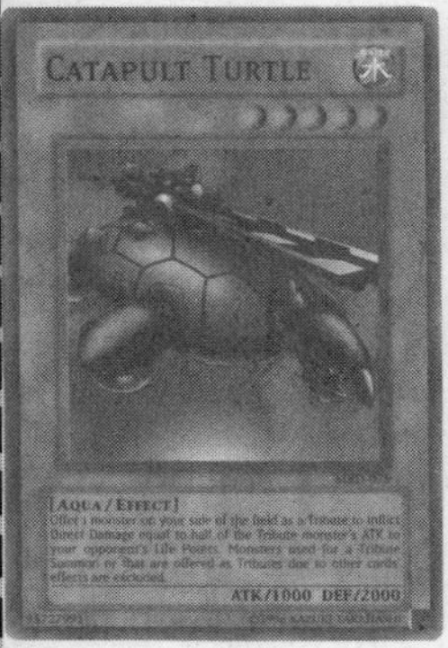
CATAPULT TURTLE
[AQUA/EFFECT]
ATK/1000 DEF/2000

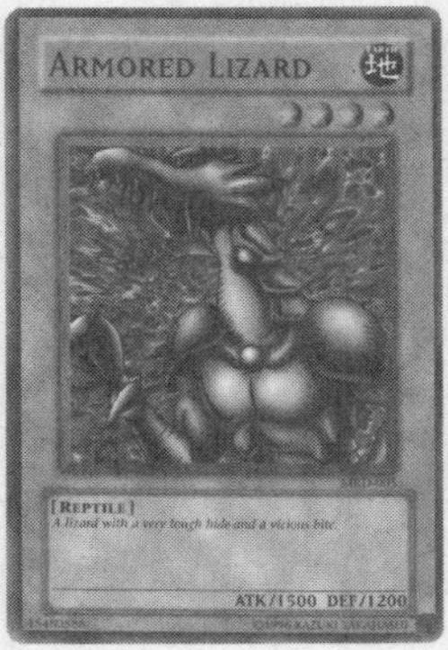
ARMORED LIZARD
[REPTILE]
A lizard with a very tough hide and a vicious bite.
ATK/1500 DEF/1200

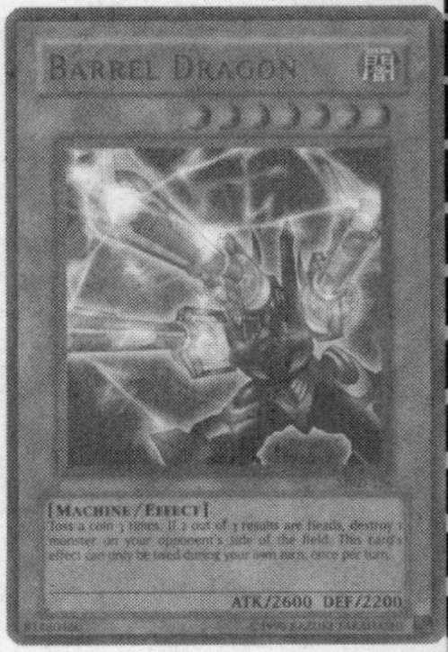
BARREL DRAGON
[MACHINE/EFFECT]
ATK/2600 DEF/2200

FIRST APPEARANCE IN THIS VOLUME	JAPANESE CARD NAME	ENGLISH CARD NAME
p.21	*Gremlin*	Feral Imp
p.21	*Dengeki Muchi* (Electric Shock Whip)	Electro-Whip
p.23	*Harpies' Pet Dragon*	Harpies' Pet Dragon
p.30	*Black Magician*	Dark Magician
p.31	*Sei naru Barrier Mirror Force* (Holy Barrier Mirror Force)	Mirror Force
p.32	*Yûwaku no Shadow* (Shadow of Seduction)	Shadow of Eyes
p.39	*Blue-Eyes White Dragon*	Blue-Eyes White Dragon
p.42	*Sennô Brain Control* (Brainwashing/Brain Control)	Brain Control
p.43	*Catapult Turtle*	Catapult Turtle
p.47	*Kuriboh*	Kuriboh
p.53	*Mangekyô: Karei naru Bunshin* (Kaleidoscope: Splendid Doppelganger)	Kaleidoscope (NOTE: Called "Elegant Egotist" in the actual card game.)

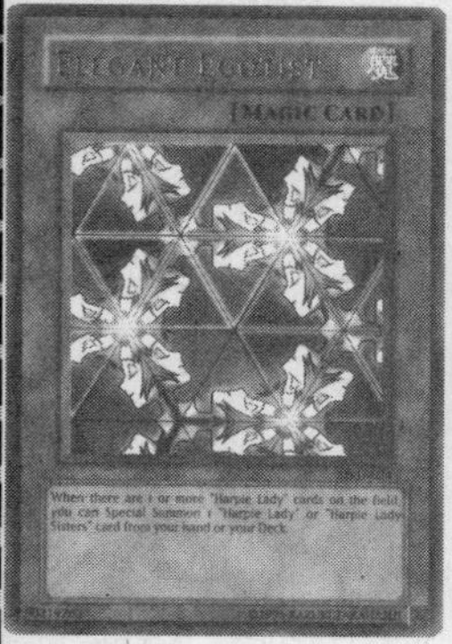
[MAGIC CARD]
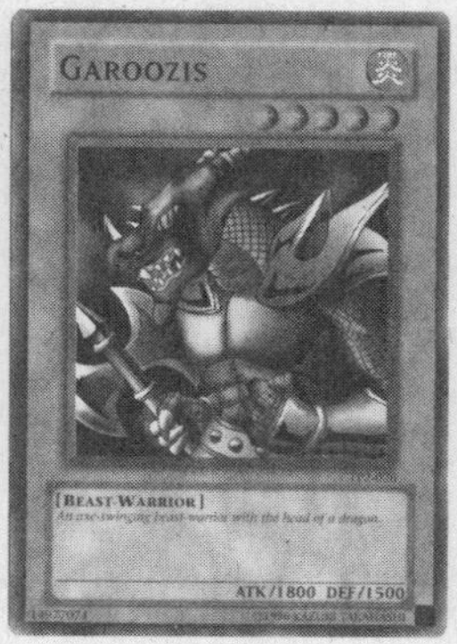
GAROOZIS
[BEAST-WARRIOR]
ATK/1800 DEF/1500
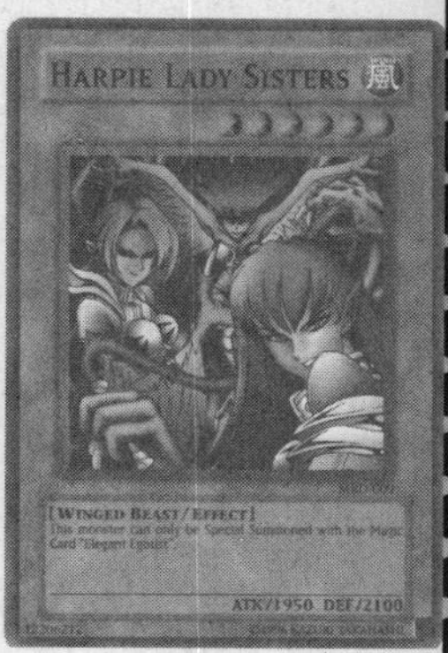
HARPIE LADY SISTERS
[WINGED BEAST/EFFECT]
ATK/1950 DEF/2100

FIRST APPEARANCE IN THIS VOLUME	JAPANESE CARD NAME	ENGLISH CARD NAME
p.53	*Monster Kaishû* (Monster Withdrawal)	Monster Recovery
p.56	*Holy Elf*	Mystical Elf
p.56	*Guriforu*	Griffor (NOTE: Not a real game card. Called "Griffore" in the video games.)
p.56	*Shisha Sosei* (Resurrection of the Dead)	Monster Reborn
p.56	*Elf no Kenshi* (Elf Swordsman	Celtic Guardian
p.64	*Hikari no Gofûken* (Swords of Binding/Sealing Light)	Swords of Revealing Light
p.65	*Chaos Soldier*	Black Luster Soldier
p.71	*Mashô no Tsuki* (Mystical Moon)	Mystical Moon
p.72	*Yûgô* (Fusion)	Polymerization
p.78	*Chaos no Gishiki* (Chaos Ritual)	Black Luster Ritual
p.107	*Furikoyaiba no Gômonkikai* (Pendulum Blade Torture Machine)	Pendulum Machine

KOJIKOCY	地	RED-EYES B. DRAGON	闇	LAUNCHER SPIDER	炎
[WARRIOR] A mad hustler with powerful arms that can cause troubles.		[DRAGON] A ferocious dragon with a deadly attack.		[MACHINE] A mechanical spider with rocket launchers capable of random fire.	
ATK/1500 DEF/1200		ATK/2400 DEF/2000		ATK/2200 DEF/2500	

FIRST APPEARANCE IN THIS VOLUME	JAPANESE CARD NAME	ENGLISH CARD NAME
p.112	*Kakuto Senshi Ultimator* (Hand-to-Hand Fighter Ultimator)	Kung Fu Fighter Ultimator (NOTE: Not a real game card. Called "Battle Warrior" in the video games.)
p.114	*Madô Kishi Giltia* (Magic Conducting/Guiding Knight Giltia)	Giltia the D. Knight
p.116	*TM-1 Launcher Spider*	Launcher Spider
p.118	*Kusaritsuki Boomerang* (Chained Boomerang)	Kunai with Chain
p.118	*Salamandra*	Salamandra
p.118	*Otoshiana* (Pitfall)	Chasm with Spikes
p.118	*Axe Raider*	Axe Raider
p.119	*Devilzoa*	Zoa
p.121	*Honô no Kenshi* (Swordsman of Flames)	Flame Swordsman
p.122	*Metalka Mahôhansha Sôkô* (Metal Change: Magic-reflecting Armor)	Metalmorph
p.125	*Shubi Fûji* (Defense Seal)	Stop Defense

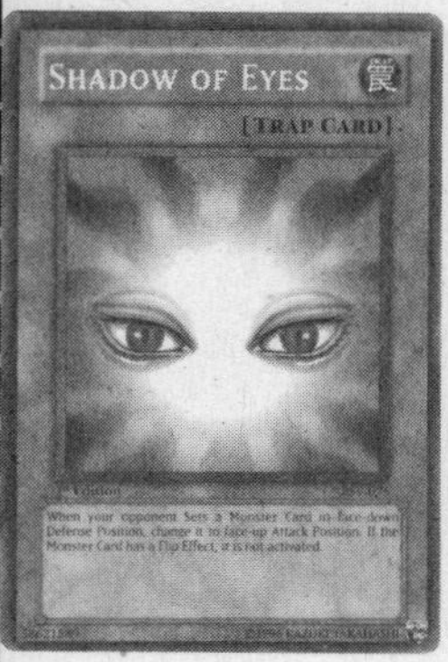
SHADOW OF EYES
[TRAP CARD]

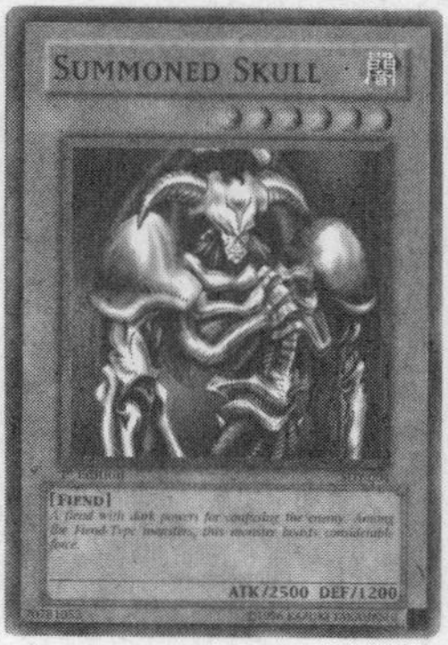
SUMMONED SKULL
[FIEND]
ATK/2500 DEF/1200

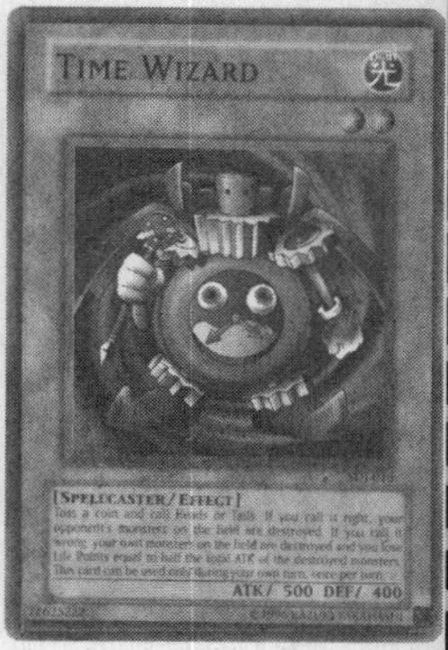
TIME WIZARD
[SPELLCASTER/EFFECT]
ATK/ 500 DEF/ 400

FIRST APPEARANCE IN THIS VOLUME	JAPANESE CARD NAME	ENGLISH CARD NAME
p.133	*Garoozis*	Garoozis
p.142	*Revolver Dragon*	Barrel Dragon
p.147	*Toki no Majutsushi* (Magician of Time)	Time Wizard
p.149	*Red-Eyes Black Dragon*	Red-Eyes Black Dragon
p.151	*Baby Dragon*	Baby Dragon
p.155	*Thousand Dragon* (NOTE: Japanese kanji reads: Thousand-year Dragon)	Thousand Dragon
p.156	*Toki no Kikai Time Machine* (Time Machine)	Time Machine
p.159	*Mamono no Kariudo* (Demon Hunter)	Kojikocy
p.160	*Slot Machine AM-7*	Slot Machine
p.161	*Tiger Axe*	Tiger Axe
p.163	*Megatron*	Space Megatron
p.165	*Monomane Gensôshi* (Mimic Illusionist)	Copycat

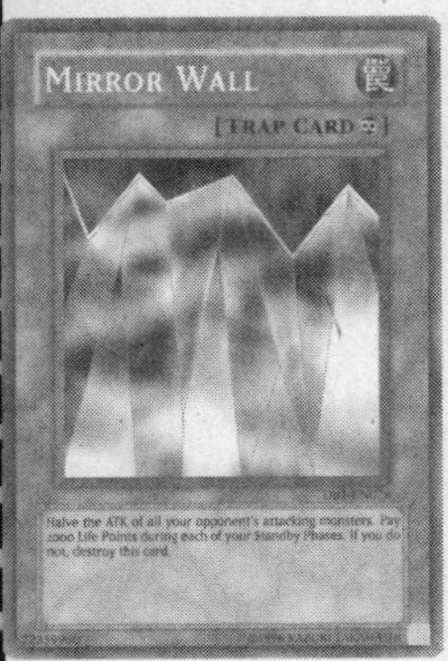
MIRROR WALL
[TRAP CARD]

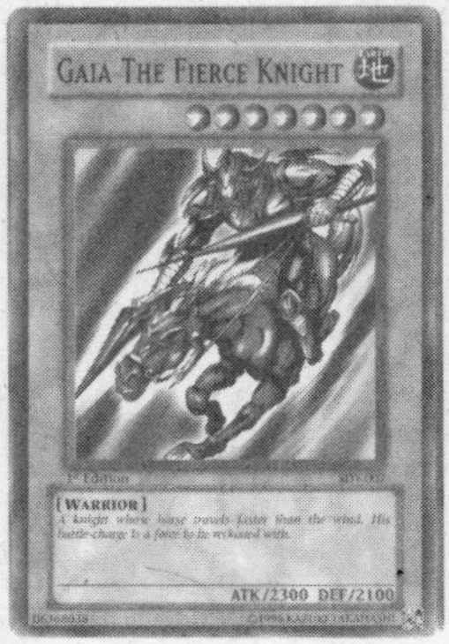
GAIA THE FIERCE KNIGHT
[WARRIOR]
ATK/2300 DEF/2100

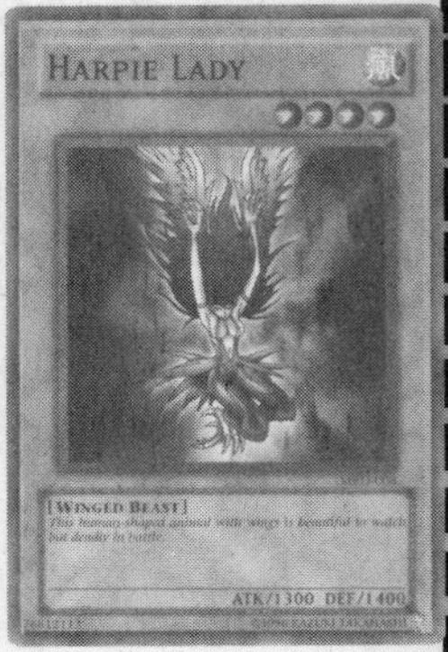
HARPIE LADY
[WINGED BEAST]
ATK/1300 DEF/1400

FIRST APPEARANCE IN THIS VOLUME	JAPANESE CARD NAME	ENGLISH CARD NAME
p.166	*Red-Eyes Black Metal Dragon*	Red-Eyes Black Metal Dragon
p.170	*Haka Arashi* (Graverobber)	Graverobber
p.170	*Yami Ryûzoku no Tsume* (Dark Dragon Clan's Nails/Claws)	Dragon Nails (NOTE: Not a real game card.)
p.170	*Gankutsu Majin Ogre Rock* (Grotto/Cave Golem/Djinn Ogre Rock)	Rock Ogre Grotto #1
p.170	*Migite ni Tate o Hidarite ni Ken o* (Shield in the Left Hand, Sword in the Right Hand)	Shield and Sword
p.174	*7 Card Slot Machine Power Unit*	7 Completed
p.176	*Sphere Bomb Kyûtai Jigen Bakudan* (Sphere Bomb/ Spherical Time Bomb)	Blast Sphere
p.181	*Uzumaki* (Whirlpool)	Whirlpool
P.181	*Armor Lizard*	Armored Lizard
p.182	*Bandit Tôzoku* (Bandit Thief)	Pillager

IN THE NEXT VOLUME...

In the final battle of the tournament, Yugi faces ultra-rich game designer Maximillion Pegasus with the soul of his grandfather at stake! As cards fly, Yugi and Pegasus turn to the darker side of their decks, unleashing sinister monsters of the netherworld. But Pegasus has the power of the mind-scanning Millennium Eye! How can Yugi defeat an opponent who knows exactly what he's going to do?

COMING SEPTEMBER 2005!